OKLAHOMA GOVERNMENT AND POLITICS:

AN INTRODUCTION

Sixth Edition

Edited by

Brett S. Sharp
University of Central Oklahoma

Jan Hardt
University of Central Oklahoma

Christopher L. Markwood
Texas A&M University-Corpus Christi

Original cover design by Jon Toney.
Cover redesign by Craig Beuchaw.

Kendall Hunt
publishing company

www.kendallhunt.com
Send all inquiries to:
4050 Westmark Drive
Dubuque, IA 52004-1840

Printed in the United States of America

To Our Students

CONTENTS

Contents

LIST OF TABLES

LIST OF FIGURES

LIST OF LEADERSHIP PROFILES

FOREWORD

Governor Mary Fallin

In 1889, thousands of pioneers came in covered wagons to Oklahoma, looking for better lives for themselves and their families. They built the tent cities of Guthrie and Oklahoma City literally overnight. In the months and years ahead, they worked to turn unsettled wilderness into fertile farmland, built schools and universities and created a democratically elected state government to serve the people.

Now in its second century of existence, Oklahoma is done with tent cities. Today we build skyscrapers and jet engines, and our researchers develop new crops and find new cures for disease. But Oklahoma remains a state of pioneers. It is a place where individual liberty and personal responsibility are valued and where hard work and ingenuity are rewarded. Above all, it is a community whose citizens work to lift themselves and each other up.

I call that attitude the "Oklahoma Spirit." It is a spirit of resiliency and of love for our neighbors and the land we call home. It propels us forward in the face of adversity, allowing our state and our people to overcome events and obstacles like the Trail of Tears, the Dust Bowl and the Great Depression, booms and busts and the horrors of the Murrah Bombing.

Through all of that adversity, Oklahoma and her citizens have emerged stronger and more prosperous. The "Oklahoma Spirit" continues to be strong. And while that spirit lives just as powerfully in our private sector, it is certainly evident in our civil servants and government leaders. Whether it is local school boards, county sheriffs or state legislators, these men and women are doing their best to improve their local schools, protect their neighborhoods and help their constituents any way they can. Whoever you are in Oklahoma, no matter what you do for a living, you have many civic leaders actively representing your interests, both in local municipal government and at the State Capitol.

I was lucky enough to see the dedication and hard work of these civic leaders as up-close as you can get; both my mother and father served as mayor in the small town of Tecumseh at different times. Few people were more dedicated to their community than they were, and they helped to instill in me the value of service at a very young age.

That appreciation for public service is something that I, in turn, have tried to pass on to my own children and to the young adults I have had the privilege of speaking to at college and high school graduations around the state of Oklahoma. I hope this book helps to pass that appreciation for service on to its readers as well.

If you are opening this book, then you have my encouragement as well as my thanks for your interest in government, in public service and in Oklahoma. In it, you will find the kind of information that will help to make you an educated and informed citizen and perhaps an educated and informed civic leader as well. We will need both great citizens and great leaders to guard the Oklahoma Spirit and to ensure that our second century of statehood is as great and as triumphant as our first.

My commendations go out to Professors Brett Sharp, Christopher Markwood, and Jan Hardt and all of the other contributing authors who took part in helping to write this book and to educate the next generation of Oklahoma students and leaders.

ACKNOWLEDGMENTS

Sixth Edition

This book is a collaboration of efforts. We are indebted to many people for their assistance on this revision. First, we want to thank the contributors to the sixth edition: Danny Adkison, Keith Eakins, Deb Ferrell-Lynn, Loren Gatch, Dana Glencross, Ken Kickham, Elizabeth Overman, Christine Pappas, Markus Smith, Tony Wohlers, Sharon Vaughan, and John Wood.

Second, we are grateful for contributions to previous editions of this book by Sharon Carney, Timothy W. Faltyn, George Humphreys, Stephen Jenks, and Phil Simpson. Their pathbreaking work continues to serve as models for our own efforts.

Third, we appreciate the able assistance of our students: Kory Atcuson, Jennifer Stringham, Paul Bashline, Donna Ita Tupa, Tiffany Palmer, Mamdouh Shouman, Michelle Stricklin, Stephen Bagwell, and Da'Mon Smith who worked tirelessly gathering and organizing data for several chapters and who contributed leadership profiles.

Fourth, we would like to express our appreciation for those many experts on Oklahoma government and politics who at various points shared their wisdom and knowledge including David Blatt, Jennifer Brock, Joe Davenport, Natasha Riley, Everett Slavik, Rick Farmer, Paul Shinn, and Trait Thompson.

Fifth, we would like to thank the Oklahoma Political Science Association and the editors of *Oklahoma Politics* for letting us republish sections of Steve Housel's article, "Oklahoma's Adoption of the Merit System: J. Howard Edmondson and Cooperative Federalism."

Finally, the graphic arts skills of Craig Beuchaw, Jon Toney, Keith Bowden, and James Barrow deserve special recognition for their assistance in designing the cover and developing many of the figures and illustrations.

OKLAHOMA IN CULTURAL AND CONSTITUTIONAL CONTEXT

Christopher L. Markwood and Brett S. Sharp

Something called "the Oklahoma Standard" became known throughout the world. It means resilience in the face of adversity. It means a strength and compassion that will not be defeated. Most of all, it means coming together as a family, the family that is Oklahoma.

Governor Brad Henry, State of the State Address, February 7, 2005.

I. INTRODUCTION

Oklahoma is one of America's youngest states. The twentieth century represented its birth and adolescence. Oklahoma had to grow up fast, not only to catch up to its elder sibling states, but also to meet extreme challenges from the Dust Bowl to the Oklahoma City Bombing. Its diverse citizenry forged a new public order within a beautiful but demanding topography. Oklahomans developed a hearty sense of community, an adventurous spirit, and a profound resiliency. They built dams and lakes and new waterways that turned a former Dust Bowl state into a western oasis. They tapped the earth's resources to become an enduring hub of the world's energy industry. They built cities literally overnight and then developed them into thriving centers of culture and commerce.

As Oklahoma moved into its second century, many of its institutions were just beginning to mature when the economy created new obstacles. The struggle now is to continue building the capacity necessary to secure the progress already made and to promote sound public policy for the next stage of this state's development. In other words, Oklahoma is coming of age. Already, leaders across the state are painting visions of a bright future for Oklahoma communities and the state as a whole. These promising possibilities will be leveraged on the efforts of generations past and the agility that contemporary Oklahomans must demonstrate to navigate the waves of change. We must recognize that the state is still in transition. Oklahoma culture is increasingly urban and cosmopolitan. After decades of being classified as part of the South or the Midwest, Oklahoma's Native American traditions and growing Hispanic influence have firmly placed Oklahoma

1

within the culture of the Southwest. On the political front, the historic domination of the Democratic Party in state and local elected offices has given way to a vigorous two-party competition that more often than not places Republicans in charge of executive and legislative positions. An economy that was once almost entirely dependent upon the petroleum industry has grown much more diversified. Yet, the state's energy industry is leading the charge on improving the economy of Oklahoma and investing in its communities. Hopefully, the stage is now set for a new era of innovation. Now is the time for state leaders to reflect on the lessons of the past, anticipate new challenges, and steer the state in the most optimal direction.

State and local governments play important, powerful roles in every citizen's life. But state and local governments are not without their limitations. Two important constraints on state and local government power are state constitutions and political culture. **State constitutions** are formal documents that detail the powers and limitations of government, as well as the rights and liberties of its citizens. **Political culture** is more of an informal limitation on government and can be defined as the attitudes, beliefs, and expectations people have toward government and toward what government should do. These two constraints are very much related. Pioneers settled America in different areas. They brought their homelands' goals, ideals, and traditions regarding how government should operate and what government should and should not do. As these settlers migrated west, they encountered new problems and new environments. These experiences, traditions, and cultural traits all influenced the development of governing documents (Elazar, 1982). In this chapter we will: (1) explore the distinctive historical background of Oklahoma; (2) examine the constitutional framework for Oklahoma government; and (3) discuss the impact political and cultural values have on Oklahoma government and politics.

II. Historical Background

An understanding of Oklahoma's Constitution requires a brief review of Oklahoma's historical beginning.[1] The land that would become Oklahoma was originally part of the 1803 **Louisiana Purchase,** the American acquisition of over 800,000 square miles from France. At the time, it effectively doubled the size of the United States. While territories and states were quickly formed all around Oklahoma, the quest for Oklahoma statehood would take a unique route.

Pre-Civil War Era

Concern over Indian presence and land possession in the Southeastern part of the United States led Congress to pass the **Removal Act** in 1830. This act called for the Cherokee, Choctaw, Seminole, Chickasaw, and Creek Tribes to be moved west. Historians often refer to them as the **Five Civilized Tribes** because their social and political development had parallels to European systems. The removal process of all of these tribes has been symbolized as the **Trail of Tears.** Historians estimate over 70,000 Native Americans were forced off their land and resettled to Oklahoma with an estimated one-fourth dying en route.

In large part, the removal and relocation of the Five Civilized Tribes was complete by 1840. Treaties were signed with the tribes thereby dividing Oklahoma, or what was then called Indian Territory, among them. The federal government established military forts to protect the tribes, and the tribes established constitutions and developed local governments. In what has been called the "golden years" of the Five Civilized Tribes, school systems, agriculture, commerce, and self-government flourished.

Civil War Era

Although initially pursuing a policy of neutrality during the Civil War, the Five Civilized Tribes ultimately signed treaties with the Confederacy in 1861. In the treaties, the Confederacy promised to provide materiel and military support, and Native American regiments were organized to defend against Union invasion. After the Civil War and the defeat of the Confederacy, the Five Civilized Tribes were forced to accept terms which included the abolition of slavery and the surrender of much of Central and Western Oklahoma for resettlement of other tribes. Caddoe, Delaware, Kickapoo, Modoc, Osage, Comanche, Shawnee, and other tribes were soon relocated from Kansas and other parts of the United States to Western Oklahoma.

Although forbidden to live in Indian Territory without a permit from the tribes, white settlers continued to push into Oklahoma. In surrounding states, especially Kansas, **Boomers** publicly advocated for opening up Indian Territory to white settlement. By 1889 the federal government was ready to open the "unassigned" lands in Central Oklahoma to homestead settlers. Knowing that there were more people interested in homesteading than land available, the government used **land runs,** whereby individuals were lined up on the border of a region of land and allowed to run for a piece of it. Those who illegally crossed before the official starting time to stake claims became known as **Sooners.** By the 1890s, Oklahoma was divided into separate areas known as the twin territories—Oklahoma Territory and Indian Territory. **Oklahoma Territory,** to the west, had been opened to non-Native American people, while **Indian Territory,** to the east, remained set aside for the Five Civilized Tribes.

The Drive for Statehood

While Native Americans were largely opposed to statehood for Indian Territory, almost immediately efforts were underway to seek statehood for Oklahoma Territory; however, several problems existed.[2] First, much of the land was temporarily not taxable because of homestead exemptions making the issue of raising revenue problematic. Second, compared to other recently formed states, the geographical composition of Oklahoma Territory was

FIGURE 1–1 The Twin Territories

significantly smaller than other Western states. Third, partisan politics contributed to the delay in statehood. National Republicans enjoyed being able to make appointments in the territory and hoped that Republican strength, if given time, would grow, thus producing a new Republican state in the traditionally Democratic South. Democrats, confident of maintaining a majority in the territory, pushed for statehood. Fourth, questions regarding statehood for Oklahoma Territory necessarily raised concerns about the future of Indian Territory and the Five Civilized Tribes.

Discussions of the future of the twin territories generally centered around four possible plans. First, Oklahoma Territory could be joined with Indian Territory to form one state. Proponents of single or joint statehood argued that a single state would have economic and geographic advantages and that, in the not-so-distant past, the two territories were previously joined. Second, the two territories could be admitted as separate states. Fearing the possibility of Oklahoma Territory politicians and interests dominating in a single state scenario, leaders of the Five Civilized Tribes favored the separate state proposal if statehood was unavoidable. In addition, some Democrats, who supported separate statehood, envied the possibility of two Democratic senators from Indian Territory and two Democratic senators from Oklahoma Territory. Third, some favored what was called "piecemeal absorption." This process would allow immediate statehood for Oklahoma Territory and allow the various Indian nations to be absorbed into Oklahoma as they were ready. The fourth option was to allow Oklahoma Territory to enter as a state, and leave Indian Territory and the Five Civilized Tribes to remain as they were.

Although the leaders of Indian Territory were opposed to joining with Oklahoma Territory for fear of being discriminated against in a state where whites would dominate, their opposition was easily overcome. In a series of congressional acts during the 1890s, Congress reduced, and ultimately eliminated, Native American governmental and tribal court authority over Indian Territory and abolished communal land ownership.

4

The transfer of land from tribal ownership to individual ownership was overseen by the **Dawes Commission,** which was created by Congress in 1893. Only after Congress gave the Dawes Commission the authority to make **individual land allotments** to the tribe members without tribal consent in 1896 did leaders of the Five Civilized Tribes begin to accept the inevitability of individual allotment. By 1901, the Dawes Commission and Congress had overcome resistance to the individual allotment. All persons whose name appeared on tribal rolls were granted an allotment of land despite the importance of communal land ownership in tribal culture. The remainder of land in Indian Territory was for designated townsites, schools, as well as coal and timber land, much of which was sold by sealed bid with proceeds credited to the tribes holding the land. Unlike Oklahoma Territory, there was no surplus land for homesteading.

The Sequoyah Convention

As the prospect of joint statehood with Oklahoma Territory grew stronger, some of the leaders of the Five Civilized Tribes, and a number of non-Native Americans and individuals with only nominal tribal ties, called for a statehood convention for Indian Territory to meet in Muskogee in August of 1905.

While many individuals had personal political goals, the stated goal of this convention was to produce a constitution for a new Native American state to be called **Sequoyah.** Delegates were selected from across Indian Territory and work began on the proposed constitution. It was similar to other state constitutions as well as the national constitution in that the document began with a preamble and created three separate branches of government. Despite a lopsided ratification vote in Indian Territory in favor of the new constitution, Congress was not interested and quickly rejected it.

As a movement to propel separate statehood, the Sequoyah movement was unsuccessful. However, the movement was significant for several reasons. First, the failure of the Sequoyah Constitution effectively ended the drive for separate statehood. As a result, members of the Five Civilized Tribes were forced to accept the inevitability of joint statehood with Oklahoma Territory. Second, the Sequoyah movement forced federal officials to speed up action on statehood. Within five months of the rejection of the Sequoyah, Congress passed, and President Theodore Roosevelt signed, the **Enabling Act,** which provided for the unification of the two territories and for a convention to develop a constitution for a new state. Third, the Sequoyah Convention gave its leaders, like William H. Murray, an Indian citizen by marriage, the opportunity and platform to push for progressive reform. While suffrage was still limited, the Sequoyah Constitution provided for corporate regulations, mine safety, consumer protection, and social guarantees for women, workers, and children. The proposed constitution also instituted prohibition and created a strong corporation commission with regulatory responsibility. Indeed, had the Sequoyah Constitution been approved by Congress and a new state

5

formed, its constitution would have been one of the most progressive state constitutions in America (Goble, 1980).

The Constitutional Convention in Guthrie

The Enabling Act of 1906 cleared the way for Indian and Oklahoma Territories to join and become the 46th state in the union. The act called for the election of delegates to a constitutional convention that was to meet in Guthrie with 55 delegates from Indian Territory, 55 delegates from Oklahoma Territory, and two delegates from the Osage Nation. While Republicans hoped to elect enough delegates to control the convention, when the election of delegates was complete, Republicans only had 12 of the 112 delegates. As a result, the Democrats were able to organize and control the convention, often ignoring their Republican opponents. In electing delegates to the convention, voters chose a very different type of representative. Few of the delegates had formal educations and most were newcomers to politics. Some scholars note the absence of most of the prominent Democrats and Republicans from this gathering (Goble, 1980). However, given the defeat of Republicans in Oklahoma Territory and the general inexperience of many would-be Democratic leaders in Indian Territory, that most of the delegates were new to politics is not surprising.

The Guthrie Convention existed in a political and social climate that sought change. The economic depression of the 1890s exposed many Americans to the reality of the unequal distribution of wealth that was associated with industrialization and economic progress. Fears of urbanization, explosive population growth, machine politics, ethnic differences, and corporate power gave fuel to populist and progressive reform movements across the country (Morgan & Morgan, 1977).

Populism developed as a potent political and social force in the 1880s out of the West, South, and Midwest. Favoring agrarian policies and fearing corporate monopolies, reformers sought social, political, and economic changes, including agrarian reform, a graduated income tax, regulation of corporations, and an expanded supply of paper money. While the Populist Party failed to become one of the two major political parties, many populist ideas were adopted by the Democratic Party in 1896 when William Jennings Bryan ran both as the nominee of the Democrats, as well as the nominee of the Populist Party.[3]

Fearful of large political machines and special interests, **progressives** in the early 1900s were reformers who "rallied for honest and efficient government" (Bowman & Kearney, 2012, p. 49) and believed in the "goodness and wisdom of individual citizens" (Janda, et al., 1997). Progressive reformers urged the adoption of **primary elections** that would give citizens the ability to choose party candidates for office rather than the traditional closed caucus of party leaders, the **initiative** whereby citizens could propose laws through signature petitions, the **referendum** as a means for citizens to approve or reject laws or questions passed by the legislature, and the **recall** to remove elected officials from office through a new vote.

From the beginning, it was clear that delegates to the constitutional convention were reform-oriented. The delegates began by electing William H. Murray as convention president. His experience as an advocate for reform, and the experiences of the other members of the Guthrie Convention who had served in the Sequoyah Convention, helped establish Murray as one of the undisputed leaders of the convention.

While most of the Democrats pledged their support to a reform oriented constitution, the issues of where to place county seats, woman's suffrage, and prohibition all carried the possibility of splitting the convention apart and required careful management. Murray used his considerable influence in the placement of county seats to extract loyalty and support from convention delegates, and secured the proposal for a reform-oriented constitution.

Ratification

Democrats orchestrated an effective campaign for ratification, arguing the necessity of the proposed constitution. Campaigning against the corruption of corporations, individual candidates for state and local offices ran campaigns associating themselves with the constitution's reforms. William Jennings Bryan, the popular reformer, even journeyed to Oklahoma to urge adoption of the constitution and many of its reforms. William Howard Taft, then Secretary of War, campaigned in Oklahoma and warned that the constitution was "flavored with Socialism" and contained too many provisions that should be decided by the legislature (Goble, 1980, 224–225).

Oklahomans ratified the constitution on September 17, 1907, with 71 percent approval and with majority support in every county. In addition, Democrats swept the executive, legislative, and judicial races, as well as four out of five congressional races. Senators were still selected by state legislatures and the new legislature would be overwhelmingly Democratic with 93 Democrats and only 16 Republicans. The election set the stage for decades of Democratic dominance of state politics (Goble, 1980, 225).

III. Significant Features of the Oklahoma Constitution

The proposed constitution was a model for populist reformers and was even championed by William Jennings Bryan himself. The framers designed a government that divided powers among three equal branches (legislative, executive, and judicial) but also limited the powers of the branches of government. The proposed constitution revealed the faith the framers had in the people, by providing avenues of direct democracy, and revealed the skepticism and distrust the framers had of government and special interests. As one of the nation's longest state constitutions, the

Oklahoma Constitution lays out the powers and responsibilities of state and local government as well as the protections and rights of the people.

Length

One of the major differences between the federal and Oklahoma constitutions is the length of Oklahoma's document. In general, constitutions can be thought of as a set of founding principles and guidelines. Much of the detail work of government is usually done by the legislature in the form of statutory law. However, the state's framers were largely distrustful of legislatures and were developing this constitution during a period of time in which prevailing political, social, and economic ideas were being challenged. As a result, the framers sought to place as much as possible outside the legislative arm of state government. One of the practical effects of this strategy was the creation of one of the nation's longest state constitutions. By comparison, the United States Constitution is only about 8,700 words and the average state constitution has about 38,000 words. The Oklahoma Constitution contains over 74,000 words and ranks fourth behind Alabama with 365,000 words, Texas with over 93,000 words, and Colorado with almost 75,000 words (see Table 1–1). Coinciding with length is extensive detail. Because the Oklahoma framers were distrustful of government but believed that government, if properly regulated, could be beneficial to the people, they sought to be specific and detailed. As a result, today's Oklahoma Constitution contains provisions specifically declaring the flash test for kerosene to be 115 degrees Fahrenheit, specifically listing maximum dollar levels of indebtedness for capital improvements for building and institutions, as well as providing a thorough description of what the state seal must look like.

Rule by the People

The Oklahoma framers joined a small number of other states and provided several avenues for direct democracy, placing some legislative authority directly in the hands of the people. The Oklahoma Constitution provides for the referendum and the initiative.

The **referendum** can be required by 5 percent of the legal voters or by an absolute majority of the legislature to allow the people to vote on a piece of legislation previously passed by the legislature. The **initiative** process allows citizens to circulate a petition and gather signatures to place an issue on the ballot. To propose a law through the initiative process requires 8 percent of the legal voters to sign the petition requesting an issue to be placed on the ballot. To propose a constitutional amendment, 15 percent of the legal voters must sign a petition requesting an amendment to the constitution to be placed on the ballot. If the required number of valid signatures are gathered, the issue will appear on the ballot, and the people may vote on it directly. These procedures put legislative authority in the hands of the people and take it away from the legislature. Oklahomans have used

TABLE 1–1
A Comparison of State Constitutions

STATE	NUMBER OF CONSTITUTIONS	DATE OF FIRST ADOPTION	EFFECTIVE DATE OF PRESENT CONSTITUTION	ESTIMATED LENGTH IN WORDS	NUMBER OF ADOPTED AMENDMENTS
Alabama	6	1819	1901	365,000	807
Alaska	1	1956	1959	13,000	29
Arizona	1	1911	1912	45,909	143
Arkansas	5	1836	1874	59,500	95
California	2	1849	1879	54,645	519
Colorado	1	1876	1876	74,522	154
Connecticut	4	1818	1965	17,256	30
Delaware	4	1776	1897	19,000	140
Florida	6	1839	1969	57,017	115
Georgia	10	1777	1983	39,526	68
Hawaii	1	1950	1959	21,440	108
Idaho	1	1889	1890	24,232	119
Illinois	4	1818	1971	15,751	11
Indiana	2	1816	1851	10,379	46
Iowa	2	1846	1857	11,500	53
Kansas	1	1859	1861	12,296	93
Kentucky	4	1792	1891	23,911	41
Louisiana	11	1812	1975	69,773	154
Maine	1	1819	1820	16,276	171
Maryland	4	1776	1867	41,622	223
Massachusetts	1	1780	1780	36,700	120
Michigan	4	1835	1964	35,858	29
Minnesota	1	1857	1858	11,734	120
Mississippi	4	1817	1890	24,323	123
Missouri	4	1820	1945	42,600	111
Montana	2	1889	1973	14,028	30
Nebraska	2	1866	1875	34,645	226
Nevada	1	1864	1864	31,944	136
New Hampshire	2	1776	1784	9,200	145
New Jersey	3	1776	1948	26,159	43
New Mexico	1	1911	1912	27,200	157
New York	4	1777	1895	51,700	220
North Carolina	3	1776	1971	16,532	34
North Dakota	1	1889	1889	19,074	149
Ohio	2	1802	1851	56,163	169
Oklahoma	1	1907	1907	74,075	179
Oregon	1	1857	1859	54,083	243
Pennsylvania	5	1776	1968	27,711	30
Rhode Island	3	1842	1986	10,908	10
South Carolina	7	1776	1896	32,541	493
South Dakota	1	1889	1889	27,675	214
Tennessee	3	1796	1870	13,300	38
Texas	5	1845	1876	93,034	467
Utah	1	1895	1896	19,366	111
Vermont	3	1777	1793	10,286	53
Virginia	6	1776	1971	21,601	43
Washington	1	1889	1889	34,300	101
West Virginia	2	1863	1872	26,000	71
Wisconsin	1	1848	1848	15,102	145
Wyoming	1	1889	1890	29,300	98

SOURCE: Adapted from Dinan, John. (2010). State Constitutional Developments. In Council of State Governments, *Book of the States 2010* (p. 11).

the initiative process to limit taxes, impose term limits on legislators, legalize parimutuel betting, and require voters to show identification.

Legislature

Article V of the Oklahoma Constitution establishes the legislative authority in state government. The Constitution provides for a **bicameral legislature,** with a House of Representatives and a Senate. The House of Representatives consists of 101 members. State representatives are elected for a two-year term, with the entire House membership up for election at the same time. The Senate consists of 48 members. State senators are elected for four-year terms with half of the Senate membership elected every two years. What is most notable about this provision is the inclusion of the initiative and referendum. Section 1 states:

> *The Legislative authority of the state shall be vested in a Legislature, consisting of a Senate and a House of Representatives; but the people reserve to themselves the power to propose laws and amendments to the Constitution and to enact or reject the same at the polls independent of the Legislature, and also reserve power at their own option to approve or reject at the polls any act of the Legislature.*

The provision of the initiative and referendum as means for allowing citizens to propose and vote on legislation or constitutional amendments is a clear expression of the distrust the Oklahoma framers had in legislative power. Believing that government had to be restrained in order for good government to work, the framers placed a number of other restrictions on the state legislature as well. These restrictions include a limitation on the length of legislative sessions, a prohibition on passing revenue bills during the last five days of the legislative sessions, and a requirement that laws be passed by an absolute majority of members rather than a majority of those present and voting.

The Executive

Expressing their distrust of strong governmental officials, governors were to be elected for four-year terms and were not allowed to succeed themselves. Like other states that had a similar provision, this restriction has now been modified to allow a governor to succeed himself or herself once. Further reducing the powers of the governor, the framers vested executive authority not only in the governor, but also in a number of other executive officers, each elected by the people. Today, the lieutenant governor, attorney general, superintendent of public instruction, state auditor and inspector, state treasurer, three corporation commissioners, commissioner of insurance, and commissioner of labor are all elected separately and independently of the governor. As a result, they may pursue policies and agendas that may or may not be consistent with those of the governor.

LEADERSHIP PROFILE

MARY FALLIN
Governor, State of Oklahoma

GOVERNOR MARY FALLIN was elected November 2, 2010, during a historic election in which she became the first-ever female governor of Oklahoma. She was inaugurated on the steps of the Oklahoma Capitol as the state's 27th governor on January 10, 2011.

After a successful career in the private sector as a manager for a national hotel chain, Fallin made her first foray into public service in 1990 when she was elected to the Oklahoma House of Representatives. This began her long and distinguished career of public service dedicated to conservative, commonsense solutions to the challenges facing Oklahoma families and small businesses.

During her time in the House, Fallin earned a reputation as a consensus builder who was willing to reach across the aisle. Serving in the Republican minority, she managed to pass more than a dozen bills that were signed into law by the state's Democratic governor, including Oklahoma's first "anti-stalker law" and measures aimed at improving the business climate in Oklahoma. She also worked to lower the health care costs of small businesses in Oklahoma and for her work in this area was honored as a "Legislator of the Year" by the American Legislative Exchange Council.

In 1994, Fallin would first make history by becoming the first woman and first Republican to be elected lieutenant governor of Oklahoma, an office she would hold for 12 years. In this capacity, Fallin focused her attention on issues affecting job creation and economic development. She served on 10 boards or commissions involving business and quality-of-life issues in Oklahoma. In 1997, she chaired the Fallin Commission on Workers' Compensation, which released a comprehensive reform plan to lower costs of workers' comp while creating a system that was fair to both businesses and workers. Fallin also used her position as president of the Oklahoma State Senate to allow the citizens of Oklahoma to vote on "Right to Work," which ended the practice of compelling workers

11

to join and pay dues to a union. In 2001, Oklahoma became the first state in the country to pass such a law in more than 25 years.

Fallin was elected to the U.S. Congress in 2006 where she represented the Fifth District of Oklahoma. In Congress, Fallin served on the committees for small business, transportation and infrastructure, natural resources and armed services. Fallin coauthored numerous pieces of legislation to lower taxes, reduce regulation on businesses and individuals, fight federal overreach, increase American energy production, create jobs and protect constitutional liberties.

As governor, Fallin has listed as her priorities job growth and retention, government modernization, education reform and protecting Oklahoma from the intrusions of Washington, D.C. Fallin serves on the Executive Committee of the National Governors Association and is Chair of the Interstate Oil and Gas Compact Commission.

The governor is a graduate of Oklahoma State University. She is married to Wade Christensen, an Oklahoma City attorney who is the state's first "First Gentleman." The couple has six children between them. They attend Crossings Community Church in northwest Oklahoma City.

Like other governors, the Oklahoma governor has the power to **veto** acts of the legislature. This power includes the **line-item veto** which allows the governor to veto specific sections of appropriations bills or legislation that seeks to impose restrictions on previously appropriated funds. While the veto is the only real power the governor has over the legislature, the state legislature may override the governor's veto by a two-thirds majority in both houses.

The Oklahoma governor may also grant pardons, paroles, and reprieves to those convicted of crimes in Oklahoma. As discussed in Chapter Four, while the governor once enjoyed exclusive power to make these decisions, this power has been limited by a constitutional amendment that created the State Pardon and Parole Board.

Judiciary

Like other state constitutions, the Oklahoma Constitution proposed a hierarchical system of courts. The lowest level of courts would be trial courts and the highest level of courts would hear cases on appeal. However, unlike most other state court systems, the Oklahoma framers proposed a separated appellate court system with a **Court of Criminal Appeals** and a **Supreme Court**. The Court of Criminal Appeals was to be the highest court for civil cases. Only one other state, Texas, has two courts of last resort. Other provisions dealing with the judiciary include the methods of selection. Rather than executive appointment, the framers decided to have judges elected. As with other positions, the justification was to keep public officials responsible to the people. However, as discussed in Chapter Six, problems with inefficiency and corruption led Oklahoma to change its judicial selection method.

Constitutional Change

Article XXIV of the Oklahoma Constitution provides a number of methods for amending the constitution. As with the national constitution, there are two steps: (1) proposal of a constitutional amendment and (2) ratification of a proposed constitutional amendment.

Proposal of a constitutional amendment in Oklahoma can be accomplished in one of three ways. First, the state legislature may propose an amendment to the constitution by a majority vote in both houses of state legislature. Second, the people may propose a constitutional amendment through the initiative petition. Oklahoma was the second state to allow amendments to be proposed by this method. To propose a constitutional amendment using this method, supporters must get the signatures of 15 percent of the voters. Third, a constitutional convention, approved by the voters, may propose amendments to the constitution. Article XXIV, Section 2 also requires that a question of whether or not to have a constitutional convention be put to the voters at least once every 20 years. Oklahoma voters have voted against calling a constitutional convention in 1926, 1950, and 1970. Interestingly, neither the legislature nor the secretary of state has placed the issue on the ballot since 1970.

The second step in the process of formally amending Oklahoma's constitution is **ratification.** All three methods of proposing a constitutional amendment require the same method of ratification. All proposed amendments must be approved by a majority of those voting in a regular or specially called election. Until 1974, the constitution required that to ratify an amendment proposed by the initiative process, the proposal had to receive a majority of all votes in the election, not just on the proposed amendment. This allowed a proposed amendment to be defeated even if it received a majority of the votes on the amendment, because of what has been termed the **silent vote**—those participating in the election, but not voting on the amendment.

The Liquor Question

The Enabling Act required that alcohol be banned in Indian Territory for 21 years after ratification. However, there were no restrictions on alcohol for the rest of the state. Constitutional Convention President Murray had supported prohibition at the Sequoyah Convention and was supported by the Anti-Saloon League in his bid for the position of president of the Guthrie Convention. While most delegates were "dry," fear that the liquor issue might cause otherwise supportive citizens to vote against the proposed constitution led Murray to propose placing the liquor question in the form of an amendment on a separate ballot to be decided at the same time the people voted on the ratification of the proposed constitution. While the feelings on both sides were strong, the amendment process passed and inaugurated prohibition throughout the entire state (Bryant, 1968). Oklahoma has since loosened the restrictions on the sale of alcohol including allowing the sale of 3.2 beer in 1933 and allowing a county option for liquor by the drink in 1986.

Individual Rights and Liberties

The use of state constitutions to itemize or list specific rights is not unique. Thus, Article II of the Oklahoma Constitution is similar to other state constitutions in that it provides individual protections and freedoms for Oklahomans. Many of the rights protected in this article are also protected by the federal constitution. For example, Section 30, which protects inhabitants against unreasonable searches and seizures, is almost identical to the Fourth Amendment of the United States Constitution. However, what is more noticeable is that many of the guarantees found in the Oklahoma Bill of Rights go further and are more specific than the federal constitution. For example, as Table 1–2 details, the protection against government establishment of religion and the guarantee of freedom of speech are much more detailed and specific than the establishment and free speech clauses of the U.S. Constitution's First Amendment.

The framers of the Oklahoma Constitution wanted to limit government's authority. As such, they gave individuals specific and often detailed protections. That the framers were fearful of government's ability to protect individual freedoms could be due in part to the fact that at the time the Oklahoma Constitution was being developed, many of the protections found in the United States' Bill of Rights had not yet been incorporated and applied to the states.

As a result of the framers' concerns about government power, in an effort to prevent state government from abusing power and restricting individual rights and liberties, the Oklahoma Constitution, like most other state constitutions, provided protections independent of the United States Constitution. The Oklahoma framers were skeptical of government power and sought to put constitutional restraints on government.

Women's Suffrage

While the Oklahoma Constitution was reform-oriented, one major reform failed to make it through the convention. Article III of the Oklahoma Constitution did not allow women the right to vote. Women's groups had been very active in promoting suffrage in the territories and had come very close to persuading the Oklahoma territorial legislature to adopt women's suffrage. Prior to statehood, women were allowed to vote

14

TABLE 1–2		
Comparison of State and Federal Constitutional Provisions		
	U.S. CONSTITUTION	**OKLAHOMA CONSTITUTION**
Freedom from Unreasonable Search and Seizure	The right of the people to be secure in their persons, houses, papers, and effects, against unreasonable searches and seizures shall not be violated, and no Warrants shall issue, but upon probable cause, supported by Oath or affirmation, and particularly describing the place to be searched, and the persons or things to be seized. *U.S. Const. Amend. IV*	The right of the people to be secure in their persons, houses, papers, and effects against unreasonable searches or seizures shall not be violated; and no warrant shall issue but upon probable cause supported by oath or affirmation, describing as particularly as may be the place to be searched and the person or thing to be seized. *Okla. Const. Art. II Sec. 30*
Freedom of Religion	Congress shall make no law respecting an establishment of religion, or prohibiting the free exercise thereof . . . *U.S. Const. Amend. I*	No public money or property shall ever be appropriated, applied, donated, or used, directly or indirectly, for the use, benefit, or support of any sect, church, denomination, or system of religion, or for the use, benefit, or support of any priest, preacher, minister, or other religious teacher or dignitary, or sectarian institution as such. *Okla. Const. Art. II Sec. 5*
Freedom of Speech	Congress shall pass no law . . . abridging the freedom of speech, or of the press . . . *U.S. Const. Amend. I*	Every person may freely speak, write, or publish his sentiments on all subjects, being responsible for the abuse of that right; and no law shall be passed to restrain or abridge the liberty of speech or of the press . . . *Okla. Const. Art. II Sec. 22.*

in school board elections. Proponents of women's suffrage viewed the constitutional convention as the best opportunity to settle the question for the entire state (Goble, 1980).

The issue of suffrage faced strong opponents. Organized by William H. Murray, opponents feared women would vote out of emotion rather than reason. At a critical moment, the issue was linked to race. Opponents claimed that allowing women to vote would increase African American political power. Opponents pointed to a February 5, 1907, Guthrie school board election to make their point. Out of all the ballots cast, 751 African American women voted and only seven white women voted. Murray quickly called a vote on the suffrage question. Delegates from areas with large African American populations generally voted against suffrage for women, and delegates from areas with small African American populations generally voted for women's suffrage. With the exception of school board elections, women's suffrage was defeated (Goble, 1980).

Corporate Regulation

Some of the most aggressive reform proposals were those that dealt with corporations and regulation.[4] Perhaps intentionally drawing on the Sequoyah Constitution, the framers detailed provisions designed to end the influence of special interests and establish the public interest as supreme.

The constitution created a Pure Food Commission, allowed for municipal ownership of utilities, prohibited corporate ownership of land, prohibited corporate contributions and influences on campaigns, and gave the state expansive taxing authority. In addition, the constitution created a powerful Corporation Commission and gave it the responsibility of "supervising, regulating, and controlling, all transportation and transmission companies doing business in this state" (Section 18). This three-member, elected commission was given investigative and enforcement authority for the state.

IV. Cultural Context of Oklahoma Government

State government is not only formally shaped and restricted by constitutions, but also informally shaped by political culture. **Political culture** can be defined as the attitudes, beliefs, and expectations people have about what government should and should not do. These attitudes and beliefs are derived from experiences and give individuals expectations about who should participate in politics and what rules should govern group behavior. Political culture has gained a great deal of attention in political science, in part as an explanation for how various geographical areas have developed different political systems. Perhaps the

FIGURE 1–2 Official Oklahoma Commemorative Quarter Issued by the U.S. Mint

leading scholar on political culture is Daniel Elazar. His work, *American Federalism: A View from the States*, argues that political culture has its roots in the historical experience of individuals. This in turn has an effect on the way individuals view government. He suggests that even though states have lost power to the national government over time, they are still important political systems. Elazar suggests that within the United States, there are three dominant subcultures, each with distinctive characteristics. These subcultures are traditionalistic, individualistic, and moralistic (Elazar, 1982).

Traditionalistic Political Culture

The **traditionalistic political culture** emphasizes the maintenance of the current social order. Government generally does not initiate a large number of new programs unless the new programs benefit the ruling elite. Political parties are generally viewed negatively in that they tend to depersonalize government. Active participation in politics is generally limited to a small group of elites (Elazar, 1982).

Individualistic Political Culture

The **individualistic political culture** emphasizes minimal government and views politics as a marketplace. Government is responsible for regulating the marketplace to guarantee everyone the chance to pursue his or her own self-interest. Government also exists to distribute favors to those who support the current regime and to help politicians get ahead. The individualistic culture looks favorably on large bureaucracies because of the patronage jobs that are available for political workers and the services that can be provided to voters. Beyond voting, political participation by the general public is not expected. Corruption in government and politics is tolerated.

Moralistic Political Culture

The **moralistic political culture** views government as a positive force for achieving social goals in the public interest. As a result, government has a much larger role. Government often initiates programs without public pressure and justifies the activity as being in the public's interest. Bureaucracies are looked upon as useful in achieving desired ends through neutral and detached processes. Unlike the individualistic political culture, which uses patronage in the staffing of bureaucracy, moralistic political cultures rely on merit-based employment practices where people are hired based upon what they know, not who they know. Active political participation by the public is encouraged, and public officials are expected to live up to high ethical standards. Corruption is not tolerated.

Impact of Political Culture

The question remains as to the impact political culture has on government, politics, and policies in different states. There appears to be a regional aspect to political subcultures in the United States. Traditionalist subcultures are generally found throughout the South, while the individualistic subculture is found throughout the middle states. The moralistic subculture is found primarily in the Northern states, although now there is a strong moralistic presence in the Rocky Mountain and Southwestern states.

There are a number of other generalizations that can be made as well. First, political participation is higher in moralistic states and lowest in traditionalistic states. Second, states with a moralistic political culture generally spend more money on welfare, produce more innovative government programs, have more lenient divorce laws, and are more likely to support same-sex marriage. Third, not as many public officials are convicted of corrupt behavior in moralistic states as they are in individualistic and traditionalistic states. Fourth, political culture appeared to play a role in the defeat of the Equal Rights Amendment. Moralistic states were more likely to have ratified the ERA and traditionalistic states were the least likely to have approved the ERA (Elazar, 1982).

Oklahoma's Political Culture

According to Elazar, Oklahoma is part of a cluster of Southwestern states with a predominantly traditionalistic culture, but with strong individualistic tendencies. Reflecting much of what Elazar generalized and what other scholars have found, Oklahoma's classification appeared accurate. Historians and political scientists initially pointed out that for Oklahoma in the past: (1) change came slowly; (2) state and local governments often acted primarily as caretakers rather than innovators; (3) state and local politics had been dominated by one political party; (4) taking care of constituents back home had been more important than party unity; (5) corruption had played a prevalent role throughout the state's history; (6) funding for many public services is below the national average (Morgan, et al., 1991, 7–9), and (7) the legislature voted not to ratify the Equal Rights Amendment (Kincaid, 1982, 20). While Oklahoma cannot be defensibly described as moralistic, many of these points can obviously be challenged. For example, the Democratic dominance in Oklahoma politics has waned significantly, especially in the higher level state positions. The state has elected its first female governor. On a number of fronts, Oklahoma communities such as Oklahoma City have made great advances in economic development through innovative initiatives and by a willingness to increase taxes under certain conditions (see the discussion of the MAPS initiative in Chapter Ten). And arguably, Oklahoma may be developing beyond its formative stage when it tolerated corruption as a matter of just getting business done. Historically, high-profile corruption in Oklahoma politics had been prosecuted by the federal government whereas now, it is increasingly prosecuted by state and local systems of justice. Perhaps the political cultures first described by Elazar in the 1960s and 1970s have since developed in directions he did not foresee.

Oklahoma's political culture has been shaped by many forces. These forces include the traditions brought by those, both Native Americans and others, who settled the area, the unique history that influenced territorial development, and the nature and use of natural resources as well as the social and political reform movement of populism and progressivism that surrounded the development of its social and political institutions. However, political culture is not bound by the past. As Oklahoma's economic base and demographic characteristics continue to evolve, the traditions and institutions of the past will face growing pressure to change.

NOTES

1. This historical account is largely drawn from Gibson 1981 and Goble 1980, 202–227.

2. This account of the development of the Oklahoma Constitution is largely drawn from Gibson, 1981, 196–197; Morgan and Morgan, 1977, 72–79; and Goble, 1980, 187–227.

3. For a detailed description of the populist movement, see Hicks, 1959.

4. For other discussions of the corporate regulation in the Oklahoma Constitution, see Goble, 1980, 214–218; Morgan, et al., 1991, 72–74.

FEDERALISM AND OKLAHOMA

Christopher L. Markwood

*The question of the relation of the States to the federal govern-
ment is the cardinal question of our constitutional system . . . It
cannot . . . be settled by the opinion of any one generation,
because it is a question of growth, and every successive stage of
our political and economic development gives it a new aspect,
makes it a new question.*

Woodrow Wilson, *Constitutional Government in the United
States* (1908), 173.

I. INTRODUCTION

Understanding the politics and government of Oklahoma requires a
basic understanding and appreciation of the American system of
federalism. **Federalism** in the United States can be defined as "a
system in which power is divided between national and subnational governments with both exercising separate and autonomous authority, both
electing their own officials, and both taxing their own citizens for the provision of public services" (Dye & McManus, 2012, p. 70). This chapter will
(1) examine American federalism and how powers are divided between
the national and state governments, (2) analyze the evolution of power as
related to the national and state governments, (3) discuss the responsibilities of both the national government and the states, and (4) explore the
interstate relationships of Oklahoma and other states in the Union.

II. DIVIDING THE POWERS OF GOVERNMENT

Almost all nations have some type of local government and thus a distribution of power among the levels of government. While there are a number
of ways to compare various forms and types of government, one way to
classify and compare governments is by the formal distribution of power
among the various layers of government. Political scientists identify three
general forms of government based on this distribution of power: confederal, unitary, and federal. All three types are very different from each other
but at one time or another, the United States has operated under each one.[1]

21

Types of Governments

Governmental systems with a central government dependent upon the unit governments for authority or power can be referred to as **confederal systems.** While the unit governments can join together for common purposes, each unit retains its independence and grants only limited authority to the central government. As a result, the central government may be weak and ineffectual. After the American Revolution (1781–1789), the Articles of Confederation was the constitutional arrangement by which the nation was governed. Under this system, the national government had very little power and relied upon the states for both administrative and financial assistance. The national government could not tax, regulate interstate commerce, or effectively enforce its laws. These weaknesses led to the constitutional convention and ultimately the adoption of a new system of government in the Constitution of 1789.

Many countries, including England, Sweden, and France, have a **unitary system** of government, which exercises centralized control over all other governmental and political subdivisions. Whether referred to as a province, republic, village, territory, or state, local and regional subdivisions in a unitary system owe their very existence to the central or national government. Each subdivision may only exercise the authority given to it by the central or national government. As a result, subdivisions tend to be administrative divisions of the central government with little power to act on their own. Prior to the American Revolution, the Colonies were subject to a unitary system under England.

Today, Oklahoma, like other states, has a unitary governmental structure as it relates to its political subdivisions, known as **counties.** However, in Oklahoma there is an interesting variation to this structure. Since the Indian nations have been given constitutional sanction and are not "local" governments, they are not subject to the unitary structural arrangement that exists between the state and local governments in Oklahoma. As a result, many areas including some issues involving taxes, gaming, and property rights fall outside the traditional unitary structure thus limiting Oklahoma's governmental authority.

In a **federal system,** both the national government and governmental subdivisions derive their authority from the people. As a system of shared powers, each level of government has authority to make some decisions free from the external control of the other. Responsibilities can be divided between the national government and subdivisions, or responsibilities can be shared. Each level of government has spheres of authority and each has limitations. The American Constitution of 1789 created a federal system of government and divided powers between the national and state governments. These powers can be classified into five categories: delegated, implied, reserved, prohibited, and concurrent.

Types of Powers

The United States federal government is strengthened by several grants of powers. Sometimes referred to as "enumerated" or "expressed" powers, **delegated powers** are those powers specifically granted to the federal government in the U.S. Constitution. For example, Article I, Section 8, of the U.S. Constitution specifically gives Congress the power to establish a post office, levy and collect taxes, regulate interstate commerce, declare war, and coin money; Article II, Section 2, specifically gives the president the power to negotiate treaties, make appointments, and serve as commander in chief of the armed forces and state militias; and Article III, Section 2, specifically gives the Supreme Court the power to resolve disputes between states.

Implied powers are not specifically mentioned in the U.S. Constitution, but can be inferred from those that are specifically mentioned. Implied powers expand the scope of delegated powers. Article I, Section 8.18 gives Congress the power "To make all Laws which shall be necessary and proper for carrying into Execution the forgoing Powers." The Supreme Court defined and justified implied powers in the case of *McCulloch v. Maryland* (1819), reasoning that since Article I specifically gives Congress the power to coin money, regulate its value, collect taxes, and borrow money, it can be implied that Congress needs a bank even though the U.S. Constitution does not expressly give Congress the power to create one. The **"necessary and proper" clause** has given the national government a tremendous amount of elasticity in carrying out its powers and has allowed the federal government to expand its role.

Despite this rather broad bestowal of power, the 10th Amendment to the U.S. Constitution provides that "The powers not delegated to the United States by the Constitution, nor prohibited by it to the States, are reserved to the States respectively or to the people." These powers are referred to as **reserved powers.** While an exhaustive list has yet to be compiled and agreed upon by legal scholars or policy makers, it is generally recognized that state governments, including Oklahoma, retain extensive control and responsibility for regulating most domestic matters, including: the operation of public schools; maintaining public services such as transportation, hospitals, and parks; conducting most criminal and civil trials; and, administering the election process.

Powers that are denied to the national government, state governments, or both are referred to as **prohibited powers.** For example, both the federal government and the states are prohibited from passing **ex post facto laws** (a retroactive criminal law imposing punishment after an act has been committed). Article I, Section 9, of the U.S. Constitution specifically prohibits the national government from giving preference to one state over another and granting titles of nobility, while Article I, Section 10, prohibits state governments from entering into a treaty or alliance with a foreign country, coining money, or interfering with the obligation of contracts.

Concurrent or **shared powers** are those possessed by both the national and state governments. For example, while the national government has the power to tax, build roads, pass legislation, establish courts, and regulate corporations, the state of Oklahoma has these powers too. As a result, people in Oklahoma can be taxed by both the national and state governments, drive on federal interstates and state highways, and be requested to appear in federal courts for violations of federal law, and state courts for violations of state law. While these powers do overlap, state laws are not allowed to conflict with federal laws.

Supremacy of National Law

Occasionally, state laws are thought to be in conflict with federal law or the U.S. Constitution. The result can be a legal battle. Article VI, Section 2, of the U.S. Constitution states:

> *This Constitution, and the Laws of the United States which shall be made in Pursuance thereof, and all Treaties made or which shall be made under the Authority of the United States shall be the supreme Law of the land; and the Judges in every State shall be bound thereby, any Thing in the Constitution or Laws of any State shall to the Contrary not withstanding.*

This clause is known as the **National Supremacy Clause.** When conflicts arise between the laws of Oklahoma and federal laws, this constitutional provision requires that federal law take precedence. Several times, Oklahoma laws have been challenged as inconsistent with federal law. The result has been a challenge to the United States Supreme Court. The cases of *Sipuel v. University of Oklahoma* (1948) and *McLaurin v. Oklahoma State Regents for Higher Education* (1950) are illustrative.[2]

Until 1949, African American students were not allowed to attend graduate or professional school in Oklahoma. While students could pursue an undergraduate education at Langston, a black college established prior to statehood, Oklahoma statutes required "separate but equal" education. Ada Lois Sipuel-Fisher was denied admission to the University of Oklahoma Law School in 1946 because she was African American. In an appeal to the United States Supreme Court, the Justices found Oklahoma in violation of the "separate but equal" doctrine because there was no option for African Americans who wanted to pursue law school. In *Sipuel v. University of Oklahoma,* the Supreme Court ordered Oklahoma to either admit Sipuel-Fisher to the University of Oklahoma or create a separate law school where she could attend. Rather than admit her to the University of Oklahoma Law School, the state of Oklahoma opted to create a separate law school for blacks at Langston. Ada Lois Sipuel-Fisher refused to attend the separate law school and reapplied for admission to the University of Oklahoma, where she was again denied admission.

In 1948, the University of Oklahoma denied admission to six African Americans to the graduate school. George McLaurin, one of the students denied admission, reapplied and was again denied admission. The Federal District Court for Western Oklahoma soon ordered his admission. However, McLaurin was still subject to blatant discrimination. He was forced to study at a separate table in the library and was separated from the other students in classrooms.

In 1949, the University of Oklahoma admitted a number of African Americans to graduate school and Ada Lois Sipuel-Fisher to law school. However, students were still segregated in classrooms, the library, and the cafeteria. In an attempt to stop this type of discrimination, McLaurin took his case to the United States Supreme Court. In *McLaurin v. Oklahoma Regents for Higher Education* (1950), the Court ruled in favor of McLaurin and banned all forms of segregation in graduate programs.

Shortly thereafter, the United States Supreme Court decided *Brown v. Board of Education of Topeka* (1954), where the justices unanimously agreed that "separate but equal" education was unconstitutional. Although slow in some areas, Oklahoma responded by obeying the Supreme Court's order to desegregate with all "deliberate speed."

III. The Ebb and Flow of Federal Powers

American federalism expects that both the national government as well as state governments will affect each other's development. What the national government does will impact Oklahoma—what Oklahoma does will impact the national government. The relationship between the national government and the states has changed over the years with the national government generally seen as gaining power and influence over the states. This increase in the national government's power is in part the result of the incorporation of the Bill of Rights, the regulation of interstate commerce, and the use of financial incentives.

Incorporation of the Bill of Rights

During the debates surrounding the adoption of the U.S. Constitution, opponents (anti-federalists) argued that there were no protections for individual rights and liberties from the national government. As a result, after the adoption of the new U.S. Constitution, the first ten amendments were proposed and ratified. These amendments became known as the **Bill of Rights** and guarantee such liberties as freedom of speech, press, religion, and the right to counsel. However, the founders were primarily fearful of the national government. As a result, the wording of the new guarantees was such that the amendments only protected citizens from the national government—not the states. Indeed, the First Amendment provides "Congress shall make no law . . ." The Supreme Court made it clear in *Barron v. Baltimore* (1833) that if the founders had intended the restrictions on government actions to apply to states they would have said so.

After the Civil War and the ratification of the 14th Amendment in 1868, this interpretation began to change. The Fourteenth Amendment provides:

> *No State shall make or enforce any law which shall abridge the privileges and immunities of citizens of the United States; nor shall any State deprive any person of life, liberty, or property, without due process of law; nor deny to any person within its jurisdiction the equal protection of the laws.*

The Supreme Court slowly used this amendment to apply protections found in the Bill of Rights to the States. Through a process known as **"selective incorporation,"** the Supreme Court has identified sections of the Bill of Rights that are essential to "ordered liberty" and has extended individual protection from state governments as well as the national government. As a result, as shown in Table 2–1, most protections found in the Bill of Rights

TABLE 2–1 Selective Incorporation and the Bill of Rights			
AMENDMENT	RIGHT	CASE	DATE
I	Free Exercise of Religion	*Cantwell v Connecticut*	1940
	Establishment of Religion	*Everson v Board of Education*	1947
	Speech	*Gitlow v New York*	1925
	Press	*Near v Minnesota*	1937
II	Keep and Bear Arms	Not Incorporated	
III	No Quartering of Soldiers in Peacetime	Not Incorporated	
IV	No Unreasonable Searches and Seizures	*Wolf v Colorado*	1949
V	Just Compensation	*Chicago, B&O RR. Co. v Chicago*	1897
	Self-Incrimination	*Malloy v Hogan*	1964
	Double Jeopardy	*Benton v Maryland*	1969
	Indictment by Grand Jury	Not Incorporated	
VI	Public Trial	*In re Oliver*	1948
	Right to Counsel	*Gideon v Wainwright*	1963
	Speedy Trial	*Klopher v North Carolina*	1967
	Jury Trial	*Duncan v Louisiana*	1968
VII	Jury Trial in Civil Cases	Not Incorporated	
VIII	No Cruel and Unusual Punishment	*Robinson v California*	1962
	No Excessive Bail or Fines	Not Incorporated	

not only keep the national government from infringing upon our rights, but keep the Oklahoma government from violating our rights as well.

Regulation of Interstate Commerce

A second way the national government has increased power is through an expansive interpretation of interstate commerce. In response to the economic growth and problems experienced as a result of the Industrial Revolution, Congress gradually began asserting power over various aspects of the economy. While Article I, Section 8, provides "Congress shall have power . . . to regulate Commerce . . . among the several States," the U.S. Constitution does not specifically detail what is meant by the term, **"interstate commerce."** In a series of court cases over a number of years, the Supreme Court gradually expanded the definition of interstate commerce, thus expanding the ability of Congress to regulate commercial activity. Some critics of increased national power thought that the Court had defined interstate commerce so broadly that Congress could regulate virtually all commercial and economic activity, even activities once thought to be under the exclusive authority of state governments.

Occasionally, the Supreme Court finds that Congress has gone too far in using its power to regulate interstate commerce. In *U.S. v. Lopez* (1995), the Supreme Court decided that Congress exceeded its constitutional authority to regulate interstate commerce when it enacted a 1990 law, banning the possession of guns on or near school property. The majority found that mere possession of a gun had "nothing to do with 'commerce' or any sort of economic enterprise, however broadly one might define those terms." This can be viewed as a significant departure from the Court's past practice. While the Supreme Court has generally upheld the power of Congress to regulate what legislators felt to be interstate commerce, even if the connection between commerce and the issue in question was distant, the Court now seems to require at least a minimum connection with commerce.

Financial Incentives

A third way the national government has increased power and influence over the states is through financial incentives and powers. The national government has used tax credits, grants-in-aid, and the threat of withholding federal funds to encourage and coerce states into adopting or changing certain policies.

Tax credits are employed by the national government to, among other things, encourage states to adopt particular policies. For example, in 1935 Congress passed the Social Security Act. In an effort to encourage states to develop unemployment compensation programs, the Social Security Act imposed a tax on all employers. However, the act granted employers a 90 percent tax credit for contributions they made to a state program. Since few states had such programs, employers encouraged state legislatures to begin unemployment compensation programs. Soon after the adoption of this law, Oklahoma, along with other states, developed an unemployment compensation program.

Grants-in-aid are transfers of money from one level of government to another, to be spent on specified programs. Grants-in-aid generally come with standards and/or requirements. Many grants are operated on a matching basis where the state government must contribute a certain percentage. Grants can be classified into two general types: categorical and block grants.

Categorical grants are targeted for specific purposes and generally have conditions and restrictions on their use. Thus, state and local governments have little discretion in selecting where they will spend the money.

Block grants are awarded for general purposes and are awarded directly to states as opposed to local governments. Block grants allow states considerably more discretion in allocating money to individual programs. For example, while a categorical grant may provide funds specifically for Native American studies in high schools, a block grant may make funds available broadly for state educational programs. Comparing the amount of money that flows from Oklahoma into the federal treasury through taxes and fees and the amount of money that Oklahoma received from federal grants and programs, Oklahoma is one of a number of states that receives more money than it contributes.

After years of receiving funds, many states have become dependent upon that money. As a result, the national government has been able to require cooperation and uniformity in certain policy areas by withholding, or threatening to withhold, funds. Several examples in which federal money is tied to changing state laws or enforcing federal rules include: speed limits, the 21-year-old drinking age, use of seat belts, and the Americans with Disabilities Act (ADA). In most cases, all that is necessary to gain compliance from states is the threat of losing a portion of federal funds. Over the years, Oklahoma has changed its laws regarding speed limits, the use of seatbelts, the drinking age, as well as compliance and enforcement of ADA to remain eligible for federal funds.

In many areas, the federal government has imposed rules and regulations to address specific problems but has not provided the funds to meet the stated objectives. These requirements are commonly called unfunded mandates. **Unfunded mandates** have been laws or regulations regarding national clean air standards, drinking water standards, as well as the treatment and disposal of hazardous waste. As early as 1994, as much as 30 percent of local government expenditures was in response to unfunded mandates. Increased competition among the states for state and local funds, a growing opposition to such government mandates as well as new Republican majorities in both the United States House of Representatives and the United States Senate, led Congress to pass the Unfunded Mandates Act in 1995, restricting the national government's ability to require state and local governments to shoulder the costs of implementing federal rules and regulations (O'Connor and Sabato, 2011, p. 108).

IV. Responsibilities and State Governments

Maintaining a working federalism relationship means that the federal government and the states must work with each other. The U.S. Constitution prescribes a number of obligations on the federal government's relations with the states and requires states to participate in the government process.[3]

National Responsibilities and State Governments

The national government has a number of responsibilities to the states. These responsibilities include the guarantee of territorial integrity, a republican form of government, and protection from both invasion and domestic violence.

The U.S. Constitution provides guidelines for the admission of new states into the union and a guarantee of territorial integrity. Article IV, Section 3, provides:

> *New states may be admitted by the Congress into this Union; but no new State shall be formed or erected within the Jurisdiction of any other State; nor any State be formed by the Junction of two or more States, or Parts of States, without the Consent of the Legislatures of the States concerned as well as of the Congress.*

Several states were once a part of other states. These states include Kentucky, Tennessee, Maine, Vermont, Virginia, and West Virginia. While some questions exist with regard to the separation of West Virginia (sympathetic to the North) from Virginia (member of the Confederacy) in 1863 during the Civil War, the other states appear to have followed constitutional procedure. Prior to statehood, the Oklahoma panhandle was once part of Texas.

Few scholars seem to know exactly what the founders meant when they wrote in Article IV, Section 4, "The United States shall guarantee to every State in this Union a Republican Form of Government." Some define **republican government** as a type of democracy where people select representatives to make decisions. According to the U.S. Constitution, Congress is responsible for judging the elections of its members. The Supreme Court, it appears, seems willing to assume that if Congress allows a state's congressional delegation to take its seats in Congress, then the United States has certified that state to have a republican form of government.

Referring to the states, Article IV, Section 4, provides "the United States shall . . . protect each of them against Invasion; and on Application of the Legislature, or of the Executive (when the Legislature cannot be convened), against domestic Violence." If a state asks for assistance in repelling an invasion or putting down domestic violence, the national government is obligated to help. But this does not mean that the national government must always wait for an invitation. If the enforcement of national law, personnel, or property is in danger, the national government may use whatever force is necessary to eliminate the threat. In addition, the orders of federal courts may also be enforced by federal authorities within state boundaries.

State Responsibilities and the National Government

State government also have responsibilities and obligations to the national government. Among those are the election of federal officials and the consideration of constitutional amendments.

The federal government does not hold elections for federal officers. Instead, it is the responsibility of states to operate and maintain election machinery, elect members to the United States House of Representatives and the United States Senate, as well as provide support for the Electoral College. Article I, Section 4, of the U.S. Constitution requires state governments to provide the election machinery for national elections. As a result, state governments have been relatively free to regulate voter registration, control absentee ballots, supervise voting, prevent voter fraud, count ballots, and publish returns. However in 1993, Congress passed the **National Voter Registration Act** (more commonly known as the "motor voter" law) which requires states to make registration available at certain government agencies as well as to make voter registration available by mail. Oklahoma adopted its own motor voter act (HB 1088) in 1993 shortly before Congress passed the national law. The National Motor Voter law went into effect in 1995.

State governments are also called upon to conduct elections for their respective congressional delegations. Today, the United States Senate is composed of 100 members, with each state responsible for electing two senators, and the United States House of Representatives is composed of 435 members apportioned to the states by population. After the 1990 Census, Oklahoma's population guaranteed it six members in the House of Representatives. This was the same number that the state had after the 1980 Census. Unfortunately, because Oklahoma's population growth has not kept up with growth in other states, Oklahoma lost a seat in the House of Representatives after the 2000 Census and the number of Oklahoma's congressional representatives stayed at five following the 2010 Census.

The national government also relies on states to provide electors to the Electoral College. Contrary to what many Americans may think, the people do not vote directly for the president and vice president of the United States. Rather, Article II, Section 1, as amended by the 12th and 23rd

LEADERSHIP PROFILE

JAMES LANKFORD
Member of Congress, 5th District-Oklahoma

JAMES LANKFORD was first elected to the United States Congress on November 2, 2010. Before being elected, he directed the Falls Creek Youth Camp from 1996 to 2009. Falls Creek is the largest Christian camp in the nation with more than 51,000 guests every summer. While Lankford directed Falls Creek, the camp experienced the greatest growth in its nearly 100-year history. In this capacity, he earned real-world leadership and business experience. Lankford has also coordinated mission and community service projects in Belize, Malawi, England, Wales, and Germany as well as many areas of Oklahoma.

He serves on the Budget, Transportation & Infrastructure, and Oversight & Government Reform Committees, where he is the Chairman of the Subcommittee on Technology, Information Policy, Intergovernmental Relations and Procurement Reform.

He received a Bachelor of Science in Secondary Education from the University of Texas and a Master of Divinity from the Southwestern Baptist Theological Seminary.

Lankford has been married to his wife Cindy for nearly twenty years. Together, they have two daughters: Hannah and Jordan. James enjoys spending time with his family, sport shooting, and reading.

Amendments, provides that each state is guaranteed Electoral College representation equal to the number of senators and representatives it has in Congress, and that the Electoral College has the responsibility to formally elect the president and the vice president. As a result, Oklahoma has seven electoral votes. According to Article II, Section I, the U.S. Constitution leaves the actual selection method to each state. By virtue of the 23rd Amendment, the District of Columbia has three votes. Some states select electors by conventions, some use primaries, and some use committees. In Oklahoma, political parties use their statewide conventions to select their presidential electors.

State are also responsible for the consideration of constitutional amendments. Article V of the U.S. Constitution states that amendments may be proposed by one of two methods: by a two-thirds vote in both houses of Congress or by a constitutional convention if two-thirds of the states petition Congress and ask for one. Amendments may also be ratified in one of two ways: by three-fourths of state legislatures, or by specially called ratifying conventions in three-fourths of the states. All constitutional amendments to date were originally proposed by Congress; the convention system has only been used once and that was to ratify the 21st Amendment. Congress submitted the repeal of prohibition to state conventions for fear that state legislatures (dominated by rural interests) would be less favorable to repealing prohibition. Since the 1980s, the Oklahoma legislature has considered two amendments to the U.S. Constitution. In 1982, the legislature voted against ratifying the proposed Equal Rights Amendment, and in 1985, the legislature voted in favor of ratifying the 27th Amendment to the U.S. Constitution, which prevents congressional pay raises from taking effect until after an election.

V. Interstate Relations

The U.S. Constitution also details the relationships that are to exist among the states. States are to grant each other's public acts and records full faith and credit, extend privileges and immunities to citizens of other states, return people who are fleeing from justice in another state, and consult Congress before entering interstate compacts.

Full Faith and Credit

Article IV, Section 1, provides that "Full Faith and Credit shall be given in each State to the public Acts, Records, and judicial Proceedings of every other State." In an increasingly mobile society, it has become very important that state governments recognize the public acts, records, and judicial proceedings of other states. This means that documents such as wills, mortgages, birth certificates, and contracts, as well as acts such as adoption, marriages, and divorces granted or issued in Oklahoma, must be recognized and enforced by other states. One of the growing problems in interstate relations is the reluctance of states to meet the obligations under the **Full Faith and Credit Clause,** particularly in the area of domestic relations. It is often very difficult for a former spouse to collect alimony and child support from a spouse or parent who has moved out of state.

A future question under the Full Faith and Credit Clause that may be decided by the U.S. Supreme Court involves the issue of same-sex marriages. If a state recognizes same-sex marriages as legal, and requires state officials to issue marriage certificates to same-sex couples, will Oklahoma recognize that marriage? In an attempt to define the position of the federal government, Congress passed the Defense of Marriage Act (DOMA) in 1996 and provided that states are not required to recognize same-sex marriages from other states, but did not prevent them from doing so if they wanted (Kersch, 1997).

Extradition

Article IV, Section 2, provides "a person . . . who shall flee from Justice, and be found in another State, shall on Demand of the executive Authority of the State from which he fled, be delivered up, to be removed to the State having jurisdiction of the Crime." Oklahoma, and all other states, have adopted the Uniform Criminal Extradition Act which unified the procedures for requesting the return of an accused criminal. However, the U.S. Supreme Court has not always required states to return individuals fleeing the justice system of another state. In *Kentucky v. Dennison* (1861), the Supreme Court ruled that Ohio's Governor Dennison was not forced to return a black man to Kentucky, a slave state, where he was accused of helping slaves escape. The Supreme Court stated governors were under a moral duty to return accused individuals, but not a legal duty.

In 1987, the Supreme Court reversed its Civil War era ruling. In the case of *Puerto Rico v. Branstad,* the Court ruled that Iowa's Governor Branstad had a legal duty to return an individual to Puerto Rico for a manslaughter trial, regardless of whether or not the governor believed that the individual could get a fair trial. In effect, the Court changed its mind and said that honoring an extradition request was a legal duty, not just a moral duty. In 2004, the state of Oklahoma entertained 91 formal extradition requests from other states and made 96 formal requests for accused criminals to be returned to Oklahoma.

Privileges and Immunities

Article IV, Section 2, provides "The Citizens of each State shall be entitled to all **Privileges and Immunities** of citizens in the several States." This means that states are not supposed to discriminate against citizens of another state or give favorable treatment to their own citizens. The Supreme Court has ruled that citizens of any state may travel freely in other states, may purchase property in other states, may use the court systems in other states, must be guaranteed equal protection of the law, and may take up residence in another state. There are, however, several exceptions where states are allowed to treat residents differently. First, states are allowed to establish reasonable residency requirements for those holding public offices. Second, states are allowed to charge non-residents more for services such as fishing and gaming licenses and for state institutions of higher education. Third, states are allowed to require individuals to obtain state licenses before practicing professions such as law and education. As such, in Oklahoma, the governor must have been a qualified voter for 10 years prior to taking office, out-of-state tuition is often double what an in-state student pays, and those wishing to be teachers, lawyers, social workers, and numerous others must be licensed or certified by the state of Oklahoma.

Interstate Compacts

Article I, Section 10, of the U.S. Constitution provides "No State shall, without the Consent of Congress . . . enter into any Agreement or Compact with another State . . ." **Interstate compacts** are formal binding agreements between two or more states. Today, there are over one hundred interstate compacts on issues including: flood control, wildlife, interstate toll highways, coordination of welfare programs, supervision of parolees, traffic enforcement, disaster assistance, child placement, and waste disposal. Oklahoma has joined a number of interstate compacts, including the Interstate Oil Compact, which attempts to monitor and coordinate the conditions and prices of the oil industry (Morgan, et al., 1991). While the U.S. Constitution requires congressional consent for interstate compacts, there is no mention as to when or how this consent is to be given. Indeed Congress provides little supervision in the development of interstate compacts and the Supreme Court has never ruled an interstate compact unconstitutional (Hardy, et al, 1995).

Suits Between States

Occasionally conflicts between two or more states cannot be settled among those involved. When that occurs, the Supreme Court has original jurisdiction and the power to resolve the dispute. As a result, the case can be heard immediately by the Supreme Court without having to begin in lower federal courts. The Supreme Court has heard and settled disputes between states that have involved issues of borders, water rights, and the disposal of garbage. Oklahoma's "Red River rivalry" with Texas has resulted in numerous lawsuits including *Texas v. Oklahoma* 457 US 172 (1982), a dispute over the Red River boundary.

Strengths and Weaknesses of Federalism

The American system of federalism has both strengths and weaknesses. As a system that seeks to decentralize powers, American federalism is a mix of national and state powers that helps manage political conflict by dispersing political power among governments. With both the national government and state governments seeking to solve many of the same problems, federalism encourages policy innovation by having many different governmental actors developing ideas and strategies. Federalism can also provide greater responsiveness by allowing state and local governments to address problems directly rather than relying on one central authority to administer the solution.

However, a federal system also has weaknesses. Decentralization and diversity creates a lack of uniformity and considerable duplication. State and local governments have different laws regarding traffic, definitions and penalties for crimes, educational requirements, and even marriage and divorce rules. These different laws and rules can cause confusion. National, state, and local governments often provide duplicate services. This overlapping of functions can be both inefficient and confusing.

VI. Conclusion

Intergovernmental relations in our federal system are important and dynamic. Federalism affects virtually every aspect of policymaking and governing. The federal government and the states must work together and the states must develop cooperative working relationships with each other. Yet, like all relationships, American federalism has experienced change. While the federal government has increased its powers over the course of two centuries, recently, it has been Congress asserting that states should shoulder a larger burden of the development, oversight, and financing of policies and programs. Whether this shift is the result of a resurgence in conservative ideology, an abdication by the national government of its leadership role, or the result of fewer federal dollars for state programs, state governments such as Oklahoma are having more expected of them. As a result, states have become leaders in policy innovation in such areas as welfare reform, tax reform, health care, corrections, affirmative action, and in the case of Oklahoma, term limits.

To understand government and politics in Oklahoma, one must understand the system within which it operates. Oklahoma and the other states have come together with the national government to form the federal system we have today. However, Oklahoma brings to American federalism a unique perspective on governing, which affects its relationships both with the federal government and with other states. In addition, Oklahoma brings to the federalism relationship a distinctive history which affects its own internal governmental structure as well as public policy.

Chapter Two

NOTES

1. For additional discussions on federalism and how it has changed, see Hardy, 1995, 5–20; O'Connor & Sabato, 2011, 90–112; Lorch, 2001, 21–48; Dye & McManus, 2012, 70–104.
2. This discussion about segregation in Oklahoma is largely drawn from Gibson, 1981, 237–239 and Morgan, et al, 1991, 27.
3. For a detailed discussion, see Lorch, 2001, 42–44.

MODERN SEQUOYAH: NATIVE AMERICAN POWER IN OKLAHOMA POLITICS

Christine Pappas

Only rarely in U.S. history has the law served as a shield to protect Native Americans from abuse and to futher their aspirations as indigenous peoples.

Walter Echo Hawk

I. INTRODUCTION

In 1905, a group of influential men met in Muskogee. They sought to protect their interests by promoting statehood. They wrote a 35,000-word Constitution, drew county borders, and designed a state seal. One of the men would become Governor of Oklahoma. One would be a U.S. Senator. Another man would serve as Speaker of the Oklahoma House of Representatives, then serve in the U.S. House of Representatives, and then finally be elected Governor. These men were attempting to create a state just for Indians. They named their state Sequoyah after the famous Cherokee scholar. The Sequoyah Constitution was ratified by the voters in Indian Territory by a vote of 56,279 to 9,073 and it was sent to Congress for consideration. Instead of creating an Indian state, Congress voted to create the state of Oklahoma, merging Oklahoma and Indian Territories (Maxwell, 1953). The state of Oklahoma entered the union in 1907. Its first governor would be Charles N. Haskell who represented the Creek Nation at the Sequoyah Convention. One of its first two U.S. Senators was Robert L. Owen, a Cherokee Attorney. Finally, William H. Murray who represented the Chickasaw Nation at the Sequoyah Convention, would write the Oklahoma Constitution, and be elected to be Speaker of the House, U.S. Congressman, and Governor.

Many native hopes were pinned on the Sequoyah Movement. The U.S. government promised in treaties that certain native lands would not be incorporated into a U.S. state without native consent. Creek Chief Pleasant Porter said, "The national government must grant us separate statehood or make a confession" (quoted in Maxwell 1953, 88). The "confession" would be that the government broke its word. However, if statehood for natives had been won, the sovereignty-based relationships that tribes hold with the U.S. federal government would have been extinguished. Sequoyah would have become a state like any other without the valuable treaty rights and sovereignty that tribes enjoy today. In fact, this chapter argues that Native America avoided a tragedy by losing the fight to become a separate state. Without retaining treaty rights and sovereignty, Oklahoma tribes would not be enjoying the renaissance that they are experiencing today.

The history of tribes in the United States in general and Oklahoma in particular is complicated. Oklahoma is unique among states. As state-issued license plates profess, "Oklahoma is Indian Territory." Per capita, Oklahoma has more Native Americans than any other state. Other states have reservations but Oklahoma is different. Our system of national tribal jurisdiction ensures that natives are not ghettoized into arid corners of the state. Over half of the state—including the entire city of Tulsa—falls within a tribal jurisdiction ensuring that native lands are suffused with people of all races. Additionally, natives are more widely dispersed in Oklahoma than any other state (Strickland, 1980). Consider the Choctaw nation. Only 10% of the population living within Choctaw National boundaries are Choctaw and 80% of tribal members live elsewhere (Lambert, 2007).

There are three identifiable phases of tribal governments in the U.S. that we can apply to the state of Oklahoma: *Original, Transitional,* and *Contemporary* (Wilkins & Stark, 2010). The first phase stretches from first contact in about 1500 to the end of the treaty period in about 1870. The second phase is marked by a decimation of original tribal governments while the U.S. federal government assumed many functions. For Oklahoma tribes, this began in 1907 with Oklahoma statehood. The third phase begins in 1934 with the Indian Reorganization Act when tribes were allowed by the federal government to write their own constitutions. However, tribal chiefs were appointed by the U.S. President until 1970. There is a special history for the Five "Civilized" Tribes of Oklahoma (Creek, Choctaw, Seminole, Cherokee, and Chickasaw). These tribes were often excluded from general tribal policy (such as the 1887 Allotment Act) and subject to special laws.

This chapter reviews the three phases of history of tribal government in Oklahoma, explains why tribal governments may now outmatch the state of Oklahoma government, and discusses some of the major conflicts tribes have with the state of Oklahoma. I conclude by theorizing that today tribes are experiencing a "Modern Sequoyah." The statehood movement may have been a failure but the growing success of tribes today surpasses any achievements that would have been possible in the state of Sequoyah. Tribes have grown tremendously in political power and economic impact and tribal members make up 13% of the population of Oklahoma. The effects of Native American success are not limited to tribes: "Tribal income had ripple effects on personal income for employees and suppliers to tribes, which some economists estimate have a multiplier effect of five times on the larger economy but also on health care, housing, bridges, roadways, and taxes paid" (Clark 2009, 16).

II. HISTORY OF OKLAHOMA TRIBES

Original Governments

Oklahoma has 38 federally recognized tribes.[1] Six tribes are indigenous to the area and the remaining tribes were relocated to Indian Territory from states as diverse as California, New York, Florida, and Texas. The Cherokee Trail of Tears is the most notable, but each tribe has its own trail and timeline. As early as 1803 Thomas Jefferson proposed the idea for a permanent native area somewhere West ... beyond white settlement. By the 1830s, hunger for land and natural resources pressed natives out of Georgia, Florida, Alabama, and Mississippi toward Indian Territory. Tribes adapted. Many sent settlers out first to tame the land and establish institutions such as schools and governments. The Cherokee "old settlers," for example, established over 100 schools and the great scholar Sequoyah wrote the Cherokee syllabary. Literacy rates in the Cherokee Nation were much higher than in surrounding white areas (www.cherokee.org). Oklahoma Choctaws were completely self-sufficient during this period. They farmed, ranched and made their own pottery and clothing (Lambert, 2007).

Tribes signed treaties with the U.S. from 1778 until 1871. The U.S. Constitution provides in Article 1, Section 8, Clause 3 that Congress shall regulate commerce "with foreign Nations, and among the several States, and with Indian Tribes." This clause is known as the **"Indian Commerce Clause"** and it is often cited as proof that the Framers presumed native sovereignty. At first Congress carried out this regulation by negotiating dozens of treaties. That treaties were the chosen form of negotiation signals that the U.S. believed itself to be interacting with independent nations.

The Treaty of Dancing Rabbit Creek in 1830 was the first removal treaty. The Choctaws pledged to exchange about 11 million acres in Mississippi for about 15 million acres in Indian Territory. This treaty is unusual because instead of placing the land in trust as would become customary, it gave the land to the Choctaw Nation in "fee simple," the most perfect legal title to land one can own. The treaty also promised that the land would never be included in any state and included the implicit promise of the rights to the waters in the land. Despite the waning of tribal power throughout much of the twentieth century, the water rights were never disturbed. In much the same way that the Tenth Amendment to the U.S. Constitution reserves powers to states that are not delegated to the federal government, tribes consider that sovereignty not signed away in a treaty continues to be reserved to the tribe. These particular rights have become the basis of disputes over the development of Sardis Lake and rights to the Arkansas River basin both of which are located within the Choctaw Nation's boundaries.

The Civil War was a devastating time for tribes in Oklahoma. Some sided with the North and some with the South. The Chickasaws and Choctaws, for example, fought with the South because the Confederate Government agreed to continue annuity payments that the Union government allowed to lapse. At the end of the war, each of the Five Tribes sent representatives to Washington, D.C. to make new treaties. The Seminoles went first and their treaty formed the pattern for the other four (Maxwell 1953). The Creeks lost one-half of their land in their Reconstruction treaty. The Choctaws lost one-third of their land, signed a treaty to let the railroad come through, and were forced to give citizenship to Freedmen (Lambert 2007).[2]

The thirst for Indian lands was unquenchable. Tribes negotiated with the federal government to find their rights and lands ever diminished. The **Treaty of Medicine Lodge** (1867) allowed the railroad through Indian Territory. Because the tribes held title to their lands, railroads were worried their interests would not be protected. They began to push for Oklahoma statehood (Maxwell, 1953). The trains brought more white settlers, who expected peace and safety. U.S. Army troops preferred the certainty of guns to the uncertainty of diplomacy. In 1868, General Custer attacked Black Kettle's village at the Battle of the Washita. As Strickland (1980) notes, the creativity of the Five Tribes was drawing to an end, replaced with the battle for survival.

The Treaty Period ended in 1871 when Congress passed a law stating, "No Indian nation or tribe within the territory of the United States shall be acknowledged or recognized as an independent nation, tribe, or power with whom the United States may contract by treaty" (25 U.S. Code § 71). After 1871, Congress would use its "plenary power" to regulate tribal relations. The phrase "plenary power" was used by the U.S. Supreme Court in the case *U.S. v. Kagama* (1886) to describe Congress's total and complete power to regulate tribal affairs. This legal arrangement was bleak for tribes. Tribes were completely subject to the whims of Congress and to Supreme Court jurisprudence that was unpredictable if not clearly hostile to Indian claims.

An assimilationist Congress wanted to end the "Indian Problem" by breaking up tribes through individual land ownership. The **1887 Allotment Act** would provide a tract of land for each tribal citizen (thus ending communal ownership of tribal lands) and allowing for the surplus land to be sold. Individual ownership would also result in individuals selling their land to speculators. The result of the Allotment Act is that most tribal land passed into white hands. Most tribes in Oklahoma were subject to the Allotment Act, but the Five Tribes were not. A separate act delayed allotment for the Five Tribes until 1906. At that time, allotments went into effect and "tribal government was eviscerated" when tribal courts were abolished and the Five Tribes lost their ability to elect their own chiefs (Lambert, 2007).

The Sequoyah Movement was launched in the context of impending allotments. It should not be a surprise that the convention was so well organized because the Five Tribes had been operating successful governments within the region for the past seventy years. Most other area residents were newcomers with no experience in public administration. Men at the Sequoyah Convention wrote the Sequoyah Constitution. Once Congress voted to allow the state of Oklahoma to join the union many of these same men, William H. Murray in particular, were able to duplicate their effort at the Oklahoma Constitutional Convention in Guthrie.

In 1953, Historian Amos Maxwell looked back upon the **Sequoyah Convention** and called it "The culminating event in the colorful history of the Five Civilized Tribes" (Maxwell 1953, 9). From his vantage point he thought the Five Tribes were through. If not for two important acts of Congress he probably would have been correct.

Transitional Governments

Between 1906 and 1970, Native American power in Oklahoma was very low. The great historian Angie Debo observed in 1970, "It was, of course, impossible for the completely pulverized tribes like the Five Tribes of Oklahoma to collect their scattered fragments" (Debo 1970, 341). What happened? The great tribal leaders, such as Robert L. Owen, turned toward non-tribal politics to express their ambitions. The allotment policies took their toll as land ceased to be held in common by tribes. The **Five Tribes Act of 1906** stipulated that Creeks, Choctaws, Chickasaws, Seminoles, and Cherokees could not elect their own chiefs and they would be appointed by the U.S. President. Tribal courts were abolished (Lambert, 2007). By the 1930s, traditions and rituals died out. According to Lambert (2007), the only thing the Choctaw Nation retained during this time was a chief appointed by the President, 10,746 acres (all that remained from the 7.5 million acres held in 1860), and porous national boundaries.

In 1934, Congress passed the critical **Indian Reorganization Act** (IRA) which ended the devastating allotment policy. It also called for tribes to reorganize their governments, made loans available, and made it easier for natives to be hired at the Indian Bureau. The IRA didn't apply to Oklahoma, but Congress passed the **Oklahoma Indian Welfare Act** in 1936 which accomplished the same goals for Oklahoma tribes. The Great Depression was raging at this time and particularly ravaged Oklahoma. In 1940 Angie Debo wrote, "Unquestionably the policy of destroying the Indians' institutions and suppressing the traits that once made them strong has degraded an overwhelming majority of the fullblood group" (Debo 1940, 394-5).

LEADERSHIP PROFILE

BILL ANOATUBBY
Governor, Chickasaw Nation

BILL ANOATUBBY is the 30th Governor of the Chickasaw Nation of Oklahoma. His career in tribal politics began in 1975 when he served as health services director. In 1979 he was elected Lieutenant Governor with Governor Overton James. In 1987, Bill Anoatubby was elected by the tribal members as the Governor of the Chickasaw Nation and continues to serve his people today. Anoatubby was born in Tishomingo in 1945. He graduated from Tishomingo High School and attended Murray State College. He  transferred to East Central University and graduated with degrees in business and accounting in 1972. Anoatubby wanted to enter the business world, but Governor Overton James asked him to come to work for the tribe. He has been there ever since.

In a recent interview Governor Anoatubby shared his views on tribal government: "I work to conduct myself to be what the people elected me to be and to do that job."

He spoke about the importance of creating unity within government, something he has been tremendously successful at doing: "When you're elected, then you become the leader; you become the government official; you need to run government, and need to quit playing politics; you need to run government, that's how I work to conduct myself." Governor Anoatubby devotes his efforts to improving the Chickasaw Nation's finances, education, economic development, environmental protection, and health care.

The Chickasaw Nation is the thirteenth largest American Indian tribe in the United States. The headquarters is located in Ada, Oklahoma. The Chickasaw Nation serves thirteen counties in Oklahoma and offers many services to its tribal members which it is able to fund due to the tribes' many successful businesses, including gaming. Tribal assets have increased dramatically, and the Chickasaw Nation has become one of the first Native American governments in the U.S. designated as an A-102 tribe, with a superior rating for both management and fiscal controls.

Governor Anoatubby chairs over more than 50 different governmental programs, 13 tribal businesses, manages over 12,000 employees and is responsible for a $350 million annual budget. Governor Anoatubby has strengthened self-sufficiency for the Chickasaw Nation and his people. The highly honored Chickasaw leader has been re-elected in every election and is currently serving his seventh term. Governor Anoatubby was also inducted into the Oklahoma Hall of Fame in 2004. He has been a Member of the Inter-Tribal Council of the Five Civilized Tribes since 1978 and has served as both vice president and president of that council. He also serves as a Member of the Greater Oklahoma City Area Chamber of Commerce Board of Directors. East Central University named him a Distinguished Alumni in 1995.

Donna Iti Tupa

Many natives served in World War II and may have expected better treatment from the U.S. government after the war. In fact, federal policy toward natives took another ruinous turn in 1953 when Congress passed **House Concurrent Resolution 108** which made the termination of tribes official policy. Several Oklahoma tribes faced termination. The Osage didn't even know they were being considered for termination when they were alerted by the National Congress of American Indians (NCAI) that a hearing was being held. They rushed to Washington, D.C., and managed to save their tribe (Debo 1970). The Choctaw Nation was also on the verge of termination. Their appointed Principal Chief Harry Belvin made promises about getting money for tribal members that were very positively received. However, the way he was going to get the money was to terminate the tribe, sell all tribal land, and disburse the proceeds to members. Without a last-minute effort by Choctaw youth in Oklahoma City, the tribe would have been terminated. Congress repealed the termination legislation just one day before it would have gone into effect in 1970 (Lambert, 2007).

Contemporary Governments

There are two acts of Congress that have led to the rebirth of tribal power in Oklahoma. First, Congress passed a law enabling the Five Tribes to elect their own chiefs in 1970 (84 U.S. Code 1091). Second, once the termination policy ended, the federal government strongly began to support tribal economic opportunities, particularly gaming. **The Indian Gaming Regulatory Act of 1988** was a lifeline for tribes.

Wilkins and Stark (2010) write that for some tribes, the contemporary era began as early as the 1930s when tribes began to reorganize their governments and write new constitutions under the direction of the Office of Indian Affairs. However, tribes in Oklahoma mainly were dormant until 1970 when they were allowed to elect their own leaders for the first time in almost 100 years. The Cherokee, Chickasaw, and Creeks each elected their governors or principal chiefs in 1970 or 1971. Tribal government capacity did not expand overnight. It was said of Choctaw Chief Belvin that "The business of the tribe fit into his top desk drawer" (Lambert, 2007, p. 80). The annual budget for the Chickasaw Nation expanded from $50,000 in 1960 to $750,000 in 1975 (Hale & Gibson, 1991). Passage of the **Indian Self Determination and Education Assistance Act** in 1975 funneled money to tribes in a block grant or "compact" to spend on projects or goals. The trend today is that tribes administer their own programs, assuming more and more of the work that had been done by the Bureau of Indian Affairs, Indian Housing through the Department of Housing and Urban Development, or the Indian Health Service.

The Indian Gaming Regulatory Act of 1988 was Ronald Reagan's attempt to create a more independent Indian country. Indeed, "Indian gaming has been the single most important catalyst for the economic advancement of Indian tribes, their reservations, and their surrounding communities" (Pevar 2012, 275). The policy was a shift because prior to this time, the federal government did not encourage tribes to engage in economic activity ... especially activity that would get in the way of the termination of the tribe. Reagan's support for tribal economic activity is an expansion of the "New Federalism" policies he supported in terms of states rights. He wanted to build both states and tribes. As his Secretary of the Interior James Watt crassly explained, "Instead of depending on the Great White Father why don't you start your own damn business?" (quoted in Bays, 2002, 186).

For tribes to have the right to begin gaming, they must enter into a compact with the state in which they are located. This process began in 2004 in Oklahoma when voters approved the **Oklahoma State-Tribal Gaming Act** in a referendum known as State Question 712. The Choctaw Nation spearheaded the campaign for the State Question 712's passage (Lambert, 2007). Once it passed, the state of Oklahoma negotiated gaming compacts with each tribe including what percentage of profits the state will take. Most states take at least 8% of the profits, but Oklahoma tribes managed to negotiate just 4% for the state of Oklahoma in most instances (http://okpolicy.org/files/gaming_2008.pdf). Tribal casinos engage in "Class II+" games which includes Vegas style slot machines and a few table games such as blackjack and poker.

By 2008, Oklahoma was second in the nation behind California in revenues from Indian casinos. In 2011, tribal casinos earned $3.48 million compared to the total budget of the state of Oklahoma of $6.7 billion in the same year (Ellis, 2013). Casinos and gaming make up just a portion of tribes' economic portfolios. Also prevalent are travel stops where tribes may sell gasoline and tobacco without collecting excise taxes from tribal members as well as a variety of manufacturing and services.

III. THE STATE OF OKLAHOMA GOVERNMENT AND TRIBES

In the period between 1906 and 1970 the State of Oklahoma had little reason to concern itself with tribes. Tribes' primary relationship was with the U.S. federal government first through the Office of Indian Affairs and now through the Bureau of Indian Affairs. One notable fact is that many tribal members were heavily involved with Oklahoma state and local governments in writing the Oklahoma Constitution (which was patterned after the Sequoyah Constitution) and as early governors and state legislators. Many of the people with longstanding ties to Oklahoma were tribal members who had been involved in building and operating tribal institutions.

Today, the State of Oklahoma seems to hold an indifferent if not hostile stance toward tribes, at least in public. Instead of negotiating agreements with tribes, disputes end up in court where it is likely that the uneven jurisprudence of the federal courts will yield unpredictable and unsatisfying results. Both sides stand to gain by negotiating agreements rather than going to court. Wildenthal concludes that tribes' relationship with the federal government is "unpredictable" and that "many state governments are unremittingly hostile to Indian sovereignty" (2003, 121).

Laurence Haupman (1995) described the attorneys for the Native American Rights Fund (NARF) as "warriors with attaché cases." Modern tribes do battle in boardrooms and election booths. Today, tribal governments have the capacity to outmatch the state of Oklahoma government. They have the political skills and finances to dominate economically and politically.

First, tribes plan for the long term—the "seventh generation" (www .ncai.org). Non-tribal governments typically only focus on the next election two, four, or six years down the line.[3]

Second, tribes can be more unified. Lambert points out, Oklahoma's state government is extremely fragmented while tribal governments have the capability of being "highly centralized" (2007, 28). Ironically, the reason that the state of Oklahoma's government is so filled with paralyzing checks and balances is because of the populist orientation of its authors like William H. Murray. Basically, tribal government *can* all get on the same page to pursue a goal. Former Cherokee Principal Chief Chad Smith advises Indians to "survive, adapt, prosper, excel" (quoted in Russell, 2010, p. 25). With Oklahoma independently electing the Governor, Lt. Governor, and several other statewide offices, even the Governor's cabinet may have different agendas or even political parties. However, just because tribe *can* coordinate, doesn't mean they always do. Tribes have extremely disruptive disputes within their governments such as the division between more modern and traditional members.

Third, tribes seek to place members in all levels of the state and federal government. The phrase **"going off the reservation"** has been used to describe this strategy. More tribal members are entering non-tribal office instead of investing their careers in tribal office. Tribal elections and governments are an invisible pipeline to power that non-tribal members cannot see. It is just as likely in Oklahoma that a candidate for legislature or even U.S. Congress got his or her political experience on a tribal legislature or with a tribal government. Two of the most powerful politicians in Oklahoma today—Rep. Tom Cole who represents the 4th District in the U.S. House of Representatives, and T.W. Shannon, former Speaker of the Oklahoma House of Representatives and U.S. Senate candidate—are Chickasaws. In the Oklahoma Legislature, in 2013, five of 48 Senators were enrolled natives, and 26 of 101 House members were native (Daffron 2013).

Fourth, tribes greatly affect non-tribal elections by encouraging get-out-the-vote drives and financially supporting friendly candidates (www.ncai.org). Tribes don't tend to lean one way or the other with their donations and often make contributions to both Democrats and Republicans. Individual natives tend to vote with the Democratic Party. However, as former NCAI President and current Lt. Governor of the Chickasaw Nation said, "We are not mobilizing for one party or for one candidate. Indians don't just vote D for Democrat or R for Republican. For us, it's 'I' for Indian" (Keel, 2012).

Fifth, tribes may band together and be unstoppable. Pan-Indian movements in the U.S. have never materialized, but the NCAI counts half of all tribes in the U.S. as members. The coordination between the Choctaws and Chickasaws on water issues is a good example of how tribes can work together to outmatch the state of Oklahoma.

IV. Issues to Watch

Several major issues implicate the State of Oklahoma and tribes although tribes primarily relate with the federal government. Currently, the stance of the State of Oklahoma does not seem to be receptive to tribes and sovereignty. Oklahoma Democratic Party Chair Wallace Collins stated that Governor Fallin "is showing a pattern of behavior of disregarding our Native American tribal members and treating them as obstacles, rather than citizens of our state" (Daffron, 2012). Several issues showcase this relationship.

First, the formal mechanism for tribal-state communication has been weakened. In 2011 the state of Oklahoma abolished the commission that advised the governor on tribal issues. The Legislature created the Oklahoma Indian Affairs Commission (OIAC) in 1967 to serve as the liaison between tribes and the state of Oklahoma. It had nine members who each represented a different region of the state. It was independent from the Executive Branch.

Governor Mary Fallin created a new position within the executive branch—Oklahoma Native American Liaison—in 2012. After one year in office the Liaison, Jacque Hensley, a member of the Kaw Nation, issued a report outlining her direct access to the governor and the many roundtable discussions she held with all 38 federally recognized tribes in Oklahoma. Tribes have not been happy with the change. In March, 2014, HB 1305 was introduced by Cherokee legislator Chuck Hosin (who also serves as Chief of Staff for Cherokee Principal Chief Bill John Baker). If passed, this bill would have elevated the position to cabinet level. Although the Liaison did meet with all Oklahoma tribes there is no assurance that this appointee will fully represent tribal interests to the governor as the OIAC was able to. Abolishing the OIAC was taken as an insult throughout Oklahoma Indian Country.

Second, the issue of water has plagued Oklahoma. This is a state which is wracked by droughts and floods on a yearly basis. Managing this "feast and famine" has always been a problem for Oklahoma. Tribes were not part of the conversation about water throughout most of the Twentieth Century because of their diminished governments, but today they are reasserting their power. In the "reserved powers" conception of treaty rights, both the Choctaw and Chickasaw Nation have claims on water such as that being held in Sardis Lake under the **Treaty of Dancing Rabbit Creek**.[4] During the administrations of Governor Frank Keating and Governor Brad Henry the state of Oklahoma and these two tribes nearly came to an agreement on how to split proceeds of the water. However, the negotiations were not completed and the issue ended up in court.[5] The Chickasaw and Choctaw Nation sued Governor Fallin in 2011 to stop the Oklahoma Water Resources Board from selling storage rights at Sardis Lake. The state of Oklahoma responded by asking the Oklahoma Supreme Court to step in and perform a stream adjudication.[6] This is a strange move because state courts do not have any jurisdiction over tribal water rights. Tribes strenuously objected and were pleased when the U.S. Justice Department intervened and moved the case to federal court. This complicated case has been granted many stays and no action is expected until summer of 2014. Lambert (2007) points out an interesting fact about the water conflict. The Choctaw Nation has been so effective in stating its claim that the non-native citizens of South East Oklahoma actually side with the tribes against the state government. Her statement is verified by the fact that both legislators who represent the Chickasaw Nation's home district have sided with the tribes against the state (Associated Press, 2011).

Third, the issue of the **Indian Child Welfare Act** (ICWA) created a surprising firestorm in 2013 with was what is known as the **"Baby Veronica Case."** ICWA was passed by Congress in 1978 in the face of evidence that as many as 25% of Indian children were being taken from their families and placed in non-tribal homes. ICWA states that tribal children must be placed with other tribal families, if possible. Baby Veronica's Cherokee father, Dusten Brown, allowed his parental rights to be terminated not knowing that she would then be placed for adoption. She was adopted by a non-native couple from South Carolina. When Dusten Brown tried to reclaim his daughter, his petition was rejected and the case finally ended up in the U.S. Supreme Court. The Court ruled that Baby Veronica should stay with the South Carolina couple. For natives in Oklahoma, the Court's ruling was demoralizing and disappointing (although not totally surprising considering the Court's checkerboard Indian law jurisprudence). However, Governor Fallin's actions were more upsetting. Instead of declining to comment on the case, she publically took the side of the South Carolina couple and signed an extradition order for Dusten Brown to face criminal charges in South Carolina saying that he had acted in "bad faith" (Hennessy-Fiske, 2013).

Fourth, it may become possible to bypass the state of Oklahoma government completely. For example, the Obama Administration granted Federal Stimulus and Disaster Relief funds directly to the tribes. Additionally, the new "Promise Zone" designation received by the Choctaw Nation creates another bypass of the state government. The Obama Administration worked with the Choctaw Nation to identify priorities for the zone and will directly fund projects that achieve those priorities (Copeland, 2014).

In summary, the relationship between the state of Oklahoma and the 38 federally recognized tribes in the state could be a source of much mutual gain. Instead, the relationship is fraught with mistrust. Issues that should be negotiated end up in federal court costing both sides millions of dollars in legal fees and lost opportunity costs. Relationships with local governments seem to be better but should be made more transparent.

V. MODERN SEQUOYAH

If the State of Sequoyah had been established by Congress in 1905 as tribal leaders wished, treaty rights would have been extinguished and tribes would not be able to enjoy the resurgence based on these rights that they enjoy today (Leeds, 2007). Russell writes, "If the Five Tribes decided to recreate the State of Sequoyah today, they could have everything but the land base, at the precise time in history when political power is coming unglued from geography" (2010, 146). In fact, it could be concluded that a Modern Sequoyah does indeed exist. Tribes exert more political power and economic impact in the State of Oklahoma than they have at any point since statehood.

NOTES

1. The 38 federally recognized tribes are Absentee-Shawnee Tribe of Indians, Alabama-Quassarte Tribal Town, Apache Tribe, Caddo Nation, Cherokee Nation, Cheyenne & Arapaho Tribes, Chickasaw Nation, Choctaw Nation, Citizen Potawatomi Nation, Comanche Nation, Delaware Nation, Delaware Tribe of Indians, Eastern Shawnee Tribe, Fort Sill Apache Tribe, Iowa Tribe, Kaw Nation, Kialegee Tribal Town, Kickapoo Tribe, Kiowa Tribe, Miami Nation, Modoc Tribe, Muscogee (Creek) Nation, Osage Nation, Otoe-Missouria Tribe, Ottawa Tribe, Pawnee Nation, Peoria Tribe of Indians, Ponca Tribe of Indians, Quapaw Tribe of Oklahoma, Sac & Fox Nation, Seminole Nation, Seneca-Cayuga Tribe, Shawnee Tribe, Thlopthlocco Tribal Town, Tonkawa Tribe, United Keetoowah Band of Cherokee, Wichita & Affiliated Tribes and Wyandotte Nation (bia.gov).

2. Civil War issues linger even today with conflict over Freedmen's citizenship rights. The Cherokee Nation also sided with the South. When the South was defeated, the triumphant North forced the Cherokee to sign a treaty giving freed slaves citizenship in the Cherokee Nation. In the 1980s the Cherokee sought to strip descendants of the Freedmen of their citizenship. Instead of allowing the Cherokee to determine who shall be a citizen, the issue ended up in federal court where it remains. The Seminole Nation, on the other hand, has two Freemen bands within their tribe because Blacks lived with the Seminole both in Oklahoma and in Florida but not as slaves. Conflicts have arisen regarding the right to share in tribal finances, but the fact remains that four of the 28 members of the Seminole Tribal Council must be from Freedmen bands (Glaberson 2001).

3. NCAI president Tex Hall explained the Seventh Generation concept in his 2003 State of Tribal Nations speech: "Tribal leaders from many of our traditions are guided by the principle that a community's leaders must consider—and are responsible for—the consequences of their actions through the seventh generation to come" (Speech by Tex Hall in 2003 found on www.ncai.org).

4. The Treaty of Dancing Rabbit Creek was signed between the Choctaw Nation and the U.S. government in 1830. The Chickasaw Nation is involved because they were removed to the Choctaw lands during 1837 and 1838. The Choctaw and Chickasaw shared national boundaries until they were separated by treaty in 1855 (Clark 2009).

5. Tribes are wary of issues ending up in court. Leading native attorney Walter Echo Hawk (2010, 4) writes, "Only rarely in U.S. history has the law served as a shield to protect Native Americans from abuse and to further their aspirations as indigenous peoples. The law has more often been employed as a sword to harm Native peoples by stripping away their human rights, appropriating their property, stamping out their cultures, and, finally, to provide legal justification for federal policies, that have, at times, resorted to genocide and ethnocide."

6. Attorney General Scott Pruitt stated, "If the tribes have any remaining water rights – which is doubtful – they would relate to the small percentage of land within the area that is Indian Country – not the sweeping power claimed by the tribes, powers which would put the economic future of the entire state in the tribes' hands" (quoted in McNutt 2012a).

OKLAHOMA'S CHANGING
ECONOMIC PROFILE

Loren C. Gatch

This would be a great world to dance in if we didn't have to pay the fiddler.

Will Rogers

I. INTRODUCTION

In this chapter we will focus on the relationship between Oklahoma's economy and its government. As one of fifty states within a federal system, Oklahoma's economic profile has been shaped by the common national experience of a constitutionally-imposed separation of powers, as well as by Oklahoma's own resources and talents. Since the 1980s, great changes have been taking place in national-state relations that have important consequences for Oklahoma. After considering briefly the consequences of federalism, we will turn to the political and economic history of Oklahoma, highlighting those experiences that have influenced the state's present-day political and economic relationships. The most important intersection of the economy and the polity occurs through the tax system, which is treated in Chapter 12. Finally, we will step back to consider the contemporary challenges that Oklahoma faces in the more globally-connected environment of the early 21st century.

The Evolution of a National Economy

As with other states comprising the national union, economic governance within Oklahoma has been shaped in basic ways by the evolving pattern of shared powers under federalism. **Federalism** means that political power is shared between the national and state governments; the result is often called a system of "dual sovereignty." At the time of America's founding, the constitution limited the economic power of the individual states by reserving interstate commerce, tariff, and treaty-making powers to the national government (Art. I, Secs. 8, 10). The constitution also prevented states from taxing or otherwise restricting the flow of goods and services across state borders. In this way, each state was compelled to be an economic market for all the other states.

The constitution also deprived states of the ability to "coin Money, and emit Bills of Credit," leaving monetary policy (but not banking regulation) in the hands of the national government (Art. I, Sec. 8). In addition to these policy restrictions, the constitution also enforced important broad limitations upon state powers through the **"Full Faith and Credit"** and **"Privileges and Immunities"** clauses of Article IV. Essentially, these clauses required each state to respect certain laws of all the other states, and to treat the citizens of other states as fairly as they treated their own citizens.

Standing above all these rules was the authority of the constitution itself as the "supreme law of the land," meaning that in the event of a disagreement between state and national constitutions, the national law had the last word (Articles III, VI). Yet this supremacy was of a limited sort. It was bounded by how the founders understood the powers of the national government. The national government was a government of *delegated* powers. Essentially, the national government was allowed powers only if the constitution explicitly granted them. In contrast, state governments were organized according to the reverse principle: any power that was not specifically denied to the states was assumed to be available to them. As a result, while the national constitution confined itself to laying out the basic structure and principles by which the national government would operate, state-level constitutions accumulated a lot of legislative detail. Over time, state constitutions grew much longer than the national one, as they sought to spell out what state governments could and could not do with their powers (Elazar, 1982).

From these beginnings, the division of labor imposed by American federalism assumed a basic pattern that lasted for nearly 150 years until the New Deal era (1933-39). Congress assured the quality of the money supply, imposed tariffs on imported goods, fought the Indians, and otherwise sponsored "internal improvements" such as new roads, canals, and railroads. Through these means, the national government carried out its basic mandate to create a nationwide economic market and promote commerce. Very little regulation in the modern sense was undertaken at the national level.

Under this federal system, each state gave up its ability to control any commerce that crossed its borders. Nonetheless, individual states retained extensive powers to regulate economic and social behavior within their borders. This division of powers was reinforced by important Supreme Court rulings that defined "interstate commerce" in a limited way (*Gibbons v. Ogden*, 1824), and that recognized the claims of state over national citizenship (*Barron v. Baltimore*, 1833). In this fashion, the federal system kept the national government from intervening in most areas of economic life. Indeed, for most practical purposes, it was the extensive "police powers" of the individual states and not any activity of the distant national government that mattered most to the average American citizen during the nineteenth century. This practical dominance by the state governments was reflected in the tendency of the states, throughout the 19th century, to revise, rewrite and lengthen their constitutions as if these documents were ordinary tools of legislation rather than frameworks of governing principles. In contrast, the national constitution has been revised relatively infrequently. By and large, changes to its contents have come about by changes in its *interpretation*, not changes in its *wording* (Sturm, 1982; Keller, 1987).

Thanks to the passage of the Fourteenth Amendment (1868) and the regulatory innovations of the Progressive Era (circa 1890-1920), the balance of power between the states and the national government began to shift in favor of the latter. During the New Deal, this shift became decisive. In order to combat the Great Depression, the national government assumed greater authority to tax, spend, and regulate economic life. People got in the habit of looking to the national government to solve their problems. After initially resisting this new trend, the Supreme Court ratified this new version of federalism. By enlarging its interpretation of "interstate commerce" to include practically all economic activity, the Supreme Court's rulings in *NLRB v. Jones & Laughlin Steel Co.* and *Stewart Machine Co. v. Davis* (both 1937) cleared the way for expanded regulatory power at the national level.

As the national government asserted its expanded powers to regulate the economy, state governments lost prestige, authority, and power from the 1930s to the 1980s. In addition, the national government used its powers to reshape the country's political and social life as well. The Supreme Court's ruling in **Baker v. Carr** (1962) forced states, including Oklahoma, to reform their electoral systems in order to better represent their growing urban majorities. The civil rights revolution was largely imposed by the national government on the unwilling states. But above all, the expansion of the national government's tax base enabled it to literally buy the states' cooperation in many policy areas by simply offering them grants-in-aid to finance various policy initiatives. States followed the national government's lead in public policy because, to paraphrase Willie Sutton, that's where the money was.

This state of affairs began to change in the 1970s, as the national government sought to renegotiate its relations with the states. Since then, the United States has shifted a good deal of responsibility for social policy back to the state level. In particular, state governments have become the sites of important new experiments in such policy areas as welfare and public education. This shift in power known as **devolution** has different causes. In part, devolution has occurred because of a growing conservative political climate that viewed large government with skepticism. This new climate has encouraged the transfer of responsibilities back to state governments (Nathan, 1996).

In addition, reinforcing these changing attitudes are new fiscal realities. The budget surpluses of the late 1990s have been replaced by budget deficits. The cost of wars in Afghanistan and Iraq, as well as the long-term fiscal problems facing Social Security and Medicare mean that money may be scarce for new programs. The hostile reactions by many states to federal health care reform passed in Spring 2010 ("Obamacare") and the resistance to national education standards (the "Common Core") underscore how assertive states have become in the face of federal policy initiatives.

II. Oklahoma in American Political Development

Within the evolving pattern of American federalism, the timing of Oklahoma's path to statehood accounts for basic features of its early political and economic life. While long a part of the nation's history, Oklahoma as the forty-sixth state is itself relatively young. At its birth, Oklahoma had the experiences and mistakes of the previous forty-five states to learn from and to repeat! As the Oklahoma historian Angie Debo wrote, "In Oklahoma all the experiences that went into making the nation have been speeded up. Here all the American traits have been intensified. The one who can interpret Oklahoma can grasp the meaning of America in the modern world" (Debo, 1987, p. ix).

What are these traits? From its beginnings, the character of the American nation was shaped by the triumphs and hardships of subjugating an unknown and unexploited world. Beckoning with the twin attractions of political freedom and untold wealth, the unconquered land rewarded restless, acquisitive individuals who were capable of breaking old ties and embarking upon new adventures. The focus of these adventures was the American frontier, as it spread westward upon waves of settlement. The settlement of Oklahoma itself marked the final disappearance of the continental American frontier. Yet as a part of American history, Oklahoma has a far older significance. As a piece of the original Louisiana Purchase, the territory fit into the new nation's land and Indian policies by serving from the 1820s onward as the destination for the forced relocation of Indian tribes. In particular, after 1840 the Five Civilized Tribes established a degree of political independence that lasted until the Civil War when the Tribes' support of the Confederacy earned them the hostility of the Union. After the war, the national government retaliated by depriving the Indians of their land in central and western Oklahoma and reducing the Five Civilized Tribes' control over their remaining eastern territories. In their weakened condition, the Tribes were ill-equipped to resist incursions by land-hungry whites and railroad speculators. As the dimensions of Oklahoma's natural wealth became evident, Native Americans were systematically cheated of their land allotments.

In its early organization, Oklahoma repeated the larger American pattern of frontier settlement, but at a vastly accelerated pace. Energized by the spectacular land run of 1889 and the subsequent discovery of vast petroleum reserves, Oklahoma became a laboratory for rapid economic development under fluid social and political conditions. According to

Debo, this early period of Oklahoma's history witnessed "the quick and ruthless exploitation of natural resources, the freedom from restraint, and the meteoric rise of individuals" (1987, p. 49).

From the start, the Oklahoma economy developed in two ways. In the southeast portion of the state comprising the former Indian Territory, where the rain was good but the soil poor, small-scale agriculture prevailed. Descendants of immigrants from the old South, these small landholders worshipped in Baptist churches and favored the Democratic Party. In contrast, white immigrants from the Northern Plains states had settled in the west and northwest lands of the former Oklahoma Territory. There they farmed wheat and raised cattle, prayed for wet weather and dry saloons, and voted Republican (Hale, 1982; Goble, 1980; Warner, 1995a). Finally, the beginnings of an urban economy sprung up along the main railroad lines, first on a north-south axis through Oklahoma City and Guthrie, and then, in the wake of the oil boom of the early twentieth century, east from Oklahoma City through Tulsa and Joplin.

Oklahoma's political system reflected its historical circumstances. The frenzy first over land settlement and then over mineral rights intersected with two national political movements of the time—Populism and Progressivism—to determine the content and character of the Oklahoma Constitution of 1907. As a national force, **Populism** emerged in the 1880s throughout the American South and West as an agrarian rebellion against low agricultural prices and monopolistic abuses by the railroads. Populists distrusted experts and other elites. Instead, they upheld the virtues of the farmer and an idealized life of agrarian simplicity against the education and wealth of the eastern cities (Hicks, 1931).

In contrast, **Progressivism** drew more from urban, middle-class roots in the municipal reform movements and "muckraking" journalism of the early twentieth century. Convinced of the corrupting effect of business on politics, the Progressive movement attacked patronage and machine politics in the name of an apolitical ideal of civic management. Far from distrusting expertise, Progressives worshipped the expert. Progressives believed that by separating business interests from politics, politics could be cleansed and made more rational and efficient. Ironically, even though they feared the corrupting effects of business interests, they thought they could borrow management methods that would make politics work as smoothly as a business. Unlike the Populists, Progressives tended to be more skeptical about the abilities of the average person, even though they claimed to be acting on his or her behalf. Progressives distrusted representative government and favored a stronger executive branch versus the legislature (McCormick, 1986).

Despite their different origins, both movements influenced the Oklahoma constitution. Populism and Progressivism joined farmer and labor forces in a common hostility to outside concentrations of corporate wealth and power. This hostility was compounded by a dim view of legislators' ability to withstand the corrupting effects of money. In the context of Oklahoma's

spectacular settlement and rapid economic development, these sentiments reinforced an overarching desire to keep land and mineral rights
out of the hands of the large corporations and under the control of local
entrepreneurs.

Reflecting these sentiments, the spirit (and sheer length) of the 1907
Constitution testified to the reformist agenda and suspicions of the time.
The document resembled other state constitutions produced in the early
twentieth century in its incorporation of detailed measures to fight public
corruption by business interests (Sturm, 1982). For example, Article IX
sought to control nearly every conceivable aspect of corporate life. It
established a Corporation Commission empowered to regulate the activity of private corporations, especially railroads. Otherwise, no consideration was too great or small for the state constitution. It addressed
everything from the safety of railroad crossings and the flash point of
kerosene to the prohibition of monopolies. In addition, the constitution
gave the state itself permission to engage in any business, apart from
agriculture. It specified the length of the working day and banned child
labor. Corporations were restricted in their ability to deal in land, while
aliens were outright prohibited from its purchase. Article V provided for
the more typical Progressive aim of direct democracy via initiative and
referendum. Yet, even as it reflected Progressive ideals, the Oklahoma
constitution also codified Populist suspicions of a strong executive. Article VI dispersed executive authority by limiting the governor's power to
hire and fire officials within the executive branch.

Produced by a Democrat-controlled convention, the constitution of
1907 also inaugurated a tradition of Democratic domination of the state
that lasted into the 1990s. Henceforth, state politics were not only Populist
and Progressive, they were Southern and Democrat too. In Southern
style, Democratic rule was quickly solidified by the disfranchisement of
African-Americans, who at the time supported the Republican Party.
Oklahoma politics quickly began to acquire something of the conservative, states'-rights outlook typical of the Old Confederacy. Attacks upon
the rights of African-Americans were followed by similar actions against
third-party challengers. While it may amaze the present-day observer, in
the years before World War I, the Socialist Party briefly emerged as a
strong third-party contender in Oklahoma state politics. Nurtured by
local conditions of farm poverty and hardship, as well as factional splits
within the Progressive movement, this rural socialism merely carried
forward the Populist-Progressive agenda into the arena of state politics.
At its peak in 1914, the Socialist Party garnered over twenty percent of the
vote for its gubernatorial candidate, Fred Holt. Yet by 1920, the Democrats had taken advantage of the patriotic hysteria of World War I to forc-
ibly suppress their Socialist rivals.

Although controlled at the outset by the Democratic Party, Oklahoma
has never entirely been a southern state. Its Populist-Progressive constitutional inheritance assured that the role of the state in the economy would

LEADERSHIP PROFILE

JULIE KNUTSON
President and Chief Executive Officer, Oklahoma Academy for State Goals

TWENTY YEARS AGO, JULIE KNUTSON made a simple but offbeat request that launched her career in a completely new direction. While working as a counseling director and assistant principal for the Norman public schools, she requested that her superintendent send her to a local conference on economic expansion in Oklahoma. She had always felt that educators—especially at the common school levels—were not keenly aware of how the economic growth of a community or a state affected education. Moreover, there was little understanding of how education affected economic growth. Her superintendent asked her why in the world she would want to attend. The very question exemplified her thought process. She promised to come back from the conference and give a workshop for her fellow educators. Her superintendent set aside any misgivings and let her go.

It was the first major conference sponsored by the Oklahoma Academy for State Goals. The organization was still in its early stages of development and this conference held at the University of Oklahoma was quite ambitious. Knutson went up to the conference leaders and complimented them on a fine program. She explained why she had come and what she intended to do with the information she had gathered. A few weeks passed and she received a letter informing her that the Oklahoma Academy was looking for an executive director. They had never had one before and were conducting a nationwide search. From an initial 250 applicants, the search committee had narrowed the field. Knutson was one of the three finalists. She believes that she was ultimately selected because of her experience in psychology. She knew it was not going to be an easy job, especially "juggling all those chiefs." In addition, she had some experience at the national level chairing a group of people from the Midwest Region of the American Counseling Association.

For the past two decades, Knutson has employed her skillful leadership to steer a statewide, citizen-based nonpartisan organization to improve the public policy of Oklahoma. Her patience has paid great dividends. "We're ultimately changing cultural thinking—that's the bottom line of what we're doing and that's never a quick process," she says. Each year, more and more people become involved in the process and become aware of the Oklahoma Academy's wonderful work in getting diverse groups of people to work collectively on major state issues. The recommendations issued each by the Oklahoma Academy are given serious attention by state policymakers.

As politics have become more polarized, the Oklahoma Academy has become something of an antidote to bite-sized campaigning. Through Knutson's leadership, the Academy has earned a wonderful reputation for credibility on both sides of the political aisle. She says, "Some years we may look like we're heading more to the right or to the left, but ultimately we get to those recommendations through an incredibly collaborative process that result in the best solution for the greater good of the state." She's the first to point out that the organization is not really run by one person, but rather an executive committee of about 25 people. Other states are now looking at the Oklahoma Academy as a model for what is possible.

In what little is left of her free time, she loves to spend in the great outdoors gardening or riding her bicycle. She likes to read for pleasure, especially mysteries and works that inspire creativity like the Harry Potter series. She's even been known to volunteer her services to help teach elementary students how to read.

She was recently recognized by *The Journal Record* as the "Woman of the Year." Knutson offers this advice for young people: "I think that if you are going into any career that's public service oriented, it's one of the most rewarding things you can do, and you'll learn more than you think you can. It's an excellent way to help make a difference."

Brett S. Sharp

be more interventionist than elsewhere. Indeed, the momentum created by Oklahoma's statehood carried forward during the early years into further enactments of the reformist agenda, including the passage of corporate and income taxes; a system of bank deposit insurance; labor codes; compulsory school attendance; and mineral conservation. Much of this agenda anticipated by fully twenty-five years key features of New Deal legislation—even though, ironically, two of Oklahoma's three New Deal-era governors (Murray and Phillips) proved largely hostile to New Deal programs.

By the early twentieth century, then, the basic elements of the Oklahoma's economic profile had fallen into place. Heavily agricultural (smallholdings in the east, cotton in the south, wheat and cattle in the west) and blessed with promising reserves of petroleum and natural gas concentrated in the center of the state, the Oklahoma economy initially prospered as a producer of natural resources. However, its exploitation of this natural wealth was both spectacular and wasteful, reflecting in part the pattern of property rights. Farmers tended to overuse the land with a single crop because the typical homesteading farm was too small for sustainable agriculture in a semiarid climate. Farmers went into debt to produce, and produced to get out of debt. One tragic result of these farming practices was the Dust Bowl conditions of the 1930s. Similarly, oil producers overpumped their wells because no one could say who owned the vast pools of oil that lay beneath the land; if one person stopped pumping, another person would take a greater share (Hale, 1982; Debo, 1987). While the state remained poor relative to the more settled parts of the country, Oklahoma nonetheless made rapid progress despite the weak farm prices that plagued the agricultural sector throughout the 1920s. In fact, until the development of Texas fields, Oklahoma remained the nation's largest producer of oil and gas. By 1916, state oil production represented a good third of the national total.

Oklahoma's Populist-Progressive legacy dovetailed with traditions of southern Democratic dominance to shape how the state's abundant natural resources would influence political life in the 1920s and 1930s. Like its economy, Oklahoma's politics were also wild: the 1920s alone saw two governors impeached and a period of martial law. The state's overwhelmingly rural constituencies responded to authoritarian and charismatic political leaders—"Our Jack" Walton, "Alfalfa Bill" Murray—who embodied the compassion and contradictions of Populism. Tax revenues from agricultural and mining activity reinforced a traditionalistic politics of patronage that sustained a level of social welfare spending which distinguished Oklahoma from other states. Governments spent in a Populist fashion, but for Progressive purposes.

True to the state's inveterate distrust of political power, the revenue streams from various sources were to a great extent **"earmarked"** for predetermined purposes in an effort to protect the state's resources from unscrupulous politicians. Article X, section 19 decreed that "Every act ... levying a tax shall specify distinctly the purpose of which said tax is levied, and no tax levied and collected for one purpose shall ever be devoted to another purpose." This sentiment was duly incorporated into subsequent Oklahoma statutes. For example, from 1933 to 1987 Oklahoma's traditionally generous social welfare policies rested upon the earmarking of sales tax revenues for public assistance programs. Thanks to this earmarking, by the early 1960s Oklahoma emerged as the leading state in per capita spending for public assistance, even though the state otherwise ranked among the lowest third of all states in per capita income terms (Klos, 1965).

At the same time, Oklahoma political traditions have emphasized grass-roots control over spending. Article V of the Constitution, like its national counterpart, places the authority to originate revenue bills with the House of Representatives. Moreover, no revenue bill may be passed during the last five days of a given session in order to avoid a gubernatorial veto. A 1933 amendment to the Constitution took the power to tax property out of the state government's hands and left it with the localities (Art. X, Sec, 9). By 1937, the hard times of the Depression era led to chronic state indebtedness and an overhang of "warrants," or short-term borrowing that was extended year after year. Thus, for good measure voters added to the constitution an amendment in 1941 mandating a balanced budget (Art X, Sec. 23). In 1985, the constitution was again amended to limit budget appropriations to 95% of the estimate of a given year's revenues. Most recently, the passage in 1992 of State Question 640 amended Article V to require that any tax increase either be approved by a popular referendum or be voted in by a three-fourths majority of both sides of the legislature. Only one other state in the Union—Arkansas—places such severe constitutional restrictions on the ability of the government to raise taxes.

In sum, Oklahoma's revenue practices as they have been embodied in its constitution reveal a great deal about the character and priorities of the state. Wary both of outside corporate interests and its own politicians, the Oklahoman political culture has sought to live up to its Progressive ideals of social welfare and economic regulation, even while its Populist suspicions have led it so maintain strict controls over the use (and misuse) of public funds. State government operates with considerable constitutional restrictions upon how much money it can spend, and how it can raise those funds.

The Changing Structure of the Oklahoma Economy: From Depression to Oil Boom

If, in political terms, Oklahoma entered statehood with a constitution ahead of the times, its economy lagged well behind them. True, along with the rest of the nation, Oklahoma was growing more urban and industrial. By 1929, Oklahoma income per capita reached nearly 65 per cent of the national average, although this figure masked sections of extreme poverty in the southeastern part of the state. Agriculture, mining, and internal trade (wholesale and retail) together comprised over 57 per cent of the source of this income, versus a mere third for the country as a whole. Compared to the rest of the country, relatively few Oklahomans made their living producing manufactured goods. This meant that on the cusp of the Great Depression, Oklahoma remained industrially underdeveloped (Klein, 1963). This underdevelopment and lack of economic diversification exposed Oklahoma to "boom and bust" cycles in commodity prices, which were far more volatile than nonfarm wages and retail prices, and left the state vulnerable to downturns in the national economy as a whole.

The shock of the Great Depression and the tragedy of the Dust Bowl are well known. During the years 1929-1933, when national per capita income dropped 30%, Oklahoma's fell significantly further. The state government responded fitfully and incompetently to the tragedy, hobbled by its divisive politics and patronage instincts (Goble & Scales, 1983). Families left the state in large numbers to escape the ecological and economic disaster. By 1945 nearly four hundred thousand people, or one-sixth of the population, had left the state. Thereafter, the population count turned up, albeit more slowly than the national growth rate, and did not return to its 1930 figure until three decades later. Relative per capita income rebounded more quickly (thanks in part to the departure of poorer residents), regaining its pre-Depression proportion by 1938 and ascending to a plateau of somewhat over 80% of the national average by the 1960s (Klein, 1963). While narrowing over time, this per capita income gap between Oklahoma and the rest of the country has persisted to the present day.

Economic recovery in Oklahoma after the 1930s meant, in a real way, that the state was simply becoming more like the rest of the country. Although wheat, cattle and cotton remained the state's three single largest areas of farm production, the proportion of Oklahoma's employment and income derived from agriculture and mining declined steadily after 1929 as the state moved towards a more manufacturing- and service-based economy. As in other rural states, Oklahoma agriculture itself took on industrial characteristics. The number of farms fell but their average size grew as farming became more capital-intensive. Again, the situation varied across the state. In the "Little Dixie" area of southeastern Oklahoma, farms remained smaller and less mechanized, while productivity and incomes stagnated. In contrast, wheat and cattle farming to the west and in the Panhandle adapted more successfully to modern conditions and methods (Klein, 1963; Lage, et al., 1977).

The oil and gas industries form a special case, since Oklahoma was blessed with resources that other states lacked. Characteristic of these industries is that while their wages are above the average, they contribute only a small percentage to the state's employment total. By the late 1920s, energy and mining activity except for natural gas turned downward, both as a proportion of national production and relative to the state's other economic sectors. While the physical volume of petroleum production recovered somewhat after the Second World War, oil made a decreasingly significant contribution to the state's output until the oil "shocks" of 1973 and 1979 (more on this below). Of longer-term significance, estimated reserves reached a high in 1955, which pointed towards the inevitable depletion of this once-bountiful source of wealth. Oil production peaked in 1969 at 225 million barrels a year, and annual production has since declined to about one fourth of that amount (Klein, 1963; Lage, et al., 1977; Dauffenbach, 2005). With the emergence of new directional drilling and fracturing technologies, however, a renewed boom has taken place in

Oklahoma's mature oil and gas fields. Since 2005 oil production has increased by over 50%, and proven reserves of natural gas doubled between 2000 and 2011. Oklahoma is ranked the 5th most important state in oil production, and the 4th in natural gas (Agee, 2011; McGuire, 2013).

After the Second World War, manufacturing, services, and government began replacing the agricultural and mining sectors as drivers of the Oklahoma economy. These shifts were paralleled by the rapid growth of the Oklahoma City, Tulsa, and (more recently) Lawton metropolitan areas. In contrast, the population of rural Oklahoma continued to decline. To a large extent, Oklahoma only experienced during the postwar period the same large-scale economic transformations that the nation as a whole had undergone. And even then, demographic recovery from the disaster of the 1930s occurred hesitantly; only by late 1950s did population growth consistently offset outmigration. Nonetheless, throughout the promising 1950s and 1960s, Oklahoma's growth in per capita income consistently outstripped that of the nation.

Despite this progress, Oklahoma's economic structure continued to differ from the nation's. Not only did agriculture and mining loom large in the state's fortunes, but government activity made outsized contributions to Oklahoma's income. The combined state and national government contribution to Oklahoma's economy exceeded that of the average state. This reflected in part the New Deal extension of federal responsibilities and the growth of revenue sharing. In addition, however, Oklahoma congressmen succeeded in placing federal installations and their payrolls (Tinker, Fort Sill, and the FAA Aeronautical Center) in the state. Furthermore, compared to the average state, Oklahoma has relied more on the national government as a percentage of its revenues. This revenue pattern is discussed in Chapter 12. In its aggregate economic impact, however, government activity during the 1960s and 1970s made a higher than average contribution to Oklahoma's employment and income. On the state and local level alone, the expansion of government payrolls continued apace throughout the 1960s and into the 1970s, even as growth in federal employment tailed off.

By the early 1970s, on the eve of the second oil boom, agriculture, mining, and government were still large sectors in terms of state employment and income compared to their relative importance within the United States economy. Economic diversification had taken place, but the state still remained behind the rest of the nation. An expanding government sector had helped stabilize the Oklahoma economy since the 1930s, but there was no guarantee that federal spending would continue. By the same token, agriculture relied upon federal price supports that shielded farmers from the worst fluctuations in commodity prices. Yet even these supports have been eroded by the deregulatory movement beginning in the late 1970s. Oklahoma's challenge has been to develop alternative sources of income that complement its traditional economic strengths. While the goals of economic development and diversification may have changed over the years—first manufacturing, then services, and now the high-tech industries—Oklahoma has faced this same underlying problem for decades.

For a while, however, the old boom times seemed to get a new lease on life. Beginning in 1971, the Organization of Petroleum Exporting Countries (OPEC) began to assert its market power by restricting the world supply of crude oil, imposing export embargoes upon selected countries, and setting ever-higher prices on the international oil market. Followed by the Iranian revolution and the second oil "shock" of 1979, OPEC pushed oil prices to levels ten times higher than those of the 1960s.

For America generally, gas lines and "stagflation" were the miserable results. For Oklahoma in particular, misery for the nation meant a windfall for the state's economy. Between 1975 and 1982, employment in Oklahoma's mining sector (which includes oil and gas) doubled; by 1982, over twenty percent of the state's economic output came from this sector, compared with barely five percent nationally (Oklahoma Department of Commerce, 2006a). In the wake of this sudden prosperity, wages and property values rose, and taxes fell even as state revenues bulged with the proceeds of oil and gas severance taxes. For a brief moment, per capita income even reached the national average.

The good times were not to last. The success of the OPEC cartel was its own undoing. By the mid-1980s, the price of a barrel of oil had fallen by nearly half from its peak, and Oklahoma was faced with the prospect of painful economic retrenchment. Not only did the mining sector collapse, but the state's population even declined. After growing fast during the 1960s and 1970s, state output now stagnated for the next decade. Thus, in a reversal of the 1970s, by the 1980s what was good for America proved very bad for Oklahoma. Cursed with temporary good fortune, Oklahoma lost precious time in its longer-term goal of developing a truly modern and diversified economy.

While these troubles were not Oklahoma's fault, its response to good fortune highlighted the state's economic vulnerabilities. Unlike Texas or Colorado, two states with similar economic roots in natural resource extraction, Oklahoma has not moved its economy as far away from natural resources and toward manufacturing and services. Oklahoma was late to enter the computer age, and much of its technology employment was concentrated in support industries for oil and gas extraction (*Economics of High Technology in Oklahoma*, 1985). Despite some success in catching up with the high-tech boom of the 1990s, a variety of studies have suggested that Oklahoma's economy is still less high-tech oriented than the economies of other states (Warner & Dauffenbach, 2002). According to the most recent National Science Foundation report, Oklahoma remains in the lowest quartile (bottom 25%) of states in terms of individuals in science and technology occupations, as well as computer specialties, as a percentage of all occupations. Although the state's record for engineers and broader categories of high technology employment is stronger, its economy is otherwise characterized by low research and development (R&D) expenditures. One bright spot is that Oklahoma ranks in the top quartile among states in producing associates degrees in science, engineering and technology categories (NSF, 2014, chapter 8).

Oklahoma in a New Century

In the words of two observers, "the last two decades of the twentieth century will probably not go down in the history books as the greatest period of economic growth in the state of Oklahoma" (Snead & Ireland, 2002, p. 9). Nonetheless, by the early 1990s, an era of sustained economic growth returned. Not only has Oklahoma's performance outpaced the nation's, but its unemployment rate has also remained consistently below the nationwide level, even during the severe economic downturn that began in 2008. During the first decade of the 21st century, Oklahoma's employment growth ranked in the top third of all states. By 2010, per capita income reached nearly 90% of the national average (33rd out of 50 states) and perhaps higher when adjusted for regional cost of living differences (Ireland & Amos, 2011; *U.S. Bureau of Economic Analysis*, 2014). Although Oklahoma's economic structure continues to converge with that of the nation, noticeable differences remain. Table 4–1 contrasts Oklahoma and the United States in terms of the distribution of output across economic sectors.

TABLE 4–1 Output (Gross Product) by Industry in Percent, U.S. vs. Oklahoma 2012		
INDUSTRY	UNITED STATES	OKLAHOMA
Natural Resources and Mining	2.9%	10.2%
Construction	3.6	3.8
Manufacturing (1)	12.0	10.9
Trade	11.9	11.7
Transportation and Utilities	5.0	6.7
Services (2)	52.4	39.9
Government	12.3	16.8

SOURCE: U.S. BEA, *Survey of Current Business* (March 2014), p. D-84. Percentages may not add up to 100, due to rounding.

NOTES

(1) Includes durable and nondurable goods.

(2) Includes: information; financial activities; professional and business services; education and health services; leisure and hospitality; and other.

This contrast illustrates both Oklahoma's progress compared to previous decades and the persistent legacy of Oklahoma's political and economic history. Stimulated by the surge in energy prices since 2004, the natural resources and mining sector continues to make an outsized contribution to the state's economy. The importance of government activity as a contributor to Oklahoma's economy is reflected in the high percentage of Oklahoma's personal income that derives from government employment (Dauffenbach, 2014). In contrast, the state has a relatively undeveloped service sector where much high-tech employment is likely to be found. In particular, the Oklahoma economy trails the nation in creating high-paying occupations of the professional and managerial type (Ireland, Snead, & Miller, 2006). Diversification away from its traditional sources of livelihood remains essential for Oklahoma's economic future.

III. Oklahoma in the Global Economy

Despite its inland location away from major trade centers, Oklahoma has always been closely tied to world markets. The prices of its raw material exports were traditionally determined in distant places like Chicago, Liverpool, and London. While its economic mix is now very different, Oklahoma's prosperity will be increasingly influenced by global conditions. Traditionally, Oklahoma has advertised itself to prospective business as a low-cost, low-wage, low-tax, non-union state (*ACE Book,* 2014). Labor union membership, which tends to increase wages, amounted in 2013 to a mere 7.5% of the work force, versus 11.3% nationwide (*US Bureau of Labor Statistics,* 2014). The perennial debates about workers' compensation costs as well as the state's passage in 2001 of a "right-to-work" (antiunion) referendum emerge from the same mindset. Yet, while low costs may attract a certain sort of labor-intensive manufacturing and service mix, low wages now do not necessarily lead to higher incomes later. Indeed, it is precisely these industries that are most likely to move jobs to even cheaper locations outside of the country. Thus, policymakers increasingly recognize the importance of nurturing Oklahoma's high-tech manufacturing and service sectors. After the last oil bust, the legislature passed House Bill 1444, also known as the **Oklahoma Economic Development Act of 1987**. Broadly speaking, the Act has sought to encourage economic development of a sort that did not engage the state in the traditional competition with other states for so-called "smokestack" industries.

Towards this end, the Act put into effect a number of measures that reflected two basic approaches to economic development. First, it created the **Oklahoma Center for the Advancement of Science and Technology** (OCAST) to encourage basic and applied research, as well as the commercialization of promising technology. Through a variety of programs, OCAST attempts to leverage modest state appropriations by attracting matching funds from federal and private sources. Most recently, the state has also sought to strengthen the links between academic research and commercialization by making it easier for universities and researchers to exploit their discoveries. Since the passage of State Questions 680 and 681 in 1998, Oklahoma colleges and universities and their faculty are now legally able to own equity in start-up firms.

Secondly, HB 1444 sought to expand the supply of investment capital by enlarging the state's role in financing high-tech startups and other small businesses whose exports would bring wealth into the state. Led by the **Oklahoma Development Finance Authority** (ODFA), this effort makes use of the state's credit to underwrite promising investments. By selling its own bonds in the capital market, the ODFA can in turn lend to borrowers that meet the agency's criteria. Alternately, the ODFA can enhance the credit, and thus lower the capital costs, of worthy borrowers by guaranteeing the interest and principal of their loans with private lenders. Through its investment affiliate, the **Oklahoma Capital Investment Board** (OCIB), the ODFA even has the authority to extend its guarantees to equity financing of startup industries. In effect, the OCIB involves the state as a stakeholder in venture capitalism. Finally, through a separate project the state has established a **Linked Deposit Program** to lower the borrowing costs for farmers and small businesses. In exchange for accepting below-market rates of interest on its own deposits, the state enables banks to make low-interest loans to qualified borrowers (Murry, 1988; Warner & Smith, 1991).

In sum, the two approaches incorporated into HB 1444 have aimed at increasing both the human and financial capital that Oklahoma has at its disposal. More recently, the passage of SB 1391 in 2002 updated the provisions of HB 1444 by establishing the **Oklahoma Science and Technology Research and Development Board** to oversee OCAST and in particular, stimulate information and biotechnology industries (Warner, 2002).

A second major program approved by the legislature in 1993, the **Oklahoma Quality Jobs Program,** focuses not upon augmenting the state's resources, but upon the direct creation of jobs through the reduction of employer costs. The Quality Jobs Program encourages the hiring of new workers by offering participating companies cash rebates of up to 5% of payrolls of new employees. Targeted at manufacturing and service firms that make most of their sales out of state, this program amounts to an employment subsidy to encourage certain kinds of desirable industry to expand in Oklahoma. Companies that do not sign up with the Quality Jobs Program can still make use of a variety of tax credits, exemptions and refunds (Oklahoma Department of Commerce, 2014).

As with the research and development (R&D) initiatives created by HB 1444, the Quality Jobs Program aims to make Oklahoma an attractive place to do business without necessarily selling the state as a source of cheap, docile labor. Both initiatives aim to cultivate the kind of high-tech, high-wage industries that hitherto have been underrepresented in the Oklahoma economy. Both initiatives are also politically attractive in that they do not involve any great upfront expenses to the state. Apart from the seed money provided by OCAST, the ODFA and OCIB merely require the state to make use of its credit standing with the financial markets to underwrite and otherwise guarantee private initiatives. As long as these initiatives are profitable, the state spends nothing and may even earn a return. While the Quality Jobs Program does require direct state payments, these payments have been rationalized by appealing to the sales and income tax revenues that these new jobs produce. As long as the state is encouraging hiring that otherwise would not take place, then in a certain sense the Quality Jobs Program can be said to pay for itself.

Do these various development initiatives work? The evidence is mixed. Some aspects, especially those concerned with education, research and development, will show results only in the long term in the form of increased high-tech employment and business startups. OCAST claims that, since its inception every dollar invested by OCAST has cumulatively generated $22.40 in private and federal investments, and other capital flows (OCAST, 2014). The fruits of venture capital investment are likewise a long way off. Although business and academic R&D expenditures in Oklahoma place it in the bottom 25% of all states, R&D financed by the state is ranked above the national average (NSF, 2014, ch. 8). As for employment effects, according to the Oklahoma Department of Commerce, the Quality Jobs Program has enrolled nearly 700 companies to which have been credited $866 million in wage rebates (ODOC, 2014). At the same time, companies that have accepted incentive payments are still able to lay off workers without any provision for paying back the subsidies (Bailey, 2013).

The great uncertainty underlying all such investment and employment projections is whether this activity would have taken place anyway even without various incentive programs. The more basic these incentives are, the more confident one can be that their expense generates a net benefit. For example, a well-educated and trained workforce is a better investment incentive than a tax break, since that workforce will attract more than one industry. All things being equal, capitalists invest in those industries, locales, and markets which promise the highest rate of risk-adjusted return. This prospective rate of return depends upon many variables, some of which are beyond Oklahoma's control. While the net benefits of such programs are hard to measure, a small state like Oklahoma that foregoes such development incentives may put itself at a competitive disadvantage relative to other states that do offer incentives (Warner & Dauffenbach, 2004a, 2004b, 2006). If in the real world all things are not equal, then what is it about Oklahoma that discourages investment for high-wage growth?

Two types of answers have been given. The first type claims that, contrary to numerous indicators that point to Oklahoma's relatively low tax burden, the existence of an income tax itself discourages work, savings, and investment; if the tax were eliminated, Oklahoma's economy would grow faster. In particular, faster growth would have "dynamic revenue benefits" that would partly make up for the decline in state revenues which eliminating the income tax would entail (OCPA & ALME, 2011). Furthermore, this perspective contends, Oklahoma's tax cuts implemented in the previous decade were actually followed by increases, rather than decreases, in state revenue as increased economic activity generated more tax revenues than the tax cuts removed (OCPA, 2013). A variant of this argument points out that, whatever the overall level of Oklahoma's taxes, businesses pay a higher percentage of these taxes than in other states (*ACE Book 2011*, Table 9).

The second type of argument contends that it is the revenue shortfalls caused by tax cuts that have worsened Oklahoma's economic prospects. In particular, these shortfalls have made it more difficult for Oklahoma's educational system to impart to its students the cognitive skills necessary to succeed in the information age. Increases in per capita income are strongly associated with increases in the percentage of the workforce with college degrees (Dauffenbach, 2006b). Based upon its students' composite ACT test results in 2013, Oklahoma is about at the national average (20.8 vs. 20.9), although the percentage of Oklahoma students who met all four of the test's College Readiness Benchmarks was below average (ACT, 2013). Oklahoma ranges in the lowest quartile of states for the percentage of college and advanced degree holders in the workforce. In the science and engineering fields in particular, Oklahoma's educational attainment is equally mediocre (NSF, 2014, chapter 8).

In primary and secondary education, the picture is even bleaker. Despite an expanding student population, larger class sizes, and enhanced instructional mandates, since 2008 the state's expenditure on K-12 education has fallen by the highest percentage in the nation. Oklahoma's K-12 expenditures per pupil now rank near the bottom of all states, while teacher salaries also rank among the lowest in the nation (Oklahoma Policy Institute, 2013; Dauffenbach, 2014).

While this chapter need not take a stance on whether tax cuts or spending increases will provide a greater benefit for Oklahoma's economy, one general observation can be made. Whatever one's policy prescription, there is no free lunch in economic development. Sooner or later, a bill comes due—whether it is for increased education costs, guaranteed loan defaults that must be made good, or tax increases/spending cuts that must compensate for funds paid out in tax expenditures of various sorts. There are no easy or cost-free policy responses to the economic challenges facing Oklahoma. Moreover, any response will necessarily have a political as well as an economic dimension.

Luckily, Oklahoma's economic structure has served the state well during the sharp national recession of 2008-9. Having never experienced a severe bubble in housing prices like Nevada or California, Oklahoma was spared a collapse in the local housing market, and thus in construction activity. Another benefit of avoiding a housing bubble is that Oklahoma's banking system remained healthy relative to those of other states. While Oklahoma did lose manufacturing employment during the most recent recession, the state's economy was bolstered by a robust natural resources sector and relatively stable employment in government. As a result, Oklahoma experienced a shallower downturn than did the rest of the nation. Whereas the unemployment rate peaked nationally at nearly 10%, Oklahoma's rate was never higher than 7%, and has even fallen to nearly 5% by early 2014. Indeed, during 2009, Oklahoma's economy grew at the fastest rate in the nation, and per capita income since then has grown at the third strongest rate (Oklahoma Employment Security Commission, 2014; Dauffenbach, 2014).

IV. Conclusion

This survey of the economic profile of the Sooner State has sought to draw links between history, politics, and economic development in order to explain certain features of present-day Oklahoma. The overarching theme of this account has been the long-term convergence of Oklahoma's economic fortunes with those of the larger nation. Variations on this theme include the legacies of Oklahoma's Populist-Progressive heritage, especially as they are embodied in its constitution. In addition, Oklahoma's experiences of economic bonanza and catastrophe highlight its precarious reliance upon natural resources as a significant source of its wealth. Most recently, those natural resources have served Oklahoma well during the most severe economic downturn the nation has experienced since the Great Depression. As more normal conditions have returned, however, the long-run puzzle of Oklahoma's economic future remains to be solved.

THE OKLAHOMA LEGISLATURE

Jan C. Hardt

Grassroots understanding of one state legislature has made me so much more tolerant of the sausage-like nature of lawmaking: It may, at times, be a less-than-appetizing procedure, but if done right, the result is extremely satisfying. The cook always makes the difference. With the legislative process it is no different. It is people, just like you and me, who make it work—heroes and cowards; the bright and the not so; the movers and shakers, and the sheep that follow.

Ralph Wright, former Speaker of the Vermont House of Representatives

I. INTRODUCTION

In a February 2010 poll, Oklahomans were surveyed about their views about smoking. 94% said that second-hand smoke was a health hazard, with 62% saying it was a serious health hazard. In addition, 71% of Oklahomans favored eliminating smoking in all public places with 56% saying they strongly favored a statewide smoke-free law (McNutt, 2010). Despite these numbers, however, any attempt to ban smoking in certain places has met with difficulty in the Oklahoma legislature with either exemptions, stipulations, or delayed deadlines preventing implementation. For example, the first major attempt to deal with public smoking came in 2003 which banned smoking in most public places. However, stand-alone bars, bingo halls, home-based businesses, and a handful of other establishments were exempted from the new law. Moreover, restaurants had until March 2006 to either build a separately ventilated smoking room or eliminate smoking in their establishments, thus giving restaurants an additional three years to comply. In 2009, the Oklahoma legislature tried to pass a bill that would have eliminated those separate smoking rooms, but this bill failed. One of the issues involved here is that 121 restaurants throughout the state had built the separate rooms by 2006 costing them anywhere from $50,000 to $150,000, and thus, they would have only had 2+ years to get the money out of their investment. The Oklahoma legislature did create a task force to study the issue of smoking in public places and its health risks.

Thus, the prospects for passage in 2010 were not great when HR 2774, the **Clean Air in Restaurants Act,** was introduced. It was very similar to the bill that had not passed in 2009 and it was only being looked at one year later. Under the provisions of the bill, restaurants would get tax breaks if they removed their smoking rooms and made their establishments smoke-free. They would also receive a rebate of up to 50% of the cost of building that smoking room, minus a depreciation fee. However, this bill was not seen as a complete victory for the Smoke Free advocates as Representative Kris Steele, the House Speaker designate and the sponsor of the bill, made compliance with the bill voluntary as opposed to mandatory. In addition, tribal establishments were exempted from this bill.

In the meantime, several new developments had taken place. First, Smoke Free Oklahoma called a press conference in February 2010 calling for the abolishment of these smoking rooms in restaurants and ending smoking in bars. In addition, Ken Selby, the owner and operator of Mazzio's and Oliveto restaurants, made several highly public statements supporting such a ban, pointing out that his restaurants actually experienced an increase in business after they went smoke-free. Third, Smoke Free Oklahoma had become part of larger movement nationwide to ban smoking in public places. Over 7,000 cities and 28 states in the United States had enacted comprehensive smoke-free laws protecting workers and the public from secondhand smoke.

In the end, the bill did pass. It went through a treacherous road to do so despite the public opinion polls supporting such a move. Yet, the results of this law were not very satisfactory to anyone. The supporters of smoke free laws, such as Smoke Free Oklahoma and the Oklahoma American Cancer Society, wished that these smoking rooms had never been created in the first place. They also wished that this law would have made accepting these rebates mandatory. The tobacco supporters and smokers were not really happy about this law as it gave these restaurants a tax break for removing the rooms that they had fought for in the 2003 law. The restaurant owners with smoking rooms were displeased because they were essentially put in a difficult position with the passage of this Clean Restaurant Act. If they did not comply, they might worry about the public's perception of their restaurants as the legislature had just passed another law encouraging the ban on smoking in restaurants. At the same time, these restaurants would not only lose more than half the money they put into these smoking rooms if they accepted the tax breaks, but they would also put their establishments through the turmoil and disruption created by a major construction project–again! Finally, the voters in Oklahoma probably will not be satisfied with this law as the legislature voted essentially to pay restaurants to undo something that they did as required by the legislature if they wanted smoking in their establishments. Although the money from these tax breaks came from a Health Department fund created by the tobacco tax and this money is supposed to go to smoking cessation efforts, it seems a bit counterproductive to

LEADERSHIP PROFILE

EMILY VIRGIN
Member of the Oklahoma House of Representatives—District 44

EMILY VIRGIN holds the distinction of being one of the youngest members of the Oklahoma House of Representatives. Elected to represent House District 44 in 2010, Virgin is a fifth generation Oklahoman and a lifelong Norman resident. She graduated Magna Cum Laude from The University of Oklahoma with a degree in Political Science and a minor in criminology. She had worked her way through school as a manager of the OU football team.

Currently, she attends The University of Oklahoma Law School. Virgin is committed to her community through service. She has volunteered in many organizations, including Thunderbird Clubhouse; Access to Justice Organization; Food and Shelter for Friends and in her church.

Virgin campaigned on a platform of education reform, fiscal responsibility and open and transparent government. Things she felt compelled to be involved in while campaigning. "When I knocked on doors, starting in March, it became clear that education was the number one issue," Virgin said. "So, I listened to the voters and made it my number one issue, too" (Lusk, 2010).

Why did she get involved in politics? "When you grow up around something, that's what you end up loving," she said. "It's really what I feel called to do. It's my passion" (Ward, 2010). Emily's grandfather, George Skinner is a Cleveland County Commissioner, so it runs in the family.

Rep. Virgin currently serves on the Appropriations and Budget Judiciary; Common Education; Higher Education and Career Tech Committees; as well as the Redistricting Subcommittee.

Jennifer Stringham

spend it on tearing something down that was required to be built if the restaurants wanted to allow smoking. Moreover, all the exemptions in the law gave the impression that the legislature was more worried about protecting special interests than making good public policy.

The extensive lobbying activity by Smoke Free Oklahoma, tobacco supporters, the American Cancer Society, restaurant owners, and various interested parties, along with the heavy press coverage of this bill all reflect the populist attitude that Oklahomans sometimes have toward their legislature. Oklahomans tend to prefer that the people, not the lawmakers, have a greater say in the decision making process. This same populist attitude can be seen in how the Oklahoma legislature is structured, how it gets its lawmakers, and how those lawmakers perform once in office.

II. How the Oklahoma Legislature is Structured

Annual Sessions

Prior to the passage of a state question in 1966, Article V of the Constitution specified that the Oklahoma legislature would meet in **biennial session**, or every other year. Today, the legislature meets annually in regular session. Annual legislatures are thought to have numerous advantages: more legislation can get passed, significant state issues can be addressed in a more timely fashion, lawmakers have more time to consider legislation, and the legislature is strengthened as an institution compared to the executive branch. The passage of a 1989 State Question shortened the sessions of the Oklahoma legislature. It still meets in annual sessions, but those sessions must start by noon on the first Monday in February and must adjourn on or before 5:00 P.M. on the last Friday in May of each year. Most current legislative sessions last 66 legislative days. In odd-numbered years, the regular session will also include one extra day in January. Because of the short session, the last few days of May are very busy for both the legislature and the governor, as typically there is a logjam of bills that must be passed and signed into law.

Numbering and Types of Sessions

To make it easier to identify a particular session, each legislative session has been numbered. Two annual legislative sessions make up a legislature and are identified by consecutive numbers. Thus, the 2013 session was called the first session of the 54th legislature, with the 2014 session being called the second session of the 54th legislature. Between annual sessions, the Oklahoma legislature meets in an **interim session**. During this time, the legislative branch is without lawmaking authority. Public hearings, committee work, bill preparations, and investigations take place during the interim period. With the passage of a 1980 State Question, Oklahoma lawmakers can call themselves into a **special session** if an emergency develops during an interim session. Prior to 1980, only the governor could call a special session. As found in the Oklahoma Constitution (Article V, Section 27), a special session does have lawmaking authority and can take place after agreement by two-thirds of the members of both houses or after a call by the governor.

Special sessions can be very controversial for a number of reasons. First, a special session called by the legislature gives the legislature added power by allowing lawmakers to maintain their influence while not in regular session. There are no time limits on special sessions, but lawmakers are limited to discussing only the issues set out when the session was called. Second, special sessions cost taxpayers money because the state has to pay for administrative overhead, salaries, and transportation costs that occur outside of the regular session. When there were rumors of a special session in 2010, the expected cost was an extra $2 million per week. Ironically, as with 2006 and the special session averted in 2010, many of these special sessions are held to deal with budget crises and so the extra costs tend to get more attention. A third controversial aspect of these special sessions is their frequency. From 1976 to 2006, the Oklahoma legislature had found it necessary to hold special sessions in 17 of those 30 years, with 7 special sessions from 1996 to 2006 alone.

More recently, the Oklahoma legislature has had infrequent special sessions. One of those includes the special session held in 2006 to discuss the FY 2007 budget which had not been passed in the 2006 regular session, but needed to pass by July 1, 2006, to avoid a state government shutdown. The Oklahoma legislature made it; on the last day of the June 2006 special session, lawmakers approved the $7.1 billion budget, the largest in the state's history. A second session was held in September 2013 for a simple reason—the Oklahoma Supreme Court had struck down a law in June 2013 arguing that it violated the Oklahoma Constitution because it contained multiple measures that were not related to each other. The special session which lasted for five days and cost $30,000 per day met to discuss each of those measures individually. Thus, there were 23 bills passed in just five days, including 11 on the last day.

A Bicameral Legislature

Article V of the Oklahoma Constitution created a legislature that is **bicameral**, or composed of two houses. In Oklahoma, these two houses are called the House of Representatives and the Senate. All 50 states except Nebraska have a bicameral legislature. A bicameral legislature offers many advantages. In a bicameral legislature, legislation needs to be passed by two different houses. Although this can cause delays, legislation is less likely to be passed hastily. Moreover, a bicameral legislature usually is more representative because typically most states follow the federal model, with the lower house having shorter terms and members representing smaller districts, and the upper house having longer terms with larger districts.

The Size of the Legislature

One of the major differences in selecting legislators is determined by the size of each house. Senate districts usually comprise several House districts, and are larger in geographic size; hence, in each state the Senate usually has fewer members than the House. This can be confirmed by looking at the minimum and maximum sizes of each body nationwide. The overall size of the state senate ranges from a maximum 67 members in Minnesota to only 20 members in Alaska, with Oklahoma almost in the middle with its 48 members. On the other hand, the lower houses nationwide range from a high of 424 representatives in New Hampshire to a low of 40 in Alaska, with Oklahoma having 101 members in its House of Representatives. Nationwide, the averages are 40.2 senators and 149.7 representatives for each state, so that puts Oklahoma almost right at the national average for both houses (National Conference of State Legislatures, 2014). The Citizens Conference of State Legislators concluded that the Oklahoma legislature was just about the right size for its population (Morgan, England, and Humphreys 1991). Because of their sizes, the Oklahoma House and Senate operate very differently, as shown in Table 5–1. Each house is allowed by the Constitution in Article V, Section 30, to create its own internal rules and judge the elections of its own members. The larger size of the House means that it tends to have more restrictive rules to make it easier to control the great number of members. The Senate, on the other hand, tends to have more a collegial atmosphere, with fewer rules that encourage longer debates.

TABLE 5–1
Differences between the Oklahoma House and Senate

	HOUSE	SENATE
Size of Legislative Body	101 Representatives	48 Senators
Qualifications for Office	Minimum age of 21	Minimum age of 25
Terms of Office	Two-year terms	Four-year staggered terms
Rules	More restricted rules and procedures	Less organized rules
Style of Debate	Less collegial atmosphere	More debate-style atmosphere

Qualifications for Office

The members of the Oklahoma House and Senate are also different in terms of their qualifications. Representatives must only be 21 or older when elected, while Senators must have reached the minimum age of 25. Both need to be qualified electors in their respective counties or districts and must reside there during their terms of office, according to Section 17 of the Constitution, Article V. Section 18 of the Constitution also prevents current United States or state government officers, as well as those persons convicted of a felony, and state legislators expelled for corruption from serving in the Oklahoma legislature. Members of both houses must take office within 15 days after the General Election in which they were elected. Moreover, Article V, Section 23 of the Constitution says that lawmakers "shall, except for treason, felony, or breach of the peace, be privileged from arrest during the session of the legislature, and in going to and returning from the same."[1] This protection is only available to lawmakers while performing their official duties in office. Lawmakers also cannot be appointed by the governor, or legislature, to a state office during their legislative terms. Lawmakers also must disclose any personal or private interest in any bill before the legislature as per Section 24 of the Constitution and are subject to a variety of ethics rules promulgated by the State Ethics Commission.

Terms of Office

State senators usually have longer terms than those of representatives. Such is the case in Oklahoma and 31 other states where senators serve four-year terms and the representatives serve two-year terms (Council of State Governments 1996). In Oklahoma, representatives are elected in even-numbered years. Senators, on the other hand, are elected for four-year terms, with half of the senators elected every two years. Senators in odd-numbered districts were elected or reelected in 2014, while senators in even-numbered districts will be elected in 2016. In five other states, all members serve four-year terms. With the remaining twelve states, all lawmakers serve only two-year terms. The 50th state is Nebraska where its members serve four-year terms in a unicameral, nonpartisan legislature. The length of a legislative term is important. With shorter terms, members of the House are up for reelection often so they are more likely to be responsive to the demands and needs of their constituents. With the longer terms, however, senators can think more about the long-term goals of the state.

Term Limits for Legislators

In 1990, Oklahoma became the first state in the country to vote for limits on legislative incumbency, by placing **term limits** on the terms that members could serve in office. Oklahoma voters through a 1990 initiative limited state legislators to a twelve-year maximum combined terms of House and

Senate service starting with the November 1992 elections. The move by Oklahomans to create term limits for state legislators attracted a great deal of attention. Not only was Oklahoma the first state to adopt legislative term limits, but after Oklahoma, 20 other states quickly adopted their own term limits, creating a national precedent. Many of these other states, including California, moved more quickly to enact their term limits, and as a result, while Oklahoma was the first state to create term limits for its legislators, it was not the first state to enact them. Term limits in Oklahoma did not take effect until 2004. This is because the Oklahoma term limit law allowed those members serving on January 1, 1991, to finish their term before their 12 years began to accumulate toward the limit. Since legislative terms start in November, those elected in 1990 were allowed to finish that entire term before being reelected under the new rules. Thus, Oklahoma's term limit law did not begin affecting state legislators until 2004.

While 21 states have adopted term limits, only fifteen states, including Oklahoma, still have term limit laws, as the supreme courts in Massachusetts, Washington, Oregon, and Wyoming have ruled term limits in those states unconstitutional, and the state legislatures of Idaho and Utah repealed term limits in 2002 and 2003, respectively (National Conference of State Legislatures, 2014). Oklahoma also has one of the more restrictive types of term limits, as it has enacted lifetime term limits as opposed to consecutive ones, as shown in Table 5–2. With the nine states that have consecutive term limits, a legislator is limited to serving x number of years consecutively, but after a period out of the legislature can serve again. Oklahoma, on the other hand, has twelve-year lifetime term limits. This means that a legislator can serve only twelve years in the legislature in his/her lifetime – whether in the House, in the Senate, or in some combination of both. The other five states with lifetime term limits include several of Oklahoma's neighbors, Arkansas and Missouri, as well as Nevada, California, and Michigan.

Many scholars, however, have speculated about the consequences of term limits. On the positive side, term limits might make state legislators

TABLE 5–2 Consecutive v. Lifetime Bans by State		
LIMIT IN YEARS	CONSECUTIVE	LIFETIME BAN
6 house/8 senate		AR, CA, MI
8 total	NE	
8 house/8 senate	AZ, CO, FL, ME, MT, OH, SD	MO
12 total		CA, OK
12 house/12 senate	LA	NV

SOURCE: National Conference of State Legislatures.

more responsive to constituents because these lawmakers know that they will only be in office for twelve years. Therefore, term limits may increase the ability of voters to make their legislators accountable. Yet, term limits may have some negative consequences as well. Term limits may increase the power of executives, lobbyists, and staff relative to members (Fowler 1992). Term limits may also not have the desired effect on state legislators because they tend to have shorter tenures than their counterparts in the U.S. Congress (Gray and Eisinger 1997; Harrigan and Nice 2008). Critics of term limits also point to the loss of experience, institutional memory, and continuity that may result if term limits are enacted (Benjamin and Malbin 1992; Copeland and Rausch 1993).

As expected, term limits in Oklahoma have had four immediate consequences. First, the average length of service of each representative and senator has decreased significantly, as one would expect. Prior to term limits in 2003, the average length of service was 8.8 years in the House and 10.5 years in the Senate. As of 2014, those numbers are respectively 6.68 and 6.54 years. Second, there has been a subsequent increase in the percentage of junior members, defined before term limits took effect as representatives with less than three terms of service (six years) in the House and less than two terms (eight years) in the Senate. The percentage of junior members in the House was only 40.4% in 2002 before term limits took effect while in 2014 it was 47.5%. For the Senate, there is a similar story with only 28.6% junior members in 2003, but 68.75% in 2014.

Third, with less seniority, it might be expected that the members are also younger in age, since now members cannot serve 20 or 30-year terms as they did in the past. That is indeed the case. The average age of representatives and senators was 54.1 and 54.6 respectively, in 2003 before term limits. Today, in 2014, those average ages are 50.5 for the House and 52.2 for the Senate (all author's calculations of data are taken from www.lsb .state.gov). Lastly, there has been substantial turnover in the leadership of both the House and the Senate. As Table 5–3 shows, there are many new members serving in the leadership, with the greatest impact occurring in the Senate. Prior to term limits, there were about 2-3 members who left the leadership every year, whereas after term limits about half of the leaders in each body are new due to turnover.

III. WHO ARE THE MEMBERS OF THE OKLAHOMA LEGISLATURE?

Membership in the Legislature

With any state legislature, it is important to look at its demographic characteristics. How many of the legislators are men? How many are women? How many are African-Americans? What are the most common occupations? These questions are important because they raise issues of

TABLE 5–3		
House and Senate Leadership Turnover		
OKLAHOMA LEGISLATURE LEADERSHIP TURNOVER NUMBER OF NEW LEADERS		
YEAR	HOUSE	SENATE
1989–1990	12 of 21	6 of 11
1991–1992	12 of 20	2 of 9
1993–1994	9 of 21	2 of 9
1995–1996	12 of 23	5 of 10
1997–1998	13 of 24	2 of 10
1999–2000	13 of 27	2 of 10
2001–2002	14 of 26	2 of 11
2003–2004	15 of 26	6 of 14
2005–2006	18 of 28	9 of 15
2007–2008	29 of 40	9 of 17
2009–2010	14 of 24	11 of 21

NOTES: Table compiled from House and Senate directories by Travis Covey and Rick Farmer, Committee Staff Division, Oklahoma House of Representatives, 5/21/07. See http://www .okhouse.gov/Research/LeadershipTurnover.doc. 2009–2010 data was compiled by the author.

representation. Can a legislature be truly representative if it does not resemble the population as a whole? While it may be impossible, and perhaps not desirable, for the legislature to match the population perfectly, the demographic characteristics of a legislator can make a difference because studies have found that certain groups vote differently. African American female legislators, for example, are more interested in education, minority issues, and health care reform (Kirksey and Wright 1992; Barrett 1995; Button and Hedge 1996). Women in general are more likely to help constituents than male legislators (Richardson and Freeman 1995). Women are also more predisposed to see women's concerns (Githens, Norris, and Lovenduski 1994; but see Dolan and Ford 1995) and perceive the causes of crime differently (Kathlene 1995).

Across the country, the most dominant profile in state legislatures is that of a middle-aged white male who is a business owner or an attorney. In fact, nationwide the state legislators are about 87% white and 76% male with an average age of 56. The percentage of lawyers, however, has fallen from a high of 25% in the mid 1970s to about 15.2% today (National Conference of State Legislatures, 2014). In fact, most of the legislators in the

1970s fit this profile, because there were few, if any racial-ethnic minorities in the state legislature nationwide and few women.

Gender

However, there have been some changes in state legislative membership, such as with the substantial increase in female legislators. There have been 180% more female state legislators in the last twenty years; in 1996 this meant that women represented 20% of all state legislators nationwide (Dresang & Gosling, 2002) and in 2002, it was 22% (Bowman & Kearney, 2012). In 2010, that average had increased to 24.2% or 1,784 of the state legislative seats available nationwide. That is an increase from several hundred, which it was in 1969 (National Conference of State Legislatures, 2014). An even more significant sign of the greater representation of women in the state legislatures can be gleaned by looking at the percentage of the legislature that is female. Nationwide, about 51% of the United States population is female, but in 2002, only six of the fifty state legislatures were more than 30% female. As of 2013, that number is now nine, with Colorado, New Hampshire, Minnesota, and Vermont having some of the highest percentages (National Conference of State Legislatures, 2014).

Oklahoma, however, is not one of those states experiencing an increase in female legislators. In fact, Oklahoma stands out in the opposite direction. As of November 2013, Oklahoma had sixteen female representatives in the House (out of 101), and four in the Senate (out of 48), with a total percentage of 13.4%. This ranks Oklahoma 48th among the states in terms of its percentage of female legislators, only below Louisiana and South Carolina, and thus considerably below the national average of 24.2% female legislators.

Ethnic/Racial Diversity in State Legislative Membership

State legislators nationwide are not a very ethnically diverse bunch and Oklahoma is no exception to that rule. In fact, 88% of Oklahoma legislators are Caucasian, compared to 86% of their colleagues nationwide. As a result, state legislators in general do not come close to matching their percentages in the U.S. population. For example, as of the 2010 census, the percentage of Americans reporting they were African American was roughly 13% and Hispanic or Latino was about 14%. But only 9% of state legislators nationwide are African American, while less than 3% are Latino (National Conference of State Legislators, 2014). In fact, the percentage of African-American legislators, has fluctuated over the years, with only 2% in 1970 to almost 9% in 1993, but dropped back to 7% in 2002 (Bowman and Kearney 2002) and then increasing to 8.1% in 2003 (National Conference of State Legislators, 2007). For Latinos, not only is the nationwide percentage of legislators small at 3%, but the picture becomes even more clear when the states of the legislators are examined. Most of the

Latino legislators come from a limited number of states, including Arizona, California, Colorado, New Mexico, and Texas, with fifteen states having no Latino legislators in 2013 (National Conference of State Legislators, 2014). However, that number was thirty-four states in 2007, so there clearly has been growth in the number of Latino legislators. In terms of African American and Latino legislators, however, the Oklahoma legislature ranks far below the national averages, with only one Latino legislator and only 4% African American legislators (two in the Senate and four in the House) as of 2013. Oklahoma also has no Asian legislators, compared to 1% nationwide (National Conference of State Legislators, 2014).

Looking at other minorities, there is one clear exception in terms of the ethnic diversity of Oklahoma state legislators—Native Americans. Oklahoma has a proud Native American tradition. In fact, the state's name Oklahoma comes from two Choctaw words, *Okla* (people) and *humma* (red), meaning "red people." Oklahoma has thirty-eight different Native American tribes within its borders and this diversity is reflected in the state legislature. 15.4% of Oklahoma's state legislators are Native American, compared to only 1% among state legislators nationwide (National Conference of State Legislatures, 2014). They are members of the National Caucus of Native American State Legislators (www.ncsl .org/collaboration/nativeamericanlegislators).

Born in Oklahoma?

One interesting statistic concerns whether Oklahoma state legislators were born in Oklahoma. By looking at the official Oklahoma state legislature website, news reports, and other sources, the birthplace of many state legislators can be determined. For the 2013–2014 Oklahoma Legislature, for example, the birthplace of 101 of the 149 legislators could be found (67.8%). The reasons for the missing birthplaces of the legislators can be numerous: state legislators may not want to reveal such private information or they may not want to reveal to their voting constituents that they were not born in Oklahoma. The Oklahoma Constitution does not require that legislators have to be born in Oklahoma; rather, they only have to be qualified electors in their respective counties or districts and must reside there during their terms of office. Yet, it is interesting to note that among who the legislators who reported their birthplace, 46 of the 67 representatives (or 68.1%) and 30 of the 34 senators (or 88.2%) in 2013 reported that they were born in Oklahoma.

Occupations of Legislators

Most Oklahoma legislators hold other jobs and are considered part-time legislators. The National Conference of State Legislatures has classified the fifty state legislatures according to their degree of professionalism based on the percentage of time legislators report doing their jobs, their annual salary, and the size of the staff as either red (most professional), white (transitioning), or blue (traditional part-time legislature). The four states in the most professional category (red) are California, Michigan, New York, and Pennsylvania. An additional six states are "red lite," meaning that they are just a bit less professional than the red states. Oklahoma is classified as a "white" transitional legislature, or a legislature moving from amateur to professional status. Along with Oklahoma, there are twenty-two other states in this "white" category including some of Oklahoma's nearby neighbors, Arkansas, Missouri, Nebraska, and Texas. In the blue category, there are an additional seventeen states, with eleven states in a "blue lite" category and another six states listed as "blue," meaning that these states have the least professional legislatures: Montana, New Hampshire, North Dakota, South Dakota, Utah, and Wyoming (National Conference of State Legislatures, 2014).

Oklahoma ranks fairly comparably to other legislatures in the white category. Its compensation level of $38,400 is slightly higher than the "white" average of $35,326. This "white" salary average, however, includes the per diem calculation but Oklahoma's does not which would make Oklahoma's salary closer to $48,300. States in this category tend to have medium-sized populations and their legislators tend to have intermediate-sized staffs, with an average of 3.1 staffers per member nationwide. Legislators in this category report that they spend 70% of their time doing legislative work, but many of them have other jobs while they are state legislators (National Conference of State Legislators, 2014).

Thus, it is not a surprise that while nationwide the most important occupation for state legislators is being a full-time legislator (16.4% of legislators), that is not true in Oklahoma with only 9.5% of its legislators reporting that as their primary occupation. Instead, in Oklahoma, these other jobs include being attorneys, non-profit consultants, educators, and farmers. Nationwide, in the 1970s about 25% of state legislators were attorneys, compared to today's 15.2% (National Conference of State Legislatures, 2014). In the House of Representatives, Oklahoma is below the national average with only 9.9% of House members in 2010 being attorneys, but in the Senate 27.1% of Senators were attorneys, which is just slightly above that national average. This compares to figures of 14.1% and 20.8% respectively for the 2004 Oklahoma legislature. Oklahoma reports more non-profit consultants (11.4%), more farmers (7.4%), and more K-12 educators (6.8%), but has a smaller number of retirees (9.5%) and business owners (7.4%) than the national averages.

Today, Oklahoma lawmakers are finding that maintaining a full-time job while being a legislator is increasingly difficult. Political scientists suggest that both full-time legislatures and part-time legislatures have their advantages. With a full-time legislature, lawmakers can be more responsive to their constituents, answering phone calls and passing legislation on a daily basis. Greater demands on the legislature, particularly in terms of budgeting and oversight, may now require year-round attention. Oklahoma's fiscal budget year, for example, goes from July 1 to June 30, yet the Oklahoma legislature is only in session from February to May. Government agencies need to be watched year-round to make sure that they are performing their proper functions. Those in favor of a part-time legislature, however, point out that full-time legislators can be more detached from the real world. Legislators can get an "inside the Capitol" mentality that may put them out of touch with the real problems and needs of working people. These seem to be the sentiments of most people in Oklahoma, given the prevailing culture of populism.

Education

Members of the 2014 Oklahoma legislature are very educated as shown in Table 5–4. In the House, 80.1% of the members have a college degree or better, while in the Senate 77.2% have a college degree or better. The national average for college educated legislators is 81%, putting Oklahoma just a bit below the national average.

Age

One might expect that Oklahoma legislators might be fairly young, given that the minimum age for representatives and senators are 21 and 25 respectively. Yet the average age in the 2014 Oklahoma Legislature for representatives is 50.5, while the average age for senators is 52.2. It is worth noting, however, that just as recently as 2004, the average age for the House was 54.1 and for the Senate, 54.6, so today's Oklahoma legislators are slightly younger. Oklahoma's legislators are also much younger than their colleagues nationwide. 10.1% of Oklahoma's legislators in 2014 were between the ages of 20 and 34, while nationwide that figure is only 4%. Oklahoma also has a higher percentage of those aged 35-49 (33.5%, compared to 24% nationwide) and a lower percentage of those over 50 as expected (56.4%, compared to 72%) (National Conference of State Legislatures, 2014).

One of the possible explanations for this is term limits. Oklahoma's term limits took effect completely in 2004, making the 2014 election class only the sixth term-limited class. Term limits should produce younger members in a legislature. Serving fewer terms limits the number of legislators who can serve in their old age since it is fairly typical for many members to start their legislative careers in their forties or fifties. As of 2014, the youngest Oklahoma representative is Justin F. Wood (R) who is 24 while the oldest is Ann Coody (R) who is 76. In the Senate, the youngest is Nathan Dahm (R) at 31 and the oldest is Jim Halligan (R) at age 77.

TABLE 5–4 Education, Age, and Tenure of the Members of the 2014 Legislature		
	HOUSE	SENATE
% of Members with College Degree or Better	80.2%	77.1%
Average Age of Members	50.5	52.2
Youngest Member	Justin F. Wood (R) at age 24	Nathan Dahm (R) at age 31
Oldest Member	Ann Coody (R) at age 76	Jim Halligan (R) at age 77
Female Members (national average = 24.2%)	16/101 or 15.8%	4/48 or 8.3%
Average Tenure of Members	6.68 years	6.54 years
Percentage of Members born in Oklahoma (of those who reported)	68.1%	88.2%
Junior Members (served three terms or less in the House, two terms or less in the Senate).	47.5%	68.8%
The percentage of current legislators who are term-limited in 2014.	7.9%	6.3%

SOURCE: Author's calculations taken in March 2014 from the Oklahoma State House and Senate websites, see www.lsb.state.ok.us.

Religion

Another aspect where Oklahoma state legislators are different from the nationwide averages is in their religious preferences. Not surprisingly considering that Oklahoma is located in the Bible Belt, Oklahoma state legislators tend to be more Protestant (54%) compared to their colleagues nationwide (34%). The Oklahoma legislature also has fewer Catholic legislators (3%) than other states, and it had no legislators that were listed as Jewish or Mormon. However, one significant limitation of this data should be noted. Religion preference data can be suspect because of the unwillingness of people to share such private information. This was true with state legislators both in Oklahoma and nationwide, where 39% and 43% respectively did not report their religious preference (National Conference on State Legislatures, 2014).

IV. Compensation and Tenure in Office

Compensation of Oklahoma Legislators

Compensation is always a controversial issue with the members of the public because they often believe that politicians are overpaid. With the state legislature, salaries are particularly problematic, because with the lifting of constitutional restrictions on legislative compensation in all but four states in 2000, most state legislators are in the curious predicament of setting their own salaries (Bowman & Kearney, 2012). It is also difficult to determine the exact yearly salaries of state legislators because of differences across the nation in how the legislators are paid. In six states, including Alabama, Nevada, North Dakota, and Wyoming among others, the state legislators are paid by the days worked. For states that use this compensation system, the pay ranges from $10 per day in Alabama to $273 per day in Kentucky with a nationwide average of $129.66 per day. All of the remaining states except one pay by the year including Oklahoma. The 50th state, New Mexico, was left out of the salary calculations because it does not offer any compensation to its state legislators, but does pay a per diem rate of $154 per day (National Conference of State Legislators, 2014).

The yearly compensation varies tremendously, with state legislators in California earning the most at $90,526 per year, and Texas paying the least at $7,200 per year, with a nationwide average of $33,448.16 in 2014. Complicating the math in computing salaries is the fact that most states pay a per diem, either by the day or month, for when the legislature is in session. These per diem amounts can range as low as $10 per day to $234 per day, and can vary depending on whether the distance traveled by the legislator, whether lodging is required, and whether or not the per diem is tied to the federal per diem rate.

In Oklahoma's case, the Constitution set legislative compensation until 1968 at $1,200 per year plus $15 per day for up to 75 legislative days during the biennial session. In 1968, Oklahoma did away with that constitutional limitation after a state question was passed creating a Legislative Compensation Board (LCB). Now, salaries are determined by a nine-member board appointed by the governor, the President Pro Tempore, and the Speaker of the House of Representatives, according to Article V, Section 21, of the Constitution. Almost half of the other states also recognized the salary dilemma creating similar commissions (Bowman & Kearney, 2012). Once the commission makes a decision, it then takes effect 15 days after the next general election.

In 1989–90, this salary was raised to $20,000, or eighth best in the nation. In 1997, the salary of legislators was $32,000 or 10th in the nation. The last pay increase for Oklahoma legislators came from the Legislative Compensation Board at its 1997 meeting. The Board gave Oklahoma legislators a pay increase of $6,400, making their salaries $38,400 effective November 18, 1998, and legislators were still at that same pay as of April 2014. Oklahoma legislators also receive a per diem rate of $150 per day which could add up to $9,900 for a typical 66-day session. This salary now makes Oklahoma legislators rank 15th highest nationwide of the 40 states that pay by the year (National Conference of State Legislatures, 2014). Moreover, the House Speaker and Senate President Pro Tempore received an additional compensation of $17,932 per year. With the pay increase of November 1998, for the first time the chairs of the House and Senate Appropriation Committees also received $12,364 as additional compensation. Furthermore, every member of the Oklahoma legislature receives a monthly allowance to purchase various insurance benefits, mileage benefits, a voluntary retirement package, a per diem for those unable to commute from home during the session, expenses for meetings, and expenses for office supplies (Council of State Governments, 2014 – www.csg.org).

A comparison of Oklahoma's compensation package with two other states, Texas and California, is shown in Table 5–5. An important fact to

TABLE 5–5 Compensation/Expenses Comparison between Various State Legislatures, Including Oklahoma, Current as of March 15, 2013.		
STATE	SALARY	PER DIEM
Arkansas	$15,869 per year	$147 per day (V) plus mileage, tied to federal rate.
California	$90,526 per year	$141.86 per day (U) each day in session.
Colorado	$30,000 per year	$183 per day for members outside 50 miles of capitol, $45 per day for inside 50 miles of capitol.
Kansas	$88.66 per day	$123 per day.
Missouri	$35,915 per year	$104 per day (U), tied to federal rate. Verification of per diem is by roll call.
Nebraska	$12,000 per year	$123 outside 50 miles of capitol, $46 inside 50 miles of capitol (V) tied to federal rate.
New Mexico	None	$154 per day (V) tied to federal rate and constitution.
Oklahoma	$38,400 per year	$147 per day (U) tied to federal rate.
Texas	$7,200 per year	$150 per day (U) set by Ethics Commission.

V = vouchered, U = unvouchered.

SOURCE: http://www.ncsl.org/default.aspx?tabid=14840

consider, however, when examining compensation levels is that the Oklahoma legislature meets only from February to May of each year. Most of the states with higher salaries, such as California and New York at $90,526 and $79,500 respectively, are year-round legislatures. Thus, the Oklahoma legislature has one of the highest compensation rates for the number of days it is in session. A particularly striking comparison can be noted between Oklahoma and its geographic neighbors. Despite the obvious population/geographic size difference, Oklahoma is often compared to Texas and yet, Texas only pays its legislators $7,200 per year. Legislators in Kansas receive only $88.66 per calendar day, far below the national average, while Arkansas legislators receive only $15,869 per year. The only Oklahoma neighbor that matches Oklahoma is Missouri where its legislators earn $35,915, but Missouri has a year-round legislature unlike the part-time one of Oklahoma (National Conference of State Legislatures, 2014).

Tenure in Office

Tenure in office is currently one of the most important issues facing today's Oklahoma legislature because of the term limit law. As shown in Table 5–4, 68.8% of the Senate and 47.5% of the House are junior members, and the average tenure of members is 6.54 years for the Senate and 6.68 years for the House. Figure 5–1 shows that many of the representatives are right in the middle of their careers right now, reflecting almost a perfect bell curve with the peak at the center of the curve. As shown in the same chart, the Senate's term limits currently are having a different effect, with many of the senators' terms loaded in the earliest years. Thus, in the future, nobody will be able to match the tenure of former Senator Gene Stipe (D-Tahlequah) who was recognized as the longest serving legislator in the history of Oklahoma. He served in the House of Representatives from 1949 to 1954 and in the Senate from 1975 to 2003. But in 2003, he resigned from office after facing federal charges relating to campaign fundraising in 1998.

V. How Oklahoma Legislators Get Into Office

Elections and Turnover

Elections are watched carefully by members of the legislature in both parties because the elections decide which party has majority control of the legislature. The party that controls the legislature has several major advantages. The most obvious advantage is that the majority party has more votes, and thus is more likely to prevail on major policy decisions. But beyond that, the entire legislature is structured by party. Members of the majority party get more staff, more seats on the various committees, better offices, and other perks. With the exception of 1921, 1922 and most

FIGURE 5–1 The Number of Representatives with their Corresponding Years of Service

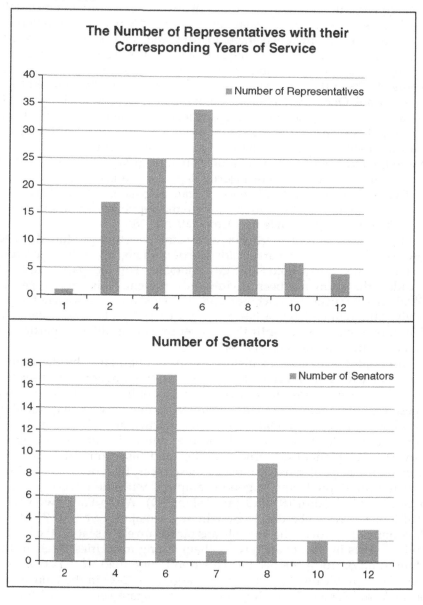

recently 2004–2014, this has meant the Democrats. But recently, the Republicans have had majority control of the legislature. Despite the Republican advantage in both houses of the legislature, there will still be many close battles to come. On tax legislation, the legislature needs a three-fourths vote, or else that legislation has to be voted on by the people. Even with non-emergency legislation, if the governor should enact a veto, a two-thirds vote of both houses would be needed to override the veto.

Comparing the partisanship of the Oklahoma legislature to other state legislatures nationwide, the Oklahoma House and Senate are more Republican than the nationwide average. In 2014, Oklahoma's House was 75% Republican. Nationwide, 28 of the House majorities are Republican representing 51.7% of the seats and 21 of the legislatures are Democrat, representing 47.4% of the seats. The remaining seats are held by Independents or are vacant. One state, Nebraska, is not included in these totals because it has a unicameral legislature. In the Senate, Oklahoma has a 72–29 advantage Republican; nationwide, 28 of the 48 state senates are majority Republican representing 52.3% of the state senate seats. With one split senate (Virginia) and Nebraska having a unicameral legislature, this meant that 58.3% of the state senates were majority Republican, and 41.7% were majority Democrat (National Conference of State Legislators, 2014). This is an exact reversal of what it was in 2010, when the Republicans controlled only 20 of the state senates, while the Democrats had 28.

Elections are also noteworthy because sometimes they produce **divided government**, where one party holds one or both houses of the legislature and the other party holds the governorship. For the past couple of decades, the norm has been divided government. This can happen in Oklahoma because the governor and the legislature are selected separately. Although Oklahoma has a straight-party ballot, fewer voters use that option and instead, **split their ticket** by voting different parties for different offices on the same ballot.

Although Oklahoma has historically been dominated by the Democratic Party for state-level offices, the general trend over the past several years has seen a substantial increase in Republican electoral success. These electoral victories mirror the longstanding success that Republicans have enjoyed from Oklahoma voters participating in national elections. In the 2010 elections, all of the statewide offices, including Governor, Lieutenant Governor, Auditor and Inspector, Treasurer, etc. went to the Republicans. In most of these races, the vote was lopsided towards the Republicans. A good example is with the governor's race between Mary Fallin (R) and Jari Askins (D). While Fallin won with 60.4% of the vote, she did so by winning a majority vote in 73 of the 77 counties. Moreover, the Republicans picked up eight seats in the House and six seats in the Senate, giving them strong majorities, 70-31 in the House and 32-16 in the Senate. This trend continued in the 2012 elections as Republicans increased their margins to 72-29 in the House and 36-12 in the Senate. Thus, Republicans once again set a record for the largest Republican majorities in the Oklahoma legislature ever. With the reelection of Patrice Douglas as Corporation Commissioner, Republicans enjoyed the second election where they held all statewide seats and both legislative majorities. Thus, at least for 2013–2014, divided government is gone in Oklahoma.

Reapportionment

Of all the factors that govern elections, reapportionment probably had the most impact on the Oklahoma legislature. Before 1964, legislative districts could be unequal in size because there was no law to prevent it. Thus, in the same state, one representative for the U.S. Congress could represent 800,000 people, while another could represent 150,000. Oklahoma was considered to be one of the "worst" states in the 1950s when it came to this because much of the power was in the rural parts of Oklahoma—particularly in the southeast portion of the state. Thus, many of the states' rural districts had been configured so that they were small, compared to the more urban districts. A combination of Supreme Court decisions successfully remedied this problem, placing sharp limits on the states' ability to control their own elections. Most important, **Baker v. Carr** (1962) gave the national government and the courts the right to rule on legislative districting. It established the **"one person, one vote" principle**, thereby making each legislative district roughly equal in size. In the second decision, **Reynolds v. Sims** (1964), the Court ruled that state legislative seats must be apportioned substantially on population.

Today, most legislative districts within a given state are of roughly equal size based on population. In fact, many districts do not follow traditional county boundaries, economic boundaries, or ethnic boundaries, but are rather artificial creations based on political concerns. These two Supreme Court decisions had a tremendous impact on Oklahoma. As a result of these decisions, the Oklahoma legislature lost some of its rural domination while the more populated areas (Oklahoma City, Tulsa, and Lawton) gained seats.

The time period after the 2000 elections was a very important one for Oklahoma because of **reapportionment,** or the resizing of districts, both in the U.S. Congress and in the state legislature, to accommodate changes in population. It is the job of the state legislature in every state to redraw the district lines, or **redistricting,** after a census. A national census is taken every 10 years in the United States. This very short, usually one-page, form is sent to all households in the United States and its goal is to count the population within each city, county, and state. Because U.S. Congressional districts must be roughly equal in population size, when a state population changes, some states may lose one or more congressional seats while other states gain. Oklahoma lost one congressional seat in 2002 because its population growth did not keep pace with other states. As a result, the Oklahoma state legislature had to engage in one of its major responsibilities—the drawing of both the state legislative as well as congressional districts. These lines were redrawn in 2002. Fortunately, for Oklahoma, the legislature resolved its differences fairly easily, unlike its neighbor to the south. There, the Texas state redistricting battle got so heated that several Democratic legislators fled the state to Oklahoma to avoid being arrested. Because Texas House rules allow the arrest of state representatives who prevent a quorum, Ardmore, Oklahoma got a temporary tourism boost!

For the 2012 elections, Oklahoma was fortunate not to lose another congressional seat, but once again, needed to redraw both congressional and state legislative district lines because of changes in population (see Figure 5–2). Despite some complaints by Democrats that they were being left out of the process, and some major changes in the state Senate and U.S. House districts, the redistricting went fairly smoothly. The Oklahoma legislature reaching final decisions fairly early in the process. Governor Mary Fallin signed the law in May 2011.

Ethics

In 1990, Oklahomans passed State Question 627 with a two-to-one vote, adding an Ethics Commission to the Constitution. The Oklahoma Ethics Commission, formerly called the Oklahoma Council on Campaign Compliance and Ethical Standards, is composed of five members appointed by the Governor, President Pro Tempore of the Senate, Speaker of the House, Chief Justice of the Supreme Court, and the Attorney General. To make sure that the commission is balanced, no more than three of the commissioners can come from the same party and congressional districts can only be represented once. The purpose of the Ethics Commission is to regulate the political and campaign activities of

FIGURE 5–2 Oklahoma House Districts 2012–2020 Elections

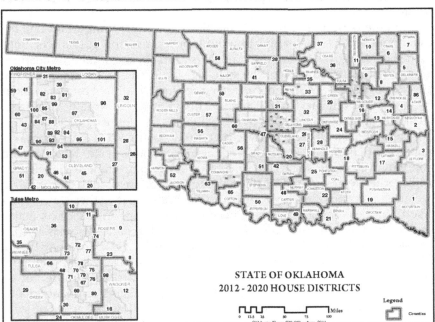

STATE OF OKLAHOMA
2012 - 2020 HOUSE DISTRICTS

state officeholders, lobbyists, and others engaged with the state government. In recent years, the ethics laws have been substantially strengthened and as a result, Oklahoma's ethics laws are stronger than those of many states.

The Ethics Commission imposes specific limitations on Oklahoma lawmakers. Lawmakers must file financial disclosure statements. Although these statements are not a complete report on legislative personal wealth or income, they must disclose individual income sources that exceed $1,000 annually. Lawmakers also cannot engage in activities nor have interests that conflict with their legislative duties. Section 24 in Article V of the Constitution requires members to refrain from voting on bills where they have a conflict of interest. Generally, these are bills that would benefit a particular interest and not a larger group.

Individual lawmakers can only receive contributions of $1,000 annually from individuals and $5,000 annually from labor organizations or Political Action Committees (PACs). Oklahoma ethics laws prohibit corporations from contributing directly to candidates and no public funds can be used to fund campaigns. This rule was no longer being implemented though after the U.S. Supreme Court decision in *Citizens United v. FEC*, as indicated by the Oklahoma Ethics Commission on its website as of 2012. Lawmakers are also required to file quarterly reports, with additional reports required as an election approaches. Moreover, lawmakers cannot receive contributions from state highway patrol members and supernumerary tax consultants. Candidates may not use their campaign funds to defray personal expenses, but rather only those expenses associated with the campaign or their duties as public officeholders. Candidates, including powerful legislative leaders, cannot give campaign funds to other candidates. Finally, individuals can receive a $100 state tax deduction for donating to state candidates.

VI. How the Oklahoma Legislature Stays Organized

Leadership

In the Oklahoma legislature, a distinction can be drawn among formal leadership positions, committee leadership, and the leadership team. The formal leadership positions include the Speaker, President Pro Tempore, and various other House and Senate majority and minority party leaders. These leaders are either elected by their respective party caucus or appointed by other leaders. The committee leadership includes those who chair the various committees. The third leadership component is relatively rare for state legislatures and exists only in the House. The leadership team consists of an informal brain trust selected by the Speaker of the House. These legislators are his/her inner circle or kitchen-cabinet and often function as a sounding board for the Speaker. Compared to the other more established leadership positions, membership in the brain trust is fluid, with members moving in and out of the circle.

The Oklahoma legislature has numerous leadership positions. Looking just at the leadership positions listed by the Council of State Governments, Oklahoma has more formal leadership positions than any other state legislature. The 2014 Oklahoma Senate has twenty-two legislators in leadership positions in both parties, while the House has twenty-four Republican leadership positions and fourteen Democratic leadership positions. Thus, 37.6% of the House and 45.8% of the Senate are in leadership positions. The leadership in both houses is organized first by party. The most prestigious positions for both houses with the current leaders as of 2014 are indicated in Table 5–6. The number of seats held by a political party will determine whether that party is in the majority or the minority for that institution.

In the Oklahoma House, the most important position is called the **Speaker of the House**, while the Senate's leader is called the **President Pro Tempore** (also called Senate Pro Tem). The Lieutenant Governor is the President of the Senate, but this has been largely a ceremonial position that calls for the person holding the post to preside over joint sessions and to cast the very rare tie-breaking vote in the Senate. These leaders get their powers from several sources: 1) the Oklahoma Constitution in Article V gives these leaders substantial power over legislative agenda setting and they both control the flow of legislation within their respective chambers; and 2) these leaders have the authority to make key legislative leadership, staff, and committee assignments for their colleagues. In many state legislatures, these leaders are also the most senior members, meaning that they have the most tenure of any member in that house. However, this is not usually the case in Oklahoma. With term limits, it is less likely to be so.

The Oklahoma House Speaker works with other leaders in the majority, including the Speaker Pro Tem, the Majority Floor Leader, Assistant Majority Floor Leader, and the Majority Whip. Only the Speaker and the Speaker Pro Tem are elected by all the members of the House. The Speaker is given additional power because not only does he/she appoint the floor leader and whip positions but he/she also has substantial control over the party caucus which selects all the other majority party positions. The **party caucus** is the meeting of all lawmakers of a party in a particular house. The Speaker of the House has substantial duties in addition to making these appointments. The Speaker presides over each day's session, assigns bills to their appropriate committees, appoints the membership of standing and special committees in the House, including the chairs, and is the chief representative of the House when working with the Senate, the governor, and state agencies. By tradition, the Speaker and Speaker Pro Tem are also ex-officio members of all standing committees. Perhaps because of this immense power, the Democratic Caucus in the past had limited the Speaker to three terms of service as Speaker. With

TABLE 5–6
House and Senate Leadership Positions as of 2014

HOUSE LEADERSHIP POSITIONS	SENATE LEADERSHIP POSITIONS
Speaker of the House— T.W. Shannon (R)	President—Todd Lamb (also Lt. Governor) (R)
Speaker Pro Tempore— Mike Jackson (R)	President Pro Tempore— Brian Bingman (R)
Majority Leader—Dennis Johnson, Fred Jordan (both R)	Majority Floor Leader—Mike Schulz (R)
Majority Floor Leader— Pam Peterson (R)	Assistant Floor Leaders—Cliff Branan, John Ford, Rob Johnson (all R)
Assistant Majority Floor Leaders— Lee Denney, Dale DeWitt, Randy Grau, Randy McDaniel, Charles Ortega, Paul Wesselhoft (all R)	Majority Whips—Rick Brinkley, Kim David, David Holt, Greg Treat (all R)
Majority Caucus Chair— Weldon Watson (R)	Caucus Chair—Bryce Marlatt (R)
Majority Caucus Vice-Chair— Harold Wright (R)	Vice Caucus Chair—A J Griffin (R)
Majority Whip—Todd Thomsen (R)	Rural Caucus Chair—Ron Justice (R)
Assistant Majority Whips—Lisa Billy, Dennis Casey, Josh Cockroft, Jon Echols, Glen Mulready, Sean Roberts, Todd Russ, Mike Sanders, Steve Vaughan (all R)	Democratic Leader—Sean Burrage (D)
Majority Caucus Secretary— Elise Hall (R)	Assistant Democratic Floor Leaders— Roger Ballenger, John Sparks, Charles Wyrick, Jerry Ellis (all D)
Minority Leader— Scott Inman (D)	Democratic Whips—Earl Garrison, Al McAffrey (all D)
Minority Floor Leader— Ben Sherrer (D)	Democratic Caucus Chair—Tom Ivester
Deputy Minority Floor Leader— Eric Proctor (D)	Democratic Caucus Vice Chair— Susan Paddack (D)
Assistant Minority Floor Leaders— Steve Kouplen, Jeannie McDaniel, Brian Renegar, Wade Rousselot, Mike Shelton, Emily Virgin (all D)	
Minority Whip—Chuck Hoskin (D)	
Assistant Minority Whip—Cory T. Williams (D)	
Minority Caucus Chair— Jerry McPeak (D)	
Minority Caucus Vice Chair— Joe Dorman (D)	
Minority Caucus Secretary— Curtis McDaniel (D)	

SOURCE: see http://newlsb.lsb.state.ok.us/

term limits operative in the Oklahoma legislature today, this has been continued with the House Republicans in the majority.

Comparatively speaking, legislative leaders in the Oklahoma Senate have less power. First, because the membership of the House is larger, the House is more centralized, thereby making it easier for the Speaker to have control. With only forty-eight Senators, such centralization is less necessary, the debates and rules are more informal, and therefore, the President Pro Tem has less power. Second, the Lieutenant Governor, with the exception of breaking ties, is given much less of a role in the Oklahoma Senate. In many states, including Texas, the Lt. Governor is called the President of the Senate and has substantial responsibilities, including managing the floor debate, controlling legislation, and other such powers. Although the Oklahoma Lt. Governor is President of the Senate, the Lt. Governor does not have these same powers, and instead functions much like the Vice-President of the United States does for the Congress— acting only when there is a tie in the Senate or presiding over a Joint Session. Third, unlike the House Speaker, the Senate Pro Tem has much less control over committee assignments and leadership selection. Committee assignments in the Senate are determined by a special committee, while the leaders are selected by the party caucus. Finally, the President Pro Tem is also limited in power because the Senate has the tradition of electing the future President Pro Tem during the terms of a sitting Pro Tem, thereby fracturing power in the Senate. No President Pro Tem has served more than three terms in Oklahoma (Oklahoma Department of Libraries, 1997).

Yet, the major leaders in the Oklahoma Senate still have power. Like their counterparts in the House, the Senate Pro Tem and the Assistant Majority leader are ex-officio members of all Senate standing committees, giving them immense power. A major source of power for both the Speaker and President Pro Tempore is that of appointing members to conference committees where the fate of important legislation is decided.

Committees

Committees are the workhorses of the Oklahoma legislature. Committees formulate legislation, hold hearings, and modify proposed legislation. Committees also are beneficial because most unimportant legislation is eliminated here and the public truly gets the greatest chance to understand the legislature through formal hearings.

Like the formal leadership, the committees have a hierarchical structure. There are four different types of committees. First, each house has permanent or **standing committees**, where most legislation is handled. In 2014, the Senate had 16 standing committees, while the House had 21 for a total of 37 (www.oklegislature.gov, 2014). The number of committees in the Oklahoma legislature has varied considerably over the years. As an example of this variance, in 2007 the House only had 10 standing committees and the Senate had 16, for a total of 26. Thus, the

Oklahoma legislature gained 11 committees from 2007 to 2014. In 2004 there were 30 standing committees in the House and 17, in the Senate for a total of 47. In 1967, each house had 36 committees, for a total of 72 (Morgan, England, & Humphreys, 1991). The number of committees is important because while committees may make the legislature more representative they can also lead to duplication and a larger workload for lawmakers.

Second, the Oklahoma Legislature has **joint committees**, composed of the members of both houses. In some states like Connecticut, Maine, and Massachusetts, these committees are used exclusively, giving the leadership more control. Examples of joint committees in Oklahoma include committees to study federal funds and state-tribal relations. The third type of committee is the **special committee**. These are created by the presiding officers of each house. Special committees are distinguished by their short tenure. Finally, there are **conference committees**. Conference committees are actually joint committees with the special purpose of resolving differences between House and Senate versions of a bill. Three members typically from each house are appointed by their presiding officers for each bill under consideration. There are some exceptions, such as the **General Conference Committee on Appropriations** (GCCA) where the state budget is written. As listed on the Oklahoma legislature website, the Oklahoma House had two special committees and one task force. There was also one joint committee, the Joint Committee on the Appropriations and the Budget. The Senate website lists about a dozen task forces, but most of those were created in 2011 and have since expired.

Certain committees are more important to legislators than others. Legislators usually try to pick committees that will be beneficial to their constituents and that will meet their own goals. In both houses, legislators submit requests for their desired assignments after a general election. The leaders of both houses do try to accommodate members' committee requests (Harrigan & Nice, 2008). Many lawmakers usually elect to continue their existing committee assignments, both to build up seniority and expertise on that committee. House members will typically serve on 4 to 6 committees, while many senators have 5 committee assignments. The most important is the **Appropriations Committee** because it makes most of the budgetary decisions for the legislature. Other committees that are considered noteworthy include Education, Revenue and Taxation, Judiciary, and Transportation. The House Speaker usually tries to give each lawmaker one major committee assignment, in addition to minor committee assignments.

A hierarchy also exists within each committee. Both the Education and Appropriation Committees are subdivided into separate subcommittees. These subcommittees are very specialized and serve to divide up the work of the various committees. The leaders for both the committees and subcommittees are called the chair and vice-chair. Senate chairs are appointed by the President Pro Tem, while House chairs are appointed by the Speaker. In the Senate, the Minority Leader appoints minority members to standing committees. This is a typical pattern in most state legislatures. The chairs schedule legislation for their committees, preside over committee meetings, and keep track of all changes to the legislation. **Seniority**, or the length of tenure, is also an important factor on each of these committees. Not only are the most senior members typically given the "best" committee assignments, but seniority also serves to distinguish members on individual committees.

Staff

Much of the work of both the legislative committees and the leadership could not get done without the legislative staff. The staff helps members with their research and constituents, gets the bills ready for distribution, and performs many other important functions in the legislature. Thus, it is no surprise that legislative staffs have increased. From 1979 to 2009, nationwide there has been an increase in the number of permanent staff from an average of 338.6 permanent staffers per legislature in 1979 to 561.3 in 2009. Legislatures, however, have reduced their session only staff, with 201.2 session-only staffers on average in 1979, and only 131.0 on average in 2009 (National Conference of State Legislatures, 2014).

The large number of bills combined with a shortened annual legislature makes a legislative staff almost imperative in Oklahoma. For the Oklahoma legislature, the staff experienced an increase from 326 staff (1979) to 394 (1988) to 415 (1996) to 433 in 2003, but then dropped a bit to 407 in 2009. This represents an increase of about one-third during the past 25 years, but it is comparable with the increase in legislative staff across the nation. In 2009, the Oklahoma legislature had only 407 staffers, with 181 in the House, and 226 in the Senate. There are also session-only staffers and Oklahoma had 114 of these in 2009, compared with the national average of 131. Texas, for example, has 298 session-only staffers, but the Texas legislature also has 2,090 permanent staffers compared to Oklahoma's 293.

Four major changes in the last two decades have influenced Oklahoma staff. First, prior to 1981, the Oklahoma legislature used centralized staff support called the Oklahoma Legislative Council. This council staffed both houses and all committees. Then in 1981, the legislature abolished this centralized staff and replaced it with separate professional staffs for both houses. A smaller centralized staff agency now exists to perform functions that are common to both houses: copy services and the sharing of computer technology. Third, senate leader Stratton Taylor in 1995 allowed every senator to have a full-time secretary/assistant instead of just a skeleton crew of secretaries who worked during the interval between legislative sessions. All but 6 of the 48 senators opted for a full-time secretary. Consequently, with one decision the Senate's full-time secretarial staff increased from 17 to 42, expanding the Senate's annual payroll by $500,000. House leaders, however, did not make the same decision; 28 full-time secretaries handle the work for 101 representatives. In 2007, there were 55 executive assistants serving 48 senators (then President Pro Tem Mike Morgan had five), and 50 permanent legislative assistants serving 101 Representatives (Interview with David Bond, Oklahoma House Communication Specialist, 2007). Fourth, there has been a trend nationwide toward the greater use of full-time staff rather than part-time staff, because of the greater complexity of legislation and the need to conduct business year-round. This can be seen in Oklahoma's increase in its permanent staff with its simultaneous decrease in its part-time staff, otherwise known as session-only staff, as noted above.

VII. THE WORK OF THE OKLAHOMA LEGISLATURE

Legislative Roles

One of the greatest demands upon legislators is the constant tension that exists between their two primary duties: lawmaking and representation. The **lawmaking function** demands that lawmakers pass laws that are best for both their state and their constituents. Not only may these demands conflict, but time spent as a lawmaker can detract from the other function, representation. The **representation function** demands that legislators spend as much time as possible with their constituents, listening to their needs, responding to their concerns, and visiting the constituents in their homes. This causes a tremendous conflict because it is much more difficult to pass laws when visiting the district than working in the Capitol. One way of looking at this representation problem is to look at **role orientation**. The three most common role orientations are trustee, delegate, and politico. **Trustees** believe that their constituents trust them to do the right thing. They believe that their constituents have given them great leeway to make the best possible decision. **Delegates** believe that they are in office to satisfy the demands of their constituents. It is very common for delegates to poll, either formally or informally, their constituents to see what decisions they should make in the upcoming legislative session. Politicos are a combination of the trustee and delegate orientations. **Politicos** believe that they are in office for their constituents, but also recognize that some decisions may have to go beyond the wishes of those constituents. These lawmakers tend to think about what is good for the state (Eulau et al., 1959).

Role Orientation in Oklahoma

Samuel Kirkpatrick in his exhaustive study of Oklahoma legislators found that most legislators tended to be trustees, with 45.8% of the Senate, and 50% of the House indicating they were trustees. The least common role orientation was delegate, with only 12.5% of the Senate and 10% of the House suggesting they were delegates (Kirkpatrick, 1978). Malcolm Jewell, a political scientist and the author of numerous works on state legislatures, however, suggests that this idea of role orientation may be more appropriate for Congress, and less appropriate for state legislatures (Jewell, 1982). As a result, others have examined the tension between the lawmaking and representation functions differently. One of the common ways to do this is to ask lawmakers what makes the most difference in their voting decisions. A 1986 survey of Oklahoma legislators found that if lawmakers could choose between voting for the district (constituents) and a legislator's conscience, most (56%) would vote with the district, while 26% said their conscience. The choice becomes much clearer, however, when political party is considered. 80% of those legislators would choose the district, while the rest would vote with their political party if there was a tension between the two (Morgan, England & Humphreys, 1991). What both of these methods of role orientation seem to suggest is that Oklahoma legislators, whether in 1978 or today, pay close attention to the demands of their constituents when making a decision. That is not surprising since it is those constituents that decide whether or not to keep a lawmaker in office.

Lawmaking

What keeps lawmakers in office is their ability to pass the laws that will meet the needs of their constituents and the state. While this can conflict with the representation function, it still remains the most important responsibility of any lawmaker. Because of the Oklahoma legislature's short session, many lawmakers develop their legislation during the period from September through January. As part of this process, Oklahoma has an **interim studies** procedure, whereby a legislator can file to conduct an interim study to allow for an in-depth exploration of public policies. These interim studies then are posted on the Oklahoma legislature's website. In 2011, legislators submitted 126 of these studies with 80 of them being approved. In 2013, the Oklahoma legislature conducted 134 interim studies. Of those interim studies, 68 were approved, 21 were combined with others, and 45 were not approved. There was a wide variety of topics covered in these interim studies, including the study of raw milk, Common Core education, Oklahoma prisons, tax credits, state employee compensation, droughts, and the transportation of mentally-ill patients by law enforcement (www.oklegislature.gov).

There are four different measures that can be passed by the Oklahoma legislature. The first is a **bill**, the most common form of legislation. A bill may be introduced in either house and must be signed into law by the governor after being passed by both houses. The second measure is a **joint resolution**. It still must be passed by both houses and signed by the governor, but is used when the measure has short-term applicability or frequently for state questions requiring voter approval. The third type of measure is a **concurrent resolution**. This type of resolution must be passed by both chambers, but does not have the force of law and will not be signed by the governor. It is often used when the legislature wants to express the opinion of both chambers. Finally, legislators can also adopt **simple resolutions** which can memorialize a prominent Oklahoman, affect the internal workings of just one chamber, express the particular sentiments of a chamber, or congratulate a person or group of persons.

The process of passing laws starts with the **formal introduction** of bills to the legislature. A chart of how this process works in the Oklahoma legislature is fully described in Figure 5–3. Bills can only be introduced by members in either house prior to the start of the legislative session unless there is a two-thirds vote of the legislature to extend the time limit. The formal introduction includes two formal **readings** of the legislation on the floor of one house. There has been some concern about the large increases in legislation in recent years. In contrast to the 1991 and 1992 sessions which considered 2,656 bills and joint resolutions, and enacted 783 of them, the 1997-8 sessions produced 3,930 measures and 872 enactments. To counter the trend, the Oklahoma House imposed an eight-bill limit on its members which was largely responsible for a drop in House bills and resolutions introduced from 1,257 in 1997 to 865 in 1999. In 2013, Oklahoma senators filed 1357 bills and 28 joint resolutions. Of those, 198 were sent to the governor and all but 6 were approved. 913 Senate bills and 31 Senate Joint Resolutions were carried over to the next session. The House of Representatives, on the other hand, introduced 1645 bills and 99 Joint Resolutions in 2010, while carrying over 1056 bills and 54 Joint Resolutions (www.oklegislature.gov). These totals do not include concurrent and simple resolutions, which do not have the effect of law. Once a bill has been introduced, it is referred to a particular committee. This **referral** is made by the presiding officer of either house, either the Speaker or the Senate President Pro Tem. Bill referral gives these leaders tremendous power because there are often times where the jurisdiction of a bill may overlap several committees. The U.S. Congress solves this problem by occasionally referring a bill to more than one committee in the same house.

Once a bill has been introduced and referred, the real work begins in committee. Most of the heated debates over legislation will probably occur in committee, because this is where the public hearings are held and where most changes are made to the legislation. If a committee votes favorably on a bill, it will send a report to the particular house. In the Senate, there is a recorded **roll call vote** and each committee makes a recommendation to the full Senate, while in the House bills may be reported out by **voice vote** or by signing a written **majority report**. If unhappy with the outcome of the committee work, members of a House committee can file a **minority report** (a rare action) opposing the position of the committee's

FIGURE 5-3 How an Idea Becomes a Law

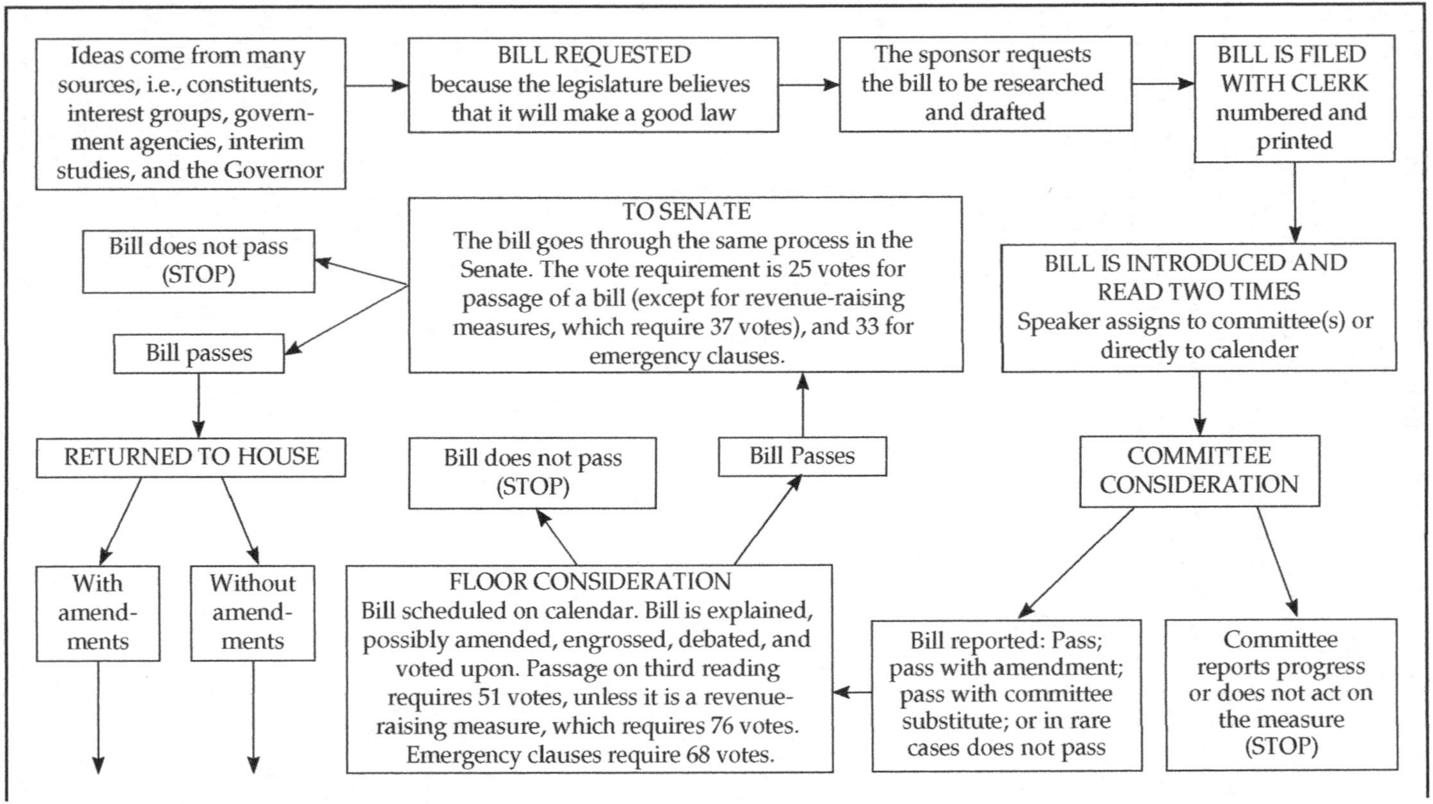

Ideas come from many sources, i.e., constituents, interest groups, government agencies, interim studies, and the Governor

BILL REQUESTED because the legislature believes that it will make a good law

The sponsor requests the bill to be researched and drafted

BILL IS FILED WITH CLERK numbered and printed

BILL IS INTRODUCED AND READ TWO TIMES Speaker assigns to committee(s) or directly to calender

COMMITTEE CONSIDERATION

Committee reports progress or does not act on the measure (STOP)

Bill reported: Pass; pass with amendment; pass with committee substitute; or in rare cases does not pass

FLOOR CONSIDERATION Bill scheduled on calendar. Bill is explained, possibly amended, engrossed, debated, and voted upon. Passage on third reading requires 51 votes, unless it is a revenue-raising measure, which requires 76 votes. Emergency clauses require 68 votes.

Bill Passes

Bill does not pass (STOP)

TO SENATE The bill goes through the same process in the Senate. The vote requirement is 25 votes for passage of a bill (except for revenue-raising measures, which require 37 votes), and 33 for emergency clauses.

Bill does not pass (STOP)

Bill passes

RETURNED TO HOUSE

Without amendments

With amendments

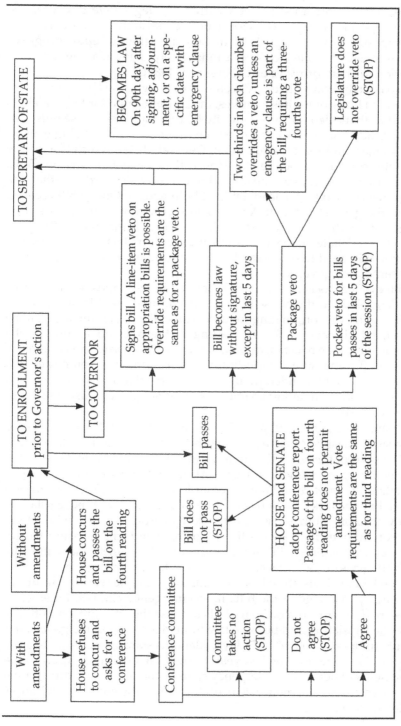

Adapted from the Oklahoma House of Representatives, http://www.lsb.state.ok.us/house/idea.gif by James M. Barrow.

majority. This report must be filed within one legislative day after the majority report is filed. The full House of Representatives can then debate and accept or reject this report. By making a motion to **report progress**, the committees of either house can indefinitely delay making a recommendation on a bill or resolution (Ferguson, 1989).

Bills passed by committees are then sent directly to the House or Senate floor. In the House of Representatives, the **consent calendar** holds all bills assigned to that calendar by a committee or the Speaker. These bills cannot be amended or debated and must stay there four days. A single member may object and send the bill to the **General Order**, which is a docket of all bills considered before the House that legislative session. Bills, however, do not need to be considered in chronological order; rather, the order is determined by the leadership of both houses. Once a bill is called up from the general order docket, it is subject to amendment. After disposing of amendments, there is a third reading of the bill on the floor followed by a debate on the legislation and a vote on its final passage. The legislation will need to be passed by both the House and Senate before it can be sent to the governor.

In the event a measure has been amended in the opposite chamber or it was "crippled" in the house of origin by striking the title of the bill, it will return to the originating house. Thus, the amendments can be accepted, which cause a fourth reading of the bill and a vote, or the amendments will be rejected, causing a measure to be sent to a conference committee. If a measure is reported out by a conference committee, the measure cannot be amended in any way (except that failure to receive a two-thirds majority in either chamber on an emergency clause will cause it to be debated).

The passed bill is then submitted to the governor who has five working days to sign. The governor can also choose to reject the entire bill (**veto**) or just reject parts of the bill (**a line-item veto**). The line-item veto, however, is only used for appropriation measures. At the end of the session, the legislature adjourns *sine dine* and the governor has fifteen working days to sign or veto a bill; the lack of action constitutes a **pocket veto** of the legislation. With a vetoed bill, both houses must seek to override the veto with a two-thirds vote in both houses or a three-fourths vote if the measure has an emergency clause. Bills will ordinarily become law ninety days after the session adjourns or five days after a session if the governor vetoes.

The Oklahoma legislature has one additional unique feature. Traditionally, a large percentage of the bills have **emergency clauses**. Emergency clauses are different from ordinary bills because they require a two-thirds vote of the legislature and become law immediately upon the governor's signature (or a veto override). Today, Oklahoma state agencies are usually funded at the same level as last year. Budget bills will then appropriate new money and hence, the emergency clause is not used very often. If the governor vetoes an emergency clause, a three-fourths vote in both houses is required to override.

These votes by lawmakers are then rated by various institutions, so that others can get an overall picture of a legislator's votes. As an example, in 2012, the Research Institute for Economic Development (RIED) rated all 149 legislators on their votes. This is a pro-business group led by Susan Winchester, a former legislator. Of the 149 legislators, 113 legislators or 75.8%, had RIED scores that were above 70%, indicating that they were pro-business leaning. Eight House members and seven senators, all Republicans, had perfect scores.

Recent Oklahoma Legislatures and Lawmaking

One of the recent trends in the Oklahoma legislature is the **backlog** of bills that tends to develop at the end of a legislative session. Usually, a large number of measures must be signed into law by the governor during the last few days of the session. A second trend that has developed during the last few years is the large number of **vetoes**. While the number of vetoes from 1991 to 1994 averaged about 17 per legislative session; from 1995 to 1998 the governor vetoed over 200 bills. Just as important, while the legislature managed to override an average of 5 bills from 1991 to 1994, there were no successful overrides during 1995 and 1996.[3] In 2003, Governor Brad Henry in his first year in office approved 488 pieces of legislation and issued 12 vetoes and one line-item veto, none which were overridden by the legislature. In his last year, 2010, Governor Henry signed 482 bills and vetoed 40. Three of those bills—all abortion-related measures—were overridden. In the 2011 legislative session, Republican Governor Mary Fallin signed 385 bills and vetoed 11 (Greene, 2011). Yet, in 2013, with a heavily Republican legislature, it is not a surprise that the number of vetoes stayed small, as there were nine House bills and six Senate bills vetoed in 2013.

A third trend is that few bills ever really receive full deliberation. The *Tulsa World* examined 2,170 bills that were introduced into the 2011 Oklahoma legislature and found that 78.7% of the bills in the House and 74.7% of the bills in the Senate died in either their original committees or did not get a vote. Thus, about three-fourths of all bills never made it out of the starting block. These bills can still be debated the following year, but they will also have to compete against all the bills that are introduced in the session as well. In the House, the second most likely place for bills to die is the floor, where 13.4% more pieces of legislation failed. In the Senate, this is not the case as only 4.1% of legislation died there. Given the Republican majority in both houses, it is probably not a surprise to learn that Republicans were more successful than Democrats in getting their legislation out of committee (Greene, 2011).

Governors now play an even larger role in shaping legislation. Not only does the governor make a State of the State address indicating his/her policy wish list, but the governor also proposes a budget and a set of budget recommendations. These create the main blueprint for the legislature's budgetary decisions during a given session.

Budgeting

One area of government control available to the Oklahoma legislature is the **appropriation process**. In the 1970s, the legislature's ability to determine the overall state budget was comparatively limited. Almost two thirds of the budget was outside the legislature's appropriation process because of federal and earmarked state fees. Thus, the legislature only controlled one third of appropriations. This was typical of most state legislatures. Today, the Oklahoma legislature has become much more of an equal partner with the governor in creating the budget. First, all revenue raising measures must start within the House, according to Article V, Section 33. Second, despite the fact that lawmakers raised taxes three times during the 1980s and again in 1990, Oklahoma remains a low-tax state. Third, and most important, Oklahoma voters passed State Question 640 in 1992 which prevents the legislature from raising taxes unless there is either a vote of the people or a three-fourths vote of the legislature. This sharply limits the amount of money legislators can use to fund state programs. Legislators raised those taxes because they found that export taxes, particularly the Oklahoma severance tax on oil and gas, was not enough to pay for the state's education system and other government programs.

In Oklahoma's budgeting process, the **fiscal year** (FY) begins July 1 and ends on June 30, so FY 2015 is the period from July 1, 2014 through June 30, 2015. All state budgets must also be balanced, according to the Oklahoma Constitution. With the fiscal year beginning on July 1, Oklahoma's state agencies must submit their budget requests, including how they plan to spend the money and how they have performed as an agency, by September of the prior year. On the first day of the legislative session, the governor proposes an executive budget recommendation. By the beginning of the session, the **State Equalization Board** also determines how much revenue the state has to spend that year and informs the legislature. Because the budget must be balanced, the Oklahoma Constitution in Article V states that the legislature cannot spend beyond 95% of expected revenues.

The real decision making process, however, does not begin in earnest until April when the General Conference Committee on Appropriations (GCCA) composed of both houses, is appointed by the Speaker and President Pro Tempore. The legislature reaches an agreement on how much will be spent on each broad area, such as education or roads. These are called **subcommittee allocations**. Once these allocations have been determined, the GCCA subcommittees can then decide how much each government program will receive. The budgets for about six agencies are then formulated into the appropriation bill which needs to be passed by a two-thirds vote of both houses (in order for the emergency clauses to be attached). The passed bill is then submitted to the governor who has five working days to sign. The governor can also choose to reject the entire bill (**veto**) or just reject parts of the bill (**a line-item veto**). As expected, Oklahoma appropriations have increased in recent years, although the growth has been somewhat limited.

In 2013, the Oklahoma legislature was expecting to have a very contentious end to its session, as the legislators still had yet to debate some of the most controversial issues. Conservative members, for example, wanted Oklahoma to be one of the few states in the country to abandon the Common Core Curriculum for common education. Native Americans and others were wondering whether the American Indian Cultural Museum in Oklahoma City would be funded, while those in Tulsa wanted the OK Pops Center to be funded as well. But alas, all of those items got shelved when a devastating tornado hit Moore, Oklahoma, on May 20, 2013, just days before the legislation session was to end. From that point forward, the Oklahoma legislature made an emergency drawdown from the Oklahoma Rainy Day Fund its biggest priority, and eventually $45 million was passed for relief funds as a result of the tornado. The only item that remained contentious was a long awaited salary increase for state troopers that many Democratic legislators had been seeking. There was the perception by some that the state trooper money had been tied to the $45 million in emergency funding, particularly given a press release issued after the tornado by Speaker of the House T.W. Shannon that perhaps raised that suggestion. But Republican leaders insisted that was not the case. In the end, the state troopers did not get their pay increases, and that issue was expected to be debated again in the 2014 session.

Oversight

Ironically, one of the jobs that students studying the legislature most overlook is oversight. Most states (41) including Oklahoma have some sort of **oversight**, whereby the legislature reviews the actions of the executive branch. The Oklahoma legislature has full responsibility for examining not only the governor, but also the state government agencies, boards, and commissions. This is an enormous task because rules passed by state agencies have the force of law, yet must be monitored by the legislature. The question for state legislatures is how to supervise those agencies. Only 25 states including Oklahoma, have given the legislature the authority to veto, suspend, or modify agency rules. In Oklahoma, the House of Representatives has a standing committee that reviews both proposed and existing rules. The membership of this committee is appointed by the House and Senate leadership. Generally, the Oklahoma legislature has 30 legislative days to approve or disapprove a rule. The lack of objection constitutes an approval of a proposed rule. The courts have ruled against one-house vetoes in several states, including Oklahoma, acting by themselves on behalf of the legislature.[5]

Unlike some states, the Oklahoma legislature has two other tools that it can use to conduct oversight—sunset legislation and the appointment process.[6] First, the Oklahoma legislature can enact **sunset legislation**. According to the Sunset Act, state agencies are forced periodically to justify their existence and demonstrate that they have done their proper jobs. The life of an agency subject to sunset review is 6 years, but there is a phase-out period of 1 year (Council on State Governments, 1996). Sunset laws across the country have rarely accomplished much of substance. Instead, they primarily serve a symbolic function in the 25 states that have such an act (Dresang and Gosling, 2002, p. 245). Of the two tools, almost all states allow the legislature to oversee the **appointment process**. Although the state agencies and commissions are part of the executive branch, the Oklahoma Senate confirms the appointments of certain agency directors and many members of state boards and commissions. The state senators control county election board secretaries, and they also choose the heads of the motor vehicle tag agencies.

VIII. The Future of the Oklahoma Legislature

Professionalization of the Legislature

One of the current trends among state legislatures is the move toward professionalization. Legislatures are considered professional when they meet several of the following characteristics: higher salaries, legislative careerism, longer sessions, more rules, fragmentation of power in the legislature, and politicization of the legislative process. This move toward becoming professional has been bolstered by several recent studies of state legislatures, including that done by the Citizens Conference on State Legislatures, who found that professional legislatures when structured properly tend to be both more representative and efficient. With the exception of the requirement for term limits, the Oklahoma Legislature has become more professional over the years. With its longer sessions, higher salaries, and extensive committee structure, the Oklahoma legislature has moved in that direction. Yet, there are several scholars of state legislatures who suggest that this may not be a good thing. Professor Alan Rosenthal of Rutgers University, one of the leading scholars on state legislatures, indicates that state legislatures when becoming professional may act more like the U.S. Congress, with its extensive delays and internal politicking (Rosenthal, 2004).

This move toward professionalization may also contradict the wishes of the people of Oklahoma. A strong populist movement in the state of Oklahoma seems to develop whenever Oklahoma politicians seem to veer too far away from the wishes of the people. According to a lengthy study of Oklahoma politics, "almost all Sooner legislators see themselves as part-time citizen legislators" (Morgan, England & Humphreys, 1991). As evidence, the increase in legislative salaries in 1989-1990 came only with a subsequent decrease in the length of the sessions. This somewhat contradictory move was supported not only by the legislators, but also by the Republican governor at the time, Henry Bellmon.

Conclusion

Overall, the Oklahoma legislature seems to be in a period of transition. During both the 1980s and 1990s, the Oklahoma legislature made substantial changes in how it conducts business. First, not only are there more permanent staff, but the legislature also has more control of the budgeting process. Second, the number of committees has been sharply reduced, as the Citizens Conference on State legislatures suggested. Third, the Oklahoma legislature has also greatly increased its information capacity. More of its activities are computerized, including the legislature's website. Fourth, members of the legislature earn higher salaries, but face tougher ethics limits on the amounts they raise and spend during their campaigns. Fifth, the Oklahoma legislature has made gradual progress in becoming more representative, with more women and minorities getting elected. Redistricting decisions forced the legislature to reallocate more of its districts to the urban areas of Oklahoma. It should be noted, however, that the Oklahoma legislature still could be far more representative. It is far under the national averages for percentages of women and minorities. Further, the drawing of legislative districts to benefit incumbents and rural interests has denied metropolitan areas greater representation in the legislature.

Yet with all these transitional changes, the most important one has not even been mentioned yet. Perhaps most significantly, the Oklahoma legislature has experienced a significant partisan shift in recent elections with Republican majorities in both houses as of 2014. With Republicans holding all state offices as well in 2014, this means that divided government, at least temporarily, is a thing of the past. This should make it easier for one party, the Republicans, to pass the public policies that they desire. It also may make it easier for the Democrats to mobilize as an opposition with a single voice. Whether this indeed happens, Oklahomans will have to wait for the future.

Most of these changes have thus made the legislature more responsive to the people. Now, the people can contact the legislature during the interim session and the staff can respond more easily. This fits in perfectly with the populist tradition in Oklahoma. The legislature is still limited, with shortened sessions and sharp restrictions on passing appropriations and taxation legislation. Yet, it can still meet the demands of the people.

What's in the future for the Oklahoma legislature? Hopefully, there will be better reporting of committee information, particularly greater details about the hearings, meetings, and votes that are scheduled. Computerizing and posting the legislature's activities online are excellent steps in the right direction. The effects of term limits also had an impact in 2014. The average tenure of legislators had dropped about 5 years, down to 6.7 and 6.5 years in the House and Senate respectively. Put another way, 47.5% of the House and 68.8% of the Senate were considered junior members in 2010 with less than three and two terms respectively. This has had the most impact on the leadership, with the 2014 legislature expecting almost an entirely new crop of leaders. Whether these limits will have a positive or negative effect in terms of the legislation that gets passed remain to be seen. In any case, the Oklahoma legislature should be interesting to watch for years to come!

R E S O U R C E S

For information, including full text of legislation, bill statutes, and links to the Oklahoma House of Representatives and the Senate, visit the web site at:

www.oklegislature.gov

The Oklahoma State Government Information Server has information and links to many areas of Oklahoma government:

www.ok.gov

For information on state legislatures throughout the United States, see:

www.ncsl.org

The Oklahoma Ethics Commission is charged with promulgating rules of ethical conduct for state officers and employees, campaigns for state elective office, and campaigns for state initiatives and referenda. See the Oklahoma Ethics Commission site at:

www.ok.gove/oec/

NOTES

1. See Article V, <u>Oklahoma Constitution</u>.
2. The states with over 30% female legislative membership are Arizona, Colorado, Connecticut, Hawaii, Maryland, Minnesota, Nevada, New Hampshire, New Jersey, New Mexico, Vermont, and Washington (National Conference of State Legislatures 2014).
3. For further information on the vetoes, see the Oklahoma legislature's web site at http://www.lsb.state.ok.us. These statistics includes measures that were line-item vetoed, but not concurrent or simple resolutions or measures filed during any of the special sessions.
4. See the Oklahoma legislature's web site at http://www.lsb.state.ok.us.
5. The other states include Alaska, Missouri, Montana, and North Carolina where the courts ruled against legislative committees acting alone on federal funds.
6. A legislative veto has been found by the courts to violate the state constitutions in most states, including New Hampshire, New Jersey, and West Virginia.

OKLAHOMA'S GOVERNOR
AND ELECTED EXECUTIVES

Kenneth Kickham

A feeble Executive implies a feeble execution of the government.
A feeble execution is but another phrase for a bad execution; and
a government ill executed, whatever it may be in theory, must be,
in practice, a bad government.

Alexander Hamilton, The Federalist, no. 70

Since the Civil War the training ground for successful presidents
has been the gubernatorial office in the states, where they seem
to serve an incomparable executive apprenticeship.

Historian Wilfred E. Brinkley

I. INTRODUCTION

It has been said that politics is show business for ugly people. On Oklahoma's political stage, leaders of the executive branch are woven into the state's history. They shoulder the responsibility of playing the lead role in the story of Oklahoma. From our first governor, Charles N. Haskall, to our current governor, Mary Fallin, Oklahoma's governors stand as solitary figures in the limelight of time passed. However, the governor's direct impact on the state's governmental process is a bit less dramatic.

The populist roots of our great state are reflected in the Oklahoma executive branch. **Populism** by definition requires direct accountability to the electorate. While some might argue the strengths and weaknesses of populism as a philosophy, the actual application of it in Oklahoma has produced a very distinctive political dynamic. The Oklahoma executive branch is responsible for initiating, implementing, and enforcing effective policies. These responsibilities must be accomplished within a uniquely **pluralistic system** that dilutes the powers of Oklahoma's governor by granting many of the powers to govern to other elected executives.

Traditionally, state government textbooks draw a direct comparison between the powers of the President of the United States and the powers of a governor of a state. However, such comparisons are not so simple when examining the Oklahoma executive branch. Unlike a president who has power to appoint executive branch administrators, an Oklahoma governor's power to direct the activities of the executive branch is diluted by the activities of the ten other separately elected executives. This seemingly simple difference in structure has a significant impact on the governor's power to govern. New Jersey's governorship, for example, is one of the most powerful in the nation. Chris Christie, the Garden State's chief executive since 2010, holds the only statewide elected office, nominates powerful office holders like the attorney general and treasurer, determines the size of the budget, fills hundreds of positions on the state's commissions and authorities, and doles out aid to hundreds of towns and cities (MacGillis, 2014). Since many of Oklahoma's other executive branch officials are separately elected, they can belong to different political parties and have different political philosophies, agendas, and power bases than the governor. Political conflicts between the governor and one or more of the separately elected executives are likely.

The writers of the Oklahoma constitution feared the concentration of power, so they held as many officials responsible to the people as possible. As a result, Oklahomans initially elected 17 members of the executive branch. Today, that number has been reduced to a total of 11, but still includes the Lieutenant governor, attorney general, superintendent of public instruction, state auditor and inspector, state treasurer, three corporation commissioners, commissioner of insurance, and commissioner of labor. More recent changes strengthening the governor have included, for example, the 2011 consolidation of several personnel and procurement functions with the stated goal of a flatter, agile, streamlined and technology-enabled (FAST) management structure (Office of State Finance, 2011).

Theoretically, a president can ensure a cohesive governing strategy when all of the administrators are required to follow the president's agenda. In Oklahoma, several other elected administrators are accountable to the Oklahoma electorate, creating a situation that is not always likely to produce a cohesive governing strategy within the executive branch. Compared with most other states, Oklahoma's pluralistic system weakens the governor's power to initiate, implement, and enforce effective policies. On the other hand, this approach assures that the large bureaucracy controlled by the executive branch is held more directly responsible to the people.

II. THE GOVERNOR

Within the existing pluralistic structure, the primary goal of an Oklahoma governor is to be the leader of the state. To be the governor of Oklahoma, one must be a citizen of the United States, at least 31 years-of-age, and a qualified voter in the state for 10 years prior to holding office (Council

TABLE 6–1				
Compensation for the Oklahoma Governor				
ANNUAL SALARY	NUMBER OF STAFF	TRANSPORTATION PROVIDED	TRAVEL ALLOWANCE	OFFICIAL RESIDENCE
$147,000	30	Automobile Airplane	Reimbursed for actual and necessary expenses	Mansion (including guest quarters)

of State Governments, 2010, Table 4.2). Once elected, the governor serves a four-year term in office with a limit of two consecutive terms. As indicated in Table 6–1, Oklahoma governors are compensated with a salary, transportation (including a driver and pilot), a travel allowance, and an official residence located near the capitol complex in Oklahoma City. The governor is provided with an approximately 30-member staff to fulfill the responsibilities of the office and make an effort to accomplish the objectives set for the administration (Council of State Governments, 2010, Table 4.3). All of these requirements and resources are designed to ensure that the governor is able to fulfill the primary roles required by the office.

III. ROLES OF THE GOVERNOR

Vested with many responsibilities, governors must use their power if they aspire to enhance the governmental process of Oklahoma. Governors are often described in terms of the policy and procedural roles they play. These roles include serving as the chief executive, chief legislator, chief bureaucrat, chief economic leader and various other roles that are often dictated by circumstances.

Chief Executive

As the chief executive, the governor provides leadership for the executive branch from the top down. The governor is responsible for protecting the public in general, enforcing laws of the state, and conducting state business with the national government and other states. However, with the exception of the power to appoint some officials within the executive branch, the Oklahoma governor is bestowed with little formal power. In the absence of real power, the governor uses influence to fulfill these responsibilities. As a result, a governor's power to impact state government can be limited in that it is indirect.

The governor as the **chief executive** can be analogized as the "head coach." While a head coach of a football team is the leader, a head coach

FIGURE 6–1 Administrative Structure

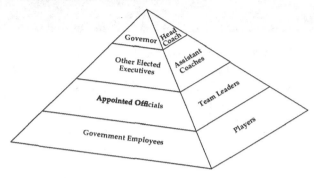

is not the individual who throws the blocks, scores the touchdowns, or kicks a winning field goal in the final seconds of a game, but, like the governor, functions as the leader at the top of the triangle-shape organization setting goals, making plans, and developing strategies (see Figure 6–1).

The circumstances in which the governor operates are remarkably similar. When the system is not meeting the objectives set, the governor (or coach) is held responsible. When things are going well, it is usually the governor who claims credit. Just as a head coach is the administrator over the assistant coaches who help the players to do the things necessary to win, the governor administers the appointed officials as they implement the policies necessary to enforce the laws of the state. Oklahoma governors do have several formal powers, including the power to issue executive orders, grant pardons and parole, participate in the selection of some judges, and extradite accused and/or convicted criminals.

An **executive order** represents the governor's policymaking power. It is best described as a policy or regulation issued by the governor having the effect of law. Executive orders are designed to allow implementation of policies and give administrative authority to enforce legislative statutes and the state constitution, and/or to establish or modify practices of state administrative agencies (Oklahoma Department of Libraries, 1998). In 2011, for example, Governor Fallin imposed a state agency hiring freeze by way of Executive Order 2011-11. Combined with the role of chief bureaucrat, this power allows the governor to effectively govern within the executive branch and impact almost all of the other areas in Oklahoma state government.

As chief executive, the governor has the power to pardon and parole. **Pardons** are defined as legal releases from punishment, while **parole** is defined as the conditional early release of a prisoner who has served a portion of the assigned sentence. From statehood to the adoption of a state constitutional amendment in 1944, governors had exclusive power to pardon or parole any individuals they deemed fit to be released. However, in 1944, the State Pardon and Parole Board was established to advise the governor on these issues. The board is composed of five members—three appointed by the governor, one appointed by the presiding Judge of the Court of Criminal Appeals, and one appointed by Chief Justice of the State Supreme Court. As a result, in order to pardon or parole an individual today, the governor must receive a favorable recommendation from the board. However, the governor can grant a **reprieve**, which is a delay in carrying out a sentence, or a leave of absence to convicted criminals (for a maximum of 60 days) without recommendation from the board (Strain et al., 1997). On June 16, 2010, for example, Governor Henry ordered a reprieve for Jeffrey David Matthews, a death row inmate who was scheduled to be executed the following day. The reprieve was granted so that defense attorneys could examine fingerprint evidence in the case.

Governors also play a role in the selection of some judges. As discussed in Chapter 8, Oklahoma uses both elections and a nonpartisan judicial selection process. For non-elected courts and for filling many vacancies, a 13-member Judicial Nominating Commission submits no more than three names to the governor for consideration. The governor then makes a nomination from the Judicial Nominating Commission's recommendations. While individuals nominated to a court under this process are eventually subject to retention votes or elections by the people, the governor does play a role in the process and is often able, over time, to have a significant influence on the judicial process in Oklahoma. In addition, governors are responsible for initiating the return of alleged criminals to the state of Oklahoma and granting extradition requests from other states.

Chief Legislator

Historically, Oklahoma's executive branch has been weak in comparison to the legislative branch. The governor's role as chief legislator is strictly limited by the state constitution to four basic functions. These "legislative powers" include delivering messages to the state legislature, preparing and introducing a state budget, calling the legislature into special session, and vetoing acts of the legislature (Strain et al., 1997).

At the beginning of each legislative session, the governor delivers a message known as the **State of the State** address. In this address to a joint meeting of the legislature, the governor outlines the objectives of his or her administration and a plan to achieve those objectives. It is important to recognize that the legislature is not required to consider or accept the governor's plan and objectives. The fact that the governor has no real power to direct the legislature usually reduces the State of the State address to an opportunity for the governor to gain exposure and to publicly posture against Oklahoma legislators. This posturing can create a tenuous relationship between the two branches, particularly when the governor is of a different political party than the leadership in the legislature.

Perhaps the most important function of state government is the development of the state budget. It is from this budget that government initiatives, programs, and jobs are sustained. It is the governor's responsibility to prepare and submit a state budget to the legislature, but the legislature is not required to accept the governor's budget. Indeed, the legislature controls all individual funding decisions. In times of divided government, when legislative and executive branches are controlled by different political parties, the threat of a budget stalemate becomes a real danger. As a result, the two branches must work towards a compromise that keeps the state functioning.

If a governor is not satisfied with the work of the legislature over a particular issue or as a whole, the power to call the legislature into **special session** to deal with specific issues can be exercised. In 2006, for example, Governor Henry called a special session to give the House and Senate more time to strike an agreement on the 2007 budget. However, once the legislature has convened, the governor cannot force action on the particular legislation or concern that led the governor to call the special session. Indeed, the governor's power is limited to calling them into session. The legislature has the power to adjourn the special session at any time.

The power to **veto** legislation is the only significant power the governor has over the legislature. Any legislation that passes the House and Senate must be presented to the governor for final approval. If the governor signs the legislation, it becomes Oklahoma law. However, if the governor does not agree with the legislation, the veto can be used. A vetoed piece of legislation is returned to the legislature to be changed, dropped, or to have the veto overridden by two-thirds vote in both houses.

There are two other types of veto power available to the Oklahoma governor. These other types of vetoes are the line item veto and the pocket veto. The **line item veto** was granted to the governor by the state legislature in 1994 (Council of State Governments, 2003). This type of veto power allows the governor to veto individual lines or items of proposed legislation without vetoing the entire bill. This power gives the governor the ability to make significant changes to legislation before it is signed into law. The **pocket veto** is exercised when the legislature passes a bill, adjourns, and the governor does not sign the bill. If the legislature adjourns, any bill not signed by the governor within 15 days is rendered invalid. By putting such legislation in a "pocket" and not signing it into law, a governor effectively causes the legislation to die. If the state legislature wishes to reconsider the bill, it must be reintroduced, and then the bill is subject to the entire legislative process all over again.

In addition to the power of "final say" on what does or does not become Oklahoma law, governors can shape legislation by threatening the author of a bill with a veto. By telling the legislature what will or will not be accepted, governors can influence legislation before it reaches their desk for approval. While a legislature has the power to override a veto with two-thirds vote of both houses, an override majority is generally difficult to secure. As a result, the legislative authors are often willing to compromise with the governor.

As chief legislator, Oklahoma governors are limited to an advisory role. Governors advise and persuade the legislature with the State of the State address, the budget process (by introducing the first draft), the prerogative to call the legislature into special session, and by the threat of a veto. The governor's ability to influence the legislative process without significant formal power is what determines his or her effectiveness in this role. The ability to establish a strong track record of accomplishment in shaping the legislative process is often how the public measures the success of the governor.

Chief Bureaucrat

The governor as the **chief bureaucrat** refers to the power to appoint over 2,500 positions to over 300 offices, boards, and/or commissions. These appointees act as the assistant coaches and players under the head coach. The governor can use this appointive power to initiate, implement, and enforce policies in furtherance of his or her objectives. While the majority of these appointments do not add to the institutional power of the governor, it is safe to say that the role of chief bureaucrat does add to the governor's prestige in a political sense.

Because each appointment is an extension and reflection of the governor, the process of choosing appointees must be carefully executed. The appointee need not share all specific views of the governor. It is important, however, to ensure basic agreement on political and philosophical principles. In addition to agreeing on these basic principles, there are usually stipulated requirements associated with appointed positions. Examples of such stipulations include, but are not limited to: professional qualifications; residence requirements; business experience; and, party affiliation in cases where appointments are to be made in the spirit of bipartisanship. Because the responsibility of appointments is so labor-intensive, governors must commit a number of staff members to handling the research and recommendation of appointments.

Chief Economic Leader

Governors also serve as an **economic leader** and developer. In today's international economy, the governor accepts the responsibility of representing the state to businesses and industries interested in building infrastructure in Oklahoma. With an increasing importance being placed on international trade and national economic development, the governor, now more than ever, must make such issues a top priority. The key to success in this role is finding a competitive edge over other states that are similar to Oklahoma in terms of geography, social, and economic, and demographic areas. Governors strive to establish Oklahoma as an attractive place for business and industry. They work with the legislature and city leaders to make Oklahoma competitive in the world economy by providing an educated workforce, tax incentives, and a high quality standard of living for employees.

Other Roles

In addition to the procedural and policy roles of the government there are also two other roles governors have: Chief of State and Party Chief. As the **Chief of State,** the governor is the ceremonial leader of the state. In this role, governors become the premier representative of the state during the times of tragedy and triumph. The role played by Governor Frank Keating in the aftermath of the Murrah Building bombing in 1995, as well as the role played by Governor Mary Fallin after the devastating Moore tornado in 2013, are excellent examples of the governor acting as chief of state. In both situations it was the responsibility of the governor to represent all of the citizens of Oklahoma, comforting those who suffered tragic losses, and facilitating a return to normality in the lives of everyone affected.

In the role of **Party Chief** the governor is the recognized leader of his or her political party. As the leader of the party, the governor can exert political power through **patronage**—appointing faithful members of the same political party—or by trying to discipline other elected officials of the same party to support the policies of the administration. Another way that the governor exerts political pressure is by agreeing to use the high profile position to campaign for a particular program or for a particular candidate. Finally, governors can reward loyal supporters in the legislature by supporting funding for local projects, or tax incentives to industries in their legislative districts.

IV. IMPEACHMENT

No account of the Oklahoma executive branch would be complete without an explanation of impeachment. The act of impeachment is authorized by Article I of the Oklahoma State Constitution. The process outlines the steps to be taken by the Oklahoma State House of Representatives and State Senate if they wish to remove the governor, or other state elective officers, for willful neglect of duty, corruption in office, habitual drunkenness, incompetence, or any offense involving moral turpitude committed while in office. The process itself consists of the House **impeaching,** or accusing the governor or other sate elective officers, in one or more of the above mentioned infractions, followed by the state Senate's decision on whether or not the governor, or other state elective officer, should be convicted and allowed to remain in office (Fischer, 1981).

The Senate impeachment trial is prosecuted by "trial managers" appointed by the House of Representatives, and the impeached official is responsible for mounting his or her own legal defense. A simplified analogy of the impeachment process would be to consider the state House impeachment proceedings as an accusation or indictment of the elective officer, and the state Senate trial proceedings as to a determination of guilt (which would result in removal) or innocence (which would result in preservation of the particular officials standing in office). Impeachment does not necessarily mean removal from office; it is possible for a state elective official to be impeached, but not removed.

The threat of impeachment is sure to gain attention and create dramatic pretense, but in practice, the act of impeachment is not all that common. Only two Oklahoma governors have actually been impeached and removed from office. In 1922, Governor Jack C. Walton was elected governor, impeached, and removed from office in the same year under 17 articles of impeachment. The charges ranged from calling out the militia without cause on three separate occasions (incompetence), corruption, and improper campaign expenditures. After a Senate impeachment trial, Walton was removed from office on 11 of the 17 articles of impeachment. The summary of the Senate's judgments stated that Walton was found to be incompetent and corrupt.

Governor Henry S. Johnston was elected in 1927 and impeached two years later on 11 specific charges of impeachment. All of the charges accused Johnston of being incompetent, since he willingly admitted doing things that the House claimed to be illegal. The specific articles ranged from granting irregular pardons and restitution to diverting funds for the purpose of hiring special agents for his office. The Senate trial lasted for almost two months and eventually concluded with the removal of Governor Johnston for incompetence. The Senate held that, while his actions were not criminally motivated, his actions proved him to be incompetent (Fischer, 1981).

V. THE CABINET

A **cabinet** is a group of formal advisors to the governor. By Oklahoma statute, a gubernatorial cabinet is created by the governor and all members of the cabinet serve at the pleasure of the governor. A governor's cabinet is generally composed of elected and appointed officials. Its primary function is to advise the governor on policy issues that arise while they fulfill their responsibilities as leaders of the state. In addition to their advisory role, cabinet members generally head state government agencies or departments within agencies. The governor's current cabinet has 14 members in addition to the Lieutenant governor and Secretary of State, and meets at the chief executive's discretion. Appointed members of the cabinet are typically close political allies of the governor and are in general agreement with the governor's agenda. The governor relies on the cabinet to initiate, implement, and enforce the policies that agree with the goals of the administration.

VI. A PARTISAN AFFAIR

When Mary Fallin became governor in 2011, she became only the fourth Republican to hold the highest office in the executive branch since statehood in 1907. The other three Republican governors were: Henry Bellmon, serving as chief executive from 1963-67 and again in 1987-91; Dewey Bartlett serving as chief executive from 1967-71; and Frank Keating, serving as governor from 1995-2003. In 2011, Mary Fallin restored the governorship to the Republican Party after Democratic Governor Brad Henry's two consecutive terms (2003-2011). Out of 27 Oklahoma chief executives, only four have not been Democrats. Like the American presidency, Oklahoma appears to have entered a new era in which control of the governor's office alternates back and forth between the two main political parties.

VII. BACK TO BACK

George Nigh, Frank Keating and Brad Henry are the only Oklahoma governors to serve two consecutive four-year terms. In 1983, Governor Nigh was re-elected to the office of governor and secured his place in Oklahoma history as the first governor to complete two full terms in office. A career politician, Nigh served as the governor for eight years, and as lieutenant governor for 16 years prior. In his retirement, Governor Nigh realized he was not governor or lieutenant governor for the first time in his 24-year career saying, "It didn't hit me until I left the house and jumped in the back seat of the car and we didn't go anywhere" (Both the governor and lieutenant governor are provided a car and a driver).

In 1998, Frank Keating achieved a truly remarkable distinction when he became only the second governor in nearly 90 years to be re-elected. Eight years later, Brad Henry joined the same exclusive club by winning re-election with 66 percent of the vote. Henry's vote percentage was the state's highest since 1958, when Democrat J. Howard Edmondson swept into office with 74 percent of the vote.

VIII. LIEUTENANT GOVERNOR

The **lieutenant governor** is elected at the same time as the governor and serves the same four-year term as the governor. Like the governor, the lieutenant governor must be a citizen of the United States, be at least

LEADERSHIP PROFILE

TODD LAMB
Lieutenant Governor

OKLAHOMA ELECTED TODD LAMB as Lt. Governor on November 2, 2010. With a campaign focused on job growth and economic development, Lt. Governor Lamb achieved an overwhelming victory and quickly began putting his forward-thinking ideas and agenda in place. He was appointed to the Governor's cabinet as the advocate for Oklahoma's small business.

An Enid native, Lamb played football at Louisiana Tech University, then returned to Oklahoma earning his bachelor's degree from Oklahoma State University and his law degree from Oklahoma City University School of Law.

In 1993, Todd Lamb worked on the campaign staff of gubernatorial candidate Frank Keating. Upon Keating's election, Lamb worked alongside the Governor for four years. During his time in the Governor's office, Lamb traveled to all of Oklahoma's 77 counties, almost half of the United States, and 2 foreign countries promoting Governor Keating's pro-growth economic agenda. Lamb served in the Keating Administration from 1994 until 1998.

In 1998, Todd Lamb became a Special Agent with the United States Secret Service. He was elected president of his Secret Service Academy class and graduated with special recognition. During his U.S. Secret Service tenure, Lamb investigated and made numerous arrests in the areas of counterfeiting, bank fraud, threats against the President, and identity theft. His duties included domestic and international protection assignments during the Clinton and George W. Bush administrations. In 2000, Lamb was a site supervisor for George W. Bush's presidential campaign. In early 2001, he was appointed to the national Joint Terrorism Task Force, where he received training and briefings at the CIA, FBI, and Secret Service headquarters in Washington, D.C. After the terrorists' attacks, he was assigned to portions of the 9-11 investigation.

Lt. Governor Todd Lamb was elected to his first term in the Oklahoma Senate on November 2, 2004 by the voters of Senate district 47 representing NW Oklahoma City and Edmond. Lamb was re-elected without opposition in 2008.

In 2009, Lamb became the first Republican Majority Floor Leader in state history. He has worked as a landman in Oklahoma's energy industry, and in addition to his Senate service, was General Counsel for an energy and wireless company in Edmond, Oklahoma.

Lt. Governor Lamb currently serves as Treasurer of the National Lieutenant Governor's Association (NLGA) Executive Committee and Vice Chair of the Aerospace States Association (ASA).

Todd Lamb and his wife Monica have been married 16 years and have two children, Griffin and Lauren. The Lambs are active members of Quail Springs Baptist Church, where Lamb serves as a church deacon. He has been a member of the Oklahoma Secondary Schools Athletic Association where he officiated high school football. He is active in many other civic and political organizations. In his spare time, Lamb enjoys fishing, hunting, reading, and spending time with his family.

31 years-of-age, and a qualified voter in the state for 10 years prior to taking office (Council of State Governments, 2003). Although they are not elected together, the lieutenant governor is required to be a member of the governor's cabinet and is held accountable to the governor for duties that the chief executive assigns.

The two primary roles of the lieutenant governor are to replace the governor when necessary and to preside over the state Senate. In the instance that the governor is removed from office, resigns, becomes permanently disabled, or dies while serving the elected term, the lieutenant governor is responsible for assuming the duties of the governor until the next scheduled general election. Interestingly, when the governor travels outside Oklahoma state lines, the lieutenant governor immediately acts as governor until the governor returns.

In presiding over the Senate, it is presumed that the lieutenant governor serves as a link between the executive branch and the legislative branch. The actual function of presiding over the Senate is an important one. When voting on any piece of legislation, the possibility of a tie exists. In such instances, the lieutenant governor breaks the tie. This is the only instance in which the lieutenant governor is allowed to vote as president of the Senate.

The year 2011 marked a breakthrough in Oklahoma history as Governor Mary Fallin assumed the highest office held by a woman in Oklahoma state politics. Her accomplishment is an extraordinary step for Oklahoma women. In addition to being the first female governor, she was also the state's first female and first Republican lieutenant governor. She was succeeded by another female lieutenant governor, Jari Askins, who later became Fallin's Democratic challenger during the 2010 gubernatorial election. Both political parties nominating women for the top office made 2010 a groundbreaking election year for women in Oklahoma politics.

IX. Other Elected Executive Officials

In comparison with other states, Oklahoma has a relatively high number of elected executive officials within the executive branch (see Table 6–2). These officials include the attorney general, the superintendent of public instruction, the state auditor and inspector, the state treasurer, three corporation commissioners, the commissioner of insurance, and the commissioner of labor.

The **attorney general** serves a four-year term and is the chief legal counsel to the state. Outside of the judiciary itself, this office is generally regarded by the people as the primary authority for interpretation of the law. In addition to the roles played by the attorney general, the office itself serves as a vital link between the executive branch and the judicial branch.

The **superintendent of public instruction** serves a four-year term and is the head administrator for all formal forms of public education in the state. In conjunction with the State Board of Education, the Superintendent supervises Oklahoma's public school system. In 2011, significant budgetary and managerial powers were legislatively transferred from the State Board of Education, an appointed body, to the Superintendent.

Table 6–2
Elected Executives and Their Agencies

Elected Executive	Agency
Attorney General	Office of the Attorney General
Superintendent of Public Instruction	Oklahoma State Department of Education
State Auditor and Inspector	Office of the State Auditor and Inspector
State Treasurer	Office of Oklahoma State Treasurer
Corporation Commissioners (3)	Corporation Commission
Commission of Insurance	Insurance Commission
Commissioner of Labor	Oklahoma Department of Labor

LEADERSHIP PROFILE

DANA MURPHY
Oklahoma Corporation Commission

COMMISSIONER DANA MURPHY has served as chair of the Oklahoma Corporation Commission. Born in Woodward, Oklahoma, Commissioner Murphy is a fifth-generation Oklahoman deeply committed to her home state. After attending the University of Central Oklahoma ("Central State"), where she received the Best All-Around Freshman Athlete award, she attended Oklahoma State University (OSU) and graduated in the top 10 percent of her class with a bachelor's degree in geology.

After practicing as a geologist for ten years, she obtained her law degree cum laude while working and attending night school at Oklahoma City University. On November 4, 2008, she was first elected to the statewide office of Oklahoma Corporation Commissioner for a partial two-year term. On July 27, 2010, she was re-elected to a full six-year term. On January 3, 2011, Commissioner Murphy became Chair of the Corporation Commission following election by her fellow Commissioners.

Commissioner Murphy's prior experience includes serving for almost six years as an administrative law judge at the Commission, where she was named co-employee of the year for 1997 and received the Commissioners' Public Servant Award in 2001. She has more than 22 years of experience in the petroleum industry including owning and operating a private law firm focused on oil and gas title, regulatory practice and transactional work and working as a geologist.

Commissioner Murphy is a member of the National Association of Regulatory Utility Commissioners (NARUC), where she serves on the Energy Resources and the Environment Committee. She is a member of the OSU Water Research Advisory Board, the Oklahoma Bar Association, American Association of Petroleum Geologists and Oklahoma City Geological Society. She also serves as the OCC representative on the Board of Trustees of the Oklahoma Public Employees Retirement System and is a member of the Salvation

Army's Central Oklahoma Area Command Advisory Board. Commissioner Murphy is a member of Energy Advocates and in March 2007 was recognized as an outstanding woman in energy. She previously served as a trustee and is currently a care chaplain for the Church of the Servant United Methodist Church in Oklahoma City.

Prior to joining the Commission, she was a member of the board of directors of Farmers Royalty Company and is a member of the Edmond Chamber of Commerce. She is also a part-time personal fitness trainer. Commissioner Murphy lives in Edmond, Oklahoma, but continues to be actively involved with her family's farm and ranch in Ellis County, Oklahoma.

The public generally regards this office as the primary authority for Oklahoma education.

The **state auditor and inspector** serves a four-year term and is regarded by the public as the "watch dog" of the state government. On the first of November of every year, the state auditor and inspector reports the findings concerning financial records of the state and county treasurers, as well as the records of all state offices, to the governor.

The **state treasurer** serves a four-year term and is the state's chief financial officer. The office is a depository for all state agencies and maintains accounts of all monies received and dispersed by the state. The public generally regards this office as responsible for the state's financial stability.

The **Corporation Commission** is composed of three elected officials serving staggered, six-year terms. Corporation commissioners supervise and regulate the rates of all utility, transportation, and transmission companies charging for their services. The public generally regards this office as the regulator of essential public services.

The **commissioner of insurance** serves a four-year term and is the administrator for laws relating to the insurance industry in the state. This office enjoys the reputation as protector of the people from insurance fraud. In doing so, the office certifies all insurance companies as well as collects and disperses taxes from those companies doing business in the state.

Finally, the **Commissioner of Labor** serves a four-year term and is the administrator of all laws that relate to labor in manufacturing, mechanical, and transportation industries in the state. The commissioner of labor enforces all provisions and regulations that affect the health and well being of the labor force in Oklahoma.

While they do not receive the same amount of attention as the governor and lieutenant governor, the other elected executives perform valuable and necessary duties by administering agencies that fall under the executive branch. It is interesting to note that until very recently only the Governor was term limited, while all other elected executives were allowed to serve an unlimited number of consecutive terms (Council of State Governments 2003). In an era when a majority of Oklahomans have supported term limits for the governor and legislators, state executive branch offices now face limits as well. Passage of State Question 747 in the 2010 general election amended Article VI of the state Constitution, thereby limiting the lieutenant governor, state auditor and inspector, attorney general, state treasurer, commissioners of labor and insurance, and superintendent of public instruction to no more than eight years in office.

X. CONCLUSION

As the most visible and popular branch of government, the executive branch sets the tone for the state. The elected and appointed executives are responsible for leading those who run our state government. As both the administrative leader and the figurehead of Oklahoma, the governor must find a way to function within a pluralistic executive branch. Oklahoma's Constitution weakens the executive branch by splintering it into several separate power bases. Numerous officials, ranging from insurance commissioner to superintendent of public instruction to Corporation Commissioners, are elected in statewide races. Add to this the fact that independent Boards and Commissions control many of the basic functions of state government, and it becomes clear how challenging it is for governors to effectively coordinate and manage state government.

In this type of governing situation, all elected executives must realize that the entire executive branch is evaluated on its ability to initiate, implement, and enforce effective policies. Such policy must be timely and must be in accordance with the needs of the people. Within the executive branch, effectiveness is measured by the use of political influence as a means to an end. The ability to be effective is vital because the roles and responsibilities of all of the executives directly impact the public and set the direction for Oklahoma.

Because of issues like pluralism and limited power, one might ask why anyone would want to be governor. The answer lies in the head coach analogy. If a team enjoys success, the coach is generally credited for promoting and creating ways to maximize achievement. Just as coaches are confident in their ability, anyone endeavoring to be governor must possess the full conviction that he or she will succeed. As fate has it, some are more successful than others. This success depends upon each governor's ability to transcend the pluralism and limited power issues, while providing effective administrative leadership.

PUBLIC ADMINISTRATION IN OKLAHOMA

Brett S. Sharp and Steven W. Housel

Collective responsibility and decentralized responsibility must go hand in hand; more than that, I think they are parts of the same things.

Mary Parker Follett, 1940

Any government in such a complicated society, consequently any such society itself, is strong in proportion to its capacity to administer the functions that are brought into being.

John M. Gaus, 1947

I. INTRODUCTION

L eta Stotts is currently working on a master's degree. In 2013 she earned a bachelor's degree. Two years earlier she completed an associate's degree with honors. Today Leta Stotts is a working professional. But in July 2010 she was a different woman—desperate, depressed and despairing. It was during that month that she walked into the Haskell County office of the Department of Human Services to apply for public assistance. She received the appropriate intake processing, but Leta received a lot more than she was expecting.

It was her good fortune on that day to have been helped by Marlyn La Vergne, a social services worker whose graciousness and continual willingness to support, guide, listen, console, counsel and encourage would be a mainstay in Leta's life for the next four years. Of course, none of these qualities are technically a part of the policies and procedures required of intake counselors. For Marlyn, however, they are integral to her character and the way she goes about her work. "When you throw people lifelines and help them understand their options," she says, "then you empower people to make choices which will better their future. Everybody has a vision and a dream. I am just a gatekeeper. I help people realize what they are capable of doing. I open the gate, provide transportation, do a lot of listening, emphasize that education is the key out of poverty, and help them understand the practical realities needed to realize their vision" (Marlyn La Vergne, personal communication, March 21, 2014).

Marlyn La Vergne was born into poverty and was raised in foster homes. She did not know what she would do with her life until she was 40 years old. Since then she has earned three undergraduate degrees. Her life experiences, her education, and her commitment to her fellow human beings have elevated her to the pantheon of great public servants, who are often poorly paid but given immense responsibilities. Leta Stots knew all of this on the day she received her associate degree. She remembered, "As I walked across the stage there was Marlyn. She was sitting next to my family with a big smile . . . and tears in her eyes" (Former Haskell County, 2013).

Leta Stots's story turned out very well. But it could have been tragic, as too many Oklahomans struggle in a state whose ranking in the areas of poverty, education, and health insurance place it in or very near the bottom 20% among the 50 states (Corporation for Enterprise Development 2014). Of course, human misfortunes and heartbreaks can also descend upon communities. For example, Oklahoma ranks third among the states in the number of federally declared disasters (Doak, 2011, p. 9A). Tornadoes, wildfires, blizzards, ice storms, severe thunderstorms coupled with flooding, heat waves morphing into droughts, and even mild earthquakes are not uncommon. And then there are some disasters that are caused by deliberate human action, such as the 1995 terrorist bombing of the Alfred P. Murrah federal building in Oklahoma City. At the time, it was the worst terrorist incident to have occurred on American soil. Ultimately, 168 people are known to have been killed.

The federal government's capacity in Oklahoma City was crippled by the attack. Public servants and nonprofit agencies from all across the state and beyond responded immediately. Fire, police, and emergency rescue personnel were on site and communicating with the incident command within the first half hour. Oklahoma's public administrators earned worldwide praise for their interagency cooperation, the hospitality they extended to rescue workers, and their commitment to keeping the public informed. The work of these public servants came to be known in the national emergency response community as **"the Oklahoma Standard."**

The public looks to government and state and local employees to directly and regularly provide services in good times and bad. Public employees implement and administer the policies and programs that support the infrastructure of government. As is the case with Haskel County's social service worker Marlyn La Vergne, public servants are committed to helping their fellow citizens pursue their dreams and improve their lives. This chapter reviews several of the most important characteristics of public administration in Oklahoma, paying special attention to recent reforms proposed by the Fallin administration, including significant changes to the merit and remunerations systems and a vast consolidation of many of the state's most important agencies.

LEADERSHIP PROFILE

WILLIAM CITTY
Chief of Police, City of Oklahoma City

AN OKLAHOMAN born and bred, Bill Citty was born in Oklahoma City in 1953. He attended North West Classen High School and graduated in 1971. After graduation, he attended the University of Central Oklahoma for a short time, with an emphasis on business and marketing. Citty soon transferred to Oklahoma State University where he changed his major to sociology. At the time, he had an interest in psychology and had served internships at several nonprofit and juvenile facilities.  Although he very much enjoyed helping young adults, he was disenchanted with the success rate of many juvenile programs.

He finished his degree in sociology, but had turned his interest back to business and marketing. In 1977, he hired on at the Oklahoma Police Department as "just a job." At this time, he had no special interest in police work, but thought it might be interesting, and was attracted to the department's willingness to pay for his graduate degree.

After working for about three years on the street, he transferred to narcotics where he worked undercover. Although he had come to enjoy working for the police department, the undercover work began to wear on him. Visiting strip clubs and bars while being required to stay on good terms with shady people was not something he wanted to do for very long. Citty was soon promoted to detective after about two years working undercover, where he mainly worked on prostitution and gambling cases. While working with Criminal Intelligence, he again went undercover to help work a major gambling operation.

After about eight years on the force, Citty was promoted to Captain and attended the FBI Academy. He considered leaving the department and going federal, but after extensive research and consideration, decided he would rather continue working in Oklahoma instead of relocating. Over the next few years, Citty held several different positions within the department. He headed up the Animal

Welfare Division for a short amount of time. He was also a hostage negotiator and even commander of the tactical team. He was appointed chief in October of 2003. Citty says that being Chief was never his conscious goal. He was just there to do his job to the best of his ability. Even so, Chief Citty is proud to head such a fine department.

Michelle R. Stricklin

II. Reform of the Merit System

A *merit system* is often thought to be synonymous with a *civil service system*. The terms are closely related but they have different meanings. In its broadest sense, a **civil service system** refers to a government's organization and management of its personnel, which can take many forms. A **merit system**, on the other hand, refers to specific human resource practices which are based on the principle that public employees are hired and promoted based on their fitness for office. Merit standards, however, have not always been a part of civil service. During the nation's first three decades the federal government's civil service was staffed by partisan elites appointed by the president—an approach that produced a workforce that was generally stable, honest and competent (Shafritz, Rosenbloom, Riccucci, Naff & Hyde, 2001, pp. 4-5).

Beginning in the 1830s, presidents started making appointments based more on patronage than ability, a practice commonly known as the **spoils system.** The first 150 years of the American experience as a constitutional republic was a period in which rural life and an agrarian economy largely dominated everyday existence. After the Civil War a new America began to emerge. Industrialization, urbanization, westward migration, and other powerful social and economic forces outstripped the administrative capacity of state and local governments (Wright, 1988, pp. 67-68, 71; Shapek, 1981, p. 6). They were neither politically nor organizationally equipped to provide such basic needs as clean water, sewerage, roads, community safety, education, and other essential services. This situation was due in large part to the patronage approach to staffing the public sector. Inexperience, incompetence, graft and corruption symbolized its worst elements.

The antidote to spoils was awarding jobs on the basis of merit, which was made law by the **1883 Pendleton Act.** Even though it initially encompassed only a small percentage of national government personnel, by the middle of the twentieth century almost 90 percent of federal employees were a part of some form of merit-based civil service. Large cities had also made substantial progress in making personnel reforms. State governments, on the other hand, were much slower to change their staffing practices. In fact, by 1950 only about a third of them had replaced patronage politics with professional personnel procedures (Mosher, Kingsley & Stahl, 1950, p. 37). In Oklahoma, except for employees of state agencies receiving national grants-in-aid, it was a fact of political life that spoils employment was the basis of public employment (Gibson, 1981, p. 6).

In 1960, the Oklahoma legislature, under the leadership of Governor J. Howard Edmondson, voted to extend the merit system to agencies throughout the state. The adoption of a merit-based civil service system was the first major overhaul of public personnel management in Oklahoma history, and was a critical component in building administrative competence in the state. Today, public employment in Oklahoma is governed by the **1982 Oklahoma Personnel Act,** whose purpose is to introduce more flexibility in carrying out the functions of human resources management while continuing strong support for merit principles.

Under the administration of Governor Mary Fallin, Oklahoma's current public personnel system is in the process of undergoing its second major overhaul. Legislation was passed in 2013 that called for a review board to study and make recommendations related to reforming and improving most areas of Oklahoma's management of its human resources. The study was carried out by the state's personnel division, many of the human resources directors of its government agencies, and the public employees association. According to the personnel agency's administrator, the reason for the undertaking was that "Oklahoma's current merit system has regressed into an antiquated, counterproductive system that creates barriers to efficient and effective human resources practices." She said the challenge is to design a new system with modernized rules and procedures while retaining the "value of the old merit principles" (Meltabarger, 2013, p. 2). The new system will be called the State of Oklahoma Career Service System. According to the study, the proposed system "is an entirely new way of administering statewide HR practices and begins with new definitions of employment" (Meltabarger, 2013, p. 3).

Currently, state employees are a part of either the Classified Service or the Unclassified Service. The procedures for hiring, promoting, disciplining, and terminating classified employees are based on merit principles, which means employment should be fair and equitable and meet fairly specific standards. Personnel actions for unclassified employees, on the other hand, permit the employer to freely hire, discipline or dismiss employees for virtually any reason, providing the action does not violate state or federal laws. This broad, discretion-based system is known as "at will" employment. The study reported problems with both services. For classified employees, the hiring process is unwieldy, compensation is set by legislatively-determined pay ranges, and discipline and termination procedures are drawn out, legalistic, and expensive. For unclassified employees, the hiring and compensating process is unruly and highly variable. It prevents the state from knowing "how many employees do various types of work . . . and whether employees performing similar functions are compensated appropriately and consistently" (Meltabarger, 2013, p. 2).

The proposed solution is to substantially reduce the number of unclassified employees from roughly 32 percent of the workforce to a much lesser proportion, perhaps as few as ten per cent. Unclassified employees will become a part of what will be called the Executive Service. Classified employees will become part of the new Career Service. Hiring for the Career Service will be simplified. The central personnel office, now known as Human Capital Management (HCM), will establish minimum state standards and provide initial review of applications. Agencies, who will be given leeway to develop specific job-related standards, will then take over the hiring process and make the final selection. The Merit Protection Commission will be replaced by a new board. Grievances will be limited to actions that affect employee pay. Appeals will be handled first by an internal review within the employee's agency. The employee may appeal to HCM for further review. The study states, "These reviews will not be quasi-judicial actions requiring pleadings, discovery, witnesses or attorney representation" (Meltabarger, 2013, p. 4). Compensation is a major piece of this overall reform effort.

Compensation-related proposals fall into three related plans. One is to increase compensation of Career Service employees so that their pay reflects 90 percent of the remuneration in the private sector for comparable work. Performance-based analysis will be included in making pay determinations. Another plan is to change the pension system from a defined-benefit to a defined-contribution system. A third is to change how workers' compensation is managed. These changes will be elaborated in a later section of this chapter.

III. A Skeptical Public

In an age of political cynicism and government skepticism, public administrators in Oklahoma may be facing less overall support than at any time in state history. The Gallup organization reported in September 2013 that fewer Americans than ever trust the federal government to handle their problems (Gallup.Com, 2013). Whereas the same polling reveals Americans express greater confidence in state and local governments, it can nevertheless be argued that Oklahomans are probably among the least trusting Americans of any level of government. Evidence for this claim is derived from three critical events that have occurred in Oklahoma in the past 25 years. The first is the term limit law. In 1990 the state became the first in the nation to limit the tenure of its state legislators. Four years later the voters approved limiting the tenure of members of Congress, but in 1995 the Supreme Court ruled it unconstitutional (Rausch & Farmer, 1998).

The second reason is the state's virtually unsurmountable limitation on tax increases. An initiative-driven vote changed the state constitution, which now requires that a three-fourths super majority of both houses is required to increase taxes. If a tax measure receives only majority legislative approval, the proposal would then need to receive majority support in a statewide vote (Lawton, 1992). The tax-limiting amendment occurred in addition to the strict system of constitutional tax and spending limits that were already in place (OKPolicy.org, 2014). More recently, Oklahoma passed another tax restriction. This 2012 law limits property tax increases to 3% per year (Prah, 2012).

Finally, Oklahoma's antipathy toward government is exemplified by its having given control of its legislative and executive branches—previously dominated for most of its statehood by the Democrats—to the Republican Party. The most visible manifestation of this relatively recent change is perhaps the depth of the majority party's philosophical aversion to government, especially to the federal government. A telling example is the about-face of the legislature toward adoption of Common Core State Standards. The purpose of the standards is to "establish clear, consistent guidelines for what every student should know and be able to do in math and English language arts from kindergarten through 12th grade" (What parents should, 2014). They were developed by the National Governors Association's Center for Best Practices, the National Conference of State Legislatures, and the Council of State School Officers. The Bill and Melinda Gates Foundation has spent in excess of $170 million in grants supporting dozens of contributing institutes, associations and universities (Strauss, 2013). Although Oklahoma was one of 45 states that adopted the standards in 2010, Republican-led House and Senate committees repealed the standards in March 2014. Their objections center on perceived federal interference. In supporting the repeal, Governor Fallin stated, "We have no interest in relinquishing control over education to the federal government or outside groups" (Oklahoma Governor's Office, 2014). As the *Daily Oklahoman* editorialized about the claim that Common Core represents a federal takeover of schools, "No real evidence exists to support that claim" (Repeal of Common, 2014). Or as the *Tulsa World* bluntly stated, such claims are simply "untrue" (Greene, 2014a).

IV. HOLDING BUREAUCRACIES ACCOUNTABLE

While politicians are voted into office by the people, they ultimately must depend upon an unelected part of government known as the bureaucracy to accomplish the work that needs to be done. The term *bureaucracy* has been associated – both fairly and unfairly – with red tape, inefficiency, waste, and corruption. In actuality, bureaucracy simply refers to a large organization composed of specialized professionals. These professionals operate according to rules established within a defined command and control structure. Bureaucracies are not institutions unique to government. Large and successful corporations such as Wal-Mart, Devon Energy, McDonald's, and General Electric are also examples of bureaucracies.

More often than not, and despite sporadic negative press coverage, governmental bureaucracies are quite successful in their endeavors. Bureaucracies have sometimes been compared to elephants. Like elephants, bureaucracies are thought of as large and cumbersome. But elephants "can run very fast" and some bureaucracies can "perform very well" (Rainey and Steinbaurer, 1999, p. 1). Many of the greatest feats of humankind— from the building of magnificent pyramids in the ancient world to the landing of a man on the moon – are the direct results of bureaucratic effort. On a daily basis, Oklahoma bureaucracies serve the public in countless ways. These organizations provide necessary institutional support for all three branches of government: executive, legislative, and judicial.

The difficulty remains as to the legitimacy of this large, powerful, unelected bureaucracy which has evolved for all practical purposes into a fourth branch of government. Fortunately, the demographic categories that make up the state government workforce roughly mirrors the state workforce overall. This diversity means that Oklahoma citizens are served by a **representative bureaucracy.** In other words, Oklahoma's bureaucracy looks like the public it serves (see Table 7–1).

Running state and local government is a labor-intensive process. According to the Bureau of Labor Statistics, one out of every seven workers in the United States works for a state, county, municipality, school system or special district—nearly twenty million state and local government employees altogether. Excluding those who work in education, state and local governments employ nearly eight million workers making this sector one of the largest in the American economy. In the state of

TABLE 7–1 Comparison of Oklahoma Workforce Gender/Ethnicity with Overall State Population 2012–2013, Excluding Higher Education		
GENDER	OKLAHOMA	STATE GOVERNMENT
Male	49%	43%
Female	51%	57%
ETHNICITY	OKLAHOMA	STATE GOVERNMENT
White	76%	76%
African American	8%	9%
Hispanic	9%	2%
Native American	9%	7%
Asian	2%	1%

SOURCE: U.S. Bureau of the Census, *State and County QuickFacts* and Data.OK.gov (2013)

Oklahoma, state government is the largest single employer with almost 34,000 employees—and that figure does not include higher education. As impressive as this figure might seem, the number of state employees working in the executive branch has seen a steady and significant decline since the early 1990s (see Figure 7–1). This decline is even more dramatic when one considers that the state population has experienced a substantial growth over the same period.

The key personnel that keep these public operations running are called public administrators. A **public administrator** is someone who is compensated by a government or not-for-profit agency for managing a program or supervising people. Public administrators, who run state and local agencies in Oklahoma are important because this state has traditionally denied strong formal powers to its governor and mayors. Career administrators fill in this power vacuum by default. Often, these public administrators use their **administrative discretion** when working under the color of vague or conflicting legislation. Administrative discretion implies a certain amount of flexibility when applying the law. For example, when stopped by a police officer for a traffic violation, we hope that he or she uses his to her discretion in our favor. In other words, we hope to receive a warning rather than a ticket. While citizens must trust their elected representatives to make laws in their stead, legislators must trust public administrators to interpret and implement laws in the face of new and unforeseen circumstances. As much judicial activity probably occurs at the administrative level than in all the courts of law in the land.

FIGURE 7–1 Number of Executive Branch State Employees
in Oklahoma by Fiscal Year (1993–2013)

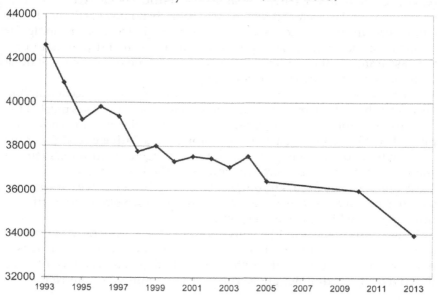

Citizens do not tend to think very much about bureaucracy when it works well. In a classic study reviewing numerous surveys conducted over time, organizational theorist Charles T. Goodsell concluded, "Most citizens are satisfied with their personal experiences with bureaucracy most of the time" (1992, p. 101). The few bad experiences that citizens have with government probably become more salient due to the fact that alternative services are rarely available. Moreover, citizens rightly believe that they are the "owners" of the public enterprise since they support it with their tax monies. Bureaucratic features take on added significance in the public sector since government agencies are not directly constrained by the bottom line of profit. Voters understandably desire to hold these institutions accountable.

The five principal methods for holding the administrative state answerable to the public are (1) elections, (2) the merit system, (3) limiting bureaucrats' political activity, (4) legislative oversight, and (5) transparent rulemaking. Elections of course are familiar to every American citizen. However, they may overlook that several of the principal administrators in the bureaucracy are appointed by elected officials, and many of these high-level administrators in turn make appointments to individuals to manage parts of their agencies. Although appointed public administrators do not answer directly to the voter, their tenure is subject to the voters' satisfaction with the performance of the government and the elected officials who lead it. The merit system, as discussed above, is a long-established, nonpartisan method of competitively hiring employees of demonstrated ability. One of merit system's founding principles is that civil servants will provide neutral competence, which means they are professionally obliged to support the policies of the elected leadership, regardless of political party. Oklahoma's "**Little Hatch Act**," which is based on a similarly-named federal law, restricts political activity of state employees. In the broadest sense, they are prohibited from running for public office or taking part in political campaigns. Its purpose is to provide assurance to the public that the actions of state employees are done without favor to politicians or political parties.

Perhaps the two least understood tools for promoting accountability are oversight and rulemaking. Ultimately, the legislature bears most of the responsibility for bureaucracies answering to the citizens, which is accomplished, as Michael Reagan explains, through **legislative oversight** or the "reviewing and controlling the operations of agencies in implementing statutes" (1987, p. 154). There are various methods for carrying out oversight, but it usually occurs through the hearings of legislative subcommittees. It is here that bureaucracies are called upon to explain and justify the programs for which they are responsible.

Rulemaking can seem like a mysterious process. Americans generally assume that legislatures write laws and agencies carry them out. This is only partially correct. As the Office of the Oklahoma Secretary of State described it: "Administrative rules, also commonly referred to as

LEADERSHIP PROFILE

JAMES D. COUCH
City Manager, City of Oklahoma City

JAMES D. COUCH was appointed City Manager of the City of Oklahoma City on November 9, 2000. He serves as the Chief Administrative Officer of the City responsible for the management and day-to-day operation of City government. Oklahoma City is a full-service city with nearly 4,300 employees and a total budget of $700 million.

Couch serves on a variety of city-related boards and agencies: Oklahoma City Airport Trust, Oklahoma City Water Utilities Trust, Oklahoma City Zoological Trust, and the Central Oklahoma Transportation and Parking Authority. Also, Mr. Couch serves as General Manager of the Oklahoma City Metropolitan Area Public Schools (OCMAPS) Trust, which oversees a half-billion dollar construction program.

Before being appointed as City Manager, Couch already had a distinguished career with the City of Oklahoma City. He served as Assistant City Manager and MAPS Director as well as Water/Wastewater Utilities Director. In those capacities he served as the General Manager of both the Oklahoma City Water Utilities Trust and the McGee Creek Authority and was responsible for the Water/Wastewater Utilities budget of $100 million annually, as well as the $390 million Metropolitan Area Projects capital construction program.

Prior to his career with the City of Oklahoma City, Couch held positions as the Assistant City Manager for the City of Edmond, Oklahoma; Public Works Director for the City of Casper, Wyoming; and Office Director for Buell, Winter, Mousel and Associates, Consulting Engineers. He received a Bachelor of Science in Civil Engineering from the South Dakota School of Mines and Technology, and is a Licensed Professional Engineer in the states of Oklahoma and Colorado.

Outside of his professional Career, Couch serves on the YMCA of Greater Oklahoma City Board of Directors and the United Way of Metro Oklahoma City Board of Directors. Additionally, he is active in various church activities at Peace Lutheran Church.

regulations, are laws enacted by state agencies, as specifically authorized by legislation, to implement the statutes created by that legislation. Before becoming effective, rules are subject to a comprehensive rulemaking process that includes review and approval by the Oklahoma Legislature" (Oklahoma Secretary of State, 2013a). This rulemaking process not only occurs under the legislature's watch, it must be done in public, made known in advance, and include opportunity for citizen input. Even though more than half of Oklahoma's laws are written by state agencies (Oklahoma Secretary of State, 2013b), the process is open and transparent.

V. Improving Bureaucratic Productivity

In the 2010 election, the voters of Oklahoma for the first time gave Republicans control of both the executive and legislative branches. Many Republican candidates, including Governor Fallin, ran on platforms that included improving the efficiency of state government. In a memorable statement, the governor said in her first State of the State address that many Oklahoma agencies were "outdated eight-track bureaucracies in an iPod world" (Carter, 2011). The governor's concern with streamlining state government and instituting similar reforms is not new.

Governmental reform efforts usually take the form of reorganization or the application of new managerial techniques. A major barrier to improving productivity in the public sector is the short tenure of elected officials. Governors have expended very little effort in preserving a sense of continuity in their productivity improvement efforts. While these activities are often short-lived, some programs do become institutionalized within the bureaucracy. For example, Governor Henry Bellmon encouraged a **"State of Excellence."** His program was likely influenced by the fashionable management strategy promoted in the book by Peters and Waterman, *In Search of Excellence* (1982). Accordingly, one of his principal legislative accomplishments was a large educational reform law. In a related initiative Bellmon's administration became one of the early champions of the **Certified Public Manager (CPM)** program, which still provides comprehensive management education and training for public administrators statewide.

Many politicians routinely advocate using the business model to run state and local governments. While sometimes helpful, its promotion demonstrates little appreciation for the stark differences between substantive and procedural issues that largely define the differences between the public and private sectors. Governor Fallin, for example, in her 2014 State of the State address said of her administration's accomplishments, "We made government run more like a business – efficient, effective and customer friendly" (Oklahoma Governor's Office, 2014b). On the other hand, Oklahoma's Preston Doerflinger, the current director of the state's Office of Management and Enterprise Services (OMES), does not lump the two models together. As he noted in a statewide television interview, "I am not one who believes we can run government just like a business. It is a different beast" (Oklahoma Forum, 2014). He went on to note, however, that many "best practices" could effectively be borrowed from business and applied to government.

Governor David Walters embraced **Total Quality Management (TQM)**, which is a set of management methods originally used to enhance business productivity. TQM has also been employed in the public sector to continuously improve customer services. Special trainers guide state employees in applying quality improvement processes and techniques. The Walters' TQM initiative was built upon a cooperative relationship between the Xerox Corporation, a recipient of the prestigious Malcolm Baldrige National Quality Award, and the state of Oklahoma. Although remnants of TQM in the state's government have persisted well beyond the Walters administration, its continued use has been due more to bureaucratic momentum than to the support of later administrations. For instance, the network of quality teams that began under Walters continued to meet even though for months they were not recognized by Governor Frank Keating.

Keating put his own imprint on Oklahoma bureaucracy by creating the document, "A Government As Good As Our People: Report of the Governor's Commission on Government Performance" (also known as the "Keating Report"), which was modeled after Vice President Al Gore's National Performance Review. Both the national and state performance reviews rode the wave of **reinventing government,** which was inspired by a book of the same name authored by Osborne and Gaebler (1992). Reinventing government promoted the use of market mechanisms, decentralization, outcomes measurement, and managerial empowerment. It emphasized revamping and even eliminating existing rules and regulations in order to increase the flexibility and capacity of public administrators to do their jobs, which assumed that public administrators were overly fearful of taking risks.

Reinventing government promoted a philosophy of tolerating reasonable mistakes when bureaucrats attempted more entrepreneurial approaches. The Governor's Performance Commission assembled numerous teams that interviewed a variety of stakeholders throughout the state. The Commission ultimately made recommendations on such wide-ranging areas as education, finance, health, human resources, management systems, social services, and transportation. Many of these recommendations were incorporated into law and policy. In "Fallin's Formal Powers in Transition," a paper presented at the 2013 Oklahoma Political Science Association Annual Conference (Nov. 7-8 in Norman, OK) Dr. John Wood of Rose State College made a convincing argument that many of Fallin's reforms have their roots in the Keating Report.

Before he was first elected to public office, Brad Henry described state government as wasteful and said it had "too many boards and agencies."

He added, "Some should be consolidated or terminated altogether" (Legislative Candidates, 1992). After becoming governor, however, Henry did not initiate a comprehensive reform of state bureaucracy, although he did tinker at the edges of reform. He issued an executive order placing the Oklahoma Employment Security Commission, the Oklahoma Workforce Investment Board, and other related agencies under the supervision of the Department of Commerce (Monies, 2003). He also advocated innovative financial management techniques such as **zero base budgeting (ZBB),** which is designed to discourage agencies from automatically assuming they should receive roughly the same amount of funding as in the previous fiscal year. Under ZBB, agencies must defend their current roster of programs as if they did not already exist.

The state legislature has also advanced its version of improving the performance of the state bureaucracy. In 1998 it passed a law creating the Quality Improvement Task Force, which requires agencies to adopt five-year strategic plans. According to the state's Office of Management and Enterprise Services, "Strategic planning is the process by which members of an organization envision its future and develop the action plans necessary to achieve the future" (Strategic Planning, n.d.). When it works well, strategic planning assists agencies in setting priorities, effectively using resources, helping employees work toward shared objectives, and strengthening overall operations (What is Strategic, n.d.).

As described above, Governor Fallin has made substantial and controversial efforts toward improving the state's productivity. The fact that there is no consensus about the efficacy of the results is not surprising. Judgment needs the leavening agent of time. For example, bipartisan support exists today among Republican and Democratic presidents that the chief executive requires managerial authority equal to the tasks assigned to the office. Yet during the New Deal, debate over the issue was acerbic in the extreme (Arnold, 1976). More recently it can be noted that scholars are still debating the value of the reforms advocated by the National Performance Review, which began in the early years of the Clinton administration and were designed to increase the efficiency and responsiveness of government (Rainey & Bozeman, 2000, p. 462). With those examples in mind, a rush to judgment over Governor Fallin's reforms would seem inappropriate, especially at this early stage of the governor's streamlining efforts.

VI. Structure of the Bureaucracy

The state of Oklahoma has approximately 300 boards, commissions, departments and agencies (Agency Directory, 2014). This patchwork of governmental subunits represents nearly a century of attempts by the state to respond to a wide variety of emerging policy problems. The situation also reflects the state's progressive heritage, which began with a fragmented executive branch and a governor that could do very little to control it (Morgan, England & Humphreys, 1991, p. 106). While there have been sporadic attempts to consolidate the executive branch, the overall trend has been in the direction of growing complexity. Currently, the state bureaucracy can be subdivided into agencies under the direction of the governor's cabinet, those under the direction of other elected officials, and numerous independent bureaus, boards and commissions.

Governors David Boren and George Nigh experimented with a cabinet system in order to strengthen and centralize their leadership. A cabinet is composed of top administrative officials, usually heads of major state departments, who work together to advise the governor on important policy matters. The legislature implemented a formal cabinet system in 1987 under Governor Henry Bellmon. State law stipulates that the cabinet system shall consist of no fewer than ten and no more than fifteen functional areas. Within these legislatively-established limits, successive Oklahoma governors have tailored cabinets to meet their individual needs. Currently, there are 13 cabinet secretaries.

Governor Fallin has accelerated the centralizing and strengthening of the executive branch by changing the composition of her cabinet. She consolidated positions and created new ones. The most significant alteration was the creation of the vast Office of Management and Enterprise Services, which is comprised of seven divisions: Central Purchasing; Division of Budget, Policy and Legislative Services; Division of Capital Assets Management; Division of Central Accounting and Reporting; Employees Group Insurance Division; Human Capital Management (comprised of remnants from the former Office of Personnel Management agency); and Information Services Division (Oklahoma Office of Management and Enterprise Services, 2011). All of the powers and duties of the divisions, some of which reflect the combination of more than one agency, are vested in the OMES director, who is a cabinet official appointed by the governor, thus "giving the chief executive considerably more control over the operation of the state bureaucracy" (Krehbiel, 2014).

Most cabinet officials have direct administrative authority over one or more state agencies. Sometimes the status of cabinet level officials is more honorific than substantive. "If a cabinet member lacks operational responsibility for an agency, that person becomes little more than a staff adviser to the governor" (Morgan, England, & Humphreys, 1992, p. 114). For example, Governor Frank Keating appointed Dr. Floyd Coppedge in 1996 to serve as Education Cabinet Secretary. The appointment provided little more than symbolic leadership since oversight of state common education is provided by the State Superintendent of Public Instruction. Higher education is of course managed by the State Regents.

In another consolidation move, the governor proposed creating a new Department of Tourism, History and Cultural Affairs, which would have combined into one department the Oklahoma Arts Council, J.M. Davis Memorial Commission, Oklahoma Historical Society, Will Rogers Memorial Commission, and Oklahoma Scenic Rivers Commission. The governor estimated the changes would save 15 percent in associated expenses. The plan narrowly passed the House committee in which it originated, but did not receive a vote by the full House in time to meet the deadline for consideration (Update on House, 2014).

These consolidation efforts are an attempt to increase both administrative and political centralization of the agencies and departments of the bureaucracy. As Berkley and Rouse point out, this can be a mixed blessing (2009, pp. 77-81). On the one hand, centralization puts more authority in the hands of the governor and her appointees. Theoretically, this should result in organizational arrangements and policies that reflect the views of the official who voters elect to lead the government. It should also produce economy, efficiency and effectiveness while reducing the fragmentation and duplication that can result from loose central control. On the other hand, Governor Fallin's centralizing moves are occurring at a time when **devolution,** or decentralization, has become one of the maxims of theorists and practitioners of public administration. Devolution contends that if line managers and others at the lower ranks of government are granted greater discretion in developing policies and administering functions, then teamwork, flexibility, adaptability and customer service are likely to improve (Milakovich and Gordon, 2013, pp. 180-181).

One of the principal criticisms of increased centralization is that it can lack the virtues of fluid communication and responsiveness. This is currently a budding problem occurring in the Fallin administration's consolidation of information technology services, which is overseen by the Office of Management and Enterprise Services. The rationale for the consolidation was that millions of dollars could be saved by the merger of the state's disparate and more or less autonomous IT systems. However, after meeting with 42 state agencies the Oklahoma Senate Committee on Select Agencies reported that "IT consolidation for all state agencies has either been cost-neutral or usually a cost burden for the agencies, with some agencies expressing much frustration with slowed service or lost data due to the conversion" ("More Work," 2013). A performance audit of the Oklahoma Nursing Board by the state Auditor and Inspector came to a similar conclusion, reporting that "IT consolidation has generated increased costs, potential security breaches and poorer service" for the agency.

Another example of centralization not being a panacea is the intense agency resistance to the governor's attempt to bring together five tourism-related agencies into a single department. The Oklahoma Historical Society described it as a "hostile takeover disguised as consolidation," claimed it would result in the Society's membership being abolished, and charged that setting Society goals and allocating its assets would be transferred to the new department ("Membership of the," 2014). The Oklahoma Arts Council stated such a move would "erode services to the state's arts and cultural industry and undermine Oklahoma's ability to compete for business and a creative workforce" ("Potential Consequences," 2014). The administrator of the Oklahoma Scenic Rivers Commission said it would simply be a "poor fit" (Oklahoma Governor's Consolidation, 2014). And the chairman of the Will Rogers Memorial Commission complained that the Commission was neither consulted in advance of the proposed merger nor been given any study that either validated the fiscal savings or provided a rationale for the move (Hartz, 2014).

VII. Employee Pay Reform

A study of Oklahoma's remuneration system released in December 2013 made extensive recommendations related to altering the state's pay system (Oklahoma Management and Enterprise Services, 2013a). The **"State of Oklahoma Total Remuneration Study"** (TRS) was conducted to serve as a resource for policy makers and agencies to use in developing a new approach. The TRS—along with the legislation and rulemaking that will follow from its recommendations—will significantly change the compensation system for Oklahoma workers.

According to TRS, "Several years of no general funding for across the board raises, coupled with increased turnover, has caused concerns to executive and legislative branch leadership, as well the employee association, regarding compensation" (Oklahoma Management and Enterprise Services, 2013b, p. 2). The TRS team included members of the state's political leadership, the state employee association, and two professional consulting organizations with national expertise in state government compensation. The market analysis they conducted used two measures with which to set benchmarks and make judgments about salary comparability. One was data from private sector sources within the state. The other used data from several regional states as a basis for assessment.

The results revealed that state employee salaries are more than 22% below the median of the private sector and 6% lower than the median of those in comparable states. The results of benefit comparisons were significantly better. When compared to the private sector, Oklahoma employee benefits were 18% above the median. As the report notes, the influence of better benefits helps to compensate for the low salary status (Oklahoma Management and Enterprise Services, 2013a, p. 8).

The recommendation of TRS is that the state begin closing the gap between current pay and the market benchmark. It suggests a target of setting aside 3% of the previous year's payroll to fund the first step toward closing the gap, which would raise approximately $40 million. Additional funding would continue until all state employees' salaries reached the TRS goal of meeting 90% of the private market (Ellis, 2014). At the 3% per year level of additional funding, it would require four years to reach 90%, which means that approximately $300 million in additional funds may have to be allocated annually to state employees in order to maintain the goal. Those who are the most underpaid would receive the largest raises and those whose wages are more in line with the benchmark would have to wait.

The bill's author, Rep. Leslie Osborn, R-Mustang, said, "Our state agencies need productive minds and ingenuity to . . . provide better services and address the problems of the future. Competitive wages will greatly enhance the state's ability to choose from the top recruits" (Ellis, 2014). As of this writing, the state House has passed the measure without debate by a 90-0 vote, and every indication supports the idea that the Senate will follow suit, although modest adjustments are first likely to be made in conference.

The remuneration plan is just one of three changes which will directly affect state employees' finances. The other reforms are new pension and workers' compensation plans. The pension overhaul calls for current employees to remain in the present defined-benefit system, but many new employees will be part of a defined-contribution plan, also known as a 401 (k)-style system. According to the Tax Policy Center, "A defined-contribution plan is a plan in which an employee's benefits during retirement depend on the contributions made to and the investment performance of the assets in his or her account, rather than on the employee's years of service or earnings history" (Gale & Harris, 2007). The new approach will require Oklahoma employees to contribute 3 to 7 percent of their wages into the system and the state will contribute a corresponding amount dollar for dollar. This method is advantageous to the state because it is funded on a pay as you go basis. Conversely, as some journalists and economists have observed, the problem for public sector employers operating defined-benefit plans is their "lack of restraint in granting extreme pension and benefit promises to government workers" (Reilly, Schoener & Bolin, 2007, p. 40). Or, as Jonathan Small concisely noted, the plans "are prone to mismanagement . . . because it is very easy for politicians to make promises and worry about funding them later" (Small, 2014). This explains at least part of the reason why Oklahoma faces the $11 billion of unfunded pension liability reported by Governor Fallin in March 2013 (McNutt, 2013).

The TRS recommends that Oklahoma's remuneration issue is not just about salary; rather, it concerns both salary and benefits. The TRS authors stated that the "primary driver" of their recommendations is to start on the path to "changing the mix" between salary and benefits (Oklahoma Management and Enterprise Services, 2013a, p. 17). The principal employee benefits are retirement, health care, sick leave, disability benefits, and death benefits. Oklahoma's overall position regarding its benefits is at or above the 75th percentile of the market. When the benefits program is considered on its own, independent of salary, Oklahoma's benefits are about 30% above market. TRS recommends a multi-year plan to change the mix between salary and benefits (Oklahoma Management and

Enterprise Services, 2013b, p. 17), which was to have started with pension reform since the state's highest level of benefit costs are for retirement and health care.

The remuneration and pension plans have become law. There was little doubt about the pay raise proposal passing because it had substantial bipartisan support, including strong backing from the governor and the Oklahoma Public Employees Association. The pension plan did not have the same broad support, in large part because it has received substantial pushback from many state employees. Representatives of the firefighters, Oklahoma Education Association, the Oklahoma Retired Education Association, and Oklahoma Corrections Professions questioned the administration's reasons for pursuing the new pension plan. The executive director of the Oklahoma Retired Educators Association charged that the state's leaders "appear to want to . . . retire many of our public employees into poverty" (Krehbiel, 2013). Even though defined-contribution would only apply to new employees, the group was concerned that funding it would shortchange financing the current system.

The third of the three reform plans that will directly affect employees' finances will only be relevant to an unfortunate few. These are the public servants who are injured on the job. The new system transfers the claims and benefits process from a judicially-based to an administratively-based procedure. Supporters of the change claim it will be advantageous to both employers and employees. While most observers agree that the new system will need "fine tuning," some are concerned that the law's permitting appeals committees to be selected by employers will not meet due process requirements for impartiality (Carter, 2014). The Workers' Compensation Commission was created in 2013 and began handling injury and illness claims in February 2014.

VIII. CONCLUSION

We could not agree more with O.C. McSuite (2002, p. 98), who said "Public service is service, and as such must always be seen in personal terms." These words echo those of Marlyn La Vergne, the Haskell County social services worker we met in the introduction to this chapter. It is just a fact of life that day in and day out, through good and bad times, Oklahoma public servants make provisions for the citizens of our state. And for the most part, state employees earn less than those in the private sector even though they generally have more advanced levels of education. The lingering recession and current fiscal policies make it hard to adequately manage the public programs that citizens deserve from their government. We can only wait to see if the reforms being implemented by the current administration supplement and lift up the conditions under which public administration is carried out in Oklahoma.

THE OKLAHOMA JUDICIARY

Keith Rollin Eakins

Scarcely any political question arises in the United States that is not resolved, sooner or later, into a judicial question.

Alexis de Tocqueville, *Democracy in America*

I. INTRODUCTION

T he Oklahoma judiciary jumps in and out of the public's consciousness in episodic fashion. We tend to focus on the courts during times of scandal, such as when revelations of bribery rocked the Oklahoma Supreme Court in 1965, or in the midst of high profile cases such as the state trial of Terry Nichols, the co-conspirator in the bombing of the Murrah Building in Oklahoma City. After the general interest in such incidents wane, the courts retreat to their usual position of low prominence (see e.g. Baum & Kemper, 1994).

But astute students of politics realize that the courts deserve more consistent attention than is given them by the public. Oklahoma courts make important decisions each year that impact the citizens of the state. The rights, duties and liability of those involved in criminal code violations, personal injury occurrences, real estate transactions, business contracts, divorce litigation, and numerous other matters are determined by decisions from Oklahoma appellate and trial courts. For example, if a college student suffers a broken nose in a barroom brawl in Norman, Oklahoma and sues the bar owner, Oklahoma tort doctrines—products of the Oklahoma Supreme Court's jurisprudence—are used to determine whether the bar owner is liable in an Oklahoma trial court. And it is an Oklahoma trial court judge who will decide the admissibility of evidence, guide the jury's decision making in a jury trial, or determine liability in a bench trial. In fact, most of the legal questions and conflicts encountered by Oklahomans are governed by the decisions and policy making of Oklahoma trial and appellate courts. Oklahoma courts are important due both to the impact they have on individual cases as well as how the totality of their case decisions shape the contours of the legal landscape that affects our lives.

This chapter first sets forth the structure of the Oklahoma judiciary examining the trial courts, intermediate appellate courts, and final appellate courts. It then looks at how criminal and civil matters proceed through the courts. Next, it discusses the various judges and justices in

Oklahoma, how they are chosen, and analyzes the advantages and disadvantages of the various selection systems. Finally, it reviews the caseloads of the Oklahoma courts and highlights the policymaking impact of the Oklahoma high courts.

II. THE STRUCTURE OF THE OKLAHOMA JUDICIARY

The judiciary of Oklahoma is unique in its design and operation (See Figure 8–1). Most notably, it features two "courts of last resort" that hear final appeals of state civil and criminal law. With the exception of Texas, all other states feature only one high court. The structure of the Oklahoma judiciary reflects both the traditions of the state's populist past as well as more modern efforts at reform. In this section, we will explain how the various Oklahoma courts operate at both the trial and appellate level, and discuss the different types of jurisdiction, or authority to hear cases, they possess.

An Introduction to the Oklahoma Trial Courts

Trial courts are the courts that consider cases as they first enter the legal system. At this level in the court system, one judge presides over a

FIGURE 8–1 The Oklahoma Court System

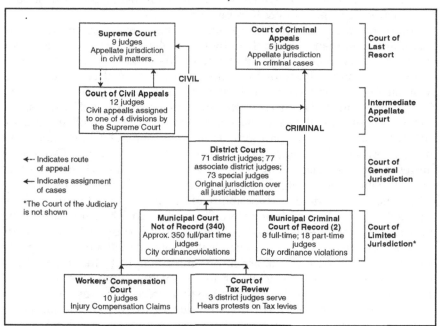

SOURCE: State of Oklahoma. The Judiciary. Annual Report, FY-94, Administrative Office of the Courts, 1994.

case involving one or more plaintiffs and defendants (both of whom can be referred to generically as "parties"). The **plaintiff** is the party who files a civil or criminal action and the **defendant** is the party who defends himself in a criminal case or denies a claim brought in a civil case. A **criminal case** is one in which the government attempts to punish someone for conduct that has been deemed a crime by a legislative body. For example, a woman was charged for violating the Oklahoma statute 21 O.S. 1971 § 22 forbidding "willfully and wrongfully committing an act injurious to public morals and openly outraging public decency" when she exposed her breasts and pubic area and danced in close proximity to a male patron's face in the "Satan's Lounge" in Tulsa, Oklahoma (see *State v. Walker 568 P.2d 286* (1977)). A civil case, on the other hand, involves any issue that is not criminal in nature. Specifically, a **civil case** is one that is brought to enforce, redress or protect the rights and duties individuals and organizations might legally owe each other. For example, if an Oklahoma man abandons his family and takes off to Alaska to work with his girlfriend on a fishing scow, his wife might file a divorce action seeking to end the marriage. Or suppose an Oklahoma concert promoter enters into a contract with the rock band "The White Stripes" to put on a show in Muskogee, Oklahoma, and the group fails to show up because the lead singer was jailed for urinating on the stage during the last concert. The concert promoter might sue the band to recover the revenue lost from the cancelled show.

Trial courts are those generally featured in cinematic legal dramas and court television reality shows such as *Judge Judy*. In a trial court, attorneys introduce evidence related to a case, whether it is civil or criminal. This may include examining one or more of the parties on the witness stand, presenting alibis for their clients, cross-examining witnesses against their clients, introducing physical evidence such as a gun found at a murder scene, or presenting expert witnesses such as a plastic surgeon testifying about a botched "extreme make-over." The judge sits as a trial gatekeeper deciding which evidence to allow the jury to consider, and which to exclude due to a lack of credibility, relevance, prejudicial impact, or other reasons. Cases are decided in either jury trials where, depending on the type of case, six to twelve members of the community determine the fate of the litigants or in bench trials where the judge assumes the role of the jury.

The Types of Oklahoma Trial Courts

The trial courts of Oklahoma are broken down into two basic types: courts of limited jurisdiction and courts of general jurisdiction. Jurisdiction is defined as the authority of a court to decide a case. **Courts of limited jurisdiction** are those that only have authority to hear specific types of cases. For example, the workers' compensation courts used to consider claims of employee-related injuries. The passage of SB1062 in 2013 replaced the workers' compensation courts with an administrative system headed by three commissioners. There are now three Oklahoma courts of limited jurisdiction: 1) the **court of tax review** that determines tax-related complaints; 2) the **court on the judiciary** that hears complaints against judges and has the authority to remove them for bad behavior; and 3) the **municipal criminal courts** that decides minor criminal violations of municipal laws (League of Women Voters of Oklahoma, 1994). The municipal criminal courts are the most common of the courts of limited jurisdiction and also hear the lion's share of cases. An example of a typical municipal court case could involve a student who is speeding down Main Street in Edmond, Oklahoma, twenty miles per hour over the speed limit and is pulled over and cited by a police officer. The speeding ticket is a formal accusation of violating an Edmond ordinance, so if the student contests the ticket his case would be heard in the Edmond Municipal Court.

Courts of general jurisdiction have the authority to consider cases involving a broad range of legal issues. The **district courts** are the only courts of general jurisdiction in Oklahoma. They decide all civil cases originating under state law and all cases involving violations of state criminal statutes. Oklahoma is divided into twenty-six judicial districts and all but four encompass more than one county (Lawler & Spurrier, 1991). However, each courthouse in Oklahoma's seventy-seven counties has an operating district court. So if an Oklahoma City woman, Crystal Method, is arrested and charged with operating a methamphetamine (meth) lab in her basement, she would appear in the Oklahoma County District Court to face the state criminal charges. Or if a Tulsa man, Cliff Clumsy, sues Wal-Mart for negligence after he slips and falls on a box of super-sized McDonalds French fries left on the floor, his civil action would be filed in the Tulsa County District Court.

An Introduction to the Appellate Courts of Oklahoma

Appellate courts have **appellate jurisdiction**: the authority to review cases that have been decided previously in a trial court. Typically, appellate courts receive cases when one or more parties is dissatisfied with the outcome in a trial court and files an **appeal**—a formal request to review the decision of the trial court. In Oklahoma, like every other state in the country, everyone is entitled to one "appeal of right." In other words, every person involved in a formal legal proceeding is guaranteed the right to have the decision reviewed by a higher court to ensure it is fair. So if the case of Crystal Method, the alleged meth lab operator, goes to a jury trial and the defendant is found guilty, she has the right to appeal the case to an appellate court and present arguments that her conviction should be reversed. For example, if her attorney showed up intoxicated in court and dozed off during the trial, the defendant may be able to get the appellate court to overturn her conviction on the grounds she was denied her Sixth Amendment right to have effective legal representation. Or if Wal-Mart loses its "slip and fall" case in a jury trial, it could file an appeal asking for a reversal alleging that the trial court jury erred as the store had put up an orange cone next to the French fry mess and the plaintiff had six toes on each foot making him uniquely susceptible to falling.

While appellate courts are decidedly different from trial courts due to their appellate jurisdiction, they are also distinct in how they operate. Unlike trial courts that have one judge assigned to a case, these courts have between three and nine judges who review the records of the trial proceedings of the lower courts and decide the appeals. Appellate courts typically do not consider any additional evidence when they review the decisions of the trial courts. For example, in the previous hypothetical case, Wal-Mart would not be allowed to have its employees testify in front of the appellate court reviewing the case. Only the attorneys representing the parties are permitted to communicate with the appellate court. The exception to this rule is if a party forgoes legal representation and chooses to represent himself.

In deciding cases, appellate court judges peruse the **record**—a transcribed recording of the proceedings from the trial court—and consider the **briefs**—written legal arguments—of the plaintiffs' and defendants' attorneys. Sometimes an appellate court holds **oral arguments** where attorneys present legal and policy arguments to the judges and respond to their questions. The judges later meet in a private **conference** where they discuss the case and vote on its outcome. For a party to win, he or she must get a majority of the judges' votes. One of the judges in the majority group is assigned to write the **opinion of the court**. Often with the assistance of one or more law clerks, the judge researches the case issues in more depth and writes an opinion giving legal and policy justifications for the case outcome. If the other judges in the majority group agree with the reasoning in the opinion, they sign it and it becomes the official opinion of the court majority. Any judges not part of the majority vote may also write a **dissenting opinion** where they express disagreement with the majority opinion. However, it is the opinion of the majority of the court that is authoritative and determines the outcome of the case.

The Types of Oklahoma Appellate Courts

There are two classifications of Oklahoma appellate courts: intermediate courts of appeal and courts of last resort. An **intermediate court of appeals** is designated so as its decisions can be appealed to a higher court of last resort. A **court of last resort**, on the other hand, is the final court of appeal in the state system.

The **Oklahoma Court of Civil Appeals** is an intermediate court of appeals that hears appeals of civil cases from the Oklahoma trial courts. There are four divisions in the Court of Civil Appeals, each having three judges. Two of the divisions are located in Oklahoma City and two in Tulsa. In most states an initial appeal is filed directly with the intermediate court of appeals. In Oklahoma, an initial appeal is filed with the Oklahoma Supreme Court, which assigns it to one of the four divisions of the Court of Civil Appeals. After receiving the case, the division's three-judge panel reviews the trial court record, the briefs of the attorneys, and on rare occasions holds oral arguments (Simpson, 2000). One of the three judges on the panel is assigned the task of writing the court's decision which must be supported by at least one of the other panel judges to be adopted as the opinion of the court. If a party is dissatisfied with the decision, he or she may seek further review with the Oklahoma Supreme Court.

The **Oklahoma Supreme Court** is the court of last resort for all civil cases involving issues of Oklahoma law. A party can appeal a decision of one of the divisions of the Court of Civil Appeals by filing a **petition for a writ of certiorari** with the Oklahoma Supreme Court. However, the court declines to hear the majority of these "cert" petitions as it has the authority to pick and choose only those cases it deems important. What types of cases do the court consider "cert-worthy?" There is no precise answer to this question but the court has set forth some considerations. Cases concerning issues of law over which there is disagreement among the lower courts, cases conflicting with Oklahoma Supreme Court or U.S. Supreme Court decisions, or cases involving important and novel issues may be more likely to be granted cert review (Administrative Office of the Courts, 1995b).

The Oklahoma Supreme Court also has the authority to hear initial appeals and thus may choose not to assign some cases to the Court of Civil Appeals if it determines that the case involves "new, first-impression issues, or important issues of great public concern..." (Administrative Office of the Courts, 1995b, p. 14). However, the vast majority of initial appeals are assigned to the Court of Civil Appeals.

Finally, the Oklahoma Supreme Court enjoys powers beyond hearing civil appeals as it has general superintending control over all lower courts and all agencies, boards, and commissions created by law. It also has original jurisdiction (i.e., it is the first court to decide) over initiative and referendum petitions as well as cases involving the executive and legislative departments of state government (League of Women Voters, 1994).

The Oklahoma Supreme Court has nine members, and decides cases "**en banc**" or, in other words, with all nine of the justices in attendance. In order for a party to win their case, he or she must attract a majority vote of at least five of the nine justices. If a party loses in the Oklahoma Supreme Court he or she can file a petition for a writ of certiorari with the Supreme Court of the United States if the case involves a question concerning the U.S. Constitution. But fewer than two percent of the petitions filed are granted cert by the Supreme Court of the United States (Epstein, et al, 2003), so the Supreme Court of Oklahoma generally has the last word on the cases it decides.

The **Oklahoma Court of Criminal Appeals** is the court of last resort for criminal cases originating in the Oklahoma district and municipal courts. Appeals of all criminal cases, ranging from traffic violations to murder, are decided by this court. There are five members of the court who, like the justices of the Oklahoma Supreme Court, hear cases en banc. In order

LEADERSHIP PROFILE

NOMA D. GURICH
Justice, Supreme Court of the State of Oklahoma, District No. 3

JUSTICE NOMA DIANE GURICH was born on September 26, 1952 in South Bend, Indiana. Although she is a Hoosier by birth, she is a resident of Oklahoma by choice. Justice Gurich's great grandparents settled near Grace-mont, Oklahoma in1904. Her grand-mother and grandfather were married on December 24, 1906 in Anadarko. Her mother was born in Anadarko in 1921. She resided in Oklahoma until 1945, when she and her husband, a returning veteran of World War II, moved to Indiana.

Courtesy Justice Noma D. Gurich

In 1978, Gurich received her Juris Doctorate degree from the College of Law of the University of Oklahoma. While at OU, she was an editor of the *American Indian Law Review* and received the Professional Responsibility Award. In 2011, OU College of Law Chapter of the Order of the Coif academic society selected her as an honorary member.

Gurich has been a judge in the state of Oklahoma for over 24 years. Justice Gurich has the unique distinction of having been appointed to a judicial office by four (4) governors of Oklahoma, after being nominated by the constitutionally created Judicial Nominating Commission. Justice Gurich was appointed to the Supreme Court, District 3 by Governor Brad Henry on January 7, 2011. She took office on February 15, 2011. She is only the third woman justice to serve on the Supreme Court of Oklahoma since statehood.

Prior to her judicial career, Justice Gurich practiced law in Oklahoma City for 10 years. In 1982, Gurich joined the firm of Abowitz & Welch, later became a partner, and remained there until her appointment to the Workers' Compensation Court. From 1978 to 1982, she was an associate with the law firm of Cheek, Cheek & Cheek in Oklahoma City.

Gurich served as a faculty member for the OU Law School Graduate School of Successful Trial Advocacy for several years. Justice Gurich is a guest speaker in both law school and college classes. She is a frequent speaker for continuing legal education courses.

Justice Gurich is also involved in service to her community. She is past President of the Kiwanis Club of Oklahoma City (2006–07). She was only the second woman to serve as President of the 90-year-old club. Gurich has been a member of the Kiwanis Club since 1998 and served as President-Elect, Vice-President and a member of the Board of Directors. She is a volunteer for many community projects including the OKC Festival of the Arts, Kiwanis projects helping children in the community and is an annual bell ringer for the Salvation Army. She serves annually on the Application Screening Committee for the Oklahoma School of Science and Mathematics. She served on the Board of Trustees for the Oklahoma Annual Conference of the United Methodist Church, Inc. from 2003–2011.

Judge Gurich is an active member of St. Luke's United Methodist Church, where she has served in various leadership roles, including Chair of the Administrative Board, Chair of the Management Council and as Trustee. She is a monthly volunteer Mobile Meals driver and TV camera operator. She served as a missionary to Russia in 1993, 1997, 2000, 2002, and 2004. Recently, Justice Gurich served as the host to a delegation of Ukrainian law professors and other legal professionals sponsored by the International Rule of Law Consortium and the Open World Leadership Center, a nonpartisan international exchange agency funded by Congress.

Justice Gurich is married to John E. Miley, General Counsel of the Oklahoma Employment Security Commission.

to win a case in the Court of Criminal Appeals, litigants must get at least three votes from the five justices.

III. The Oklahoma Criminal Court Process

The Formal Stages of the Oklahoma Criminal Court Process

Criminal cases begin with a district attorney (DA) filing one or more charges against a defendant. A **charge** is a formal accusation that one has violated an Oklahoma statute forbidding a criminal activity such as bestiality, murder, driving under the influence of alcohol, etc. The next step is the **arraignment**, in which a judge reads the charges alleged against the defendant and the defendant enters a plea of guilty or not guilty. If the accused faces a possible sentence of incarceration, she has a constitutional right to have an attorney represent her. Typically, those who can afford it hire private counsel and those who cannot get an attorney appointed to them by the trial court free of charge. Defendants usually plead not guilty at this stage, and most are freed with the understanding they must return for subsequent court proceedings. Some of those freed pending trial may be required to post a bond, a sum of money that is forfeited if they fail to return. In considering the amount of the bond that must be posted, a judge will consider the severity of the crime, the defendant's criminal record, her ties to the community, and the danger she may pose to the community.

After arraignment, the vast majority of the criminal cases are resolved without ever going to trial. At least 90 percent of all criminal cases in state and federal courts are resolved through plea bargaining (Carp & Stidham, 2004, p. 218). **Plea bargaining** is an agreement reached between the prosecutor and the defense counsel whereby the defendant agrees to plead guilty in exchange for some leniency promised by the DA. If a plea bargain cannot be reached, then most cases go to a preliminary hearing. At the **preliminary hearing** the judge decides whether there is enough evidence against the defendant to force her to stand trial. Specifically, the prosecutor must present evidence and testimony to prove that there is sufficient "probable cause" that the defendant committed a crime. Sometimes, the defendant's attorney will cross examine the prosecution's witnesses and cast doubt upon the evidence in an attempt to make the prosecution's case look weak and get the charges dismissed. If the judge decides that probable cause has been met, the case will be set for trial and pre-trial motions.

Before the trial, the DA and defense attorney usually appear before the trial court judge and make **pre-trial motions**. At this stage, the attorneys argue that some evidence should be kept out of the trial, that some witnesses must or cannot testify, or that the case should be thrown out. For example, in drug trafficking cases it is common for the defense attorney to move to suppress the evidence of drugs purportedly found by police. The Fourth Amendment requires that police conduct searches properly. If a police search was done illegally, such as a home search without a valid warrant, the trial judge may rule, for example, that the twenty-five pounds of marijuana discovered are inadmissible in court. Or in a rape case, the DA may argue that an alibi witness for the defendant, who claims the defendant was not at the rape scene, is mentally ill and incompetent to testify. After the pre-trial motions are decided, the case is ready to go to trial.

During the **trial**, the prosecution presents its evidence against the defendant and asks for a "guilty" verdict and conviction. The defendant also has the opportunity to discredit the physical evidence and testimony introduced by the prosecution, and may choose to offer its own evidence. After both sides have presented their cases, the jury (or judge if the defendant has requested a "bench trial" instead of a jury trial) meets to determine the guilt or innocence of the defendant. Members of the jury will find the defendant guilty if they believe the prosecution has proven "**beyond a reasonable doubt**" that the defendant committed the crime. Under Oklahoma law, if the case involves a "petty" crime that is punishable by incarceration of six months or less, then the "guilty" verdict of the jury need not be unanimous. However, if it is a serious crime punishable by more than six months in prison, then a jury finding of "guilty" must be unanimous— i.e. all of the jurors must agree to find the defendant guilty.

If a defendant has been found guilty by a jury or judge, she must be sentenced by the trial court. In a jury trial, juries may recommend a punishment. Typically, **sentencing** occurs right after convictions for minor offenses, or when a defendant has pled guilty. In more serious cases, such as those involving felonies, formal sentencing will occur at a later hearing after the judge receives a pre-sentence report. **Pre-sentence reports** are sentence recommendations prepared by the probation department reflecting assessments from the prosecutor, the defense attorney, and the probation officer. The judge also must consider the legal range of punishments for the crime. For example, if a defendant is convicted of participating in a riot and encouraging other riot participants to engage in acts of violence, he faces imprisonment for two to ten years according to Oklahoma sentencing statutes. In determining the length of the sentence the judge, in addition to considering the pre-sentence report, would also take into account any criminal record of the defendant, his prospects for rehabilitation, his remorse, the societal harm stemming from the criminal act, and any other factors he considered relevant.

Finally, a defendant who has been found guilty has the right to appeal his or her conviction to the Oklahoma Court of Criminal Appeals. In his or her **appeal,** the individual convicted asks the Court of Criminal Appeals to overturn the conviction or sentence imposed. Typically the convicted individual, now known as the **"appellant,"** has an attorney to represent him who files an **appellate brief** with the Court of Criminal Appeals arguing that the conviction and/or sentence was unfair or based upon legal mistakes. The DA, now known as the **"appellee"** also files a brief with the Court of Criminal Appeals arguing that the conviction and sentence should be upheld. The court also may schedule oral arguments in important cases. During the **oral arguments**, the defense attorney and DA present their legal arguments to the judges who probe them with legal questions. This procedure only involves the court and the attorneys from each side arguing the legality of the original trial. In other words, no new evidence of any kind is submitted—neither the defendant nor any other witnesses testify. After reviewing the briefs from the appellant and appellee, the transcript of the trial (every word and piece of evidence from the trial is carefully recorded), and hearing the oral argument (if one was scheduled) the Court of Criminal Appeals meets in a conference to make a decision. The court's **decision** need not be unanimous—a majority vote of the five judges is all that is required to reverse or affirm the trial court (see *The Appellate Courts* section above). This decision is final unless the case is appealed to and accepted by the Supreme Court of the United States, an occurrence which is highly unlikely since the Court rejects more than 98 percent of the cases appealed to it.

Plea Bargaining: The Norm of the Oklahoma
Criminal Court Process

While it is important to understand the formal steps of the Oklahoma Criminal Court process discussed above, it is at least equally important to understand the process of plea bargaining since the vast majority of cases never make it to trial. Generally, prosecutors and defense attorneys strike a plea bargain that allows both sides to resolve the case with some certainty as to what charge, if any, the defendant will be convicted of and what type of penalty he or she will receive. These "deals" may be scrutinized by the trial judge who examines them for appropriateness and gives approval generally. Plea bargaining involves either charge bargaining, sentence bargaining, or a combination of both.

Charge bargaining involves either **charge reduction**, where a prosecutor agrees to reduce a charge to one less serious, **charge deletion**, where a prosecutor drops one or more charges against a defendant formally accused of multiple crimes, or a combination of both (Carp & Stidham, 2004). For example, in 1992, while serving a sentence in an Oklahoma state prison, Gary Ray Preston and three co-defendants murdered another inmate. Preston was charged with first-degree but pled guilty to a reduced charge of second-degree murder. If he had been convicted of first degree murder he would have been eligible to be punished by death, but as the charge was reduced to second-degree murder the worst possible sentence was imprisonment for life (Preston received an eighty-year sentence). Here, the prosecutor and Preston entered into a charge reduction plea bargain.

Sometimes DAs will agree to drop, or delete, a criminal charge in order to get a conviction on other charges. In 1999, Mississippian James Harold Smith pled guilty to felony counts of kidnapping and assault in exchange for the Assistant DA of Woodward County, Oklahoma, dropping a maiming charge. Smith had locked up his common-law wife in the sleeper cab of his truck, denied her food and water, and periodically beat and tortured her with a modified cattle prod. Smith received a suspended sentence, a fine, and was ordered to receive mental health treatment (Associated Press, 1999a).

Sentence bargaining occurs when the DA promises to request that the judge impose a lighter sentence if the defendant agrees to plead guilty. A defendant and his attorney can expect that a DA's sentence recommendation will be considered seriously by the judge. If DA sentencing recommendations held no sway, then the plea bargaining system upon which all parties, including judges, rely would break down.

In the case of James Harold Smith, it appears that both a sentence bargain and charge deletion bargain were made. The victim had fled back to Mississippi, was in hiding, and refused to testify against Smith. Facing a very shaky case without the victim's testimony, the prosecution stated, "Under [the] circumstances we felt that obtaining the two major felony convictions with the treatment provisions was as good as could reasonably be expected" (Associated Press, 1999a). In other words, faced with the very real possibility of acquittal, the prosecution most likely recommended a suspended sentence as an inducement to obtaining guilty pleas, which amount to convictions, on two of the three felony charges.

The realities of the criminal justice system are that all of the players—district attorneys, defense attorneys, and judges—depend upon a system of plea bargaining. Plea bargaining offers distinct benefits to everyone involved in a criminal case. First of all, going to trial is risky for both sides. As one Oklahoma County District Court judge recounted, "You never know what will happen. Sometimes I preside over cases where I would have bet my house that the jury would have convicted the defendant and did not. And then other cases where I thought the D.A. had a weak case, the jury finds the defendant guilty." So plea bargaining guarantees the prosecution a conviction in the case, while at the same time guaranteeing defendants that they will not get the most severe punishment that is possible. The judge and the DA benefit as plea bargaining saves time and allows faster resolution of the case docket. A jury trial can be very lengthy, and judges constantly feel the pressure of an overwhelming caseload, so the more plea bargains that are reached the more efficiently judges can do their jobs.

Finally, the victims of crime may prefer to resolve a case through plea bargaining to save them the agony of reliving the experience through a prolonged trial. A victim of rape, for example, may need to testify against the accused and face a humiliating and emotionally painful cross-examination by a defense attorney. Defense attorneys in rape cases often take the **"nuts and sluts" tactic** of defending their client by portraying the victim as promiscuous and consenting to the sex act, claiming the accuser is mentally unstable and fabricating her story, or both. In summary, since all of the parties often have much to gain from the certainty and expediency of resolving a case through plea bargaining, it is not surprising that the norm of "let's make a deal" predominates the legal culture of the criminal justice system of Oklahoma and the rest of the United States as well.

Despite its prevalence, the practice of plea bargaining has some strong opponents. Some decry it as a deal that lets criminals "off the hook" receiving less punishment than is fair. Others concerned with the rights of the accused attack the system as one that pressures those in a vulnerable position to give up their constitutional rights to confront their accusers and be judged by a jury of their peers. Yet some scholars who study plea bargaining view it as a rational and efficient way of resolving cases. They suggest that the outcome is generally fair since the final "deal" reflects the reasoned judgment of professional lawyers who consider the strength of the evidence against the defendant, the defendant's prior criminal record, the likelihood of conviction, and the preferences of the victim (Padgett, 1985).

IV. THE OKLAHOMA CIVIL COURT PROCESS

The majority of cases filed in the Oklahoma courts are civil matters. This is typical in other state courts as well as civil cases encompass a wide spectrum of issues from abandonment to zoning. Yet, civil cases tend not to attract the same attention as criminal cases, probably because the issues involved are often not as dramatic and salacious as those in criminal cases. On the other hand, civil cases sometimes spring from the very same incident that gives rise to a criminal case because the criminal action also violates civil laws designed to protect personal rights. For example, after O.J. Simpson was acquitted for the murders of Nicole Brown Simpson and Ronald Goldman, he was found liable in a civil action against him for "wrongful death." In losing the civil case, Simpson did not face incarceration, a penalty in criminal cases, but was ordered to pay the victims' families millions of dollars to compensate them for the loss of their loved ones.

The following section explains the formal stages of how civil cases move through the Oklahoma Courts. While reading, keep in mind that the legal system in our society has a way of filtering out cases early on due to a settlement agreement of the parties or summary judgment. In fact, approximately ninety percent of the civil cases in Oklahoma and the country never make it to a formal trial.

The Formal Stages of the Oklahoma Civil Court Process

In Oklahoma, most civil cases begin when one or more parties involved in a dispute file a petition in a district court. A **petition** is a formal legal statement that briefly sets forth the grounds for the lawsuit and asks for some kind of relief in the form of money, specific performance, etc. The party who files the petition is designated as the plaintiff and must **serve** the petition to the defendant either pesrsonally or by certified mail so the defendant has notice of the lawsuit. The defendant files an **answer** to the petition which either: 1) denies the allegations in the petition; 2) offers defenses to the petition; 3) makes counter-claims against the plaintiff; or 4) alleges any combination of the three. At this point the defendant could also file a motion to dismiss the petition alleging the plaintiff failed to state a claim recognized by law. These formal allegations by the parties of their claims and defenses are referred to as **pleadings**.

Imagine that Brittany Notsobright, an Oklahoma college student who wanted to get a base tan for Spring Break, went to a tanning business, "Leatherfaces Unlimited," fell asleep in the tanning bed and woke up two hours later with first degree burns on her face. Her lawyer, Petty Fogger, files a petition in the district court making these allegations against the company and seeks $3 million in damages for pain and suffering, medical expenses, and compensation for Brittany's physical disfigurement due to the company's negligence. After being served the petition, Leatherfaces Unlimited files an answer denying some of Brittany's allegations and claiming that Brittany was already burned when she came in to tan, was intoxicated, and set the timer herself so Leatherfaces Unlimited was not responsible for Brittany's misfortune.

If the petition is not dismissed, then the case goes to the discovery phase. During **discovery**, parties try to get useful evidence from each other to use at trial. The purpose of discovery is to allow both sides to get evidence related to the case so the trial can be fair and one side won't be surprised with new evidence at the time of trial. It is also designed to facilitate settlement of the case without a trial. Mechanisms of discovery used by attorneys typically include depositions, interrogatories, requests for production of documents, requests for permission to enter upon property to conduct inspections, requests to admit facts or authenticate documents, requests for an examination of a party by a physician, and subpoenas for witnesses to appear with documents. Some of these discovery tools are self-explanatory, but others require brief explanation.

Depositions involve lawyers from one side questioning the party or witnesses from the other side under oath. The depositions are recorded and transcribed and copies are given to both sides. In addition to the useful information provided by depositions, attorneys may use them to discredit a witness if he or she makes contradictory statements during the trial. **Interrogatories** are questions given to the opposing side asking for written responses. This is also useful for finding information and discovering documents relevant to the case. And requests for an examination of a party by a physician may be ordered by a court if the physical or mental health of a litigant is at issue (Carp, Stidham, & Manning, 2004).

In our hypothetical case, there are a number of potential discovery requests. Brittany's lawyer, Petty Fogger, would want a copy of her tanning contract to see if she agreed to assume any risk in tanning or to see whether Leatherfaces Unlimited followed the contract's stated tanning procedures. And Petty Fogger may want to have a tanning bed expert visit the business to examine the tanning bed in question for defects. Leatherfaces Unlimited may want to depose Brittany to ask her questions such as how much alcohol she consumed before tanning, how much tanning she had done before the incident, whether she really fell asleep or just purposely reset the timer for an extra ninety minutes, etc. And the tanning company may also want its own physician to examine Brittany to see if she really suffered injuries as severe as she claimed. If there are any disagreements between the parties on providing evidence during discovery, it is the responsibility of the district court judge to resolve them.

Because the process of discovery often eliminates the uncertainty over what evidence each side has most cases are settled and some are resolved through summary judgment. A **settlement** occurs when both parties agree to resolve the dispute in lieu of proceeding to a trial. A **summary judgment** occurs when a judge grants a party's motion to decide the case in his or her favor because no legitimate issues exist necessitating a trial.

If the parties are unable to reach a settlement, and the matter is not resolved through a summary judgment, the case gets scheduled for a pre-trial conference. A **pretrial conference** is set by the trial court judge to discuss the case with the lawyers and to allow the lawyers to share a list of witnesses and evidence that they wish to present at trial. The conference is also used to get both sides to stipulate or agree to certain uncontested facts in order to narrow the focus of the trial to only those issues in dispute. So the lawyers for Brittany and Leatherfaces Unlimited may stipulate that Brittany entered the tanning establishment at 2:00 p.m., signed in, and then left at 4:15 p.m., so these facts will not have to be established at the trial. These conferences are also used by many judges to try to persuade the parties to resolve the case before trial. Many district court judges face heavy caseloads and desire to resolve their case dockets efficiently, and the easiest way to do this is to avoid a time-consuming trial.

Sometimes parties in a dispute are unable to negotiate a settlement and opt to take the case to **trial** which is conducted in a manner similar to the criminal trial mentioned above, yet is guided by different rules of procedure. In a typical civil trial, the judge or jury will decide in favor of a party's claim if it is supported by the "preponderance of the evidence." It is important to note that this standard of proof is much lower than the criminal standard of "beyond a reasonable doubt." To prove a case by a **preponderance of the evidence** one must establish only that it is "more likely than not" that a claim is valid. Criminal cases require a higher standard of proof because conviction often carries with it a unique stigma and severe punishment, such as incarceration. Thus, it is not surprising that in some cases, such as that involving O.J. Simpson discussed above, one is acquitted of criminal charges yet found liable in a civil case stemming from the same incident.

In a civil case decided by a jury, Oklahoma law requires that only three-fourths of the jurors agree in order to render a verdict. If the defendant is found liable by a judge or jury then a **judgment** is issued. In other words, a remedy must be determined or damages must be assessed in the case. For example, let's assume that Petty Fogger was able to convince a jury that Leatherfaces Unlimited was negligent in allowing Brittany Notso-bright to be burned by a defective tanning bed. The jury would then decide the **damages**—the amount of money that must be awarded to Brittany.

Since it lost the case at trial, Leatherfaces Unlimited may now file an appeal which will likely be assigned to the Oklahoma Court of Civil Appeals. Both parties will file briefs arguing their sides of the case, and the litigant receiving the majority of the votes from the three-judge panel will win the case. If the Oklahoma Court of Civil Appeals affirms the trial court decision and decides in favor of Brittany Notsobright, Leatherfaces Unlimited can file another appeal with the Supreme Court of Oklahoma through a petition for a writ of certiorari. However, unlike the first appeal which the court must consider, the second appeal is up to the discretion of the nine-member court and is typically not granted. If the Oklahoma high court chooses to "grant cert," it will review the briefs of the parties, the decisions of the lower courts, the trial court transcript, and may hold oral arguments where the attorneys for both parties present their sides of the case. The court then issues an opinion either reversing or affirming the decision of the Court of Civil Appeals (see *The Appellate Courts* section above).

Pre-Trial and Out-of-Court Settlements: The Norm of the Oklahoma Civil Court Process

Typically, only about 3% of all civil cases are "actually disposed of by jury or bench trial verdict" (U.S. Department of Justice, 2004, p. 2). Civil cases tend to be resolved through **pre-trial** and **out-of-court settlements** for reasons similar to those explaining the prevalence of plea bargains in criminal cases. Namely, parties may feel pressure to settle a case for fear of "losing it all" if they go to trial (Smith, 1999). Resolving cases before trial reduces uncertainty and allows the parties to control the outcome since the matter is removed from consideration by a judge and jury. Furthermore, trial judges in civil cases face the same pressures to process their crowded case dockets. The typical civil case is assigned to an Oklahoma district court judge with a sizable criminal caseload in addition to his or her civil case docket. Thus, trial court judges may take an active role in facilitating settlement of the cases pending before them. In fact, attorneys often complain of judges being "overbearing" during pre-trial negotiations, and may feel "coerced" into accepting settlement offers (Melone and Karnes, 2003, p. 187). Civil litigation also can be very time-consuming and expensive. The average civil suit takes nearly two years from start to finish (U.S. Department of Justice, 2004). And those involved in lawsuits may often pay exorbitant legal fees and endure other costs in the form of psychological stress, lost productivity, and general disruption of their daily lives. So there are several important incentives for litigants to resolve their disputes before taking the costly and uncertain step of going to trial.

Using a previous example of Cliff Clumsy who sues Wal-Mart for negligence after he slips and falls, both Cliff Clumsy and Wal-Mart may be better off to settle their case. If Wal-Mart offers to pay Cliff's medical expenses and a reasonable amount for his pain and suffering, it avoids an expensive trial and a potentially large damage award it loses. And if Cliff accepts the settlement, he will avoid the risk of losing the case, be able to pay his outstanding bills and maintain his household until he can get back to work. However, saying that both parties may be better off does not imply that the outcome is necessarily fair. It is often the "big guys" like Wal-Mart who come out ahead in litigation because, being able to withstand the inevitable delays in civil litigation, they are in a superior bargaining position compared to the "little guys" like Cliff Clumsy who cannot afford a lengthy legal battle (see Galanter, 1974). Cliff may feel forced to settle for an amount less than he considers fair because the fall made him unable to work and pay his bills and he will lose his house and car if he doesn't get money soon. On the other hand, Wal-Mart, a large corporation with "deep pockets," has the ability to keep operating its business without disruption and will not be bothered by any case delays that operate to the detriment of Cliff Clumsy.

V. JUDGES AND JUDICIAL SELECTION IN OKLAHOMA

Introduction: The Scandal and Resulting Reform

In Oklahoma, a variety of methods are used for selecting judges. Depending on the type of court on which they serve, judges may be chosen through non-partisan elections or various appointment methods. However, the current multiplicity of selection systems did not always exist. It is the result of a compromise produced from a political cauldron bubbling over from a judicial modernization movement, a major scandal in the highest echelon of the Oklahoma judiciary, and a clash over reform between state lawmakers (Simpson, 2000).

Prior to 1969, most state judges were elected on partisan ballots much in the way that a state representative or governor is chosen. From the office of supreme court justice down to the now defunct office of justice of the peace, Oklahoma judges were elected to terms of two to six years depending on the type of court on which they served. Elections made judges somewhat accountable to the people, but their inherent partisan and political nature made some question whether the system produced judges who could maintain fairness and impartiality in deciding cases. Thus, in the early 1960s, a national judicial reform movement took hold in Oklahoma. Prominent public organizations, such as the Oklahoma Bar Association and Oklahoma law schools began to endorse changes such as the "Missouri Plan" of judicial selection, which placed nominations of judges in the hands of a commission (Simpson, 2000).

Coincidentally, while reformers were pushing for an end to partisan judicial elections in Oklahoma, a shocking scandal erupted in the Supreme Court of Oklahoma. Three justices on the Supreme Court were accused of taking bribes which influenced their decisions in key cases. N.S. Corn, a former justice convicted of income tax evasion admitted to taking bribes while on the court. Corn also testified that two of his brethren on the court, justices Earl Welch and Napoleon Bonaparte Johnson, had similarly accepted bribes. Corn's revelations ended the careers of Welch and Johnson. Welch resigned his position to avoid imminent impeachment, while Johnson was impeached and removed from office by the Oklahoma legislature (Lawler & Spurrier, 1991).

This scandal was almost perfectly timed for those seeking changes in the Oklahoma courts, as it stoked the embers of reform into a raging fire. In 1966, Earl Sneed, a former law school dean from the University of Oklahoma, spearheaded a court reform initiative that was well-received by the press and would appear on a ballot for voter approval in 1968. Leaders in the Oklahoma legislature were now under enormous pressure to develop their own reform proposal, although many state lawmakers remained adamantly opposed to changing the status quo. In general, rural lawmakers wanted to keep the ability to elect their own local judges, whereas urban lawmakers favored the Missouri Plan which would take away selection decisions from the voters. Eventually, a compromise proposal was reached where the Missouri Plan would be implemented for appellate court selection, and non-partisan elections would operate to choose district court judges. This proposal was presented to voters as an amendment to the state constitution, and passed in the summer of 1967. Beaten to the punch by the legislature's compromise reform, Sneed's initiative went down in defeat in 1968 (Simpson, 2000).

Selection in the District Courts: Nonpartisan Elections

The judges serving in the district courts of Oklahoma hear all cases arising under state law. There are 71 district judges and 77 associate district judges, and they are chosen through nonpartisan elections for four year terms. In **nonpartisan elections**, voters choose district judges and associate district judges without the benefit of viewing party labels on ballots. If a district court judge draws no challenger after serving a term that judge is, in effect, retained for an additional term and the office is not listed on the ballot. When a district judge or associate district judge position becomes vacant then it is filled by the Judicial Nominating Commission and governor in the same way an appellate judgeship is selected (League of Women Voters of Oklahoma, 1994).

Judicial elections tend to be staid, uneventful and lacking in substance. Judges are restricted from discussing actual cases and how they would rule on specific issues so the campaign rhetoric is typically limited to vague claims of candidates possessing "solid experience" or being "a law and order " judge. Voters typically know very little about the candidates and, since Oklahoma judicial races are nonpartisan, they do not have party cues to guide their voting decisions. Consequently, voters may base their decisions on considerations such as which candidate has a last name that sounds familiar or bespeaks a favorable ethnic background (see e.g. Baum & Kemper, 1994).

Occasionally judicial races involve feuds and campaign shenanigans just as colorful and "down and dirty" as the scrappiest of non-judicial races. A case in point is the 1998 Pottawotomie County, Oklahoma race for associate district judge between Paula Sage and John D. Gardner. Campaign fliers were distributed showing Ms. Sage baring her breasts at a Halloween party. The flier claimed Sage would be "a disaster and embarrassment" if elected and listed "10 reasons ranging from allegations of unprofessional behavior to having a temper and a foul mouth." Ms. Sage claimed that the woman who took the photo worked for her opponent. "It was just kind of a lark deal. You grab the bottom of your shirt and flash a little bit. Someone grabs a camera and...I'm evidently the most unlucky woman in the world." Sage explained further, "I think people are going to see this for what it is, which is extremely, extremely dirty politics." Sage ended up losing the race by 355 votes (Associated Press, 1998).

Moreover, judicial candidates may not always follow the letter of the law that limits what they can say on the campaign trail. Oklahoma County District Judge Susan Caswell, a former prosecutor, waged an aggressive and ultimately successful campaign in 1998 by chiding her opponent, touting her experience prosecuting cases involving crimes against children, and vowing to continue to fight for victims if elected. Her campaign literature stated that she believed "justice requires a fair system for all, especially little children who may be too small or unable to speak for themselves." Because of this campaign, Caswell received a great deal of unwanted attention after she took office. Judge Caswell was investigated for ethics violations related to her campaign statements, and in a separate proceeding was ordered by the Oklahoma Court of Criminal Appeals to disqualify herself from a child abuse trial. The court justified its decision stating, "In this case...the facts demonstrate Judge Caswell's impartiality might reasonably be questioned." The court elaborated: "Because of the close proximity of the election and the filing of charges in this case and the campaign rhetoric exuded in this election, we understand appellant's concerns about getting a fair trial before this judge" (Associated Press, 2000a).

Selection in the Courts of Limited Jurisdiction

Municipal judges are selected for two-year terms according to the provisions of the charter of a particular city. A common practice is appointment by the mayor subject to approval by the city council.

The Court of Tax Review and the Court on the Judiciary do not employ their own judges. Judges serving on these courts come from the district courts, the Court of Criminal Appeals, and the Supreme Court of Oklahoma and are provided "necessary expenses" for their duties. The Court of Tax Review is comprised of district court judges chosen by Oklahoma Supreme Court. The Court on the Judiciary is divided into a trial division and an appellate division. The trial division is comprised of eight district judges chosen by the secretary of state, and one attorney chosen by the Oklahoma Bar Association board of governors. The appellate division is comprised of five district judges picked by the Secretary of State, two Supreme Court justices chosen by their fellow justices, one Court of Criminal Appeals judge tapped by that court, and one attorney selected by the Oklahoma Bar Association Board of Governors (League of Women Voters of Oklahoma, 1994).

Selecting Judges in the Appellate Courts of Oklahoma

Today, judges in the appellate courts of Oklahoma—the Court of Civil Appeals, the Criminal Court of Appeals, and the Supreme Court—are chosen through an appointive process. Named after the state where it was first adopted, the **Missouri Plan** features a Judicial Nominating Commission, an appointment by the governor, and a retention election for the appointee.

The **Judicial Nominating Commission** is made up of fifteen members who serve without pay. The Oklahoma Bar Association elects six members for staggered six-year terms, one from each congressional district as they existed in 1967. The governor selects six, one from each "old" congressional district, not more than three from one particular political party, and none may have lawyers as immediate relatives. The state legislature chooses two at-large members for two year terms. One is selected by the Senate President Pro Tempore, the other by the Speaker of the House of Representatives, and neither can be a lawyer or have a lawyer for a close relative. Finally, the Commission chooses one at-large member for a two-year term. No more than two of the three at-large members can be members of a specific political party (Oklahoma State Courts Network, 2014).

When a vacancy occurs in one of the appellate courts, the nominating commission interviews applicants and prepares a "short list" of their top three or four candidates for the open slot. Eligible candidates must be at least thirty years of age and a licensed practicing attorney or judge for at least five years. The list is then forwarded to the governor who chooses one of the three for appointment to the position.

If the successful appointee is in office for at least one year before the next general election, he or she must face a retention election. The **retention election** is nonpartisan in that there is no party label on the ballot, and noncompetitive in that the judge is not running against any other candidates. Voters must decide whether the judge or justice should be retained in office—they mark the ballot either "yes" or "no." If the majority of votes favor retaining the judge or justice, he or she can serve the remainder of the six-year term. Thereafter, judges and justices sit for retention elections every six years if they wish to serve additional terms. There are no term limits for judicial offices in Oklahoma (Lawler & Spurrier, 1991).

If job security is a central concern in one's career choice, one could do much worse than serving as an appellate court judge or justice. To date, no judges or justices in Oklahoma have lost a retention election. Such electoral safety is not an anomaly unique to Oklahoma. A study found that out of 4,588 such elections nationwide, only 52 judges were unseated. In other words, judges lose retention contests only about 1% of the time (Aspin, 1999).

Yet as the statistics show justices occasionally lose retention elections. And often these losses are the result of interest groups and others taking aim at individual judges for political reasons. For example, Tennessee high court justice Penny White lost her first retention contest after the Tennessee Conservative Union, the Republican Party, and Republican governor Don Sundquist all actively campaigned against her (Carp, Stidham, & Manning, 2004). While judicial seats are relatively safe under the Missouri Plan, judges unlucky enough to be the target of organized, moneyed political opposition are vulnerable.

Recent Republican Efforts to Change to the Appellate Courts

Recently the Republican-controlled Oklahoma legislature has made significant efforts to alter the Oklahoma appellate courts. The first successful maneuver was their changing the make-up of the state Judicial Nominating Commission. From 1967 until 2010 there were only thirteen commission members: six lawyers chosen by the Oklahoma bar, six non-lawyers chosen by the governor, and one at-large member chosen by the commission. In 2010, Republican legislators drafted a state question for voter approval adding two additional non-lawyer, at-large members to be chosen by the state legislature. The Oklahoma Chamber of Commerce vigorously supported State Question 752 and provided 82% of the financing aimed at passing the measure (National Institute on Money in State Politics, 2014). The provision easily passed, weakening the influence of attorneys in selecting appellate judges and increasing the likelihood of the selection of appellate judges with pro-Chamber judicial philosophies.

In 2012, the Oklahoma Supreme Court granted certiorari in a case challenging the validity of the Republican-supported **Comprehensive Lawsuit Reform Act of 2009.** Later that year, the Oklahoma Chamber of Commerce responded by issuing evaluations of individual Oklahoma Supreme Court justices according to their tendencies to broaden or restrict civil liability, a move viewed by many as an attempt to intimidate the high court justices. In June 2013, the Oklahoma Supreme Court struck down the tort reform law as unconstitutional and immediately afterward a furious T.W. Shannon, the former Republican Speaker of the Oklahoma House of Representatives, chastised the Court decrying them as judicial activists making policy as a "super legislature" (Justice at Stake, 2014).

Shannon matched his angry rhetoric by sponsoring a flurry of bills intending to dramatically change the Oklahoma courts. To summarize, these measures called for: requiring Senate confirmation of appellate judges; making lower court elections partisan; establishing performance reviews of appellate judges; mandating 12-year term limits for appellate judges; establishing a mandatory retirement age for judges; and diluting or even disassembling the Judicial Nominating Commission. Shannon's legislative retaliation against the courts proved to be short-lived and a casualty of his political ambition. When incumbent U.S. Senator Tom Coburn announced in early 2014 that he would retire, Shannon immediately resigned his Speaker position to run for Coburn's Senate seat. Shannon's judicial vendetta was not a high priority to the succeeding House Speaker, and the "court-packing" bills subsequently died (Justice at Stake, 2014).

The Effects of Selecting Judges Through Elective and Missouri Plan Systems

The elective and Missouri Plan systems are used to select judges in the Oklahoma district and appellate courts, respectively, and each places different emphases on two features: judicial independence and judicial accountability. **Judicial independence** means that judges are insulated from political pressures and have the freedom to apply the law as they see it. **Judicial accountability**, on the other hand, is the principle that judges in a democratic society are responsible to the people through mechanisms that allow popular control. In reality, there is a distinct tension between independence and accountability. One way to view it is as a continuum or trade off: the more independence judges are given, the less accountable to the people they become and vice versa. Figure 8–2 shows where the elective and Missouri Plan systems fit on this continuum.

The clearest example of a high independence and low accountability system can be seen in the lifetime appointment of federal judges (and a small number of state judges). These judges can act freely with little fear of political repercussions or losing their jobs as they are rarely removed from office. In fact, in the history of the United States only seven have been impeached and removed from office. The potential downside of lifetime appointment is that bad judges are nearly unaccountable. For example, a federal judge can be verbally abusive to litigants and lawyers, have a serious drinking problem, and ignore clear case precedent in making decisions, all with relative impunity. Yet on the upside, this freedom also allows a federal judge to make decisions he or she strongly believes are morally right without regard to political consequences.

Conversely, the more accountable judges are to the people, the less leeway they have to act according to their own beliefs and the more they have to consider their political environment. This is the case for elected judges. For example, an elected judge might feel pressure to make decisions against her conscience and sense of justice and may favor the prosecution in certain criminal cases fearing challengers or political groups will attack her as "soft on crime" in the next election. But the electoral check on judges also allows for easier removal of those who abuse their power or engage in dubious conduct on the bench. As judges are important policy makers, many argue that the elective system makes them more representative of and responsive to the values of the community in which they serve.

In between the extremes on the continuum of judicial accountability and independence lie the Missouri Plan judges. Their accountability is relatively low since they routinely win retention elections, yet it is greater than that of federal judges as some Missouri Plan judges, albeit in states other than Oklahoma, have been removed after being targeted by political

FIGURE 8–2 The Methods of Judicial Selection on the Continuum of Judicial Independence and Accountability

Independence			Accountability
Lifetime Appointment	Missouri Plan	Partisan Elections	

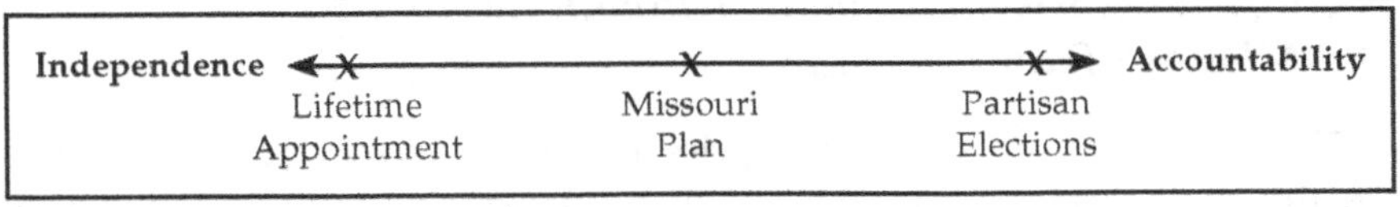

groups seeking to further their policy goals. Their independence is considerable as they are not constrained by the prospect of a contested election, yet it is less than of federal judges who need not consider the political ramifications of their decisions.

Which System is the "Best"—Elective or Missouri Plan?

Academics and politicians alike disagree on the question of which method of selection leads to the most fair and just legal system. As noted previously, this debate played out in the Oklahoma legislature decades ago and the resulting political compromise produced a variety of selection processes in the state. This debate resurfaced when Brad Henry, the former governor and state senator and chairman of the Judiciary Committee, sponsored bills in 1999 and 2000 to change the selection method of district judges from nonpartisan elections to the Missouri Plan. Henry's bill was precipitated by nasty incidents in 1998 such as the improper, bare-fisted campaign rhetoric splashed about in Judge Caswell's successful race and the indecent, bare-chested fliers flashed about in Paula Sage's unsuccessful judicial bid. While the bill looked promising and enjoyed some support, it faced great opposition and ultimately died after failing in two legislative sessions as many legislators preferred the local control of elections which the Missouri Plan lacked (Associated Press, 1999b, 2000b).

The current multiplicity of selection systems in Oklahoma bespeaks the difficulty in determining which method is "the best." Like most important questions, there is no simple answer. What is "fair" and "just" is not agreed upon by all. So a worthwhile approach may be to examine the *impact* of the elective and Missouri Plan systems. In other words, what differences result from the two selection methods? Interestingly, when one analyzes both systems, what becomes most evident are their similarities (Baum, 2004).

One striking commonality is the influence of the governor. Even the elective system for the district courts is impacted by the governor because a judicial vacancy is filled in accordance with the Missouri Plan: the governor selects one of the nominating commission's three candidates. After the governor appoints a replacement, that judge is typically successful in winning re-election for as many terms as he or she desires. Considering that a large number of district judge slots are filled in this way, the governor's imprint on the composition of the court can be considerable. Another notable similarity can be found in characteristics of the judges selected. Proponents of the Missouri Plan often suggest that it produces judges with stronger qualifications than those elected. However, studies have found no significant differences attributable to selection systems in judicial traits such as experience and education (Baum, 2004; Glick & Emmert, 1987; Smith, 1999). This has led scholars to conclude that there is no single system that is clearly superior in recruiting to the bench the best legal talent in the state (Porto, 2001).

So what of decision making? Are there significant differences between the behavior of elected versus Missouri Plan judges? On this question, there is not a great deal of evidence, but it seems likely that both systems make judges somewhat conscious of public opinion when they decide high-profile cases. For example, because voters care greatly about criminal justice issues, and death penalty cases tend to be the most prominent in voters' minds, judges facing retention or competitive elections are probably more likely to approve death sentences than those who do not face election (Baum, 2004). Although judges facing retention elections have a lower probability of defeat than those running against challengers, they are aware that their seats are not completely safe. They know of the potential for bad publicity and the prospect of organized political opposition if they make unpopular decisions on high profile issues. Nevertheless, it is very likely that elected judges who face great political pressures will consider more strongly their constituents and political supporters in their decision making than their Missouri Plan counterparts.

Does the Missouri Plan Remove "Politics" from the Selection Process?

The Missouri Plan is often touted as a process that modernizes judicial selection and cleanses it of political considerations. However, judicial scholars who have studied the operation of the Missouri Plan note that such an assertion is naive (see, e.g., Watson and Downing, 1969). In theory, the task of the plan's nominating commission is to choose nominees solely on the basis of merit, which is why the Missouri Plan is often referred to as a "merit selection" system. The reality is that the work of the nominating commission tends to be influenced by other considerations such as personal and family ties, partisanship, and political loyalties—especially to the governor. Because the governor typically appoints the non-lawyer commission members, they may often be sympathetic to the governor's selection goals (Baum, 2004). One study found that a number of commissioners surveyed believed their commissions to be "controlled by gubernatorial appointees whose commission membership is a political 'thank-you' and who select whomever the governor wants" (Henschen, et al, 1990, p. 334).

Other studies cite bar association politics at work in the selection of the attorney members to the nominating commission. Researchers found that while some attorneys are interested in judgeships personally, and work to get their commission member selected whom they think will favor their candidacies, most are concerned with "policy payoffs," not patronage. That is, they want to get persons on the bench who will be sympathetic, or at least not hostile to their clients' interests" (Watson et al., 1967:67). The stakes of the policy payoffs tend to pit the corporate attorneys, who favor judicial decisions and policies benefiting businesses, against the plaintiff attorneys, who desire court policies and outcomes favoring individuals (Watson, et al, 1967). Interestingly, these same factions tend to clash over the same "policy payoffs" in elective judicial systems.

The politics involved in the Missouri Plan system was also evident to some Oklahoma legislators who opposed Henry's plan to change district judge elections to Missouri Plan selection. Representative Opio Toure from Oklahoma City said, "The [Missouri Plan] system is essentially a political process and it's closed door. We need to open it up so we can have a wider pool to select from" (Associated Press, 1999b).

VI. Cases and Policy Making in the Oklahoma Courts

Cases in the Oklahoma Courts

The trial and appellate courts of Oklahoma decide cases spanning a wide range of issue areas from abandonment to zoning. Each year more than 500,000 new cases are filed in Oklahoma, most of them flowing into the district courts. Criminal cases account for more than half of the filings. However most of these do not involve events that tend to come to mind for when one thinks of a "criminal case." Gruesome murders, brutal beatings, savage rapes, daring bank robberies, and even small-time burglaries make up a small percentage of criminal case filings. The boring reality is that the majority of criminal case filings are simple traffic cases. In fact, traffic cases usually account for roughly a third of all the cases filed in Oklahoma (Administrative Office of the Courts, 1994, 1995a, 1999, 2011). This prevalence of traffic cases is not unique to Oklahoma. It is characteristic of the composition of state court dockets throughout the country.

Civil matters comprise about 40% of the cases filed in Oklahoma. The greatest number of civil case filings arise from **small claims**—cases that involve claims of less than $4,500. Small claims comprise approximately 37% of the civil case docket and 17% of the entire case load of Oklahoma courts. **General civil cases**—involving matters such as breach of contract, property rights, personal injury, or civil and privacy rights—typically represent approximately 30-40% of the civil case docket and 12-18% of the total case load of Oklahoma courts (Administrative Office of the Courts, 1994, 1995a, 1999, 2011). Table 8–1 presents some summary statistics of cases filed in the Oklahoma Courts in 2011.

Policy Making in the Oklahoma Courts of Last Resort

The number of cases decided by the Oklahoma Supreme Court and Court of Criminal Appeals is miniscule compared to that heard by the lower courts—but the policymaking power of the high courts is considerable. Through their case decisions, these courts create precedents that the lower courts are legally obligated to follow in numerous important areas of law. In other words, the Oklahoma courts of last resort have the final word in interpreting and deciding all issues of Oklahoma law. For example,

TABLE 8–1		
Summary of District Court Cases Filed July 1, 2010–June 30, 2011		
Civil Cases:		
General Civil:		96,163
Small Claims:		89,128
Divorce:		23,755
Victim Protective Order:		5,548
Domestic (Other than (Divorce, VPO):		12,045
Adoptions:		2,305
Probate:		7,948
Mental Health:		4,751
Guardianship:		4,887
Marriage Licenses:		27,323
All Other Licenses:		4,264
Criminal Cases:		
Felony:		46,020
Misdemeanor:		62,815
Traffic:		175,965
Juvenile Cases:		11,350
Total All Cases:		537,301

SOURCE: Administrative Office of the Courts (Oklahoma). (2011). The Judiciary. Annual Report, FY-2011.

on March 30, 2004 in a unanimous opinion, the Oklahoma Supreme Court upheld the constitutionality of a ban on cockfighting approved by Oklahoma voters several months earlier. Nevertheless, James Tally, president of the Oklahoma Gamefowl Breeders Association, vowed to continue the fight. "This is going all the way to the U.S. Supreme Court," he exclaimed in an interview with the *The Oklahoman* newspaper ("Court upholds," 2004). Oklahoma high court decisions which raise federal constitutional issues can be reviewed by the Supreme Court of the United States, but this occurs infrequently. Only about 2% of all state high court decisions are appealed to the Supreme Court of the United States (Glick, 1991, p. 87) and only a very small fraction of these cases are heard by the Court on the merits (Kagan, et al, 1977, p. 121). It was unlikely the Supreme Court of the United States would consider a state ban on cockfighting to be a legitimate federal constitutional issue and, not surprisingly, the Supreme Court denied cert review without comment (Greiner, 2004).

The policymaking influence of the Oklahoma courts of last resort is considerable outside of the state as well. Although precedents made by Oklahoma high courts are legally binding only within the state, they often have great *persuasive* value outside of Oklahoma. It is common for judges on state supreme courts to borrow or reject the reasoning from decisions of other state high courts when grappling with making and justifying a difficult decision of their own. Especially when addressing legal issues uncharted in his or her state, an appellate judge may seek out solutions provided by the courts of respected sister states. In a study of the reputation of state supreme courts, the Supreme Court of Oklahoma fared relatively well. It ranked sixteenth among the fifty states in its tendency to have its decisions cited by other high courts (Caldeira, 1983).

Oklahoma high courts have also distinguished themselves nationally and internationally through their progressive and innovative jurisprudence. For example, a study of state judicial innovativeness showed that Oklahoma ranked fifth among the fifty states in adopting new tort law doctrines in the postwar period (Canon & Baum, 1981). More recently, the Oklahoma Court of Criminal Appeals received world-wide attention for a ground-breaking decision in which the high court acknowledged that international treaties and their interpretation by the International Court of Justice (ICJ), the highest court of the United Nations, were binding upon state courts. On May 13, 2004, the Oklahoma high court halted the execution of Osbaldo Torres—a Mexican national who was not informed of his right of access to the Mexican consulate. In reaching its decision the court relied upon a decision of the ICJ which had held that pursuant to the Vienna Convention on Consular Relations (VCCR), a treaty ratified by the United States, German nationals sentenced to death in the United States must be informed of the right of access to their consulate. The Oklahoma high court extended this ruling to the case of Torres, holding that his failure to be notified of the right to access to the Mexican consulate constituted a violation of the VCCR. This case is significant in that the court makes a strong statement, which may be echoed in the future by other state high courts, that international law is enforced in the United States. It signals to the world community that the United States respects the rights of non-citizens (Leavitt, 2004).

VII. CONCLUSION

The purpose of this chapter is to provide students of politics an overview of the Oklahoma judiciary by examining its structure, methods of judicial selection, processing of cases, and impact on public policy. Although much of the discussion focuses on the courts without reference to other political players and institutions, keep in mind that this was a heuristic choice made for the sake of clarity. The Oklahoma courts do not operate in a political vacuum—they are very much a part of, and affected by, the greater political arena. This was demonstrated when the Oklahoma State Legislature changed the courts selection systems in 1967 after a major scandal and considered further changes in 2013 as retaliation against the Oklahoma Supreme Court's nullification of the Lawsuit Reform Act of 2009.

Yet the influence of politics on the Oklahoma courts is not limited simply to the ability of outside political forces to impose institutional change. The *decisions* of judges and courts are also affected by external political considerations as well as internal beliefs and attitudes. The common perception that courts are bastions of objective, rational, and formalistic decision making unaffected by political factors may be a comforting notion to some but it is clearly inaccurate. Judges are political actors with distinct policy preferences who pursue self-interested goals. Their decisions are made within a complex and politically-charged environment where they are often called upon to interpret broadly-written laws and apply them to novel and unforeseen situations. Armed with case precedents proffering various and conflicting policy interpretations that may be only tangentially related to the specific issue at hand, judges, particularly at the appellate level, enjoy great flexibility in employing these cases as rhetorical tools to justify decisions which are distinctly political. Stumpf describes the nature of judicial decision making aptly:

> *Each and every judicial decision rewards some interest or viewpoint and deprives another. Decisions are thus allocative of society's scarce resources, making them, by definition, political. This is the great paradox of the judicial role. (1998, p. 50)*

Despite the inevitable wading into political waters to make legal policy, the courts enjoy a high degree of public support. Polls show that the public holds favorable views of American courts (Stumpf, 1998), and Oklahoma and other state judges are routinely retained by large margins and receive scant criticism unless they become embroiled in a public scandal or are targeted by outside interest groups. Their popularity and ability to weather controversial decisions are partly due to the "mythology of the court": the persistent notion that judges are different from other politicians and "above politics." And the courts are steeped in a culture that is quite adept at perpetuating this myth. Judges are presented as a select group of sages who alone are capable of divining and interpreting the law. They wear majestic black robes, sit in elevated benches, and use a special language unfamiliar to the general public. And the "engrained need of the people for assurance, security, stability—a need to know all is well—sustains the myth" (Stumpf, 1998, p. 49).

Not everyone, however, has a sanguine view of the judiciary as objective interpreters of the law. A person's view of the courts may be less favorable if he or she has a stake in a matter that ends up on the wrong side of a court's policy decision. As a case in point, after being informed of the unanimous vote of the Supreme Court of Oklahoma to uphold the state's ban on cockfighting, state Senator Frank Shurden exclaimed "I didn't have any doubt. I think they've been prejudiced all along" ("Court upholds," 2004).

The reality that courts are inherently political institutions similar to the other branches of government should not be a cause for alarm. History has shown that the American judiciary is quite adaptable and responsive to the needs of society. The courts are generally in step with the values and policy preferences of the public, yet at times they rise to protect the rights of disfavored groups against the "tyranny of the majority."

OKLAHOMA AND
THE U.S. SUPREME COURT

Danny M. Adkison

The federal Constitution is perhaps the greatest of human experiments.

Louis D. Brandeis, Associate Justice, U.S. Supreme Court

I. INTRODUCTION

At one time or another, all states, in different capacities, find themselves before the highest court in the United States. Article VI of the nation's Constitution makes that document (along with constitutional federal laws and treaties) the "supreme law of the land." Article III describes the jurisdiction of the Supreme Court and lower federal courts the Congress may create. Some states may find themselves or citizens of their state in federal court due to the presence of a "federal question." States are one of the parties cited in Article III that can be in federal courts even if the issue they raise does not involve a federal question. Furthermore, long ago it was decided that decisions by a state's highest court (civil or criminal) could be appealed to the Supreme Court (if the case raised a federal question or if the state were a party to the dispute).

The state of Oklahoma has been involved in some important, even landmark, decisions issued by the U.S. Supreme Court. In some the state is an actual party in the dispute. In others, residents of Oklahoma have been parties to cases that have had far reaching consequences.

Below are the facts surrounding some of these cases (room does not permit discussing every case). Those cases discussed deal with the Fourteenth Amendment's stipulation that states not deprive citizens of "equal protection of the law," issues pertaining to criminal justice, the notion of fundamental rights, and the constitutional right to "keep and bear arms." As is sometimes the case, some of the cases deal with more than one constitutional issue.

II. EQUAL JUSTICE UNDER LAW

There are four words etched in stone on the front of the U.S. Supreme Court building: Equal Justice Under Law. The Supreme Court did not get its own building until the 1930s, making it one of the newest. Likewise, guaranteeing equality came late to the U.S. Constitution. There was no specific reference to constitutional guarantees of equality until ratification of the 14th Amendment in 1868.

Although Oklahoma would not become a state until 1907, it would play an important role in the development of the legal protection of equality, on two different occasions.

In the 1940s it was illegal in Oklahoma for a public university to enroll students of different races. State law also provided for fining any professor in a public university who taught a class containing different races. Finally, any student attending such a class could also be fined.

Like many other states, Oklahoma did provide public education for African-Americans. Langston University, centrally located near the center of the State, was just such a school. In doing this Oklahoma, again like many other states, was merely following the doctrine of **"separate but equal"** which had been the law of the land since 1896.

In 1946 Miss Louise Sipuel, having graduated from Langston University, applied for admission to the University of Oklahoma School of Law. President Cross informed Miss Sipuel that although she was academically qualified, state law prevented the University from admitting her. There was no separate law school for African-Americans and therefore, Miss Sipuel would have to go elsewhere to earn a law degree.

The NAACP approached Miss Sipuel about initiating a suit against the University of Oklahoma Law School. The NAACP often used the tactic of **"test cases"** to challenge the constitutionality of state laws. Miss Sipuel agreed to allow the NAACP lawyers to initiate the case. They supplied her with a lawyer—Thurgood Marshall—to assist her in her lawsuit.

Marshall argued before the Oklahoma courts that Miss Sipuel's rights to equal protection of the law, as guaranteed by the 14th Amendment, had been violated. The Oklahoma courts ruled against Miss Sipuel. Marshall appealed her case to the U.S. Supreme Court. The U.S Supreme Court disagreed with the Oklahoma court, ruling that Oklahoma was required to provide Miss Sipuel (and by implication all African-Americans who were qualified) with a legal education as soon as it would provide one for whites. The Court probably assumed that Oklahoma would respond by admitting Miss Sipuel to the O.U. law School. The Oklahoma Regents, however, came up with a different response.

In the few weeks prior to the beginning of the Spring term, the Regents created the Langston University School of Law to be located at the State Capitol building in Oklahoma City. The school had two Professors and one Dean, Thurgood Marshall.

Viewing Oklahoma's actions as a sham, several other African-Americans enrolled in several different graduate programs at the University of Oklahoma leaving the Regents with the option of either admitting them or denying them admission (time and expense prevented the State from creating the many new graduate schools). One of these students was George McLaurin.

Oklahoma University did admit Mr. McLaurin, but it seated him in a janitor's closet (with a view of the blackboard) and assigned him his own table to use in the Library and the Cafeteria. Neither McLaurin nor Sipuel thought these responses satisfied the requirements of the 14th Amendment which stipulated that no state was to deny and individual the equal protection of the law. In the end, the U.S. Supreme Court agreed.

It is important to note that both of these cases reinforced the "separate but equal" doctrine. That doctrine would not be successful challenged until the *Brown* v. *Board of Education* decision in 1954. Yet, these two Oklahoma cases were very important. They put states on notice that although the doctrine of "separate but equal" endorsed by the Court in *Plessy* v. *Ferguson* (1896) was still the law of the land, the Court was going to place greater emphasis on the "equal" component of that doctrine. Looked at in this way, these two Oklahoma cases, along with similar cases in other states, indicated that the Court was becoming increasingly dissatisfied with "separate but equal."

* * * * *

In 1971 the U.S. Supreme Court, for the first time in its history, struck down a state law because it treated men and women differently (*Reed* v. *Reed*). In striking down laws mandating racially segregated public schools the Supreme Court relied on a very tough standard. For a law treating races differently to be upheld the government had to convince the Court that the State was, due to the circumstances involved in the case, compelled to pass such laws. As decades of cases would demonstrate, this standard would result in nearly all laws treating races differently as unconstitutional.

Would the Court use the same standard when judging the constitutionality of laws treating men and women differently? The Court did not give a definitive answer to this question until a 1976 case originating in Oklahoma, *Craig v. Boren*.

In the mid-1970s Craig, an Oklahoma State University student, left a party to purchase more beer. When he went to purchase the beer he was told that he had to be 21 years old to purchase the beer; he also learned that state law treated males and females differently concerning purchasing intoxicating 3.2% beer. The minimum age for females to purchase 3.2% beer was 18; males had to be 21. Craig was enrolled in an introductory American government course at the time, and he complained to his instructor about the different ages established in Oklahoma law. His instructor explained the law to him and sensing that he was very upset nonchalantly suggested he could always sue if he was that passionate about the issue.

Craig did sue. How could Oklahoma justify treating males and females differently when it came to purchasing 3.2% beer? The lawyers arguing on behalf of Oklahoma's law argued that statistics proved that more males than females were arrested for driving under the influence of alcohol, and that more males than females were injured or killed in automobile accidents. Oklahoma's law was predicated on the assumption that when couples are together, it is more likely the male will be driving; hence the greater (and by assumption more maturity) desired in males. The lower court agreed with this logic and upheld Oklahoma's law.

Five members of the Supreme Court, however, voted to overturn this decision. They noted that the arrest differences between males and females were slight (2% to 1.8% respectively) and had other shortcomings.

When *Craig* v. *Boren* was decided in 1976 the Supreme Court had two tests it used when judging the constitutionality of laws treating people differently. It used the rigorous **"strict scrutiny"** test in cases where the law treated different races differently or where a law treating people differently deprived someone of a constitutional right in the process. The "strict scrutiny" test was a very difficult test for any law to pass since the Court required the government to demonstrate a compelling need for the different treatment. The other test used to judge laws treating people differently was the **"rational basis"** test. Under this test the Court tended to defer to the lawmaker (state legislatures or Congress) as long as there was a rational basis for the law. Most laws would be able to pass such a test.

With *Craig* v. *Boren* the Court articulated a test that it had begun to form in its 1971 *Reed* v. *Reed* decision. Some had hoped the Court would use the same test for gender discrimination cases as it was using in race discrimination cases. The Court refused to do so, but neither did the Court leave laws that discriminated on the basis of gender to be judged in the same way that all other laws treating categories of people differently ("rational basis"). Rather, the Court articulated its new test for gender discrimination cases: **"heightened scrutiny."** Under this test, for a law treating males and females differently, the government would have to show that the law furthered important governmental objectives and must be substantially related to the achievement of those objectives.

III. KEEP AND BEAR ARMS

The Second Amendment to the U.S. Constitution is one of the briefer amendments. It consists of a single sentence: "A well regulated Militia, being necessary to the security of a free State, the right of the people to keep and bear Arms shall not be infringed."

In spite of its brevity, the Amendment has been subject to a great deal of controversy. Why did the First Congress include this in the twelve amendments it proposed in 1789, ten of which when ratified would be called the Bill of Rights? What does the amendment actually protect? It is common for pro-gun forces to rely on this amendment as proof that Americans have a right to purchase guns, and to attack any attempt by the government to regulate the purchase or use of guns.

While the amendment has been passionately debated in recent decades, very few cases dealing with the meaning of the amendment have reached the U.S. Supreme Court. One of the most important cases on this issue started with two individuals in Oklahoma.

In 1934 Congress passed a National Firearms Act. This Act made it illegal for certain types of guns to be transported across state lines except under certain specific conditions. Congress' authority for passing the law was based on the clause in Article I, Section 8 stipulating that Congress can regulate commerce among the states. A few years after this law was passed Jack Miller and Frank Layton were stopped by Oklahoma authorities as they left Claremore, Oklahoma on their way to Siloam Springs, Arkansas. They had in their possession a double barrel 12-guage Stevens shotgun with a barrel less than 18 inches in length.

Miller and Layton were charged with violating the federal law. Their lawyers made two arguments to the District Court. First, they argued the National Firearms Act was a violation of the Constitution by allowing Congress to regulate matters that should have been regulated by the states. In other words, the federal law violated the police powers of the states. Second, the lawyers argued that the federal law violated the Second Amendment by depriving their clients of their right to "keep and bear arms." The federal District Court was sympathetic to the Second Amendment argument. On direct appeal, the U.S. Supreme Court issued its decision in 1939.

There are two major interpretations as to what the First Congress meant when it proposed the Second Amendment. One is called the **individual right interpretation.** According to this view, the Amendment clearly allows states to have militias, but it also recognizes an individual's constitutional right to own a gun. Another interpretation of the Amendment, the **collective right interpretation,** asserts that it was inserted in the Bill of Rights because states feared the newly created national government would first use its extensive powers to disarm a state's militia and then use its newly authorized standing army to march on the states.

If the individual right interpretation is correct then the 1934 national firearms act probably would violate the Second Amendment. If, however, the collective right interpretation is the accepted meaning of the Second Amendment, individuals would have to base their argument that they have a right to own a gun to something other than the Amendment.

The Supreme Court, in what was previously regarded as the definitive interpretation of the Second Amendment, surveyed the history of the writing of the Amendment and concluded that it was designed not to protect each individual's right to own a gun but as a guarantee to states that Congress could not disarm their militias (now referred to as the National Guard).

Neither Mill nor Layton was a member of the National Guard of Arkansas or Oklahoma. Furthermore, a double-barrel sawed-off shotgun would not ordinarily be the type of weapon issued by a state's militia. Therefore, Miller and Layton could not rely on the Second Amendment to challenge the constitutionality of the 1934 National Firearms Act.

Interpreted this way, the Second Amendment recognizes a collective right: the right of the people of a state to establish and arm a militia. It should also be pointed out that by taking this interpretation of the Second Amendment as the correct one, the Supreme Court was not denying that people have an individual right to own a gun. It merely meant that an assertion that individuals do have a right to a gun must rely on some authority other than the Second Amendment. Nor did the decision mean that all guns (except those issued by the state) are illegal. States can, as Oklahoma has, make possession of guns legal. But, if the government were to decide it wanted to strictly regulate possession of guns, the Second Amendment would not stand in the way. Recently, the Supreme Court in the cases of **District of Columbia** v. **Heller (2008)** and **McDonald** v. **Chicago (2010)** reversed its own ruling stating that individuals have a right to possess a firearm and that the Second Amendment applies to both the federal government and the states.

IV. Privacy Rights Issues

Few are surprised today to hear a reference to the right to privacy. Yet, just a few decades ago the U.S. Supreme Court had not specifically recognized the constitutional right to privacy. It did so in a 1965 decision dealing with an individual's right to procreate (*Griswold* v. *Connecticut*). But the stage was set for this decision by *Skinner* v. *Oklahoma*, a 1942 case that also raised questions about the state's control over an individual's right to procreate.

In 1935 the Oklahoma Legislature passed into law the Habitual Criminal Sterilization Act. The law sought to address the problem of repeat criminal offenders. Its solution for such "habitual criminals" was to sterilize the repeat offender, preventing him or her from producing offspring. What might have made the State Legislature think such a law would be judged constitutional by the U.S. Supreme Court?

The answer to that question can be traced to the Court's 1927 decision of *Buck* v. *Bell*. In that case the Court relied on eugenics and upheld a Virginia law allowing the sterilization of individuals held in state institutions for mentally insane (or, in this particular case, the feeble-minded). In upholding the law, Justice Holmes asserted, "Three generations of imbeciles are enough."

Not only was the Court relying on what it thought was the best science of the time, but clearly the Court was also influenced by Social Darwinism, which was the dominant way of thinking in America in the late nineteenth century.

The Supreme Court was given the chance to judge the constitutionality of Oklahoma's Habitual Criminal Sterilization Act when Oklahoma sought to sterilize a man named Skinner following his conviction of three felonies. Skinner was convicted of three crimes: (1) stealing chickens; (2) robbery with a firearm; and, again (3) robbery with a firearm. He was serving time in the penitentiary when Oklahoma initiated proceedings, under the Habitual Criminal Sterilization Act, to force him to undergo a vasectomy. Under that law, all the government had to prove to a jury in order to mandate the surgery was that the operation would not be detrimental to his general health. Having convinced the jury of this, the State ordered the surgery and Skinner appealed to the Supreme Court.

Skinner argued the Habitual Criminal Sterilization Act was unconstitutional for two reasons. First, the law was founded on the faulty notion that criminal behavior could be transmitted genetically (and thus was a violation of the Fourteenth Amendment's due process clause), and second, the law was a violation of the Eighth Amendment's prohibition against cruel and unusual punishment.

Perhaps as an indication of the difficulty the Court was having struggling with the decision in this case, the Court, after noting the arguments made by Skinner, stated, "We pass those points without intimating an opinion on them." The Court had found another reason for ruling that the law was unconstitutional. The Court ruled that since some crimes were included in determining which criminals were "habitual offenders" while others (like embezzlement) weren't, the law was a violation of the Fourteenth Amendment's equal protection clause.

The Court in the Skinner case seemed tempted to rule that procreation was too fundamental a right for the government to be allowed to regulate. The opening sentence in the decision began, "This case touches a sensitive and important area of human rights." The decision ends by asserting, "We are dealing here with legislation which involves one of the basic civil rights of man."

It would be over twenty years later, however, before a majority of the Court, ruling in *Griswold* v. *Connecticut* (striking down a Connecticut law making it illegal to use birth control devices) would explicitly recognize privacy as an unenumerated right protected by the Constitution. The *Skinner* decision was a precursor to that decision and the many privacy rights cases that followed.

V. Criminal Justice

The Fourth Amendment to the Constitution prohibits the government from conducing unreasonable searches and seizures. What makes a search or seizure reasonable?

The Amendment itself provides the answer to this question. First, a search or seizure must be based on **"probable cause."** The Amendment does not define "probable cause" but we know from Court cases that it is greater than a "high suspicion" but less than an "absolute certainty." Second, there must be a warrant issued by a magistrate. Finally, the warrant must provide specificity concerning the place to be searched and the persons or things to be seized.

This much concerning the Fourth Amendment is fairly straightforward. Complexity enters in the execution of this Amendment in particular circumstances. The case law dealing with the subject of this amendment is

LEADERSHIP PROFILE

MICHAEL C. TURPEN
Attorney and Counselor at Law

MIKE TURPEN is a partner at Riggs, Abney, Neal, Turpen, Orbison, and Lewis, a prestigious law firm with several offices throughout Oklahoma and one in Denver, Colorado. He graduated with a Bachelor of Science in History and went on to graduate from the university's College of Law in 1974. Among Turpen's many accomplishments, he received the Oklahoma Bar Association Outstanding Young Lawyers Award. He began teaching law at the Oral Roberts University College of Law and proceeded to teach at the National College of District Attorneys. He served as Police Legal Advisor for Muskogee County, and later became the District Attorney for the same county. Turpen served as the President of the Oklahoma District Attorney Association for a year. Afterwards, he was elected Oklahoma Attorney General where he served from 1982 to 1986. In that capacity, he argued before the U.S. Supreme Court on a death penalty case.

He grew up in north Tulsa where he was mentored by his parents, "Aunt Mildred," and his gym teacher, Mr. Hales. Turpen was a down-to-earth guy who worked as a waiter at Steak-n-Ale. This work experience taught him the significance of service and humility. He was even Santa Claus one year at the local Sears which helped him to learn about humor and kindness. E.M. Guillory, an older African American man from Muskogee, is the person Turpen credits for teaching him the most about leadership. Guillory was very creative and told Turpen a story:

> A young child goes to an older man and says, "Oh wise man, I wrote my name in the sand on the beach, but when the tide came in, my name was washed away. I carved my name in the bark of a tree, but when the tree grew, my name was gone. I chiseled my name in stone on the side of a mountain, but when the wind blew it eroded my name away. Oh wise man, what really matters in this life? Give me a reason for living and dying." The old wise man replied, "Inscribe your name in the

hearts of your fellow man and you shall live and endure forever and ever and ever."

Turpen says, "We leave our name in the hearts of others by how we treat each other, how we help each other, how we respect each other" (2007). The most important leadership trait is to lead by example—with passion and purpose. It is far more important to live it than to just talk about it. Turpen says, "If you catch on fire with enthusiasm and spirit, people will come from miles around just to watch you burn." People do come from miles away to see Turpen's ability to lead others as an authentic charismatic leader. Thousands of other Oklahomans just stay in their living rooms and on Sunday mornings watch Turpen verbally duke it out with his conservative counterpart, Kirk Humphreys. Both have leveraged their former political careers into perhaps the most successful political commentary show on state politics in the nation, the award-winning *Flashpoint*.

Turpen has become very well known for his time in public office, his political campaigns (who could forget his "It's Turpen Time!" campaign slogan?), his legal accomplishments, and his late blooming career as a colorful television personality.

Tiffany Palmer

vast, due to the fact that there are so many unique situations calling for unique solutions. Because of this it is very difficult to state a general principle that summarizes the Court's application of the conditions specified in the Amendment. The Court has created numerous "exceptions" to these conditions. For example, the Court does not require a warrant if the police are engage in "hot pursuit." Another noted exception is the **"automobile search"** (which would include not just automobiles but any easily moved vehicle). Police may search a vehicle if they have, in their opinion, probable cause to do so, but without having to get a warrant from a neutral magistrate. Police may also search a person subject to valid arrest and seize any evidence in the suspect's immediate surroundings that is in plain view. This can be done without a warrant and any evidence that might establish the guilt of a suspect can be used in court. Another exception the Court has recognized is the so-called **"stop and frisk"** rule. Under this rule a police officer could, without a warrant and with only a "high suspicion" stop an individual and pat down the outer garment (without reaching inside a pocket) in order to detect any illegal behavior.

While the Court has recognized other exceptions to the conditions specified in the Fourth Amendment, one that played an important role in a case from Oklahoma is the public school environment. Probably the most noted case dealing with the public school exception is the 1985 case of *New Jersey* v. *T.L.O.* Noting that the public school environment was unique and thus school officials could conduct warrantless searches as long as the search, under the circumstances, was reasonable.

This exception was extended in *Veronica School District* v. *Acton* (1995). In *Veronica* the Court upheld suspicionless random searches of students participating in competitive athletics. This too was extended in a 2002 case from Oklahoma.

In 1998 Pottawatomie County in Oklahoma adopted a Student Activities Drug Testing Policy. This policy required all students who participate in competitive extracurricular activities to submit to drug testing. Students participating in such activities as choir, marching band, and Academic Team were required to take a drug test and then be subject to random testing while participating. Two students at the Tecumseh school (located in Pottawatomie County) sued challenging the constitutionality of the policy. Lindsay Earls was a member of the choir, marching band, Academic Team, and Honor Society. Daniel James participated in Academic Team. One argument they used against the policy was that there was no drug problem at the Tecumseh school.

Relying on earlier rulings like Veronica, the U.S. District Court upheld the policy but the Tenth Circuit Court in Denver, Colorado reversed, indicating that suspicionless searches should not be allowed where there was no evidence of a drug problem. The Supreme Court took the case and ruled in favor of the school policy.

Writing for the Court, Justice Thomas noted that it was already established in law that public schools need not be bound by the Fourth Amendment's requirement for a warrant based on "probable cause." To require this "would interfere with the maintenance of the swift and informal disciplinary procedures that are needed" at public schools. What of the privacy rights of students? The Court noted that when students participate in competitive extracurricular activities they waive some privacy rights. In summary, Thomas explained, "Finally, we find that testing students who participate in extracurricular activities is a reasonably effective means of addressing the School District's legitimate concerns in preventing, deterring, and detecting drug use."

Four of the Court's Justices disagreed with this gradual erosion of student privacy rights. Their view was expressed in a dissent by Justice Ginsburg: "Although special needs inhere in the public school context, those needs are not so expansive or malleable as to render reasonable any program of student drug testing a school district elects to install."

These Justices might agree that the Court had moved a long way from the position it took in *Tinker* v. *Des Moines Iowa School District* in 1968 when in upholding the right of students to symbolically protest the Vietnam War by wearing black armbands to school the Court asserted that students do not shed their constitutional rights at the schoolhouse gate.

C A S E S   C I T E D

Board of Education of Independent School District No. 92 of Pottawatomie County v. *Earls*, 536 U.S. _____ (2002).

Brown v. *Board of Education*, 347 U.S. 483 (1954).

Buck v. *Bell*, 274 U.S. 200 (1927).

Craig v. *Boren*, 429 U.S. 190 (1976).

District of Columbia v. *Heller* (2008) and *McDonald* v. *Chicago* (2010).

Griswold v. *Connecticut*, 381 U.S. 479 (1965).

McLaurin v. *Oklahoma State Regents*, 339 U.S. 637 (1950).

New Jersey v. *T.L.O.*, 469 U.S. 325 (1985).

Plessy v. *Ferguson*, 163 U.S. 537 (1896).

Reed v. *Reed*, 404 U.S. 71 (1971).

Skinner v. *Oklahoma*, 316 U.S. 535 (1942).

Sipuel v. *Board of Regents of the University of Oklahoma*, 332 U.S. 631 (1948).

Tinker v. *Des Moines School District*, 393 U.S. 503 (1969).

U.S. v. *Miller*, 307 U.S. 174 (1939).

Veronica School District v. *Acton*, 515 U.S. 646 (1995).

RECOMMENDED READINGS

1. Danny M. Adkison and Lisa McNair Palmer, *The Oklahoma State Constitution* (Westport, CT: Greenwood Press, 2001).

2. Ellen Alderman and Caroline Kennedy, *In Our Defense: The Bill of Rights in Action* (New York: William Morrow and Company, Inc., 1991).

3. Gene Aldrich, *Black Heritage of Oklahoma* (Edmond: Thompson Book and Supply Co., 1973).

4. *The Constitution of the United States of America: Analysis and Interpretation*, edited by Johnny H. Killian (Washington, D.C., U.S. Government Printing Office, 1987).

5. Arrel M. Gibson, *Oklahoma: A History of Five Centuries* (Norman: University of Oklahoma Press, 1981).

PARTIES, ELECTIONS, AND POLITICAL PARTICIPATION IN OKLAHOMA

Jan C. Hardt

I'm not a member of any organized political party. I'm a Democrat.
Will Rogers

I. INTRODUCTION

Oklahoma is a hard state to categorize when it comes to politics. Going all the way back to statehood, most Oklahoma voters have registered as Democrats. Although Republicans are swiftly gaining ground in voter registration in the state (McNutt, 2012b), the latest statistics still show a slight Democratic edge (Oklahoma Election Board, 2014). Throughout most of Oklahoma's history with few exceptions, the state legislature has been majority Democratic. Most state offices have been held by Democrats, and most Oklahoma governors have been Democratic. Yet, since 1960 Oklahoma has voted only once at the presidential level for a Democratic candidate—Lyndon Baines Johnson in 1964. Moreover, many of its congressional seats have been held by Republicans. And, if most Oklahomans were asked, except in the Southeast corner of the state, they would probably say that there are more Republicans than Democrats in Oklahoma. They would also talk about some of the more well-known Republicans that have held state office in Oklahoma, including Frank Keating who was governor from 1994 to 2002, and Mary Fallin who served as Lieutenant Governor, as a member of Congress from the 5th district, and more recently as Governor.

Despite this difficulty in categorizing Oklahoma's party preferences, the state has lots of rules that govern both its political parties and its elections. Sometimes, these rules have given Oklahoma national attention. After the chaos of the 2000 presidential election, Oklahoma was one of the few states applauded for its election process. Oklahoma's sophisticated method of tabulating its votes would have eliminated almost all of the problems that happened in Florida. In the 2004 and 2008 presidential elections, Oklahoma again captured national attention. The Oklahoma legislature moved the date of Oklahoma's primary up to the third week of the presidential nomination season, instead of in the middle for both elections. Thus, relatively small Oklahoma became a major player in helping to determine the presidential nominees in those elections. Suddenly, all of the major party candidates wanted to visit and spend money in Oklahoma.

At times though, some of the national attention has not been desired. In 1998, Oklahoma attracted national attention because there was concern that Oklahomans would vote for a dead candidate whose name appeared on a ballot and could not be removed by state law, and because nude pictures of a female candidate showed up during a judicial campaign. Then, in the 2004 presidential election, some national pundits poked fun at Oklahoma because the endorsement of John Edwards (NC) by Barry Switzer, a former college football coach, seemed to be a deciding factor in voting for Edwards.

One of the cardinal rules of politics is that political rules are never neutral. Someone always wins when a new rule is established, and someone always loses. New rules change how the game is played. That is certainly the case in Oklahoma. This chapter will seek to examine some of these rules and many others that have consequences for how Oklahomans participate in politics.

First, this chapter will examine political parties in Oklahoma and the rules that govern them. Not surprisingly, the rules have kept certain candidates from getting on the ballot, and might have determined the outcome of some races. This is particularly true in state legislative races in Oklahoma after 2004, as one of Oklahoma's new rules, a term limit for state legislators took effect. This has already brought change to the state legislature in the form of open seats, very competitive races, and the subsequent turnover in both houses of the legislature. Second, this chapter will examine redistricting. Redistricting after the 2000 Census changed many of the rules that govern Oklahoma elections. Oklahoma not only lost one congressional seat, but also saw the shapes and thus the constituencies of its congressional districts, its state House districts, and its state Senate districts, change. This was a process that saw the redistricting map decided in the courts, rather than the state legislature, where it is supposed to be decided. Third, this chapter will examine some of Oklahoma's election rules. Oklahoma is a bit of puzzle when it comes to election rules. On certain aspects, the state leads the country such as in voting technology. But in other aspects, it has older rules that many other states have long abandoned. Fourth, no chapter on parties and elections could be complete without looking at voter turnout. No candidate or party can win unless the voters turnout to the polls. In Oklahoma, voter turnout varies considerably depending upon the geographic region. Finally, this chapter will examine the outcomes. Who has won elections in Oklahoma? Who has lost? Which party seems to be getting more candidates elected to office?

II. POLITICAL PARTIES IN OKLAHOMA

Political parties are regulated by both the federal and state governments. Without party regulation, voters could face hundreds of candidates on any given ballot. In order to regulate political parties, it is necessary to define them. In Oklahoma, a recognized **political party** is a political organization whose candidates' names appeared on the general election ballot in 1974 "and those parties which shall be formed according to law" (Strain, Reherman, & Crozier, 1990). New parties can be formed in Oklahoma after filing a statement of intent, and then filing a petition containing the signatures of registered voters equal to at least 5% of the total vote cast in the last general election for governor or for presidential and vice-presidential elections.

Party Structure and Organization

In the United States, the political parties are organized on three levels: national, state, and local. Although most people believe that the **national party organizations**, such as the Democratic National Committee or the Republican National Committee, have all the power, this is far from the case. The national party organizations do hold presidential conventions every four years to select the presidential nominees. The national parties also provide their candidates with services best done at the national level. The national organizations might provide polling information on current issues to their candidates or produce national campaign ads to be run in most districts. The national organizations also create policy platforms at their conventions to guide their candidates. Moreover, in a very competitive race the national parties might help their candidates with campaign funds.

Yet, despite these responsibilities, national party organizations in the United States do not have that much power. Most of the major rules and decisions are made by the **state party organizations**. This has led some political scientists to call the national party organizations "loose confederations of state organizations" (Morgan, England, & Humphreys, 1991). Although the national party organizations create policy platforms, no major party has required its members or its candidates to support the platform. Each state party may create its own **platform**, a list of policy goals designed to appeal to the public and maintain consistency with party principles. The state platform can be different and sometimes in opposition to that of the national party. Moreover, states decide who can get on the ballot. For major party candidates this is usually not an issue, but it concerns independent and third-party candidates who must petition their way onto each ballot.

State parties also determine the type of **party nomination elections**. These elections are used in the United States to determine who will be the nominee for each political party. There are currently two types of party nomination elections. The first is the **direct primary**, where voters go on a specific day and vote for a presidential nominee in a voting booth.

About 75% of states use some sort of primary system. Direct primaries can be either open or closed. An **open primary** allows both Democrats and Republicans to vote for either party, and sometimes independents are included. A **closed primary** means that only Democratic registrants can vote for the Democratic nominees, and only Republicans registrants can vote for the Republican nominees. Independents cannot vote in a closed primary. Oklahoma has a closed primary.

The remaining 25% of the states, including Iowa, one of the most important early presidential contests, hold the second type of party nomination election, a **caucus**. Caucus elections usually occur over several states, and usually involve a series of meetings among the voters supporting each of the candidates. These meetings are designed to create coalitions of voters that winnow the field and rally support behind just a few candidates. There is typically one final vote at the end of a caucus weekend which reveals the winner.

Sometimes an uneasy tension remains between the national- and state-party organizations. On one hand, national organizations do not discipline state parties that deviate from the national platforms. In fact, the state parties contain diverse groups and individuals making it difficult to write one national platform for the state parties. Each of the fifty state parties has thus developed its own identity. Yet, the state parties are also supposed to be united by one common national party organization. For the most part, the two major parties are separated by their past histories and their different views on certain political issues.

In Oklahoma, each of the two major parties has its own structure and organization as shown in Table 10–1. The Oklahoma Democratic Party began in the 1880s and as of April 2014 is chaired by Wallace Collins and its vice-chair is Dana Orwig. The Democratic Party elects its officers every two years, and holds a convention every year.

The Oklahoma Democratic Party has a simple, but effective, mission statement: "to elect Democrats in Oklahoma." On its website, the Oklahoma Democratic Party emphasizes that it is the moderate party in Oklahoma. As it states, "We are the party squarely in the center of the political spectrum. Unlike the far left, we know that less government is sometimes a better government and that government cannot solve every difficulty faced by our society. But, unlike the far right, we understand there is a role for government to play in finding solutions to our country's problems. We firmly believe that government at every level has an absolute responsibility to encourage opportunity for success to all of its citizens. However, government has no responsibility to guarantee success itself" (http://okdemocrats.org/mission-bylaws/).

To help achieve these goals, the Democratic party in addition to its Chair and Vice Chair has several officers, Dave Ratcliff as Secretary and Donna Russell as Treasurer as of April 2014. It also has four staff members: Trav Robertson as Executive Director, David Scott at IT Director, Christine Byrd as Political Outreach/Ofiice Manager, and Aaron

TABLE 10–1		
The Democratic and Republican Parties in Oklahoma		
	OKLAHOMA DEMOCRATIC PARTY	OKLAHOMA REPUBLICAN PARTY
LEADERS	Chair: Wallace Collins Vice-Chair: Dana Orwig	Chair: Dave Weston Vice-Chair: Sara Jo Odom
CONVENTION	Elects its officers every two years. Holds a convention every year.	Elects its officers every two years. Holds regular state conventions every year except the gubernatorial election year, or every three out of four years.
STAFF	An executive director, IT director, political outreach manager, office manager, development director, and usually a few interns.	A political director, office manager, finance manager, member services representative, two national committee liaisons, and three or four interns during busy periods.
STRUCTURE OF THE PARTY	Democratic National Committee State Executive Board State Party Organization 5 Congressional District Organizations 77 County Organizations 2115 Precinct Organizations	Republican National Committee State Executive Committee Republican State Committee 5 Congressional District Committees 77 County Central Committees 2115 Precinct Organizations

Wilder as Development Director. The party also usually hires a few interns per semester.

The Democratic Party has a hierarchical structure. It has an executive board consisting of the state party officers and the leadership of the five congressional district party organizations (chair, co-chair, and secretary). The Democratic Party has 77 county organizations and 2115 precinct organizations each with its own separate chair, co-chair and secretary. The party includes in its leadership all Democratic state House and Senate members as well as all Democratic officials elected statewide (Oklahoma Democratic Party, 2014). The Oklahoma Democratic Party also has two organizations specifically devoted to younger people, the Young Democrats for those aged 13-35 and College Democrats, which includes the College Democrat organizations on every college campus in Oklahoma.

LEADERSHIP PROFILE

BRITTANY M. NOVOTNY
President, Young Democrats of Oklahoma

BRITTANY M. NOVOTNY has recently made a name for herself in Oklahoma politics, as the first openly transgender woman to run for public office. Novotny challenged incumbent, Sally Kern for the Oklahoma House District 84 in 2010. Although Novotny lost the race, she became known for successfully using social media during her campaign.

She was born the youngest of five children on March 6, 1980 in Chickasha, OK. She grew up in Oklahoma City. Novotny graduated from Westmoore High School in 1998, where she learned the value of team work while playing on the Jaguar football team. A member of the Westmoore academic team, Novotny received a full scholarship to the University of Science and Arts of Oklahoma. There, she studied sociology, while working at a local youth shelter and becoming politically active in student government. Novotny graduated *magna cum laude* from USAO in 2001 with a B.A, in Sociology.

Looking for new adventures, Novotny attended law school at the University of California-Hastings. There, intrigued by the school's close proximity to the founding place of the United Nations, Novotny began to entertain public service as a career path. While finishing law school, she kept up with the evolving business and political climates in Oklahoma. She earned her *juris doctorate* from UC-Hastings in 2005.

Novotny returned to Oklahoma City and was admitted to the Oklahoma Bar in 2005. She began her own law practice in Oklahoma City in 2007, concentrating on employment and civil rights law. During this time, a chance luncheon with politically like-minded women encouraged Novotny to become active in Oklahoma politics. She began to attend meetings of the Oklahoma Democratic Party and became an active member of the Young Democrats of Oklahoma organization.

In 2008, Novotny was elected National Committee Woman for the Young Democrats of Oklahoma organization. While serving in this capacity, she worked to build strong national connections for Oklahoma. She became the YDO Executive Vice-President in 2010, being called upon to complete the term of the previous vice-president. In 2010, Novotny was elected president of the organization, becoming the first openly transgender person to hold office at either the state or national levels of the official Young Democrats organization. Her vision for the YDO organization includes invigorating the young people of Oklahoma and encouraging them to become involved in the political process. She believes that Oklahoma's laws regarding term limitations give young people with the desire to serve their communities many opportunities to do so.

In addition to her activities in Oklahoma politics, Novotny is active in her community as well. She was awarded the Leadership Award for Community Action in 2009 by RAIN Oklahoma. She also serves on the community advisory board for S.K.I.L. (Supporting Kids in Independent Living).

Jennifer S. Stringham

The Republican Party dominated pre-statehood politics, officially forming as a party on June 12, 1892, in McAlester, Oklahoma. The Republican Party today has several stated beliefs: "We believe in limited government, individual liberty, and personal moral responsibility.

We believe Oklahoma should be a place of opportunity where people who work hard and abide by the rules can pursue their own dreams with a reasonable expectation of success" (Oklahoma Republican Party, 2014). To achieve these beliefs, Oklahoma Republicans hold state conventions every year except the gubernatorial election year, or every three out of four years. The convention elects a chair and vice-chair for two-year terms.

As of April 2014, the Chair of Oklahoma Republican Party is Dave Weston and the Vice-chair is Sara Jo Odom. Other members of the leadership include a man and woman from each county, county chairs and vice chairs, and several other chairs. As part of its organization, Oklahoma Republicans also include all Republican statewide officials, Republican members of the legislature, Republican members of Congress, and their past party chairs. The Oklahoma Republican Party in 2014 had several additional staff members: John Roberts as Political Director and Lauree Beth Stedje as Office Manager, Sarahi Wilson as Finance Director, Kati Harris in charge of Member Services, and Robert Ary as its Northeast Field Representative. Its National Committeeman was Steve Fair while its National Committeewoman was Carolyn McLarty. It is also not uncommon for the party to have three or four interns at any one time.

LEADERSHIP PROFILE

ELISE HALL
Member of the Oklahoma State House of Representatives–District 100

Representative Hall grew up in the district she now represents, House District 100. While attending the University of Central Oklahoma in Edmond, Elise Hall began her campaign for House District 100 and used traditional campaign methods as well as social media to great effect, winning a three-way primary easily.

Elected in 2010 at the age of 21, Elise Hall became the youngest legislator in Oklahoma history. After winning the election in 2010, she went on to finish her education at UCO and received a Bachelor's Degree in Business Administration.

Courtesy Elise Hall

In the Oklahoma House of Representatives, she has helped pass more than 20 government modernization bills that will save an estimated $170 million over seven years. Representative Hall has been a featured conference speaker at the 2013 regional Conservative Political Action Conference in St. Louis and was recognized by the American Conservative Union as a rising star in the conservative movement.

Regarding why she became interested in politics, Representative Hall said, "I've always had an interest in the history and purpose of our government and politics. As a freshman in college, I had the opportunity to travel across the U.S. with a nonprofit and teach high school students the political process. Observing state governments across the nation gave me a healthy appreciation of how state government best represents its people. When I decided to run for office in 2010, I did so in order to stand for the conservative principles I hold true, bring a small business background, and the passion of a 21-year-old to represent the younger generations."

Regarding young Oklahomans getting involved in the political process Hall said, "There are people who would say that young people cannot make a difference and that young people are too young to actually get elected. If a young person wants to get involved in the political process by running for office, they need to be willing to work hard to communicate with voters their positions and background. My hope is that the hard work necessary to run for public office does not deter young people from putting their name on the ballot and standing up for their generation."

When not in session, Representative Hall is a partner in The Hall's Pizza Kitchen as well as provides contract marketing services to individuals, small businesses, and non-profits. She is also active in her local church and community.

Kory Atcuson

Third Parties in Oklahoma

Third parties do exist in Oklahoma. Third parties face several substantial challenges when competing against the two major parties, the Democrats and the Republicans. The first challenge is to get their candidates on the ballot. Unlike the major party candidates who receive an automatic place on the ballot, third parties must collect petition signatures to get on the ballot in Oklahoma. In 1996, the Reform Party was able to be officially recognized as a third party in Oklahoma by getting more than the 49,751 required signatures on a petition seeking ballot recognition. The U.S. Taxpayers Party also sought ballot recognition in 1996, but its petition was declared insufficient. In 2002, both the Reform and Libertarian parties were no longer recognized by the state to field their party candidates on the Oklahoma election ballot.

As a consequence, the third parties have had troubles fielding candidates in recent elections, with neither the Reform nor Libertarian parties fielding candidates since the 2002 elections. Thus, it is not surprising that in the 2004 U.S. presidential elections, Oklahoma was the only state in the nation whose voters were limited to just two choices for president, Democrat and Republican. Half of the states had at least 6 names on the ballot, and Colorado had 12 names (see www.oklp.org/obar/issues.html). Thus, voters in 49 states had the opportunity to vote for Libertarian nominee Michael Badnarik, and voters in 36 states had the opportunity to vote for independent/Reform candidate Ralph Nader on the ballot. Oklahoma voters, however, were not given these choices, despite attempts by Libertarians in Oklahoma to get on the ballot in 2004. The problem for third-party voters came down to the ballot access laws. Oklahoma has the toughest set of ballot access laws of any state. It requires that party officials file petitions with voter signatures equal to 5% of those voting for governor or president in the last general election.

To remain on the ballot, a new party's candidate for governor or president must draw at least 10% of the vote in the next election. Thus, it took a petitioning requirement of 51,781 signatures for a third party to secure full party ballot access, and 37,027 signatures to place a presidential candidate in the 2004 elections.

Despite several failed attempts to pass Oklahoma Ballot Access Reform (OBAR) laws in the state in 2004 and 2005, not much has changed, and in fact it has gotten worse. Because of the daunting odds facing a third party and the belief that the rule is unfair, the Libertarian Party took Oklahoma's ballot-access law to court in March 2007. The Oklahoma Court of Civil Appeals turned down claims that the state's requirements for gaining recognition for a party are constitutionally restrictive. In the 2008 election, the Libertarian Party failed to field a candidate due to the burdensome petition signature requirement which meant 48,500 signatures in order to get a presidential candidate on the 2008 election ballot.

As a result, Oklahomans for Ballot Access Reform (OBAR) made a serious effort to try to amend the petition signature requirement in 2009-2010. In contrast to Oklahoma's steep 5% petition signature requirements, almost all states require 2% while Alabama requires 3%. By dropping Oklahoma's petition signature requirement to 3%, third parties would have been required to get 30,000 fewer signatures to be on the ballot in the 2010 elections. Early on, OBAR's efforts to get HB 1072 into law were successful. It passed in both House and Senate committees, but there was disagreement about how the votes were to be counted. As a result, it went to a conference committee where 28 legislators decided its fate. Despite a press conference by OBAR at the Oklahoma capitol and substantial lobbying efforts, HB 1072 failed to make it out of the conference committee.

In October 2012, OBAR held a rally at the Oklahoma state capitol to draw attention to the fact that Oklahoma's ballot included only the two major parties for president. Thus, this was the *third* presidential ballot in a row in which Oklahomans could only vote for the two major parties. The last time that this happened in a state was from 1952-1964 in Ohio. OBAR also pointed out that in addition to the limitations on ballot access, Oklahoma is also only one of five states that ban all write-in candidates.

In November 2012, the Oklahoma Americans Elect Party sought to get its presidential and vice presidential nominees on the general election ballot, but lost a decision in the Oklahoma Supreme Court. Those candidates were not placed originally on the ballot after election officials got advice from the state attorney general's office. The Oklahoma Americans Elect Party had not been authorized by the national party organization nor had it completed the requisite paperwork to be recognized as a political party in the state. Thus, in the 2012 elections once again, the only alternative to the two major parties were the few independent candidates scattered throughout the ballot.

Once on the ballot, third parties face a second challenge–getting their voters to the polls. Many voters view a third party vote as a wasted vote, and as a result third parties have had to work hard to overcome these impressions. The Reform Party was so worried about its outcome in the 1996 elections that it filed suit in October 1996 alleging that the Election Board and the state of Oklahoma had made some serious errors. The party alleged that the state failed to notify voter registrars of the existence of the Reform Party. Reform party state chairwoman, Dale Welch Barrow of Tulsa, also noted that the Election Board failed to list the Reform Party on voter application forms and failed to post notices at registration sites recognizing the party.

Finally, the third challenge faced by third parties comes on Election Day — getting enough votes. In Oklahoma third parties experienced one of their best years ever in 1992, when Ross Perot as an independent was on the presidential ticket. He received 319,878 votes that year, while the Libertarian party received 4,486 votes. In 1996, however, Ross Perot in conjunction with the Reform Party was only able to get 130,788 votes, while the Libertarian party received 5,505 votes (Oklahoma Department of Libraries, 1997). With the continued inability to get on the state ballot, third parties in Oklahoma mostly exist on the web and in their private meetings, but not on Election Day.

Party Competition

Having party competition in a state is important. First, without at least two competitive parties, voters often find themselves without a choice of candidates. In such a state, the minority party may not even field candidates, forcing those voters in the minority party to either not vote, or switch to the other party. Second, competition is the fundamental basis for a democracy. Without competition, voters can effectively lose their right to vote. Third, competitive parties serve a crucial function for the state government as well. Without an opposition party, the majority party can often run unchecked, making policies that perhaps may be unwise. The opposition party, therefore, can often serve as a watchdog for the interests of the people.

Nationwide, there definitely has been true party competition at the state legislative level. In 2004, there was only a 62-seat difference between the two parties, out of 7,382 total seats—or less than a 1% margin. Republicans controlled this seat edge so it is not surprising that they also had an advantage in terms of the number of states controlled, with 21 states controlled by Republicans, and only 17 controlled by Democrats. But the parity among the parties can be seen if one does some math. Only 38 states were controlled by either the Republicans or the Democrats, and if Nebraska is eliminated because of its nonpartisan elections, 11 states are left where party control was divided. One of those states was Oklahoma in 2004. After the 2006 elections, the national trend seemed to shift towards the Democrats. The Democrats seized control in all of the chambers that changed hands outright in 2006; thus, the Democrats led 23 states, while the Republicans only led 15 and 11 were split (National Conference of State Legislatures, 2007).

The 2012 elections were expected to be a bad year for Democrats in Oklahoma and a good year for Republicans, so the results of these elections were really not a surprise. After all, Democrat Barack Obama was seeking a second term as President, and he has not ever really been that popular in Oklahoma, as one of the redder states in the nation. Moreover, the economy nationally still had not rebounded from the tremendous downturn in 2009-2010 and so there was great instability in housing prices and unemployment, although Oklahoma did fare better than some other states. In addition, several of the national policies produced by the Democratic Congress, particularly the stimulus bill and President Obama's health care plan, did not sit well with voters. This was especially the case in Oklahoma where the state threatened to sue over the Obama health care plan. But few political pundits expected the results to be as bad for the Democrats as they were. The party lost six seats in the U.S. Senate, retaining control, but just barely at 53-47. The real damage occurred in the U.S. House and the states. In the U.S. House, the Democrats lost a massive 63 seats, losing not only majority control but giving the Republicans a substantial 242-193 majority. At the governor's level, the Democrats lost 6 seats, with a final outcome of 29 seats held by Republicans, and 21 held by Republicans. The state legislatures also went Republican with 26 states now having Republican majorities and 19 states having Democratic majorities. The remaining 4 states were split. While this suggests a large Republican advantage, the distribution of seats in the legislatures nationwide tells a different story. Republicans still do have an advantage, holding 3,829 seats to the 3,440 held by the Democrats, but that is an advantage of only 2.5% of the seats (National Conference of State Legislatures, 2014).

Today Oklahoma is known as a "red" state, meaning that it votes Republican, but this has not always been the case. In the past, the Democratic Party seemed to dominate. Oklahoma was thus classified as a Democratic-majority state. Oklahoma's classification does need some explanation. After all, some people could look at the Oklahoma legislature and notice that since statehood, the legislature has been majority Democrat all years except 1920, 1921, and 2004-2010 making it a state traditionally dominated by Democrats. The question of party competition, however, depends heavily on how party competition is measured. One needs to look at not only the party composition of the state legislature, but also whether a party won the vote for President, the congressional seats, and most state offices.

In looking at the vote for president, the picture is very clear in Oklahoma. The average presidential vote in Oklahoma from 1960 to 1996 was 55.3% Republican, considerably above the national average of 48.1%. The 2000, 2004, 2008, and 2012 presidential elections were nationally contested elections, but not in Oklahoma. In 2000 Republican George W. Bush got 60.3% of the vote in Oklahoma, while Democrat Al Gore received only 38.4% of the vote. In 2004, Bush did even better, winning with 65.6% of the vote in Oklahoma, compared to John Kerry's 34.4%. In 2008, Oklahoma became unique as it was the only state in the country with each of its counties voting for McCain. Thus, McCain clearly won the state with 65.65% of the vote, and it was also his second highest vote total (Wyoming was first). In 2012, there was a similar result with this time Barack Obama losing to Mitt Romney in Oklahoma. Romney won the election 66.8% to 33.2%, but that does not tell the full story. In 52 of the 77 counties in Oklahoma, Romney won with more than 70% of the vote, with one county as high as 90.4%. Only four counties in the entire state gave Romney less than 60% of the vote. This time Oklahoma was the third reddest state in the country behind Utah (#1) and Wyoming (#2).

With Congressional seats, the picture historically was a bit more mixed as Oklahoma had a split delegation with some Democrats and some Republicans. But in 1996 Oklahoma elected its first entirely Republican delegation to the U.S. Congress (Oklahoma Department of Libraries, 1997; Wayne, 1997). These results were repeated in 1998 as again Oklahomans elected the same delegation to the U.S. Congress. Yet in 2000, Democrat Brad Carson won the open seat vacated by Tom Coburn (R) due to self-imposed term limits. Carson won again in 2002. In the 2004 elections, Carson's 2nd Congressional district seat became open when he vacated that seat in an unsuccessful bid to capture the U.S. Senate seat. Several candidates competed to take his place, and Dan Boren, a Democrat, emerged as the victor with 65.9% of the vote. In the 2006 and 2010 elections, four of the five incumbents including Dan Boren decided to run for re-election, so there was only one truly competitive race. That was for the 5th Congressional district. In 2006 Republican Ernest Istook vacated the seat in a failed bid for Governor and in 2010 Mary Fallin, his replacement, also left the seat to run for governor. Fallin, the Republican won with over 60% of the vote in 2006, and James Lankford after winning a seven-candidate Republican primary won the 2010 general election with 62.5% of the vote. Thus, after the 2010 elections, four of the five congressional seats were held by Republicans, with the lone Democratic seat held by Dan Boren. After the 2012 elections, however, the U.S. Congressional delegation became entirely Republican again as Dan Boren chose not to run for re-election and his seat was captured by Markwayne Mullin. In fact, the major drama in those elections occurred in the 2nd Congressional seat, where the incumbent, Republican John Sullivan, lost in the primary to Jim Bridenstine, who easily won the general election in November 2012.

With statewide offices in Oklahoma, however, another picture appears. Until just the last decade, most of the statewide offices and the legislature were held by Democrats. Oklahomans did elect some Republicans, including Tom Daxon as Auditor/Inspector in 1978, Henry Bellmon as Governor in 1986, Robert Anthony and J.C. Watts as Corporation

Commissioners in 1988 and 1990, and then Claudette Henry as State Treasurer in 1990, but these were the exceptions rather than the rule. The real change, however, came with the 1994 general elections when Oklahomans elected Republicans for Governor, Lieutenant Governor, Commissioner of Labor, Insurance Commissioner, Corporation Commissioner, and to the U.S. Senate. For the first time, a majority of statewide offices were now held by Republicans. Yet the 2004 elections brought another change with most of state offices held by Democrats. Democrats not only captured the governor's office in 2002 with the upset of Brad Henry over Republican Steve Largent, but also control every other major state office except Lieutenant Governor and the Corporation Commission. In 2006, the Republicans also lost the Lieutenant Governor seat when Jari Askins, a Democrat, beat Todd Hiett, a Republican, in a bid to replace Mary Fallin, who ran successfully for the 5th Congressional district seat.

Given the national changes as noted above, Oklahoma's statewide offices were not going to remain Democratic for long. In the 2010 elections, the Republicans experienced the equivalent of a partisan tornado, winning every single statewide election for the first time in Oklahoma history. The closest election was for Insurance Commissioner where the Republican won with 54% of the vote. In the much anticipated race for Governor featuring two female candidates competing against each other, Republican Mary Fallin easily defeated Democrat Jari Askins with over 60% of the vote.

Most measures of party competition focus not only on statewide offices, but also on those for the legislature. Until recent years, Oklahoma has not been very competitive. Prior to the 2004 elections, Oklahomans had a Republican legislature in only two years, 1920 and 1921. In 1996, Oklahoma Republicans held out hope that they might capture the state legislature, but it did not happen. Republicans continued to be in the minority in the 1998, 2000, and 2002 elections although the party made small gains. By the eve of the 2004 election, the combined number of seats for Republicans stood at 68, their highest number ever, which would have seemed to bode well for the November elections.

Indeed, it did. Oklahoma Republicans had one of their most victorious moments in Oklahoma history in 2004, capturing the Oklahoma House with 57 seats, with the Democrats having only 43 seats. Thus, the Republicans now controlled the state House for the first time in in over 80 years. While hopeful that they could win the Oklahoma Senate, the Republicans only gained two seats. In 2006, the Republicans again almost reached the ultimate victory, control of both the Oklahoma House and the Senate. But the Republicans were only able to pick up four seats in the Senate, instead of five, creating a 24-24 tie in the Oklahoma Senate. With a Republican in the Lieutenant Governor's seat, the Republicans would have held the advantage in any tie vote, but that office went to Jari Askins, a Democrat. It wasn't until 2008 that the Republicans finally gained majority control of both houses. Consistent with the Republican landslide nationally in the

2010 elections, Oklahoma Republicans gained even more seats. The party picked up six seats in the House increasing their edge over the Democrats from 62-39 to 68-33. In the Senate, the Republicans knew they would retain their majority even before the November 2010 election was held as they had 25 seats. But they picked up seven additional seats on the day of the election for a 32-16 majority. The 2012 state legislative elections just continued the Republican trend. The Republicans picked up four seats to gain a 36-12 edge in the Oklahoma Senate and picked up two seats and both vacancy seats in the Senate to have a 72-29 edge in the House.

With these recent gains, Republicans have improved their ranking in one of the most commonly used measures of party competition, political scientist **Austin Ranney's party index**. This index looks at four factors: the vote by Democrats for governor, the seats held in the state House, the seats held in the state Senate, and all terms in which Democrats controlled the governorship, Senate, and the House. According to the most recent calculations, Oklahoma is now classified as a competitive two-party state (Maxwell, Crain, & Santos, 2010, p. 124).

III. REDISTRICTING IN OKLAHOMA

One of the major events affecting politics in Oklahoma for the 2002 elections was redistricting. **Redistricting** is the redrawing of both congressional and state legislative district lines to reflect the shifts in populations between states. Because of *Baker v. Carr* and several other Supreme Court decisions decided in the 1960s, one person equals one vote, and thus, districts must be roughly equal in population. Every ten years, the U.S. Census measures those changes in population and determines whether a state has gained or lost population relative to other states. According to the 2000 Census, Oklahoma actually gained in population, but lost in population relative to other states. Thus, Oklahoma was destined to lose a seat in Congress in 2002. This meant that all the congressional districts needed to be redrawn to move from six seats to five. Simultaneously, state legislative districts were also being checked for population changes, and some of those districts needed to be redrawn as well. According to the U.S. Constitution, state legislatures are responsible for redrawing these district lines.

Thus, the Oklahoma legislature had two major goals to accomplish after the 2000 Census and before the 2002 elections: drawing the district lines for the congressional districts and drawing the state district lines as well. This was not going to be an easy process because there were numerous players who had a stake in the system and wanted their political interests protected. Besides the 101 incumbent state legislators and six incumbent members of Congress, then-Governor Frank Keating, a Republican, the state Democratic and Republican parties, and potential challengers to those incumbents, all wanted to control the outcome. Numerous redistricting plans, several court decisions, and several lawsuits later, Oklahoma did get two redistricting plans, but only after the Oklahoma legislature agreed to turn over the decision to the courts. Oklahoma did avoid some of the embarrassing situations that befell other states in their attempts at redistricting. Just south of the Red River in Texas, Democratic state legislators actually left the state en masse on several occasions so that they could protest the Republican plans. Yet at the same time, it is probably safe to say that few people are happy with the final Oklahoma redistricting plan. But that is politics!

Why all the controversy? Because in redrawing the districts, the Oklahoma legislature had to consider numerous factors: protecting incumbents, dealing with Democratic versus Republican interests, retaining Oklahoma's seniority in Congress, individual election decisions, and rural versus urban power. Moreover, redistricting means that not only did the congressional districts need to change, but the state House and Senate districts changed as well. Many state legislators had to face fairly new districts with new voters, new concerns, and new issues. They had to campaign harder than ever to meet their new constituents while making sure that they didn't isolate their old ones. This was not easy for some and as a result, nine seats, five in the House and four in the Senate, changed parties in 2002.

For the 2012 elections, redistricting went much easier, and generally without much controversy. Although Oklahoma's population growth rate was below the national average of 9.7%, it avoided a repeat of the 2002 redistricting process where Oklahoma lost a congressional seat. As a result, the redistricting process for 2012 was bound to be less politically contentious and for the most part it was. Despite complaints by the Democrats that they were ignored in the process and despite some major changes in state legislative seats as the redistricting panels redistricted from west to east, most of the redistricting went fairly smoothly until the November 2010 election intervened. It was during this election that voters passed ballot initiative SQ 748, which altered the structure of Oklahoma's redistricting commission to make it more bipartisan. This upset a Libertarian voter who filed suit, claiming that third parties were now being left out of the process. Regardless, the Oklahoma redistricting process continued and the final redistricting plan was signed into law by Governor Mary Fallin on May 20, 2011. The final plan (see Figure 10–1) leaves state House incumbents basically untouched, making minimal changes to district boundaries and not forcing two incumbents to vie for the same seat. The Senate redistricting was slightly more controversial including complaints about a six-figure consultant, the slight advantage given to suburban areas, and concerns about two districts where one incumbent from each major party would be vying for a single seat. The Congressional districting map was also passed fairly easily, and it too was done far ahead of schedule, with it not needing to be completed until 2010.

FIGURE 10–1 Oklahoma Congressional Districts 2012–2020 Elections

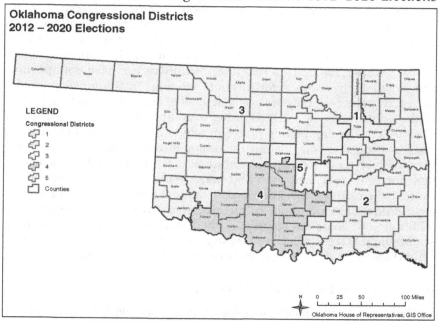

SOURCE: http://www.okhouse.gov/Documents/Districts/2012/Congressional%20District%20Map%202012-2020%20Elections.pdf

IV. OKLAHOMA ELECTION RULES

Rules on Election Day

Oklahoma has a number of rules that govern the election process. Electioneering is prohibited within 300 feet of a polling place, while intoxicating liquor is prohibited within a half mile. To prevent further undue influence, voters cannot disclose how they vote to any other person within a precinct polling place and ballots cannot be removed or brought into a polling place. In 2006, Oklahoma voters passed State Question 733 which lifted the ban on package stores selling alcoholic beverages on election days while the polls were open.

Oklahoma Polling Places

According to the U.S. Election Assistance Commission Report of 2010, Oklahoma had fewer registrants (953 as compared to 1,680 nationally) and fewer Election Day voters (433 as compared to 515 nationally) per polling place. The location of Oklahoma's polling places, though, has occasionally caused concern. In Oklahoma, many of the polling places are located inside religious institutions such as churches or temples. In fact, of the 1961 polling places in Oklahoma, 978 of those are at religious institutions, or 49.9%. In the two most populous counties, Oklahoma County is at 59.4%, while Tulsa is at 62.9%. While no systematic study has been done on this issue nationwide, in North Carolina's study of its polling places, only 500 of 2800 polling places were in religious institutions, or 17.9%. Locating the polls in religious institutions can have both positive and negative effects on voter turnout. Religious institutions have often been chosen because they are easily accessible and they do not have some of the security issues, such as siting a polling place in an elementary school. Thus, having polling places in religious institutions may make it easier for voters to vote, thereby increasing turnout. Yet, at the same time, there may be those who feel uncomfortable voting in a religious institution different from their own and may decide not to vote. The federal courts have ruled on this issue and stated that polling places in religious institutions do not amount to an excessive government entanglement with religion. There are some published guidelines, however, for siting such polling places, including keeping them at a minimum, using a non-consecrated portion of the building or covering religious symbols.

Instruments of Direct Democracy

The populist movement in Oklahoma is very evident in the state's active initiative and referendum processes. These measures allow Oklahomans the right to change the state constitution and statutes directly. Unlike citizens of some other states, Oklahomans can use both the initiative and the referendum, and in the past has used them often. There are usually eight to ten such measures on the ballot each year, dealing with everything from property taxes to wine making.

Oklahoma Ballots

While many other states have adopted an **office-column** ballot where a voter votes separately for each office, Oklahoma has a **party-column** ballot. With this type of ballot, it is much easier to vote for a single political party for all candidates because the ballot is organized that way. Oklahoma is the only state in the nation, however, where a voter must mark the party for each office in order to vote a straight-party ticket. For example, in 2012 an Oklahoman voter wanting to vote for all candidates of the same party needed to vote four times—for president, congress, state offices, and the state legislature. This can make it much more confusing for voters because they have to remember to vote multiple times for their party. The Oklahoma Election Board usually makes a special effort to remind voters of this process, through news reports and at the polling booth. The party-column format may influence the outcome of elections by actually discouraging a straight-party vote. Oklahoma Democrats were convinced that this happened in the 2006 elections in the House District 25 race when Democrat Darrell Nemecek was declared the initial winner by two votes over Todd Thompsen of Ada. But a recount was conducted shortly after the election and four votes were thrown out because incorrect ballots were mistakenly given to four voters for in-person absentee voting. The loser in that recount, Nemecek, blamed the straight-party voting system, saying that it was confusing to some voters who may have marked straight-party voting for statewide offices, but not for local offices which included the legislative races.

At the top of an Oklahoma ballot, the traditional symbols for the major parties are also missing. Rather than use a donkey for the Democrats and an elephant for the Republicans, an Oklahoma ballot features a rooster for Democrats, an eagle for Republicans, a statue of liberty for the Libertarians, and for the Reform party, a five-pointed star in 1996. The rooster and eagle symbols were chosen by the first state legislature so they remain today. The legislature believed ballot symbols were necessary because at that time, many voters were illiterate. Thus, symbols would make it easier to understand the ballot. In filing their candidacies in Oklahoma, candidates cannot adopt or assume famous names, nor can they take the names of persons in office or publicly declared candidates for office, under election law. Candidates are also not allowed to place titles or prefixes before or after their names on the ballot. Such titles as Mr., Mrs., Miss, Dr., Rev., Prof., Judge, Sen., Col., or Sgt., are not allowed on the ballot (Strain, Reherman, & Crozier, 1990).

Absentee Ballots in Oklahoma

At first glance, Oklahoma's absentee ballot procedure would appear to encourage voter turnout. After all, Oklahoma introduced in-person absentee balloting in 1990 and is now one of 32 states (and the District of Columbia) to use that procedure. Oklahoma is also one of 27 states (and DC) that allows for no-excuse absentee balloting by mail. Twenty-one other states require that voters provide a written excuse before submitting an absentee ballot, which tends to discourage voter turnout.

Yet, Oklahoma's absentee ballot procedure is not as simple as it first appears, particularly the procedure by mail. Oklahoma requires that every absentee ballot be notarized and the ballots also need to be returned by mail with a service that requires delivery documentation. According to the U.S. Election Assistance Commission, only 9.1% of Oklahoma voters cast domestic civil absentee ballots in the 2010 elections, compared to a national average of 15.1%. The notary signature makes a big difference. According to the same 2010 U.S. Election Assistance Commission report, Oklahoma had 1,209 absentee ballots rejected in 2010. Of those, Oklahoma was fairly similar to the national averages in the percentage of ballots that were rejected for not being received on time—32.2% in Oklahoma compared to 33.0% nationwide. Oklahoma even had a lower percentage of its ballots, 4.4% as compared to 17.6% nationwide, rejected for a lack of voter signature. But what was striking was the comparison of ballots as reported by the Oklahoma Election Board that were rejected for the lack of witness signature. A whopping 604 ballots or 50.0% of all absentee ballots were rejected for this reason. The percentage nationwide was significantly smaller, only 1.3%. (U.S. Election Assistance Commission, 2010). The Oklahoma legislature in April 2012 made this procedure even more difficult by passing a law which limited a notary public to only sign a maximum of 20 absentee ballots. Given that the Oklahoma legislature has now made this procedure even harder with the limitation on notary publics, the number of absentee ballots rejected should only be expected to increase.

Voter Registration

In order to vote in Oklahoma, one must register with a political party or as an independent. According to registration figures available from the, Oklahoma Election Board, the percentage of Democrat registrants has decreased, while the percentages of Republican and independent registrants have increased. As of January 15, 2014, 885,609 (44.8%) of voters were registered as Democrats, compared to 999,943 (47.8%) in 2011. The Republicans, meanwhile, increased from 849, 332 (40.6%) voters in 2011 to 854,329 (43.2%) in 2014 (Oklahoma Election Board, 2011 and 2014). These numbers could lead many Republicans (and Democrats) to wonder if in a future election Republicans could not only maintain their majorities in the Oklahoma Legislature, but also beat the Democrats in terms of voter registration. As of January 2014, the Republicans only have 31,280 fewer registrants.

In looking at the independents, however, it is much harder to calculate the number of "true" independents. This is because several third parties, most notably the Reform and Libertarian parties, lost their officially recognized status with the state in 2004, and thus by state law, any voter that registers with an unrecognized party by the state is automatically recorded as an independent. But the 2014 registration figures (as of January 15) showed 238, 870 voters registered as independents (12.1%), which is an increase in percentage from 10.8% in 2007 (Oklahoma Election Board 2014).

In looking at Oklahoman registration since 1960, more Oklahomans have registered as Democrats than as Republicans every year. Given the higher percentage of Democrats, it is not surprising that a large percentage of counties are majority Democratic as well. But here there has been a major change since January 2004. In January 2004, all but eight of Oklahoma's 77 counties were majority Democratic. These eight Republican counties were mostly in the northwestern part of the state, with the exception of Tulsa and Washington counties in the northeast. Counties in the southeast were particularly Democratic, with Choctaw, McCurtain, and Pushmataha having less than 6% Republican registered voters. In 2007, 2010, and 2014, however, registered Republicans increased significantly the number of majority Republican counties—21 in 2007, 24 in 2010, and 29 in 2014. The Republicans now have an electoral majority in the Panhandle counties, the other northwestern counties, the highly populated center of the state (Oklahoma, Cleveland, Canadian, Logan, and Noble counties), and several counties near and including Tulsa. Democrats, on the other hand, hold an electoral majority in the northeastern counties, all the southern counties, and all the southeastern counties. In the November 2012 election, Oklahoma ranked 38th of the 50 states in voter registration rates with about 64.3% of Oklahoman citizens registered to vote, compared to 65.1% nationally. Unfortunately, this means that Oklahoma dropped in its voter registration compared to other states as Oklahoma was 70.0% registered and ranked 36th (including DC) among the states in 2008 (http://www.census.gov/hhes/www/socdemo/voting/).

Voter registration can be done at tag agencies or in local government offices. Oklahoma also allows registration by mail for all voters. The closing date for registration before an election is 24 days. One must be a resident of the county where one is registered to vote for at least 30 days. Moreover, Oklahoma is one of just twenty one states to allow **absentee voting without an excuse**. Oklahoma registered voters can vote by absentee ballot for any reason and without notarization. Oklahoma is also one of thirty-two states to offer **early voting**. First used by Texas in the 1988 presidential election, early voting allows voters the chance to vote in person at their county clerk's office or a satellite office usually twenty to forty days before Election Day. Oklahoma is one of 27 states to offer both of these forms of voting (National Conference of State Legislatures, 2014, January 27), which together tend to encourage voter turnout (Busch, 1996).

In 1995, the **National Voter Registration Act** became effective in Oklahoma. More commonly known as **motor voter**, this law allows voters to register by mail at any tag office, welfare office, or disability office, with the burden placed on the voter to give the correct information. During its first eighteen months, the law resulted in a record registration of 20-million people, or nearly a million per month (Wayne, 1997). A news station in Tulsa sought to show in 1996 that motor voter's failure to request identification when registering to vote could lead to voter fraud. The news station successfully registered several animals to vote, including those with such names as Rover and Muffy. Unfortunately for the station, it faced some temporary legal problems as a result of this investigation. It is illegal to misrepresent a voter when registering to vote. To guard against voter fraud, several U.S. Attorneys in Oklahoma created special election boards in 1996 to monitor election fraud in both the Tulsa and Muskogee areas ("Unit to Target Voting Rights Infractions").

Like most states, Oklahoma does **purge** its voter registration records to remove voters who have either died or moved away from their county. Purging records can also substantially reduce voting fraud (Wayne, 1997). Traditionally, the **Oklahoma Election Board**, which governs elections in Oklahoma, has removed nonvoting voters after a four-year time period, but in 1994 the Board purged the rolls of voters after purging in 1992.

These two purges sharply reduced the number of registered voters in Oklahoma from 2.3 million in 1992 to about 1.98 million in 1996. Every few years, Oklahoma has done an additional purge, and thus in March 2013, over 145,000 registrations were removed from the voter rolls in this way. Of those voters, nearly half were registered as Democrats, one-fifth were registered as Independents, and the remaining voters were registered as Republicans (http://okvoterchoice.org/2013/09/as-the-state-purges-voter-rolls-independent-registrations-surge/).

In its January 2004 presidential primary, Oklahoma also implemented a federal law, **the Help America Vote Act**. This law requires that voters show identification the first time they vote in a federal election. Without an acceptable form of identification, voters have to sign an affidavit, and their votes are considered provisional, meaning that their votes are not counted until election officials can verify the information on the affidavit. In the 2010 elections, Oklahomans voted on an initiative, SQ 746, which required that each person appearing to vote had to present a document that verified that person's identity. That document had to have the person's name and photograph, had to be issued by a federal, state or tribal government, and could not expire until after the date of the election. An expiration date exemption was allowed for those voters 65 or older on their identity cards. This initiative passed easily with over 74% of the vote. As of January 2014, thirty-four states had passed some form of photo identification law. Oklahoma is considered by the National Conference of State Legislatures to be one of those in the "least strict" category, as Oklahoma will allow voters to show either a valid government identification card OR a voter registration card, which in Oklahoma does not contain a photo (http://www.ncsl.org/research/elections-and-campaigns/voter-id.aspx). Oklahoma's voter identification law, though, has been challenged in the Oklahoma courts, and as of February 2014, the Oklahoma Supreme Court had agreed to reinstate a challenge to the law by a Tulsa voter who claimed that the law was unconstitutional. So, the future of this law may be uncertain.

Party Nominations

Each election year, the political parties select candidates to represent that party for each office. These are called **nomination elections**. The type of election is determined by the political parties in the fifty states. Prior to the 1890s, most nomination decisions were made by party elites. Political parties typically used conventions open only to elites to select candidates for the major offices, with almost all recommendations for the nominations coming from the elites as well. The **Progressive Movement** rose as a result. Many believed that politics had become too corrupt. Not only did the political process seem to ignore the masses of people who were not party elites, but there was massive political corruption as well. Dead people voted, ballot boxes were stuffed, and alcohol from nearby pubs was used to bribe votes. Much of this kind of power rested with **political machines**, urban party organizations that doled out jobs and other services in exchange for party loyalty, a system known as **patronage**.

The Progressive Movement sought to give power to the masses by taking the power away from the political machines. First, the movement encouraged the adoption of the Australian ballot. The **Australian ballot** is a secret ballot that is not color coded or otherwise marked to reveal candidate preferences. Second, the movement strongly recommended that many government employees be hired on the basis of merit and *not* party loyalty. The end result was that many states, including Oklahoma, began to add a **merit-based system** for selecting government employees. Finally, the Progressive Movement urged the adoption of a **primary election** in all states. A primary allows the voters to select the candidates for the party nominations directly through a ballot. From 1902 to 1955, the existing 48 states all adopted some sort of primary election.

There are basically three types of primaries today. Thirty-five states including Oklahoma have some type of **closed primary**. A closed primary specifies that only those who registered to vote in the party can vote in that party's primary election. With this type of primary, a candidate is more likely to be acceptable to the party, because only those registered with the party can vote for that candidate. In five of these states, the political parties can call a convention instead of holding a primary. The second type of primary is an **open primary**. Eleven states have an open primary where voters can vote for candidates of either party, regardless of how they are registered. In these states, voters typically do not register with a particular party. Those supporting an open primary suggest that the eventual winners of these primaries are more likely to appeal to all the people—whether Democrat, Republican, or independent—because voters can vote for all candidates. Finally, four states have a **top-two primary**, in which all candidates regardless of party run in a single nonpartisan primary. For example, Louisiana voters can vote for candidates of both parties on the same ballot during the primary. Instead of holding general elections, Louisiana then holds a runoff between the top two candidates for an office. California and Washington have similar systems. Nebraska also uses the top-two primary for its nonpartisan state legislative races and some of its statewide elections (Bowman & Kearney, 2015, pp. 76-77).

How Oklahoma Conducts its Primary Elections

Oklahoma's primary elections are relatively late compared to most states. Rather than in April or June of each election year, the Oklahoma Republican and Democratic parties hold their primaries on the fourth Tuesday in August in each even-numbered year, including presidential election years. Primary runoff elections also exist in Oklahoma. If either candidate fails to receive a majority of the votes, a runoff election will take place. The runoff election is held between the top two candidates in the primary election. Primary runoff elections usually occur in states in which the voters are predominantly of one party (Abramson, Aldrich, & Rohde, 2011). These two rules often make it difficult for challengers to compete against incumbents. With a late primary and a potential runoff, as well as a general election, this usually means that candidates have to compete in two or three elections in the short time span between August and the first week in November. This makes it easier for candidates who have substantial campaign funds and built-in name recognition to win their races, because there is not a lot of time to campaign. Thus, incumbents typically have the advantage.

A recent change in Oklahoma statutes authorizes the two parties to allow independents to vote in primary elections, but neither party has done so. Hence, most people register with one of the two major parties. In 2014, Oklahoma's polling hours were from 7:00 a.m. to 7:00 p.m. All citizens of Oklahoma, who are citizens of the United States, age 18 or over are eligible to vote, with only a few exceptions. The Oklahoma Constitution declares ineligible citizens who have been judged guilty of felonies (until their sentences are expired), persons in prisons, and persons committed to mental institutions or who are patients in institutions for the mentally retarded. Persons in the military services do not satisfy residence requirements merely because they are stationed in Oklahoma. Nor do they lose their residency in this state because they are located elsewhere in the line of duty (Strain, Reherman, & Crozier, 1990).

In 2011, Oklahoma was forced to make major changes in its primary elections to comply with both a new federal law, as well as changes enacted by both the major party organizations. First, the new federal law requires that election officials e-mail ballots early enough so that military members stationed overseas as well as registered voters living abroad can have plenty of time to return their ballots in order to be counted. Thus, the Oklahoma legislature moved the filing period for statewide and legislative candidates about 45 days earlier, from early June to mid-April and the primary election has been moved up a month, from the last Tuesday in July to the last Tuesday in June. Thus, the filing period will occur on the second Wednesday, Thursday, and Friday in April. For the 2014 elections, Oklahoma's primary was held on June 24, 2014, and its primary runoff date was held on August 26, 2014. This was quite a change for the candidates because not only was the filing period held at the capitol during its busiest month, but now candidates in a primary runoff only had two months between the original election and the runoff election to campaign instead of just one.

Second, Oklahoma was also forced to change the date of its presidential primary. In the 2008 elections, Oklahoma held its presidential primary on February 5, 2008, meaning that it was held on **Super Tuesday** with almost two dozen other states, giving Oklahoma more of a role to play in the election process because of its early primary date. But several states in the 2008 elections, most notably Michigan and Florida, got penalized by the Democratic National Committee (DNC) because they moved up their primary dates early than the DNC rules allowed and almost lost their delegates at the DNC convention as a result (Abramson, Aldrich, & Rohde, 2011). To avoid this controversy for the 2012 elections, both the DNC and its counterpart the RNC (Republican National Committee) set very clear guidelines for states to follow for their primary dates. Any state that holds its primary date before March 1, 2012, could lose half of its delegates at the national convention. Not wanting to risk that possibility, the Oklahoma legislature passed a law in 2011 that moved its 2012 primary date from February to the first Tuesday in March.

Oklahoma Presidential Elections

Presidential elections essentially consist of three stages: 1) the presidential nomination season, which runs typically from February to June of a presidential election year, 2) the national party conventions typically held during the summer, and 3) the general election season, which usually starts after the conventions are over and runs until the election in November.

Although the candidates usually start campaigning in states much earlier, the first stage is the presidential nomination season in which each state holds an election from February to June of a presidential election year so that its parties can select their nominees. Oklahoma adopted a **presidential preference primary** as its preferred form of election in 1986 and such a primary was held for the first time in March of 1988. Each vote for a candidate on the primary ballot actually represents a slate of delegates committed to vote for that candidate at the presidential convention. The political parties in each state can decide whether their presidential primary contests will use winner-take-all or proportional representation. Most Republican state party organizations, including Oklahoma, have chosen **winner-take-all**, meaning that the winner of each presidential primary receives all of the delegates to the convention for that state. For the 2012 election cycle, states that schedule GOP primaries prior to April 1 had to use proportional representation (Vigdor, 2011). Most Democratic party organizations have chosen **proportional representation**, meaning that candidates who do not win the primaries can still receive some representation at the convention depending on how well they do in that primary. In Oklahoma, Democratic presidential candidates who receive 15% of more of the vote are entitled to receive delegates, with the proportional representation system.

The second stage of a presidential election is the convention season. The **national convention** is where each party chooses the presidential nominee who will represent the political party in November. The convention for each party is typically held in August or September, or about two months prior to the date of the general election. The incumbent president's party usually gets the later date for the convention, giving that candidate an advantage before the general election starts.

The third stage, the **general election,** is much less straightforward. In the United States, voters essentially cast two votes in November—a popular vote for president and the selection of **electors** to represent Oklahoma at the **Electoral College**. The framers of the U.S. Constitution did not trust the masses in voting for President and Vice-President of the United States. They thus created the Electoral College as an institution where party elites, or electors, could choose the president and vice-president based mainly on the wishes of the masses. The winner of the popular vote of the state receives all the electors for that state, with those electors committed to vote for that candidate at the Electoral College. The electors are selected by the state delegate conventions of the political parties in Oklahoma. It is a misdemeanor in Oklahoma for a presidential elector to vote for someone other than the candidate he/she nominally represents. All electors in Oklahoma must sign an oath at least ninety days before the presidential election. The state of Oklahoma has seven electors after redistricting with the 2000 census. The number of electors is equal to the number of U.S. Senators and members of the House of Representatives who represent Oklahoma in the U.S. Congress. Oklahoma electors meet at the State Capitol in December following the general presidential election (Strain, Reherman, & Crozier, 1990).

V. POLITICAL PARTICIPATION IN OKLAHOMA

Because of populist attitudes in Oklahoma, political participation for Oklahomans goes far beyond just turning out to vote. The strong populist tradition in Oklahoma suggests that citizens should have more control over the political affairs in Oklahoma. In Oklahoma, this can be seen through turnout rates higher than the national average.

Voting Turnout in Oklahoma

One of the measures of political participation is **voting turnout**. It is measured by the percentage of voters that are age-eligible to vote that actually turnout at the polls. Voting turnout in Oklahoma has been just slightly higher than the national average with 57.5% for the ten presidential elections between 1960 and 1996. The national average for that same time period was 55.3%. In recent presidential elections, Oklahoma's turnout has been both higher and lower than the national average. In 2000, for example, Oklahoma's turnout rate was 55.3%, which was higher than the national turnout rate of 51.2%. In 2004, Oklahomans set a voting record when 1,463,875 voters cast ballots, the most voters ever. In November 2008, when all 77 Oklahoma counties voted for John McCain, Oklahoma ranked 45th in turnout at 58.8%, compared to the national average of 63.6%. Overall for the 2004-2008 elections, Oklahoma ranked 42nd, with a voter turnout rate of 60.5% (Oklahoma Election Board, 2008). In the 2012 elections, Oklahoma ranked 44th among the 50 states in terms of the percentage of its total citizens who voted, at 51.0%, compared to the national average of 56.5%.

Voting turnout varies substantially by geographic region in Oklahoma. Typically the northern sections of the state tend to have the highest voter turnout, while southern Oklahoma tends to have the lowest voter turnout. This is particularly true in the southeastern section of Oklahoma known as **"Little Dixie."** This geographic area closely resembles the South in terms of its voting patterns, with less voter participation and more support for Democratic candidates. Education and income usually are strongly correlated, and as a result, the southeastern part of the state has the lowest voter turnout. The county with lowest percentage turnout of registered voters in the 2008 presidential elections was Adair, which was the only county below 55% voter turnout of registered voters. Other counties with lower turnout include Haskell, Latimer, Pushmataha, Choctaw, Bryan, Johnston, and Coal–all counties which are south of I-40 and east of I-35. The counties with the highest percentages of turnout were generally in the northern and southwestern sections of the state, with Major County at over 76% turnout of registered voters in the presidential election. On the other hand, the northeastern part of the state has some of the highest levels of education, with wealthier voters and more Republicans. All of these factors encourage the higher voter turnout found in that region.

Yet, party competition must be measured by another factor–competition for elected seats–and Oklahoma does have a problem with making sure its legislative elections are contested. This has become a problem in the last elections in particular. As an example, in 2010, there were 125 races for the state legislature on the ballot in the 2010 elections, and 53 of these only had one name on the ballot. In 2012, even more seats were uncontested in the Oklahoma legislature. In the Oklahoma Senate, 24 seats were up, but in eight of those (or 33.3%) the candidates went completely unopposed, meaning that they did not face a candidate either in the primary or general elections. An additional four candidates only faced a primary opponent, meaning that there were a total of 12 seats out of 24 (or 50%) where the seat was not contested at all in the general elections. Perhaps even scarier for those who desire competitive elections in Oklahoma, the average margin of victory among the ten Senate candidates in 2012 with the *smallest* margin of victory was 31.3%. Yes, elections in Oklahoma are not very competitive!

The lack of competition only increased for the Oklahoma House seats in 2012. With 101 seats up in 2012, 54 of the candidates, or 53.5%, faced no challenger whatsoever. An additional 13 seats saw the candidate being contested in the primaries, but again not in the general election. Thus, 67 of the 101 seats faced no competition in the general election, and thus only 34 seats of the 101 were truly competitive.

Unfortunately, it is not only at the state legislative level where elections fail to be competitive in Oklahoma. The Center for Voting and Democracy rated all 50 states from the 1982 to the 2010 elections in terms of their competitiveness at the congressional election level. Oklahoma was scored on six different aspects of competitiveness, including the amount of competition, whether its elections were landslides, and the amount of representation. Oklahoma ranked 50th among the states, meaning that it had the least competitive congressional races in the nation from 1982 to 2010.

VI. INITIATIVES, REFERENDA, AND RECALLS

Besides turning out to vote, Oklahomans can participate in Oklahoma's initiative, referendum, and recall process. An **initiative** gives voters the right to take direct action by placing questions directly on an election ballot. With an initiative, Oklahomans can change either state statutes or the Oklahoma Constitution itself. While 21 states give their voters the right to change state statutes, only 16 states including Oklahoma allow voters to change the state constitution through the initiative process. In order to create such an initiative, voters would need to circulate a petition among other voters gathering the required number of signatures. Oklahoma requires 15% VH to change the Constitution and 8% VH to change state statutes. **VH** is a designation which stands for the total votes cast for the office receiving the highest number of votes in the last election. These signatures can be gathered for 90 days, and a completed petition should then be delivered to the Oklahoma Secretary of State. Once placed on the petition, signatures cannot be removed, but they do not have to be verified before submission. There is however, a $1,000 penalty for falsifying petition signatures in Oklahoma (Council of State Governments, 1996).

With a **referendum**, the legislature is reluctant to vote on a question and instead places it directly on the ballot, allowing the voters to decide. The Oklahoma Constitution provides for two kinds of referenda. The first type of referendum allows for a change to the Constitution to be made. All 50 states but Alabama have this type of referendum. The second type of referendum deals with the state statutes. The Oklahoma legislature may place a proposition on the ballot or an unhappy group can gather enough signatures on a petition to force a public vote on some legislative act. This type of referendum, called a citizen petition referendum, is rarely used. Nevertheless, 22 states allow for both types of statute referenda. The unhappy group will need to gather signatures equivalent to 5% **VG**, or 5% of the total votes cast for governor in the last election. All types of referenda can occur within 90 days of the legislative session and are not restricted to subject matter (Council of State Governments, 1996). In Oklahoma, a large percentage of legislation in the Oklahoma legislature carries an **emergency clause**, meaning that legislation requires a two-thirds vote to pass and goes into effect immediately upon the signature of the governor. If no emergency clause is attached legislation in Oklahoma then has 90 days after the legislature adjourns before becoming effective. During that 90-day period, the citizen petition referendum can take place. With enough signatures, the people can vote on that issue.

Oklahoma's initiative and referendum process is very active. Oklahoma faces an average of eight to ten such measures every year.

The 2010 elections were unusual, not only in the sheer number of state questions on ballot (eleven), but also their variety, including questions on everything from Sharia law to spending on common education. There was even a referendum that dealt with initiatives and referendums, SQ 750, which was designed to lower the signature requirement for initiatives and referendums. SQ 750 got 50.4% of the vote. But one of the more unusual features of these eleven state questions was their length. With all 11 state questions, there were nearly 2000 words. When combined with the nine statewide offices, a U.S. Senator seat, a U.S. House seat, and all the judge positions, some worried that voters might experience **ballot fatigue**, where the number of voters voting for each position/state question drops as they move down the ballot (Bisbee, 2010). In fact, this was the longest ballot that Oklahoman voters had experienced since 1984. In 2012, the ballot was considerably shorter, as there were only six initiatives on the ballot, all of which passed. Once again the topics of these state questions varied tremendously, with two on ad valorem taxes, and other state questions on affirmative action, parole, water infrastructure, and creating a welfare department.

Like other election campaigns, efforts to get initiatives and referenda are monitored by the Oklahoma Election Board. In many initiative or referendum campaigns, special interest groups, like the elderly or educators, will contribute money to influence passage of the measure. Although the Oklahoma Constitution prohibits corporate contributions to elections, the U.S. Supreme Court has held recently that corporations have a first amendment right to contribute to initiative and referendum campaigns. According to Oklahoma's ethics laws, groups campaigning on state questions must report contributions in excess of $200 annually. These disclosures have revealed corporate contributions in excess of $20,000 to certain state question campaigns. In 1990, the Oklahoma legislature passed legislation that would require more stringent reporting of such campaigns so that contributors could be known. This legislation, supported by both Oklahoma Common Cause and the Oklahoma League of Women Voters, was vetoed by Governor Henry Bellmon. The Governor thought that it would hinder the public's use of the initiative and the referendum.

Oklahoma's recall process is limited compared to some other states. A **recall election** allows voters the chance to reject an elected official through a direct vote of the people after that person has already served in office. Nineteen states currently have a process whereby citizens can petition their government to recall officials in various positions, including governors, legislators, and Supreme Court judges. The state of Oklahoma does not have a recall system at the state level. Therefore, no recall elections are held for governor, state legislators, school board officials, county officials, or other state positions. This lack of a voter recall caused problems for some Oklahoma voters when Democrat Governor David Walters was governor from 1991 to 1994. Voters sought his removal in 1991 because he had illegally solicited campaign contributions. While in office, Governor Walters plead guilty to a misdemeanor election violation. Oklahoma voters found, however, that he could not be removed from office because the state had no recall process for governors. Given that Governor Walters would be facing a Democratic legislature, impeachment was considered as an option, but only briefly, by those unhappy with his term in office.

This has led occasionally for calls to institute such a recall procedure at the state level. Representative Danny Morgan (D-Prague), for example, introduced an amendment in February 2012 that would allow such an occurrence. His amendment would have applied to all elected officials in Oklahoma. Citizens who wanted to recall an official would have 90 days to gather registered voters totaling at least 15% of the number of voters in the most recent general election. If the petition had been successful, the recall election would feature two questions: should the official be recalled and who should replace the official if the recall is successful. Under the language of the amendment, the official being recalled could not be placed on that list. Unfortunately for Morgan, this amendment failed in the legislature, but was however re-introduced in the 2014 legislature and was still pending as of April 2014.

There is, however, a recall option for voters in some municipalities. Of the 50 to 55 municipal governments organized under a home rule charter, about 15 to 20 have recall elections at the municipal level (Myers, 1996). The larger cities in Oklahoma have a home rule charter. One example of such a recall election took place in Del City, Oklahoma, where a city council member faced a recall election in 1997, allegedly because of that member's effort to seek a grand jury investigation into the actions of fellow council members. In a more recent recall election, a Piedmont, Oklahoma, councilman in August 2013 upset some of his constituents after meeting privately with a company that was interested in building a wind farm in Northern Piedmont. He ended up losing the recall election.

VII. RECENT ELECTIONS IN OKLAHOMA

Presidential Elections in Oklahoma

Unlike 1996 and 2000, when candidates barely visited the state, Oklahoma in 2004 became one of the presidential candidates' prime destinations because of the early February primary. Senator Edwards, for example, made fourteen separate visits to Oklahoma. A major debate was held in October in Stillwater, Oklahoma, and several candidates debated health care just a few days before the Oklahoma primary in Edmond, Oklahoma. The weekend before the primary saw a flurry of campaign ads, including one 30-minute spot by General Wesley Clark, and numerous campaign rallies daily by the candidates. The eventual winner was Clark (AR) who ended up spending the most of any the candidates on campaign ads and mail circulars. Senator John Edwards (NC) who received an endorsement from former University of Oklahoma football coach Barry Switzer came in second, while Senator John Kerry (MA), the winner of the Iowa and New Hampshire elections came in third. Democratic voter turn-out for the race, the only one on the ballot, was 29%, while Republicans had only 9% with George W. Bush easily defeating a Los Angeles t-shirt maker to win Oklahoma's Republican delegates. In the 2004 General Election, George W. Bush easily defeated John Kerry, the eventual Democratic nominee in Oklahoma, taking 65.6% of the vote.

With several states moving up their presidential primary dates in 2008, most notably California, the 2008 presidential election race started fast, with about twenty candidates declaring early, roughly split between the two parties. Notable early candidates included Hillary Clinton, Rudolph Giuliani, Barack Obama, John McCain, Fred Thompson, Mitt Romney, and John Edwards. Several candidates visited the state in early 2007, including Rudy Giuliani, John Edwards, Barack Obama, and Bill Richardson, all before May 2007. Thus, Oklahoma seemed to have not only more presidential candidates visit the state, but they also visited earlier than usual. This was not a surprise given the early primary dates of California, Oklahoma, and many other states for the 2008 presidential elections. Oklahoma had its election on February 5, 2008, which was **Super Tuesday**, which meant that nearly two dozen states were also holding their election contests on this particular day. Yet, by the time the Iowa and New Hampshire elections had passed, the choices of candidates for Oklahomans had been whittled down from eleven original Republican candidates who were on the ballot to only seven still in the race. For Democrats, they lost four of their seven candidates the same way, so only Hillary Clinton, Barack Obama, and a perennial Oklahoma candidate, Jim Rogers, were actual candidates in the 2008 Democratic primary. Hillary Clinton (D) and John McCain (R) ending up winning the Democratic and Republican presidential nominations respectively in Oklahoma, and it was not a big surprise in this "red" state that Oklahoma voted for John McCain with 65.65% of the vote, or a 31.3% margin of victory over the eventual nationwide winner, Barack Obama.

As stated previously, Oklahoma's 2012 presidential primaries were held on March 6, 2012, which was about month later than they had been held in the 2008 elections. This had several consequences for Oklahoma. First, Oklahoma was not one of the first states, as twelve states had held their primaries before Oklahoma. Second, this also meant that the selection of candidates had effectively been already narrowed by the previous states. Thus, while the 2012 elections started with seven Republican presidential candidates on the ballot in Iowa, the first state, by the time the voting took place in Oklahoma, only four candidates were left: Mitt Romney, Rick Santorum, Ron Paul, and Newt Gingrich. Despite being on March 6, however, Oklahoma's primary got plenty of attention from the Republican candidates. Given Oklahoma's status as one of the "reddest" states, all four candidates wanted to win Oklahoma, and thus made sure to visit here. Romney's October 2011 event was directly across the street from the state GOP headquarters, and he had county chairs in the top 10 counties and volunteer teams in all five congressional districts. Ron Paul attracted 1300 voters and Newt Gingrich attracted 500 voters to their rallies respectively before the March primaries. When the voting was completed, Rick Santorum had won the state, despite the fact that Mitt Romney was trending as the winner nationally at the time. Santorum won with 34% of the vote, Romney had 28% of the vote, and Gingrich had 27%, while Paul only had 10% of the vote. On the Democratic side, incumbent President Barack Obama won easily as expected with 57.1% of the vote, but not without some drama. Not only did this represent one of his lowest vote totals, since he was running basically uncontested as the Democratic presidential nominee, but the candidate in second place with 18% of the votes was Randall Terry. In January 2012, the Democratic National Committee thought so little of Randall Terry that it sent out a letter declaring that he was not a "bona fide" candidate for the Democratic nomination. Yet in Oklahoma, he still managed to get second place.

The Oklahoma Democratic Party sent 50 delegates to its national convention in September 2012 in Charlotte, North Carolina, where eventually Barack Obama was chosen as the Democratic nominee, despite the fact that some Oklahoma delegates were pledged to vote for Terry. The Oklahoma Republican Party, on the other hand, sent 43 delegates to its August 2012 convention in Tampa, Florida and used winner-take-all as its method. Of the 43 delegates, fifteen were allocated by district, with each district winner receiving automatically all three pledged delegates. Ten at-large delegates and three bonus delegates were all pledged to vote for the statewide winner. The final three delegates were party leaders who were not pledged to vote for a particular candidate. In Oklahoma, Santorum had 14 of the pledged delegates, Gingrich and Romney each had 13, and 3 were uncommitted. On the convention floor, 34 of the delegates eventually went to Romney (79%), 6 delegates went to Ron Paul, and 3 were unannounced. There had been tension between the Oklahoma Romney and Paul campaigns all the way back to the Oklahoma convention which had been held in Norman in May 2012, when the Paul supporters accused the Romney supporters of physically attacking them as well as violating the rules of the convention. In November 2012, Oklahoma voters cast their ballots for their favored presidential candidate during the general elections. With no surprise, Mitt Romney won easily with 66.8% of the votes in Oklahoma, while Barack Obama lost with 33.2% of the votes. Also not a surprise, every single county in Oklahoma gave a majority of its votes to Romney over Barack Obama.

Congressional and State Elections

The last twenty years (1994-2014) have not been good for the Democrats in Oklahoma, but they have been good for Republicans. Although Oklahoma has voted for Republican presidential candidates since 1960, it usually was considered a Democratic state because most of its state offices, including a majority of the legislature, were held by Democrats. Yet in 1994, for the first time, Oklahomans voted in Republicans for a majority of the state offices, including Governor Frank Keating and Lieutenant Governor Mary Fallin. The 1996 and 1998 elections brought more changes. After the 1996 elections, for the first time in Oklahoma history its congressional delegation was represented entirely by Republicans. In 1998, the Democrats lost 4 seats in the State House, raising the hopes of Republicans that they could capture the House in 2000. Alas, that did not happen. In fact, while Republicans celebrated as George W. Bush won the most competitive race in presidential election history, Democrats cheered because they picked up another prize—the 2nd district seat in the U.S. Congress won by Brad Carson. Yet Republicans did console themselves with their gains in the state legislature. They won three open seats formerly held by Democrats and defeated five incumbent Democrats, making Republicans just five seats short of the Democrats' 53-seat majority in the legislature.

More recent elections, such as those in 2002, have brought some political turmoil to Oklahoma in more ways than one, as shown in Table 10–2. First, Oklahoma's gubernatorial election was a surprise to most political experts. Former Representative Steve Largent had resigned his House seat to campaign for governor and spent $3.18 million, more than any of his competitors, and was viewed as the clear frontrunner for most of the race. But then independent Gary Richardson entered ended up spending $2.63 million on the race, mostly from his own funds. That money bought campaign ads which Richardson aired on television at least one year before the race and before most of his competitors. On the Democratic side, there appeared to be more disarray at first than a strong challenger. Brad Henry, although a state legislator, was relatively unknown throughout the state and faced well-financed businessman Vince Orza in a primary that was close enough to need a runoff election. But Henry won the runoff election, and was able to use that momentum to carry him to the governor's office. Henry ended up spending the least of the three major competitors with only $2.28 million. He probably benefited greatly from a ballot proposition on cockfighting which increased voter turnout particularly in the Democratic counties, and Gary Richardson as the independent candidate mostly attacked Largent, the frontrunner. What was the end result? Oklahoma had its closest gubernatorial election in 32 years, with Henry getting 43.3% of the vote, Largent with 42.6% of the vote, and Richardson with 14.2% of the vote.

	TABLE 10–2				
Changes in Oklahoma Congressional and State Seats					
	2004 ELECTIONS	2006 ELECTIONS	2008 ELECTIONS	2010 ELECTIONS	2012 ELECTIONS
1ST SEAT IN CONGRESS	John Sullivan (R)	John Sullivan (R)	John Sullivan (R)	John Sullivan (R)	Jim Bridenstine (R)
2ND SEAT IN CONGRESS	Dan Boren (D)	Dan Boren (D)	Dan Boren (D)	Dan Boren (D)	Markwayne Mullin (R)
3RD SEAT IN CONGRESS	Frank D. Lucas (R)	Frank D. Lucas (R)	Frank D. Lucas (R)	Frank D. Lucas (R)	Frank D. Lucas (R)
4TH SEAT IN CONGRESS	Tom Cole (R)	Tom Cole (R)	Tom Cole (R)	Tom Cole (R)	Tom Cole (R)
5TH SEAT IN CONGRESS	Ernest Istook (R)	Mary Fallin (R)	Mary Fallin (R)	James Lankford (R)	James Lankford (R)
OKLAHOMA SENATOR	Tom Coburn (R)			Tom Coburn (R)	
OKLAHOMA SENATOR			James Inhofe (R)		
GOVERNOR		Brad Henry (D)		Mary Fallin (R)	
LIEUTENANT GOVERNOR		Jari Askins (D)		Todd Lamb (R)	
CORPORATION COMMISSION CHAIR			Dana Murphy (R)		
CORPORATION COMMISSION COMMISSIONER		Bob Anthony (R)			
CORPORATION COMMISSION VICE-CHAIR	Denise Bode (R)		Jeff Cloud (R)	Patrice Douglas (appointed 9/2011)	Patrice Douglas (R)
STATE TREASURER		Scott Meacham (D)		Ken Miller (R)	
SUPT. OF PUBLIC INSTRUCTION		Sandy Garrett (D)		Janet Barresi (R)	
COMMISSIONER OF LABOR		Lloyd L. Fields (D)		Mark Costello (R)	
ATTORNEY GENERAL		Drew Edmondson (D)		Scott Pruitt (R)	
INSURANCE COMMISSIONER		Kim Holland (D)		John Doak (R)	
STATE AUDITOR & INSPECTOR		Jeff A. McMahan (D)		Gary Jones (R)	
TOTAL SEATS HELD BY EACH POLITICAL PARTY	8 seats Democrat 10 seats Republican	9 seats Democrat 9 seats Republican	9 seats Democrat 9 seats Republican	1 seat Democrat 17 seats Republican	0 seats Democrat 18 seats Republican

NOTE: A blank space indicates the seat was not up for reelection that year. The officeholder thus remains the same as the previous year.

In 2004, there were very few statewide races in Oklahoma—only those for corporation commissioner and U.S. Senator. The former was very uneventful; Denise Bode, the Republican, won as predicted with 63.6% of the vote. The exciting race instead was the race for U.S. Senator between Democrat Brad Carson, Republican Tom Coburn, and independent Sheila Bilyeu. With Don Nickles (R) retiring, this became an open seat featuring high-quality candidates. Both Carson and Coburn had represented the state of Oklahoma before as U.S. House members. Thus, this was widely predicted to be a competitive race. One of the more interesting features of this race was the involvement of the national parties. By the time the race was finished, both the Democratic National Committee and the Republican National Committee had given about $600,000 each to their respective candidates because it was feared by both parties that this race could decide the U.S. Senate. With some well-placed campaign advertising including one featuring Brad Carson as a puppet of the Democratic Party and one that called Brad Carson too liberal for Oklahoma, Tom Coburn was able to overcome some mistakes during the campaign to defeat Brad Carson, 52.8% to 41.2%. Perhaps because of all the negative campaigning during this race, Sheila Bilyeu was able to surprisingly do well for an independent candidate, getting 6% of the vote.

In 2006, Oklahoma statewide races were also generally uneventful. This even included the Governor's race which at one point featured 5-6 Republican candidates vying to spar against the incumbent Brad Henry (D) for his seat. But in the end, Henry easily defeated Ernest Istook (R), the former member of Congress, 66.5% to 33.5%. Other races such as that for attorney general, state treasurer, superintendent of public instruction and all five US congressional seats followed a similar pattern, with one candidate typically getting at least 60% of the vote. The exceptions to this during the 2006 came with the Lieutenant Governor's race, where Jari Askins (D) won with only 50.1% over Todd Hiett (R) who had 47.5% and the Insurance Commissioner and State Auditor and Inspector races where both Democratic candidates, Kim Holland and Jeff McMahan, won their races with about 52% of the vote. The closest statewide race came with the Commissioner of Labor seat where Lloyd Fields (D) competed against the incumbent Brenda Reneau (R). This was a rematch of the 2002 election when Fields lost to Reneau by only 44,000 votes. This time Fields was victorious, but winning by just over 2,700 votes.

In the 2008 elections, mostly Republicans triumphed. There was no suspense in the congressional election seats as the four incumbents for U.S. Representative retained their seats (three Republicans and one Democrat), and the lone open seat was an easy win for Republican Mary Fallin. A close race for U.S. Senate also did not materialize with incumbent Republican James Inhofe easily defeating Andrew Rice, 56.6% to 39.1%. In fact, the only close race was the short-term Corporation Commissioner seat, where Republican Dana Murphy defeated Democrat Jim Roth with 52.6% of the vote. The Republicans easily won the long-term Corporation Commissioner seat with Jeff Cloud winning with 60.98% of the vote.

All of the stars aligned for Republicans in the 2010 elections. President Barack Obama has never been very popular in Oklahoma, and the stimulus plan and Obamacare bills that he helped get through Congress did not help his popularity. When combined with the fact that this was a midterm election where Democrats were expected to lose, the 2010 election was never going to be a banner year for Democrats statewide in Oklahoma. But even some Democratic pundits hoped that they might pick up 3-4 statewide seats. Alas, that did not happen, with Democrats losing every statewide seat they contested in 2010–from Governor to Superintendent of Public Instruction. There were nine seats in all and when combined with the two Republican holdover Corporation Commission seats, the Republicans after the 2010 elections held all eleven statewide seats for the first time in Oklahoma history.

In the 2012 elections, there was only one statewide seat—Corporation Commissioner—and that did not turn out to be a contest. The governor appointed Patrice Douglas to the Corporation Commissioner seat in September 2011 when Jeff Cloud left office. She was reelected in 2012 easily when she did not get an opponent to run against her. Thus, most of the suspense in the 2012 concerned the margin of victory in the Oklahoma legislature and the congressional seats. With the Oklahoma legislature, Republicans were widely expected to retain their majorities in both the House and the Senate, but they were also hopeful that they would gain seats. Indeed, they did. In the Oklahoma House, the Republicans increased their majority advantage from 70-31 to 72-29. In the Oklahoma Senate, the Republican majority also increased from 32-16 to 36-12. With the congressional seats, the suspense was really not about which party would capture the five congressional seats. They were all widely expected to go Republican. The first and second congressional district seats, however, made the 2012 elections a lot more interesting, but for different reasons. The first congressional district seat was expected to be a fairly boring race. After all John Sullivan (R) was a five-term incumbent who had definitely outraised his opponent, and there wasn't expected to be much of a Democratic challenger. Well, the second part of that did come true, but unfortunately for Sullivan, he lost his Republican primary election to Jim Bridenstine in a shocking upset. Sullivan received only 46% of the vote to Bridenstine's 54%.

In the second congressional district, Dan Boren (D) chose not to run for reelection, creating an open seat. Despite the fact that the seat had been held by Democrats for over a decade, Republicans were once again expected to win the seat. After coming in first but only getting 42% of the vote against George Faught in the Republican primary, Markwayne Mullin defeated him again in the runoff and then defeated Democrat Rob Wallace, 57 to 38% in the general election.

Term Limits in Oklahoma

In 1990, Oklahoma became the first state in the nation to adopt term limits for its state legislators. These **term limits** require that state legislators can only serve twelve consecutive years in the either the Oklahoma House and/or Senate. As adopted, term limits apply only to state legislators, but did not completely take effect on Oklahoma's state legislators until 2004. Fifteen states including Oklahoma circulated petitions in the states to examine term limits at the congressional level. In ***U.S. Term Limits vs Thornton***, the U.S. Supreme Court held that the states cannot impose term limits on Congress. To maneuver around this ruling, 14 of the 15 states, including Oklahoma, have adopted **instruct and inform laws**. Candidates for state legislative and congressional races, under these laws, would be required to sign a pledge that they will do everything in their power once elected to adopt a constitutional amendment to limit congressional terms. Failure to adhere to the pledge exacts a price: the words "disregarded voters' instruction on term limits" will appear next to their names on the ballot when they run for reelection (Rafool & Warnock, 1996).

The impact of term limits on the 2004 elections was substantial. In the Oklahoma House alone, there were 28 seats that were left open because of a term limits, and when combined with the 9 members who left office or who lost in other primary races, that meant the Oklahoma legislature experienced 37 new House members after the 2004 elections. The impact of term limits has continued even with the most recent elections.

With the 2012 elections the large number of open seats continued, with 13 open seats in the House of Representatives and 7 open seats in the Senate. Of those 20 open seats, 8 were the direct result of term limits, with 6 representatives and 2 senators being term-limited. In other states, like California, where the states adopted term limits earlier, there has typically been substantial rotation of seats, with term-limited candidates just seeking other offices. This is particularly likely to be the case in Oklahoma with its state legislative term limits as Oklahoma has **permanent term limits**, meaning that once a candidate has reached the end of his or her term, he or she can no longer run for any state legislative office ever. After the 2010 elections, this possibility got more interesting when Oklahoma passed SQ 747. This law limits the terms for all statewide offices, with most of those term limits set at eight years, except for the corporation commissioner positions which were limited to twelve years. That initiative passed with nearly 70% of the vote. There is evidence that "office-hopping" is already taking place in Oklahoma. Many former state legislators ran in the 2010 elections for other offices including Fallin and Askins for Governor, Lamb and Corn for Lt. Governor, and Paddack for Superintendent of Public Instruction, among others.

There is, however, one more option for term-limited state legislators; they can work as lobbyists and lobby their former colleagues in the institution they just left. This is known as the **revolving door** of lobbying.

These former members clearly have an advantage in lobbying as they are known by their former colleagues and they also know the institution well, having served it just previously. On the 2014 list of registered lobbyists in the state of Oklahoma, there are dozens of former Oklahoma legislators, including Thad Balkman, Fred Morgan, Bill Nations, and Greg Piatt.

Some Conclusions

Oklahoma is a strong state politically. In recent years elections have become more competitive, providing genuine competition for most state-wide offices in Oklahoma. The two major parties themselves have also been strengthened considerably, with more resources, more organization, and more staff. Recent elections in Oklahoma have seen major changes with Republicans capturing most state offices and congressional seats. Most Oklahomans have also continued to vote Republican at the presidential level.

ONLINE RESOURCES

Oklahoma Election Board:	www.ok.gov/~elections
Oklahoma Democratic Party:	www.okdemocrats.org
Oklahoma Republican Party:	www.okgop.com
Democratic National Committee:	www.democrats.org
Republican National Committee:	www.rnc.org
Libertarian Party:	www.lp.org
New Party:	www.newparty.org
Patriot Party:	www.patriotparty.us/
Socialist Party:	www.sp-usa.org
Tulsa World:	www.tulsaworld.com
Lawton Constitution:	www.lawton-constitution.com
Daily Oklahoman:	www.oklahoman.com
OBAR:	www.okvoterchoice.org
Initiatives and referendums in the states:	www.pirg.org/aapc/platform/init.htm

INTEREST GROUPS AND CAMPAIGN FINANCE IN OKLAHOMA

Jan C. Hardt

Successful lobbyists, without exception, know the bill under discussion in any committee as well or better than most of the members. They have dissected every sentence and phrase and know what a difference the "will" and "shall" can make. They also are well aware that the lobbying process is long and often convoluted, calling for patience and often cunning. There's a rhythm to the legislative dance, and lobbyists have to become masters of the steps. Like the seasons, the ebb-and-flow of legislation changes and occupies different venues.

Ralph Wright, former Speaker of the Vermont House of Representatives

So much money is being spent on the campaign that I doubt if either man, as good as they are, are worth what it will cost to elect him.

Will Rogers

I. INTRODUCTION

Oklahoma has a number of very active interest groups. Interest groups help Oklahomans to participate in politics by organizing citizens around groups of particular interests. Many citizens have also raised concerns about the power, influence, and growing activity of interest groups. Fortunately, the Oklahoma Ethics Commission has placed more effective restrictions on these groups and how they can lobby the legislature, as well as other aspects of the government. The Ethics Commission, for example, has tightened its definition of who is a lobbyist, meaning that more lobbyists are now regulated. It has also enacted very specific laws about how these interest groups can be involved in campaigns, and how much they can donate to politicians.

Oklahomans also participate in politics by donating money. The more money a candidate receives, the more likely that candidate is going to win the race. The money spent varies tremendously with the type of seat being sought, whether there is an incumbent, the type of challenger, and the amount of competition in the race. This chapter will examine the growth of interest groups, their lobbying efforts, and the role of campaign finances in Oklahoma politics.

II. Lobbying In Oklahoma

What is Lobbying and Who Does It?

Lobbying is most often done by interest groups seeking to influence decisions made by the executive, legislative, or judicial branches of government. **Lobbying** can be defined as the communication of data or opinion by someone other than a citizen to a governmental decision maker in an effort to influence a specific decision. **Interest groups** are individuals with common needs who seek changes in public policy. Oklahoma tends to be an active state in terms of both the numbers of lobbyists and the numbers of interest groups participating.

Lobbyists and Interest Groups in Oklahoma

In 1948 American journalist John Gunther identified some of the earliest interest groups in Oklahoma politics. He found that the most active interest groups were the Baptist Church, oil interests, the elderly, the education lobby, and "county rings" (Green, 2004, p. 201). In 1960 the five same groups were still influential, but Stephen Jones, an Enid lawyer, added labor unions and newspaper organizations to the list as well.

In order to represent their interests, most groups rely on **lobbyists**. Lobbyists are individuals who are usually paid by interest groups to represent their interests to the legislature or other government entities. Lobbyists tend to be highly educated with 46.5 percent having a bachelor's degree, and another 46.5 percent having a master's degree (31.4%), doctorate (5.0%), or law degree (10.1%) according to a 2006 survey. The same survey found that 72% of the lobbyists surveyed in Oklahoma were male, that their average age was a little more than 51 years of age, and that they averaged over eleven years in lobbying (Davis, Metla, & Herlan, 2006). The annual income from lobbying in Oklahoma is $86,525, which is low compared to most states since Oklahoma ranks 44th among the fifty states in the average yearly income for lobbyists (Coleman, 2006).

The number of registered lobbyists in Oklahoma has grown steadily, with 83 lobbyists in 1976, 343 lobbyists in 1986, 410 lobbyists in 1997, and 417 lobbyists in 2004, but only 374 in 2007, 322 in 2011, and 321 in 2014. Of the 321 lobbyists in 2014, 76.3% came from Oklahoma, while 23.7% were from out-of state, meaning that 6% more are in-state lobbyists compared to both 2004 and 2007. Lobbyists can represent single interests such as

Michael Means who works for the Oklahoma State Home Builders Association and lobbies the Oklahoma legislature. Or a lobbyist can work for multiple interests, such as Jami McAnulty Longacre who works in Kellyville, OK, for 21 different interests. Many of the lobbyists, including Longacre are with consulting firms who not only lobby for multiple interests, but these interests can also be very diverse, and not necessarily in the same field of expertise. Longacre lobbies for Oklahoma-based PACs such as the Oklahoma Pork Council, the Oklahoma Agricultural Education Teachers Association, and the Oklahoma Grocers Association, but also for several interests with a more national focus, such as Monsanto and Johnson & Johnson. Longacre also lobbies for purely municipal interests, such as the Jenks Public Works Authority, TRUST (Transportation Revenues Used Strictly for Transportation), and the Tulsa Regional Chamber. Of the 321 registered lobbyists in 2014, 102, or 31.8% work for multiple interests, with an average of 11.8 interests per lobbyist among those with multiple interests. These numbers are consistent with those of 2011 as in that year there were 108 lobbyists working for multiple interests for a percentage of 33.5 with 9.2 interests per lobbyist.

In contrast to the early years of studying lobbyists (1976 and 1986) when oil and gas companies had the most lobbyists, today the "other" category has the most lobbyists, as shown in Table 11–1. The percentage of "other" lobbyists in 2014 (31.3%) represents a decrease from 2011, when they represented 59% of all lobbyists.[2] Over the years, there has been some variation in terms of which group has the most lobbyists

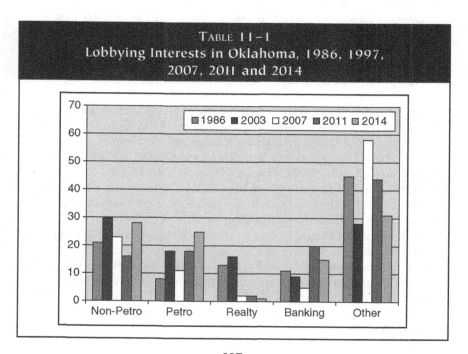

TABLE 11–1
Lobbying Interests in Oklahoma, 1986, 1997, 2007, 2011 and 2014

after business. In 1986, the second and third largest lobbying groups were real estate organizations and the banking community, with 13.4% and 11.7% respectively. Surprisingly, given the fact that Oklahoma has the reputation of being an oil and gas state, the petroleum community in 1986 had only the fourth largest group of lobbyists, representing 7.3% of all lobbyists registered in Oklahoma. In 2014, however, oil and gas came in third place. What has really dropped is the number of lobbyists representing only real estate organizations with only twenty in Oklahoma in 2014 (Oklahoma Ethics Commission, 2014; Morgan, England, & Humphreys, 1991).

This categorization, though, while used by political scientists for almost forty years in Oklahoma does not appear to be the best fit anymore. What it obscures are several interests in Oklahoma that clearly have a large number of lobbyists that can get lost in some of these other categories. A good example of this are the "health" interests in Oklahoma, which represented 15.5% of all interests lobbied for in Oklahoma. Education was also another key category, with 5.5% of all interests. But another upcoming category, although small in size, is the category representing municipal interests. These interests can include the Tulsa Regional Chamber, the Lawton Chamber of Commerce, the Woodward Industrial Foundation, and City of Oklahoma City.

Over time, some have asked whether there are too many lobbyists in Oklahoma. One way to measure this is to look at the number of lobbyists in a state versus the number of legislators. A smaller ratio means that there are fewer lobbyists in that state, but that could also mean that those lobbyists might have more influence since there are fewer people lobbying. Davis, Metla, and Herlan found in their sample in 2006 that there were 2.6 lobbyists to each legislator. In 2014, that number had dropped to 2.2 lobbyists per legislator, with 321 lobbyists and 149 legislators. According to a study conducted by Rawls (2005), only seven states had fewer lobbyists per legislator, with four being in the Northeast (New Hampshire, Pennsylvania, Vermont, and Maine), and only one of these, Pennsylvania, considered to be a large state. The three states with the most lobbyists per legislator were all large, including New York (18:1), Florida (13:1), and Illinois (12:1), but being a large state does not necessarily guarantee a large number of lobbyists per legislator as indicated by the example of Pennsylvania (Rawls, 2005). Thus, Oklahoma with its 2.2:1 ratio is actually on the small side in terms of the number of lobbyists per legislator, ranking it about 40th in the nation, and under the national average of 5:1 lobbyists per legislator (Rawls, 2005).

Having more lobbyists, however, does not always mean that an organization has more influence. In 1986, legislators were asked their perceptions of the most influential lobbyists. The three most influential groups have not even been mentioned yet—education, labor and professional groups. Banking and finance, public employees, oil, and business lobbyists round out the list of lobbyists legislators think are most influential (Morgan, England and Humphreys, 1991).

Recent Oklahoma Legislation and Lobbying

This list by no means exhausts the types of interest groups active in Oklahoma. By looking at only the most numerous or influential groups listed in a broad survey, one can miss other advocacy or single-issue interest groups that can be very influential when activated. For example, one powerful interest group lobby includes Indian tribes. Nineteen different Native American groups have their interests represented by lobbyists. These include those of the Chickasaw Nation, the Muskogee (Creek) Nation, the Osage Nation, the Citizen Potawatomi Nation, and the Cherokee Nation, just to mention a few. In 2004, a gaming issue came up before the legislature. In order to save the horse racing industry in Oklahoma, proponents argued that more gaming would have to be present at the race tracks. This issue featured an unusual combination of lobbyists arguing for the measure: education interests who would get some of the profits, the horse racing industry, and Native American gaming interests. More recently, Native Americans, business interests, and others were active in bringing a state lottery to Oklahoma. The state lottery became a state question on the 2004 election ballot which passed, and thus Oklahoma had its first state lottery starting in 2005.

On occasion, there can be a heated battle between lobbyists on different sides of an issue. That is certainly the case between Oklahoma grape growers and vintners who are trying to get the legal ability to sell their wine directly to retail outlets who are competing against a few, but well-funded liquor wholesalers. Under current Oklahoma law, any wine produced in the state must go through a wholesaler who can then sell the wine directly to the retail outlets. In 2000 the voters of Oklahoma approved overwhelmingly the right for in-state wine to be sold directly to retail outlets, bypassing the wholesaler. But in November 2006, the U.S. District Court ruled that the state question was unconstitutional, saying that by extending a privilege to in-state wine growers to sell directly to retail outlets, and not out-of-state growers, the Oklahoma question violated the interstate commerce law. The 2007, Oklahoma legislators considered more than a dozen bills regulating wine sales, with eight measures directly addressing the subject of wine shipment. Some of the bills were designed to give Oklahomans the ability to have wine shipped directly to their doors, as is available in 38 other states. But all of these measures except one died in committee. The lone remaining bill, HR 1753, reaffirmed the existing system of alcohol distribution, but also allowed Oklahoma wineries to ship their products to customers in other states, but not to customers within the state of Oklahoma. According to Danny Morgan (D-Prague), the minority leader in the Oklahoma House, this created another inequity between Oklahoma wine growers and those of other states, and just seemed to make the problem worse. In grappling with this issue in the future, state legislators will need to consider many interests: the needs of 48 state bonded wineries who produced more than 200,000 liters of bottled wine in 2006 alone, the fact that the current system allows for the efficient collection of $13 million in taxes on wine purchases, the large wholesale industry in Oklahoma with its extensive payroll, including one company, Central Wholesalers, who has an Oklahoma payroll of $25 million, and the state's need to control excessive alcohol purchases, including those by minors. Thus, it does not look like this issue will be decided soon. Indeed, as of 2014, these same wine growers were still waiting for their wine bill. Well, there is always next year...

One of the major issues in both the 2010 and 2011 legislative sessions was whether or not under certain circumstances people with concealed carry licenses can carry guns onto a public college campus. This was one of several bills introduced into the Oklahoma legislature dealing with guns. Others included an "open carry" law, allowing licensed college faculty and administrators to carry concealed weapons on campus, and allowing licensed concealed carry users to bring their weapons on campus under certain circumstances. However, none of these bills passed in either 2010 or 2011. The only bill that passed, HR 1652, now permits students, teachers, and visitors who have permits to carry concealed weapons to take their guns to CareerTech centers and leave them locked in their vehicles. Governor Mary Fallin signed this bill into law in May 2011.

With all of these pieces of legislation, lobbyists on both sides were very active. In support of the legislation Oklahoma Students for Concealed Carry on Campus (OSCCC) argued that these measures would make campuses safer by allowing certain concealed carry owners to bring their guns on campus. They also asserted that these laws would give people their second amendment right to defend themselves. Supporters of concealed carry on campus laws also cite statistics which show that 70 colleges and universities nationwide already permit concealed weapons on campus and there have been no incidents of gun violence on these campuses. The OSCCC leaders lobbied on behalf of these arguments in a number of different ways. They created a Facebook page and they met with most of the Oklahoma legislators in April 2011 personally. But one of their more unusual actions occurred on April 4, 2011, when they encouraged their followers to wear empty gun holsters to show support for the concealed carry laws being changed and to allow others to see that there are respectable people with concealed carry licenses.

Others lobbied against these pieces of legislation. Opponents of the CareerTech bill included the CareerTech superintendents who worried about the safety of others on their campuses. The 54 Oklahoma CareerTech campuses handle a large number of secondary students and have about a dozen childcare centers in their facilities. Thus, some critics have suggested that it might be similar to recommending concealed carry laws for elementary school campuses, which would obviously cause tremendous concern. College administrators also met with the legislators and expressed their concerns that concealed carry on campus would not only bring more guns to campus, but that it would make it more difficult for campus police to identify the original shooter. Oklahoma college presidents, including those at OU, OSU, and UCO, as well as Higher Education Chancellor Glen Johnson, spoke against the measure saying that it would make their campuses more danger-ous. They expressed confidence in their campus security to keep campuses safe, rather than unknown concealed carry holders. These issues will con-tinue to be active in Oklahoma for years to come. The Student Government Association at Rogers State University voted in April 2011 to become the first public Oklahoma campus to approve of concealed carry on campus, and it is a good bet that the Oklahoma legislature will consider more reforms of the concealed carry laws in the future.

Level of Interest Group Activity

How active are Oklahoma's interest groups compared to those of other states? Two political scientists, Thomas and Hrebenar (1999), sought to mea-sure the impact of interest groups in each of the fifty states by looking at how interest groups are able to work with other political actors in the state. They came up with five categories of effectiveness: dominant, dominant/complementary, complementary, complementary/subordinate, and subor-dinate. In a dominant interest group state, interest groups play a large role in setting the policy agenda. There are many active interest groups and they make their presence known in all three branches of government. New Mexico is an example of a **dominant state**, where there are many active interest groups. Dominant interest groups typically come closest to being true **pluralism**, with multiple, competitive actors all fighting for and win-ning the attention of policymakers. In a **complementary state**, interest groups and lawmakers need to work together. Neither is stronger than the other, and the interest group's impact on policy making is moderate. Finally, in **subordinate states**, interest groups are fairly weak. They do not have much of a presence and nor do they have much of an impact on making public policy. Oklahoma is classified as a **dominant/complementary state**. Interest groups in Oklahoma are strong as indicated above, but face some limitations because of the strengths of the legislature and the governor. Oklahoma is usually listed among the strong interest group states because of the power of economic interests (particularly oil and gas) as well as the historic lack of a strong two-party system (Thomas & Hrebenar, 1999).

III. What Do Interest Groups Do?

The Functions of Interest Groups

The wide variety of interest groups in Oklahoma serves several impor-tant functions. First, interest groups make it easier for people to partici-pate in the political process, and may often give voters their first introduction to active politics. People will often need to join interest groups because of their jobs. Many occupations, including education, labor, and the health care profession, have established interest groups so that those employees can be aware of legislation affecting their interests. Individuals may also join interest groups because of their hobbies, activities, or interests. Perhaps a person who recycles gets upset with the lack of recycling facilities in his or her community and decides to join the Sierra Club. Perhaps a gun owner may decide to protect the right to have a gun by joining the National Rifle Association. On the opposite side of the fence, a gun control advocate might also decide to join Handgun Control Incorporated. Interest groups, however, can be distinguished from certain recreational groups by looking at the amount of political activity involved. Most boating groups, for example, are not considered political, unless they decide to fight for a change in boating laws such as placing limits on those boaters who drive their boats drunk.

Second, interest groups provide key information about specific policy areas. This information may be provided to the public, to legislators when crafting legislation, or to other government officials. In June 1997, for example, the Southern Baptist Church decided to call for a boycott against the Disney Corporation because of the benefits that it gives to gay employees and its sponsorship of activities for the gay community. The public who heard about this boycott found out not only that Disney provides these benefits, but also that it is a major media conglomerate. The Disney Corporation includes the theme parks and films as well as several sports franchises, ABC television and radio networks, and 80% of ESPN.[3] Thus, a potential boycott of Disney meant not only the theme parks but the other companies like ESPN that it owns as well. On the other side, several gay rights organizations informed the public about what gay benefits mean to the gay community. Finally, interest groups can advocate the needs of a certain group of individuals. Whether it is education policy, boating policy, or crime policy, interest groups help to meet the needs of members and to articulate those needs to both policymakers and public.

What Do Interest Groups Do?

Most political interest groups are involved in some sort of lobbying. There are two types of lobbying: direct and indirect. **Direct lobbying** refers to efforts made by interest groups to convince policymakers through personal contact. This personal contact can include talking to policymakers directly, giving them information, sending information through the mail, or testifying before legislative or executive hearings. A 1986 survey of professional lobbyists in Oklahoma found that 98% of them use personal contacts; another 84.5% help in drafting legislation, appear before committees, and present research results. 85.1% of lobbyists also engage in contacts with executive branch personnel (Morgan, England, & Humphreys, 1991). Interest groups can also rate the legislators they lobby in terms of how well the legislators vote for particular interests. As an example, the Sierra Club of Oklahoma, an environmental organization, rates legislators yearly on whether not they have voted for environmental interests. For the 2013 session, the Sierra Club rated fifty-six Oklahoma legislators with a grade of A- or better, while only twelve legislators received a failing grade. Thus, it is not a surprise that in its 2013 summary, the Oklahoma Sierra Club was pleased with its activities in 2013, as it had been able to defeat seven different anti-environmental bills before the Oklahoma legislature (Oklahoma Sierra Club, 2013).

One method of direct lobbying in Oklahoma is to **hold a rally** on the steps of the Oklahoma state capitol. At these events, their supporters are not only trying to capture the attention of legislators, but they are also trying to get media coverage of their causes. For example, Oklahoma colleges, universities, and their students usually hold a Higher Education Day at the capitol every year to rally for state spending on higher education so that tuition rates can be kept at a reasonable level. There is also usually a Common Education Day as well, representing the interests of K-12 schools, with parent teacher associations urging parents to attend since the teachers are typically in school on that day. One rally that took place in February 2014 was when independent pharmacists rallied to get HB 2100 passed which would place regulatory controls on pharmacy benefit managers so that they could not force a pharmacy to dispense a prescription at a lower cost than the pharmacy paid for it.

Another common form of lobbying is for interest groups to give money to candidates or other election campaigns. Most interest groups will form a **political action committee**, or a PAC, for this purpose. PACs segregate campaign donations, meaning that it legally separates campaign funds from other organizational finances on behalf of its sponsoring organization seeking to influence the political process. PACs according to Oklahoma law can only give $5,000 per candidate per calendar year.

An additional type of activity by interest groups is to use the courts. Often an interest group will not like the way that a law is being interpreted and may **file a lawsuit** or file an *amicus curiae* or friend of the court brief in a court case to state its position. As an example, Domestic Energy Partners is an interest group in Oklahoma that represents oil and gas companies along with royalty owners. It along with Oklahoma Attorney General Scott Pruitt filed suit in March 2014 against the federal government accusing the Department of Interior and the U.S. Fish and Wildlife Service of "colluding" with environmental groups to bypass public procedures to enact endangered species regulations.

Lobbyists may also give gifts directly to legislators, under Oklahoma law. In the past lobbyists could spend up to $300 per year on each state employee or non-elected state official, but now that amount has dropped to only $100. The amount for elected state officials, thus including state legislators, however, has remained unchanged at $300 per year. Lobbyists are required to report gifts that total more than $50 in a six-month period, according to Oklahoma Ethics Commission rules. All the reported gifts given to lobbyists can be seen online at the Oklahoma Ethics Commission website.

In 2014, for example, there were a total of 2,922 separate gifts reported that were given by lobbyists, which is a 31.3% decrease from 2010. Of those, 698 went directly to senators and 1,545 went to representatives, but several more went to their staff and their spouses. The gifts in 2014 totaled $187,804.56, with 85.5% of that amount, or $160,530.85 for 2,305 gifts coming between January 1 and June 30, 2014. This hefty percentage in the first half of the year makes sense given that the Oklahoma legislature is in session from February to May. The average amount for the gifts that went to individual legislators was $34.51, with the total for each legislator mostly in the $600-$1,000 range. There were some notable exceptions to this, however. Representative Jon Echols, for example, received 44 gifts totaling $1,692.16 for an average gift of $38.46. Representative Brian Bingman also received 36 gifts for a total of $1,489.26. Some of the lobbyists who gave the most represent varied interests, including James Dunlap who lobbies for Hewlett-Packard, the Oklahoma State Medical Association, and Lilly USA, among others. Another lobbyist who donated was Tammie Kilpatrick who lobbies for Health Care Services Corporation, Chesapeake Energy, Avalon Correctional Services, and American Fidelity. Although these two lobbyists were some of the largest donators, neither of these two gave more than $6,000 total in 2014.

Most of the gifts consisted of meals, for such events as a caucus breakfast, lunch, or dinner. There were also movie tickets, football tickets, chocolates, and books given. The Chickasaw Nation, for example, gave out 146 gifts of $50 Bedre Chocolate and also hosted a sine dine event for legislators after the end of the 2013 session. The Association of County Commissioners hosted a $3.15 breakfast for several legislators along with a $19.47 lunch for a total of $3,652.87 given. Given that this is Oklahoma, it is not surprising that college football tickets were a popular gift as well. At $100 each, the University of Oklahoma gave 49 individuals season football tickets. Its in-state rival, Oklahoma State University, did not give tickets this year but OSU did give season tickets to 28 individuals in 2010.

Interest groups in Oklahoma are also asked to testify before the legislature about the potential impact of a bill on the community, whether it be farming interests or those representing the horse racing industry in Oklahoma. For example, one of the bills that has had difficulty getting passed through the Oklahoma legislature deals with insurance reforms to provide services for those with autism. For the last several years, including 2010, numerous families have made repeated trips to the capitol to testify about their children and their battles with autism. Alas, so far all these efforts have not borne fruit, as the Oklahoma legislature has not passed an autism bill yet, and most have even failed to get out of committee.

Indirect lobbying, on the other hand, refers to the activities of interest groups designed to influence policymakers indirectly, usually by using an intermediary. The most common form of indirect lobbying involves using the public. Some interest groups hope that by influencing the public through campaign advertising, news reports, or mailings, that the public will be so moved that they will immediately call their public officials to get them to change some public policy. A 2006 survey of professional lobbyists seemed to suggest that both inside and outside lobbying strategies have been used in Oklahoma. Asked which lobbying techniques are used most often, the professional lobbyists stated that political fundraising (60%), directly trying to persuade officials (59%), getting influential constituents to contact officials (52%), engaging in informal contacts with officials (49%), and mounting grassroots lobbying efforts (48%) were the most common. Getting influential constituents to contact officials directly (an inside technique) and mounting grassroots lobbying efforts (an outside technique) were used very often 52% and 48% of the time, respectively (Davis, Metla, & Herlan, 2007). In Oklahoma, it is very common to see various interest groups using television advertising to make their voices heard. It is hard to live in Oklahoma more than a week without seeing commercials for the Chickasaw Nation, a Native American tribe located within the state.

IV. Lobbyists And Lobbying Regulation

Who Are the Lobbyists?

There are many different types of lobbyists. The type of lobbyist depends heavily on how that lobbyist was acquired. First, some lobbyists are **in-house** lobbyists. These lobbyists are usually members of interest groups or employees of a corporation and are hired to lobby for a particular interest. In-house lobbyists represent 15-25% of all lobbyists in state capitals. Many lobbyists are **contract** lobbyists. These lobbyists are professionals, hired by an interest group or corporation solely for the purpose of lobbying. Often, contract lobbyists may work for several different lobbying organizations at one time, particularly if they are part of a lobbying firm. Much different are **volunteer** lobbyists. While they are usually members of an interest group, they are usually not paid and have agreed to lobby because they were asked to by their interest group. Volunteer lobbyists may not have the professional experience of some paid lobbyists, but often volunteer lobbyists are more devoted to their issue, and use emotion to effectively persuade policymakers. Finally, there are **government** lobbyists, or lobbyists who are hired by a government to represent its interests before policymakers. The governors of all fifty states and even mayors have organizations that represent their interests in Washington, D.C. Similarly, local communities in Oklahoma may send representatives to the Capitol to lobby for policy changes.

Lobbying Regulation

Why is lobbying regulation necessary? Without it, members of special interest groups could spend money and seek to influence officials in the state without any regulation. Lobbying or **ethics laws** make it possible for the public to know how much is being spent, which organizations have lobbyists, and which candidates have received the money or other services from lobbying. According to the Council of State Governments, Oklahoma's ethics laws fall into the moderate category, along with 14 other states. There are 12 states that have tougher ethics laws than Oklahoma. One example of such a state is Kentucky. After a federal investigation in Kentucky called BOPTROT, several lawmakers and lobbyists were sent to prison. One of them was the House Speaker Don Blandford, convicted of both extortion and racketeering. Because of these scandals, Kentucky changed its ethics laws so that they are now the toughest in the country. Lobbyists in Kentucky cannot contribute to legislative campaigns, hold fundraisers for candidates, or serve as campaign treasurers. Legislators also face a two-year **revolving door** restriction on lobbying the legislature after they leave it. One last law allows lobbyists to spend up to $100 per legislative year for meals and drinks. However, this same law also requires *complete* disclosure. The result is that during the first month after the law took effect, legislators in Kentucky received a grand total of $26 in lobbyist spending for food and drink for the month.

Oklahoma ethics laws are not this stringent, but since 1990 when the Oklahoma legislature revamped its commission on ethics, the lobbying laws in Oklahoma have clearly changed. Formerly the Oklahoma Council on Campaign Compliance and Ethical Standards, the **Oklahoma Ethics Commission** in 1990 not only shortened its name but also strengthened the state's ethics laws. There are specific statutes to regulate the activities of those that lobby members of the Oklahoma legislature. Under state statutes, any person who spends in excess of $250 in a calendar quarter for lobbying activities, who receives compensation in excess of $250 in a calendar quarter for lobbying services rendered, and/or whose employment duties in whole or part require lobbying is considered to be a **lobbyist**. Every quarter, lobbyists also must file expenditure reports with the commission when an expenditure on any one member of the legislative, executive, or judicial branch exceeds $50. These lobbying rules satisfy the requirements for **disclosure**. Disclosure is important because it can give the citizens of Oklahoma and other candidates the chance to see how lobbying money is being spent.

Unfortunately, despite these reporting requirements, there were few readily available published records of PAC or lobbyist contributions in Oklahoma. Prior to the 2006 elections, Oklahomans seeking information on lobbying and PAC contributions, needed to either visit the Ethics Commission in the state capitol and copy each report by hand or rely on newspapers which provided only ad hoc information at best on PAC contributions and lobbying disclosure. This, despite the fact, that many other states such as California, had made their lobbying/PAC information available online allowing it to be easily searched. The Oklahoma Ethics Commission started in the summer of 1997 to allow web access to ethics information. Unfortunately, after an initial trial period, the state legislature recalled its earlier mandate that campaign finance information must be disclosed, and made that information voluntary for candidates instead. As a result, only about 15-18% of the candidates made their campaign finance information available on the web from 1997 to 2006. Any full study of Oklahoma campaign finance required a trip in person to the State Capitol and extensive digging through paper documents to get the material desired. Fortunately, this has now changed starting with the 2006 elections when the Oklahoma Ethics Commission began to require mandatory online filing from all candidates.

V. Oklahoma Campaign Finance

Campaign spending by candidates in Oklahoma is regulated by two distinct sets of laws. Candidates for the U.S. Congress seats in Oklahoma are federal election candidates so they are governed by the **Federal Election Campaign Act of 1971** and **1974**. This law was largely amended by the **Bipartisan Campaign Reform Act of 2002** (BCRA), which increased the $1,000 individual donation to $2,000 which is indexed to inflation and banned soft money contributions, among other provisions. For the 2013-2014 elections, that amount is now $2,600. Since these laws only deal with federal election candidates (president, U.S. House, and U.S. Senate) all other candidates in the states, including Oklahoma, are covered by separate state laws created by each state. All fifty states now have some regulation over campaign finance for state and local elections. All states, for example, require that election campaigns disclose their sources of funds. State campaign finance laws vary considerably, however, on how much must be disclosed, what the candidates can spend, the sources of campaign funds, and when they must disclose that information.

The campaign finance laws of a state are important because they determine how much money candidates can receive from various groups in society. One of the more significant decisions was decided by the Supreme Court in 1976, *Buckley vs. Valeo,* which set specific restrictions on the federal government and states in terms of how campaign finance can be regulated. This decision said that candidates can spend as much of their own personal money as they need to run their campaigns. Therefore, governments are only allowed to limit the personal spending of a candidate if the candidate agrees to accept public funding. Thus, for the few states that have public financing, they can place an overall limit on how much a candidate may spend on the campaign. Otherwise, all overall limits on campaign spending were eliminated by the *Buckley* decision. This decision also stated that governments could put limits on other sources of funds, such as those from a family member, from labor organizations, and other groups. Governments can also limit the use of leftover campaign funds; a state can specify, for example, that money raised for campaign purposes may not be used later by a candidate to defray personal expenses.

The Buckley decision, FECA, and BCRA have guided the campaign finance laws of Oklahoma and the 49 other states. Only eight states have regulations that equal or exceed the existing federal limits established by FECA. The toughest state law is in Florida and places $500 limits on both individual and group contributions to candidates. Eight states place no limits on individual or group contributions, including three of Oklahoma's neighbors: Missouri, New Mexico, and Colorado.[4] Oklahoma's campaign finance laws are classified as moderate by the Council of State Governments. Oklahoma's laws for state and local elections are slightly weaker than those established for federal elections. Unlike the federal government, Oklahoma provides no public funding for its campaigns. Thus, there are no limits on the overall amount of money that candidates can spend for their races for governor, state legislature, and other seats. Few states have opted for public funding. The truest comparison between Oklahoma's laws and that of the federal government comes in the area of contributions. The contribution limits on individuals in Oklahoma are certainly weaker than the federal limits. While individuals can only contribute $2,600 per candidate per election in 2013-2014 federal races under the new BCRA law, Oklahomans can donate up to $5,000 to a candidate in a calendar year.

Oklahoma's campaign finance laws, however, are tougher than federal election laws in several aspects. First, there are more restrictions on the donations that can be made by Oklahoman interest groups. Labor organizations in Oklahoma can spend only $5,000 to a candidate committee in a calendar year, while the federal law allows for $5,000 per candidate per election. Since most candidates will have a primary, a general, and maybe even a runoff election, this can more than double the amount that labor organizations can spend on federal elections. PACs at the federal level are allowed to donate $5,000 per candidate per election, usually meaning that they can spend $10,000 on a candidate. PACs in Oklahoma can only spend $5,000 per calendar year per candidate. Second, there are also stricter laws on who can donate. State highway patrol officers and supernumerary tax consultants are prohibited from making contributions, while state officials, state employees, judges, and classified employees *should* not make contributions (Council of State Governments, 1996). Third, Oklahoma also prohibits the use of leftover campaign funds for personal use. The federal government has been relatively slow in applying this law to presidential and congressional candidates.

In January 2004, the Oklahoma Ethics Commission changed the amount that a contributor can give to a state political party under certain circumstances. The state limit on contributions to a state political party is still $5,000 per family per year. But with the enactment of BCRA at the federal level, a new category of contributions was created called **Levin Funds**. These contributions must be earmarked to help a party with registering voters or getting them to the polls, otherwise known as get-out-the-vote activities. A contributor may now give up to $10,000 to a state political party if that amount is earmarked for Levin Funds. This new change in the law took effect July 1, 2004.

Independent Expenditures

One of the most difficult types of campaign activity to regulate is the **independent expenditure**. This occurs when a person or group campaigns either positively or negatively on behalf of a campaign, without that campaign's knowledge or cooperation. These independent expenditures commonly take the form of campaign advertising, but can often result in flyers, mailings, and newsletters. Independent expenditures are difficult to regulate because it is often hard to tell whether a given activity truly occurred independent of a campaign. Independent expenditures can often pose problems for candidates as well. Interest groups can run a negative campaign against a candidate, thereby forcing that candidate to spend large amounts of money responding to the attack. This money could have been spent on other activities, including positive ads run by that candidate. Only six states currently have laws requiring public disclosure. Of those only Florida has a law specifying that the creators of independent expenditures notify all candidates within twenty-four hours of obligating the funds. This specific disclosure law allows the receiving campaign the chance to respond without infringing upon the original group's right to freedom of speech. Oklahoma's ethics laws allow independent expenditures, but those independent expenditures cannot be made by candidates on behalf of another candidate.

The Costs of Oklahoma Elections

A recent U.S. Supreme Court decision might have an impact on the costs of Oklahoma's elections. In the case, *Citizens United v. Federal Election Commission* (2010), the Supreme Court ruled that the federal government may not prohibit direct corporate or union spending on advertising for candidates' elections. When the law was passed, Oklahoma was one of the 24 states that prohibited both. In order to avoid legal challenges to these laws, many states chose not to enforce the laws. The Oklahoma Ethics Commission, for example, as of June 2012 has a "resolution not to enforce statement" on its website, indicating that it will not enforce the ethics rules dealing with the ban on corporate donations until the legislature takes a stand.

As a result of *Citizens United* and the decisions not to enforce, campaign spending in the 2010 and even 2012 elections substantially increased.

The costs are highest in the most populous states and in states where there is heavy use of electronic media (Center for Responsive Politics, 2010). Oklahoma as a smaller state has seen remarkably consistent spending in its recent state level elections, although it did experience a significant increase in election costs starting with the 2006 elections. Thus, candidates for the state House and Senate, for example, spent $8.9 million in total in 1998, $8.9 million in 2000, and $9.0 million in 2002, but then spent $15.0 million in the 2006 elections, $14.7 million in 2008, $10.5 million in 2010, and $11.3 million in the 2012 elections.

This same increase in spending can be seen with a glance at overall spending for all it the major election years are non-presidential election years (i.e. 2002, 2006, and 2010), as this is when most of the statewide races are contested, including governor and lieutenant governor. This obviously has a significant impact on how much is spent on Oklahoma elections because those in statewide races (governor, corporation commissioner, etc.) tend to spend more than those in non-statewide races. Thus, there was only $17 million spent for state-level races in 2008 and only $13.7 million spent in 2012 which were both presidential election years, but there was $29.3 million spent in 2002, $41.1 million in 2006, and $38.3 million spent in 2010. Thus, while the recent trend has been an increase in overall spending, the 2010 and the 2012 elections at the state legislative level both show a slight reverse in this trend.

That slight trend is exhibited in Table 11–2 which shows how much the candidates spent on average for each type of race in Oklahoma in elections ranging from 1998 to 2012. This is most notable for Senate races where candidates spent $110,563 on average in the 2008 elections, but only $67,980 in 2010 and only $61,378 in 2012. But in the House races in 2012, the candidates actually spent more on average than they spent in 2010, spending $35,175 in 2012, but only $30,707 in 2010. The only races where candidates spent more than $100,000 in non-presidential election years on average were those for statewide seats (Governor, State Auditor and Inspector, etc.). In the 2010 elections, there were eight statewide elections where candidates spent substantial sums of money: Attorney General, Governor, Insurance Commissioner, Labor Commissioner, Lieutenant Governor, State Auditor and Inspector, and Superintendent of Public Instruction. Thus, there were fifteen candidates in Oklahoma who each spent over $500,000 on their races and five of those spent over $1 million, including five candidates for Governor and Lieutenant Governor as might be expected, but also a candidate for the Superintendent of Public Instruction.

Even with the same type of seat, though, there is still considerable variation in campaign spending. Some of the variation can be explained by the quality of the challenger and the number of years the incumbent has been in office. One example of this has been Mary Fallin's major statewide campaigns, for Lt. Governor in 1998 and 2002 and for Governor in 2010. In 1998 when she was first elected for Lt. Governor, Mary Fallin faced a tough challenger, and as a result the Lt. Governor's race was an expensive one,

TABLE 11–2

Average Money Spent by Type of Seat Sought for the 1998, 2002, 2006, 2008, 2010 and 2012 Elections

	1998	2002	2006	2008	2010	2012
Attorney General			$385,493.86		$781,418.23	
Corporation Commissioner			$412,301.03	$597,653.08	$80,269.69	$200,188.71
District Attorney	$32,340.20	$30,163.50	$412,301.03		$57,049.64	
Governor	$577,095.90		$1,220,915.88		$1,841,055.72	
House	$25,969.55	$24,062.36	$33,571.75	$40,917.61	$30,707.33	$35,174.51
Insurance Commissioner	$168,056.80	$185,327.28	$258,487.77		$368,407.48	
Judge—Supreme Court	$67,220.59	$30,673.63				
Judge—Associate	$4,424.78	$5,101.84	$8,788.54		$13,522.28	
Judge—District	$19,467.66	$11,798.68	$17,031.29		$41,026.16	
Labor Commissioner	$102.746.50	$63,085.15	$146,035.12		$117,092.12	
Lieutenant Governor	$843,953.50	$236,734.50	$700,250.33		$380,271.77	
Senate	$57,082.29	$71,954.59	$86,397.48	$110,562.74	$67,980.11	$61,377.94
State Auditor and Inspector	$224,756.10	$79,467.85	$367,010.95		$315,168.59	
Super. of Public Instruction	$2,724.92	$71,954.60	$168,773.57		$272,392.90	
Treasurer			$1,002,452.34		$199,646.25	

with $843,953.50 spent on average. But in 2002, with Fallin having more experience in that seat, only $236,734.50 was spent on average. In the 2010 elections, Mary Fallin ran for Governor and was considered the candidate to beat after having been a member of Congress in the meantime. However, she faced a significant opponent in Democrat Jari Askins and several Republican primary challengers and as a result, the candidates spent over $1.8 million on average on this race. Fallin alone spent $4,099,098 on the 2010 Governor's race while Askins spent $4,055,656.

What can also be seen in Table 11–2 is that state senate candidates spent considerably more than state house candidates during every election. Senate candidates not only have more constituents because they have larger districts, but they are elected every four years instead of every two. Because of the greater prestige, senate seats also tend to attract better candidates (those with state house experience, those with name recognition, etc.) than the house seats. In the 2012 elections, the average amounts raised by house and senate candidates respectively were $36,033 and $61,869, for a difference of $25,836. For the 2010 elections, the average amount raised by House candidates was $30,707, while the average amount raised by Senate candidates was $67,980, for a difference of $37,203. Senate candidates were particularly frugal during the 2010 and 2012 elections spending less than 2006 and 2008 ($138,637 on average).

Even more interesting is when the amounts raised and spent are divided even further by looking at the type of candidate who won the race, i.e., whether the candidate was in the House or Senate, a winner or loser, a Republican or Democrat, or an incumbent, challenger, or in an open seat race. The 2008/2010/2012 election state legislative receipts and expenditures are shown in Table 11–3 divided by the type of candidate.

Table 11–3 shows five significant results, the first of which is evident in the way the table is structured. Given the significant difference in house versus senate fundraising shown above, all of these results were done looking at the house and senate fundraising separately. Second, the losers simply could not compete with the winners, both at the ballot box and in raising money. Typically, the winners raised and spent approximately 3-6 times that of the losers, no matter which office is examined. Thus, in the 2012 elections the house winners raised $49,110, while the losers raised only $22,793. The senate winners raised $104,537, while the losers raised only $37,751 on average. This gap in money raised can buy advertisements, circulars to deliver door-to-door, and other campaign essentials that make it much harder for the loser to be competitive.

A third trend noted in the chart is that incumbents do better than challengers, with the differences here at 2:1 but sometimes more than that. The most notable difference was in 2012 when senate incumbents outraised senate challengers $96,601 to $29,735 and outspent them $98,623 to $28,310. As can be seen with the 2008 and 2010 election data, this is not an anomaly, as this same trend existed also in those elections. Fourth, there are significant chamber differences between the Republicans

Table 11-3
2008, 2010, and 2012 House/Senate Receipts and Expenditure Averages Shown by Type of Candidate

	Dems	Repubs	Indeps	Winners	Losers	Incumbs	Challs	Open Seats
2012 House Receipts	$33,292	$37,543		$49,110	$22,793	$39,701	$22,624	$44,451
2010 House Receipts	$29,350	$35,576	$11,993	$47,600	$18,265	$457,207	$19,043	$28,369
2008 House Receipts	$36,110	$57,083	$3,419	$67,612	$24,597	$62,658	$22,545	$48,792
2012 House Expenditures	$35,065	$35,235		$47,107	$22,426	$38,734	$20,380	$43,827
2010 House Expenditures	$30,971	$31,205	$11,861	$44,304	$18,117	$44,557	$17,728	$25,491
2008 House Expenditures	$30,584	$52,593	$3,184	$60,245	$22,207	$55,021	$21,288	$44,233
2012 Senate Receipts	$66,638	$65,078	$1,828	$104,537	$37,751	$96,601	$29,735	$61,626
2010 Senate Receipts	$86,099	$81,754	$200	$153,727	$37,394	$136,479	$29,288	$79,184
2008 Senate Receipts	$173,042	$120,242		$194,508	$86,365	$185,243	$116,428	$116,976
2012 Senate Expenditures	$57,499	$67,296	$2404	$95,090	$42,324	$98,623	$28,310	$60,512
2010 Senate Expenditures	$72,508	$67,120	$200	$120,033	$35,623	$99,132	$26,689	$71,633
2008 Senate Expenditures	$137,909	$102,211		$149,775	$82,069	$130,811	$112,086	$107,556

LEADERSHIP PROFILE

ROBERT STEM
Lobbyist, Capital Gains, LLC Executive Director, Association of General Contractors

ROBERT STEM is an Oklahoma lobbyist and association director who responded to a charge from his mentors to be become involved in the things he felt passionate about while maintaining respect for the opposite side. After checking into his dormitory room as a freshman at the University of Central Oklahoma in 1993, Bobby brazenly walked into the office of then university President (and former Oklahoma governor) George Nigh and gave him his phone number, telling him if he or Mrs. Nigh ever needed a ride, an errand run or their oil changed, he was the man to call. When President Nigh called a few weeks later to hitch a ride to Altus so he could give a speech, Bobby agreed and began a first career as a chauffeur for Nigh and his wife.

Bobby received a B.A., in Political Science from UCO in 1993. While he was at UCO President Nigh helped him get a position as an errand boy working for Governor David Walters at the National Governor's Conference in 1993. He chose political science because it kept him in the mix of the two things he was passionate about: politics and Oklahoma. Stem worked for Sen. Stratton Taylor (D-Claremore) after he graduated from UCO. Sen. Taylor exposed him to politics and encouraged him to put something on his resume that wasn't Democratic. Stem enrolled in the Oklahoma City University School of Law and earned his *juris doctorate* in 2002.

A law degree, according to Sen. Taylor, was a "broad degree" and allowed Stem to pursue any avenue that interested him. Stem used it to his advantage and formed his own lobbying firm, Capital Gains in 1998. Capital Gains is consistently ranked the top lobbying firm in the state of Oklahoma. The firm represents the interests that are important to Stem and his colleagues—the Oklahoma Fraternal Order of Police, the District Attorneys Council and the Choctaw Nation. In addition to running his own lobbying firm, Stem is also the Executive Director of the Association of General Contractors, a group of Oklahoma road and bridge builders.

Stem believes that everyone should be involved in their community. His involvement in Oklahoma politics came about because one man gave him a chance and then introduced him to the world of politics. By continuing to be active in the Oklahoma political process, Stem knows that the things that he values are part of the dialogue and what moves Oklahoma forward.

As a lobbyist he has the ability to refocus the agenda of leaders, a responsibility he takes seriously. One lesson he learned early in his career is that it is important to know and understand the people on the other side of the issues and to view them not as the enemy, but as good people with different ideas. It is important to be a person who is able to compromise and be reasonable (a skill he gained while in law school). His motto in his office is "fight with intense vigor and do it like a gentleman."

A husband to Kimberly, an author and father to two daughters, Reyna, 18 and Annebella Grace, 5, Stem lives the example, "treat others like you want to be treated." He advises young people, who want to be involved in the political process to hustle, listen and be humble. Hustle to your way into a first opportunity; be willing to volunteer and to work long hours to earn your stripes. Listen to everything around you. Be humble and teachable. If young people heed his advice Stem says, "You can be successful."

Jennifer S. Stringham

and the Democrats. In all three elections, the House Republicans raised and spent more than their Democratic colleagues; in the 2012 election House Republicans spent $37,543 on average while the House Democrats spent $33,292. But in the senate, the opposite is the case, as the Democrats beat their Republican colleagues in both receipts and expenditures for two of the three elections. In the 2012 election results, however, show that fundraising gap narrowed in the senate with a $66,638 to $65,078 fundraising advantage for the Democrats and the Senate Republicans actually outspending their Democratic colleagues $67,296 to $57,499 for the first time in four elections. Finally, this chart shows that Oklahoma is still a two-party state with the independent candidates having little ability to match the fundraising ability of either the Republicans or Democrats.

Given these results, it should be no surprise that most of the top recipients of campaign contributions for both the 2010 and 2012 elections are senators, not representatives, since the Senate usually raises more money on average than the house. The top recipients with their expenses as well for the 2010 and 2012 elections are listed below in Table11–4. In

Table 11-4
2010 and 2012 Top Recipients/Spenders in Oklahoma State Legislative Races

2010 Elections				2012 Elections			
Candidate	Office	Contributions	Expenses	Candidate	Office	Contributions	Expenses
Jay Paul Gumm	S	$298,185.67	$293,096.90	TW Shannon	H	$305,465.24	$215,193.64
Mark Allen	S	$289,182.80	$238,165.75	Dan Newberry	S	$271,208.46	$269,404.14
Daniel Sullivan	H	$253,881.78	$260,128.01	Charles McCall	H	$246,261.23	$239,276.00
Cliff Branan	S	$252,278.34	$122,982.37	Susan Paddack	S	$225,307.94	$156,794.03
Josh Brecheen	S	$247,392.01	$226,462.94	Jack Beller	S	$201,696.00	$199,665.22
John Sparks	S	$238,818.56	$213,980.23	Clark Jolley	S	$197,910.25	$396,327.88
Brian Bingman	S	$221,784.16	$78,027.65	Kay Floyd	H	$169,699.58	$157,942.35
Frank Simpson	S	$217,134.97	$204,372.43	Rob Standridge	S	$167,501.27	$154,700.45
Eddie Fields	S	$211,445.32	$211,240.32	Jabar Shumate	S	$145,160.00	$124,094.26
Kim David	S	$202,382.24	$191,570.89	AJ Griffin	S	$142,234.52	$32,752.02

the 2010 elections, only two House candidates cracked the top 17, Daniel Sullivan of House district 71, and Kris Steele, who was named as House Speaker. In the 2012 elections, though, six House candidates were in the top 17. This can be explained by the fact that many of these candidates were in open seat races, which are often the most competitive seats. During the 2012 election, many incumbents went unopposed, and thus did not have to raise nearly as much money. Therefore, it is not surprising that there are only a few incumbents among the top recipients of 2012 campaign money. Many of the incumbents listed were either leaders in the legislature or soon to be leaders. An example of this is T.W. Shannon who as Speaker of the House was listed as the #1 recipient of campaign money in 2012, with $305,465.24.

The Role of Political Action Committees, or PACs

One of the keys for a candidate to be competitive at the state legislative level is receiving political action committee (PAC) money. PACs are the organizations that allow corporations and interest groups to give money to candidates in Oklahoma. In Oklahoma, because of their strong influence, one other type of group needs to be included, even though they are technically not labeled as PACs by the Oklahoma Ethics Commission. These groups are Native American organizations, which as shown in Table 11-5, were the top three contributors in the 2010 elections, with the Chickasaw coming in first with $306,300 in donations, but the Choctaw and Cherokee close behind in second and third. In the 2012 elections, once again the Chickasaw Nation came in first in PAC donations at $318,700, the Choctaw Nation was again second at $194,250, but the Cherokee Nation came in ninth this time at $96,000. As a result, an effort was made to include all Native American organizations in Oklahoma in the PAC totals listed for these elections.

Besides Indian tribes, there are three other strong influences in Oklahoma as seen in the 2010 and 2012 top 10 PAC contribution lists as six of the PACs on the two lists are the same. Oklahoma is known as an oil and gas state as well as a state with a strong agriculture presence, and it shows on these two lists as seen in Table 11-5. The Oklahoma Independent Energy PAC (OKIEPAC) is on both lists (#6 in 2010, #5 in 2012), but there is also Energy for Oklahomans (#7 on 2010) and Devon Energy Corporation (#4 in 2012). There are a few other organizations on both lists including OK Ag Fund (#9 in 2010, #7 in 2012) and the Oklahoma Public Employees Association (#3 in 2010, #4 in 2012).

The top 10 average donation list for the 2010 and 2012 elections as shown in Table 11-6 has some similarities to the Top 10 PAC list (Table 11-5), but it also has some differences as well. The top 10 average donation list was by taking only those PACs that gave a minimum of 20 donations. This is to create a list of the true "players" among PACs, as

TABLE 11-5
Top 10 PAC Contributors in State Legislative Races, 2010 and 2012 Elections—Total Amount Donated

2012 Elections

1. Chickasaw Nation	$318,700
2. Choctaw Nation	$194,250
3. Oklahoma Public Employees	$124,000
4. Devon Energy Corporation	$116,800
5. Oklahoma Independent Energy PAC (OKIEPAC)	$114,250
6. Center for Legislative Excellence	$110,250
7. OK Ag Fund	$106,250
8. Okla State AFL-CIO Political Action Committee	$101,800
9. Cherokee Nation	$96,000
10. ROI PAC	$95,250

2010 Elections

1. Chickasaw Nation	$306,300
2. Choctaw Nation	$273,400
3. Cherokee Nation	$167,700
4. Oklahoma Public Employees	$142,250
5. Oklahoma Society of Anesthesiologists	$123,000
6. Okla Independent Energy PAC (OKIEPAC)	$113,250
7. Energy For Oklahomans	$109,500
8. Realtors PAC	$104,900
9. OK Ag Fund	$96,550
10. Working Oklahomans Alliance	$96,000

it is very easy to give one maximum donation of $5,000 to a single Oklahoma legislator, but a much different thing entirely to give large donations to multiple legislators. That's what this list seeks to measure. Once again on this list are some of the same Top 10 PACs as would be expected: several Indian tribes, the Oklahoma AFL-CIO PAC, energy PACs, and Oklahoma Public Employees. This indicates that these organizations are not only giving a large aggregate donation, but are donating large individual amounts as well.

TABLE 11-6
Top 10 PAC Contributors in Oklahoma State Legislative Races, 2010 and 2012 By Average Donation (Minimum of 20 Donations)

2012 Elections

1. Chickasaw Nation	$2,678.15
2. ROI PAC	$2,215.12
3. Devon Energy Corporation PAC	$2,203.77
4. Center for Legislative Excellence	$2,004.55
5. Choctaw Nation	$1,982.14
6. Tulsa Firefighters PAC	$1,975.00
7. Prosperity PAC	$1,972.00
8. Oklahoma Republican Party	$1,893.94
9. Cherokee Nation	$1,882.35
10. Okla State AFL-CIO	$1,817.86

2010 Elections

1. Cherokee Nation	$3,354.00
2. Devon Energy Corporation PAC	$2,303.00
3. Choctaw Nation	$2,087.00
4. OK Public Employees Association	$1,871.70
5. Center for Legislative Excellence	$1,822.60
6. OK Society of Anesthesiologists	$1,757.10
7. Chickasaw Nation	$1,750.28
8. Okla Independent Energy PAC	$1,690.30
9. Greater OKC Chamber PAC	$1,636.40
10. OK State AFL-CIO	$1,635.10

Political Party and Ideological PAC Donations – Where are the Democrats?

But there are several newcomers on the top 10 average donation list that have not appeared in past elections, such as in 2008 or 2010. For the first time since the 2006 elections, a political party PAC and ideological PACs made return appearances, all to the benefit of Republicans. As an example, the Oklahoma Republican Party was listed as #8 on the top 10 average donation list in 2012, with an average donation of $1,893.20. Similarly, ROI PAC and Prosperity PAC, two ideological PACs which gave only to Republicans in the 2012, also appeared on the 2012 list, with average donations of $2,215.22 (#2) and $1,920.00 (#7), respectively. For Republicans, this had to be great news. First, these donations are fairly large, since the maximum donation on this list was $2,678 and the maximum donation in Oklahoma is only $5,000. Getting such a large donation at once is always helpful to a candidate, as it is much easier to raise money through these big donations rather than acquiring dozens of $10 or $20 donations. Large donations can even sometimes make the difference between winning and losing. Second, it is important to note that there were no Democratic Party organizations on these lists, obviously giving the Republicans an advantage. The closest to that was the Oklahoma State AFL-CIO PAC which did give mostly to Democrats, but only ranked 10th on this list and was the only organization of its kind.

So, that brings up a very good question: where are the Democrats? The answer to this question reveals the true lack of balance that exists between the two political parties in Oklahoma right now, at least in terms of campaign contributions. It also probably explains why Democrats have not been successful lately in Oklahoma legislative elections. As shown in Table 11-6, the various Republican Party organizations gave large donations in 2012, particularly when compared to the Oklahoma Democrats. Democratic Party organizations in the 2012 elections gave $14,245 to 32 candidates, for an average donation of $445.16. Unfortunately for them, the Republicans gave more–a lot more. Republican Party organizations gave $124,500 to 81 candidates, for an average donation of $1,355.37. Thus, no matter which way it is viewed, it is bad news for the Democrats. The Republicans gave nine times more money to more than twice as many candidates, and the average donation was about three times as much.

But this is not the end of the bad news for the Democrats. PACs based on ideology donate either entirely or almost entirely to one party over another. The Democrats also fare terribly with these types of PACs. In the 2012 elections, the ideological Democrat PACs gave an average donation of $1,074.33 while the ideological Republican PACs gave $1,754.61. Now, for Democrats, this might look like some good news, because at least these numbers are bit closer. Yet, that is not the case, because here it is important to look at the number of donations and the total amount as well. For the Democrats, that average was based on only 30 donations, and a total amount of $32,229. With the Republicans, however, ideological Republican PACs gave to a whopping 149 candidates a total amount of $201,950. Yes, Republicans gave over six times the amount the Democratic PACs did to almost five times the candidates!

Unfortunately for the Democrats (and happily for the Republicans), this is not a new phenomenon in Oklahoma elections. In the 2010 elections, the two political parties gave about the same amount on average,

LEADERSHIP PROFILE

DAVID J. BOND
Director, OCPA Oklahoma Policy Solutions, Inc.

DAVID J. BOND was born in 1981 in Dallas, Texas. An only child, David's family moved to Oklahoma where he attended Christian Heritage Academy in Del City, Oklahoma. After graduating high school he attended Oklahoma State University in Stillwater to which he received a Bachelor of Arts Degree in Political Science. David made, as he said, "pretty good grades" as well engaging in many extracurricular activities.

David had always been interested in the subjects of politics, political history, and campaign and elections. He became even more engaged in politics during the 2000 presidential election. It was at this time that he switched his degree track from a degree in journalism to a degree in political science. Less than a week after graduation, he started a job with the political action committee of the Oklahoma State House Republican Caucus.

David is currently the director of the OCPA Oklahoma Policy Solutions, Inc., which is a 501(c)4 organization that advocates at the state capitol for free-market policy solutions, as well as for public policy proposals that limit the size and scope of state government and encourages individual liberty. Was this the job he had envisioned for himself? No. He never envisioned himself as a registered state lobbyist. But having done so, he now lobbies for important initiatives such as across-the-board-tax cuts, meaningful reductions to the size and scope of government, and allowing for the individual to be empowered and become more involved in the political process. These are the concepts and beliefs that allow David to sleep well at night—knowing he is helping to move Oklahoma into a bright future.

David has high hopes for Oklahoma and all her citizens. He hopes that Oklahoma becomes one of the top target destinations in the country for people to start a new business, or better yet, to remain here to expand their businesses and hire more employees. For this to happen, David believes that it is important not to pick "winners and losers" but rather to level the playing field for all business—both large and small. Likewise, David hopes Oklahoma can appropriately apply some of these same free-market principles to areas such as state government and education.

Although David is grateful for his college educational experiences and believes his coursework laid the foundation to help him reach his goals, David believes that most of what he has learned about the nation of politics and elections in Oklahoma, he learned by working within the process itself. College gave him the framework and some historical prospective, but his real-world experiences has allowed himself to grow successfully as the director of OCPA Oklahoma Policy Solutions, Inc.

What will Oklahoma be like in ten years? David believes that most people agree that we are at a transitional period in the history of our nation. In the next few years, we will have to decide whether we want to continue on the current collectivist trajectory or shift back to the concepts of free markets and individual initiatives that allowed this country to develop into the greatest, freest nation in the world. The individual states are each microcosms of this pressing reality, and Oklahoma is no different. Those states that seek to show how success can be achieved by taking restraints off private individuals have the opportunity to set the standard for other states. David believes Oklahoma is one of those states. The overarching goal of the organization he works for, is to advance these ideas and help policymakers act on them; thus, allowing Oklahoma to be a great state.

David looks to his grandparents for inspiration. He believes they are his link to past generations of self-sufficiency, personal responsibility, and steady consistent faith. Attributes younger Oklahomans should aspire to embrace. David Bond listens to music, is an avid photographer, enjoys reading, watching the occasional movie, and conversing with friends. However, his greatest enjoyment in life is being a father to his son.

Paul M. Bashline

about $900 per candidate, but the Democrats gave only to 39 candidates for a total of $33,505, while the Republicans gave to 162 candidates for a large total of $152,401. Further back, in the 2008 elections, the Republican Party PACs, typically gave 7-10 donations, for an average amount of about $45,000 per PAC, but the Democratic Party PACs in the 2008 election were basically non-existent, giving only about 15% of what the

Republicans gave in 2008. But prior to the 2008 and 2010 elections, the party and ideological PACs of both parties were regular visitors to the top 10 average PAC donation list. They were 7 out of the 10 PACs in 2006. Party PACs were also the top two PACs in the 2002 elections and along with ideological PACs, made up 6 of the 10 PACs on that list.

Thus, for two consistent elections, 2008 and 2010, the parties and ideological PACs were not successful in giving large average donations or making a large aggregate donation, but that clearly changed for the Republicans in 2012. Now, they are making appearances on the top 10 lists, while the Democrats are not. This indicates the lack of parity between these organizations in terms of campaign fundraising and could have significant implications down the road. This is because the political parties' main goal is to win seats in office. Thus, they and the ideological PACs associated with them will often give very large average contributions hoping that the money will make a difference in the outcome. This party money often represents the seed money for challengers and open seat candidates. While this money was not as strong for either party in the 2008 and 2010 elections, in the 2012 elections the Republicans came back with a vengeance while the Democrats did not. Thus, the Democratic Party in Oklahoma truly has become a disappearing act, at least in terms of campaign finance, and that does not bode well for the Democrats in the future.

The Number of PAC Donations

In looking at the list of PACs that give the most contributions in terms of the number of contributions donated, however, a completely different set of PACs emerges as shown in Table 11–7. While the Native American organizations are still there (Chickasaw at #2 and Choctaw at #7 for 2012), PACs that give a lot of contributions tend to give smaller amounts, typically either $250 or 500, but will distribute their money to many more candidates. These include PACs that encourage employee contributions as well as PACs from professional associations.

Thus, the 2012 list includes organizations such as the Oklahoma Optometric PAC, the Thoroughbred PAC, the Oklahoma Osteopathic PAC, the ONEOK Inc. Employee PAC, and the Farmers Employee & Agent PAC, with the optometrists giving the most at 197 contributions in the 2012 elections. These top five PACs, however, gave an average contribution of only $436.29, which is considerably less than the $2,000 or $3,000 contributions given by the party PACs. Similarly in the 2010 elections, the #1 contributor was the Oklahoma Optometric PAC which gave 222 contributions, far more than other PACs on the list. Its average donation, however, was only $384.68. Other low-average contributors ($300-$600) on the list include ONEOK, American Electric, SURE (Speak up for Rural Electrification) and the Thoroughbred PAC, both tied at #7, and AT&T PAC. The Native American organizations, the OK Ag Fund, and the energy organizations, by contrast, had a much higher average of $1,463.50.

TABLE 11–7
Top 10 PAC Contributors in Oklahoma State Legislative Races, 2010 and 2012 By Total Number of Contributions

2012 Elections

NAME OF PAC	# OF DONATIONS
1. Okla Optometric PAC	197
2. Chickasaw Nation	119
3. Thoroughbred PAC	118
4. OK Ag Fund	114
5. Oklahoma Osteopathic PAC	113
6. OHA_PAC (Oklahoma Hospital Association PAC	100
7. Choctaw Nation	98
8. ONEOK Inc. Employee PAC	98
9. Oklahoma Medical PAC	95
10. Farmers Employee & Agent PAC (FEAPAC)	94

2010 Elections

NAME OF PAC	# OF DONATIONS
1. Okla Optometric PAC	222
2. Choctaw Nation	131
3. ONEOK Inc. PAC	125
4. Chickasaw Nation	116
5. American Electric	114
6. SURE – Speak Up for Rural Electrification	111
7. Thoroughbred PAC	111
8. Energy for Oklahomans	110
9. OK Ag Fund	106
10. AT&T Employee PAC	104

It is probably not a surprise, but many of the same state legislators who are on the top recipient list for 2012 also received the most PAC contributions for 2012 as well, as shown in Table 11–8. But this list revealed some changes from the 2010 elections as well. First, it should be noted that there were no repeat candidates from 2010 to 2012. Most of these are Senate

TABLE 11–8
Top 10 State Legislative Recipients of PAC Contributions

2010 Elections

NAME	TOTAL PAC	AVG PAC	H OR S	PARTY	Won?
1. Sullivan, Daniel	$159,750.00	$892.46	House	R	Won
2. Fields, Eddie	$149,200.32	$1,113.44	Senate	R	Won
3. Gumm, Jay Paul	$148,550.00	$983.77	Senate	D	Lost
4. Aldridge, Cliff	$132,650.16	$1,096.28	Senate	R	Won
5. David, Kim	$128,600.16	$1,067.10	Senate	R	Won
6. Bingman, Brian	$124,850.16	$1,070.40	Senate	R	Won
7. Steele, Kris	$108,110.79	$813.70	House	R	Won
8. Sparks, John	$100,085.59	$943.57	Senate	D	Won
9. Johnson, Rob	$97,100.00	$985.00	Senate	R	Won
10. Coates, Harry	$95,300.16	$2,004.09	Senate	R	Won

2012 Elections

NAME	TOTAL PAC	AVG PAC	H OR S	PARTY	Won?
1. Shannon, TW	$154,891.50	$1,194.14	House	R	Won
2. Newberry, Dan	$142,050.16	$974.68	Senate	R	Won
3. Jolley, Clark	$99,000.18	$1,185.56	Senate	R	Won
4. Rousselot, Wade	$88,950.00	$805.08	House	D	Won
5. Crain, Brian	$88,800.16	$1,011.21	Senate	R	Won
6. Paddack, Susan	$87,225.00	$812.10	Senate	D	Won
7. Boggs, Larry	$86,050.00	$1,956.67	Senate	R	Won
8. Barrington, Don	$84,098.91	$651.92	Senate	R	Won
9. Shumate, Jabar	$73,150.00	$725.22	Senate	D	Won
10. Cooksey, Marian	$67,150.16	$875.98	House	R	Won

candidates, and they are only up every four years. All of these candidates with the exception of Jay Paul Gumm (#3 in 2010) won their seats, suggesting perhaps that receiving a large amount of PAC money might help with the election outcome. In addition, these two lists both have a preponderance of Republicans, not a surprise given the high Republican legislative majorities in 2012. But, there is one important detail that should be noted. 2012 was apparently not a big election for PAC donations, as evident in the fact that eight of the candidates raised over $100,000 from PACs in 2010, but only two did in the 2012 elections. As pointed out in Chapter 10 on elections and political participation, one of the other new trends in Oklahoma elections is the lack of contested seats, with 33% of the Senate seats and 53.5% of the House seats totally unopposed in the 2012 elections. As a result, many PACs might have needed to spend less money in 2012 because of these uncontested seats.

Trends Among PAC Donations in Oklahoma

PACs in Oklahoma tend to follow certain trends. Most PAC money comes from in-state PACs. For both the 2010 and 2012 elections, 88.3% of all PAC money came from in-state PACS, while only 11.7% came from out-of-state PACs. In-state PACs also gave a lot more money on average ($888.91 in 2012 and $832.31 in 2010) than out-of-state PACs ($534.01 in 2012 and $553.10 in 2010). Yet certain candidates count on the out-of-state PAC contributions because they come from particular interests, especially oil and gas as well as health interests. Examples of these include Center Point Energy Corporation, BP North America, and Spectra Energy Corporation as well as Merck, Wyeth, Pfizer, and Johnson and Johnson. It is important to note, however, that the name of the PAC does not always denote where it is located. While the Sooner PAC is definitely located in Oklahoma, several nationally based PACs may have "Oklahoma" in their titles but are located elsewhere including the AFL-CIO COPE Treasury Account Oklahoma PAC, the Arvest Oklahoma PAC, and the Gay and Lesbian Victory Fund Oklahoma PAC.

The amount that PACs give varies considerably depending on the political party, the type of office contested, and whether the candidate was a winner or a loser. With the political parties, PAC money in 2006 constituted a higher percentage of the money raised by Democratic candidates (32.2% PAC) compared to Republicans (23.3%), by house candidates (29.3% PAC) more than senate candidates (26.3%), and by winners (32.1% PAC), more than losers (20.1%). By the 2010 and 2012 elections, two major changes had taken place. First, not surprisingly Republicans who now controlled the legislature also defeated the Democrats in PAC fundraising, with 38.3% of the money raised by Republicans in the 2012 elections coming from PACs, but only 28.2% of the Democratic money. Second, the winners had a much stronger advantage over the losers in raising PAC money in the 2012 elections, as a whopping 53.1% of their money came from PACs, but only 15.6% of the losers' money came from PACs. PACs will often give a larger share of their money to winners, as these were the better-quality candidates in the first place and PACs want to give to candidates who can implement their policies once in office. The only similarity from the 2006 to the 2012 elections came with the House versus Senate difference as house candidates still got more of their money (37.2%) from PACs than did the senate candidates (27.7%).

What was really surprising, though, was the average PAC contribution. As seen in Table 11–9, of those candidates who received any PAC contributions, Republicans got more on average from PACs in 2012 in both the House and the Senate, with Republicans getting about $150 more on average in the Senate ($997.16 to $849.69) and about $80 more on average in the House ($800.72 to $719.66). Most of the average PAC contributions also increased from 2010 to 2012. Although the PACs actually spent less in aggregate, i.e. total amounts, they could spend more per candidate because they had fewer candidates on which to spend their money, thanks to the increase in uncontested seats in the Oklahoma legislature in the 2012 elections.

TABLE 11–9 AVG PAC CONTRIBUTIONS – BY HOUSE & SENATE LOOKING AT ONLY THOSE STATE LEGISLATIVE CANDIDATES WHO RECEIVED PAC CONTRIBUTIONS		
2010 Elections		
	HOUSE	**SENATE**
Winners	$656.00	$973.43
Losers	$915.11	$1,167.09
Democrats	$678.19	$956.49
Republicans	$695.40	$1,051.28
Incumbents	$622.02	$851.34
Challengers	$1,004.91	$1,520.71
Open Seats	$981.92	$1,241.32
2012 Elections		
	HOUSE	**SENATE**
Winners	$742.48	$897.55
Losers	$1,120.64	$1,285.74
Democrats	$719.66	$849.69
Republicans	$800.72	$997.16
Incumbents	$692.12	$842.00
Challengers	$1,138.06	$1,432.69
Open Seats	$1,040.79	$1,067.50

The real surprises came with the winners and losers. Although PAC donations constitute a smaller proportion of the money raised by losers, losers do manage to receive a larger contribution on average than do winners, and this is true in both houses. This difference was magnified in the House where house winners in 2012 received only $742.48 on average, while house losers received a substantial $1,120.64. In the Senate, the comparison was a bit less, with senate losers only receiving $1,285.74 compared to the winners' average of $897.55. These differences can probably be explained by looking at the type of PAC money received. The winners are getting contributions from almost every PAC, including those that give large donations like the parties, but also the employee and professional PACs which typically donate smaller amounts. However, the losers who received PAC money, got most of their money from the parties and ideological PACs, who typically give $3,000 or $4,000 donations. Why? These two groups know that these candidates represent the potential to pick up a seat from the other party, and so they will donate heavily to these candidates hoping to provide the seed money to make that happen.

The same results happen when incumbents versus challengers are examined. The 2012 House incumbents received $692.12 on average from PACs, while House challengers received $1,138.06. House open-seat candidates received an amount in between at $1,040.79. But in the Senate, incumbents received only $842.00, which is more than the house incumbents, but certainly far less than the senate challengers at $1,432.69. The senate open-seat candidates received $1,067.50. It is important to look at the number of donations here as well. Those senate challengers who received almost twice as much on average only received 92 contributions total, while the senate incumbents received 1,111 contributions. The Senate open-seat candidates received 665 contributions. Thus, while senate challengers may have received much more from each contribution, they received fewer contributions compared to the Senate incumbent or open-seat candidates.

Another huge difference between the winners and losers and the incumbents versus challengers appears when the total number of PAC donations to candidates who received PAC donations are examined, as shown in Table 11-10. Basically, the losers and challengers, who are often the same candidates, were able to garner very few donations. In the 2012 elections, the house losers got only 10 donations on average per candidate, while the winners got 41. The incumbents got 40.3 donations on average per candidate, while the challengers got 9.4 donations and the open-seat candidates got 24.2 donations. These differences are even more magnified in the Senate, where the incumbents received 69.4 donations on average per candidate, but the challengers received only 10.1, and the open seat candidates fared better as expected with 23.6 donations on average. The huge difference between the losers and winners is easily explained after one looks at the percentage of candidates receiving PAC money. Among the winners in both the House and the Senate, only Representatives Mark McCullough and Corey Williams did not receive PAC

TABLE 11–10
Average PAC $, Average Number of PAC Donations, Average PAC Donation Amount, to All State Legislative Candidates in the 2010 and 2012 Elections

2010 Elections

HOUSE	# OF CANDIDATES	AVG PAC$	# OF PAC CONTRIBS	AVG PAC AMT
Democrat	92	$13,748.07	19.7	$582.74
Republican	112	$18,593.97	26.6	$581.50
Winner	100	$27,280.47	41.7	$685.09
Loser	108	$5,234.26	5.8	$465.10
Incumbent	85	$29,108.36	46.0	$639.34
Challenger	69	$5,289.13	5.2	$422.68
Open Seat	54	$9,640.66	9.7	$652.43

SENATE	# OF CANDIDATES	AVG PAC$	# OF PAC CONTRIBS	AVG PAC AMT
Democrat	22	$35,520.47	37.1	$762.36
Republican	37	$35,298.68	33.3	$896.16
Winner	23	$69,499.45	70.9	$1,002.30
Loser	37	$13,216.60	11.4	$726.41
Incumbent	16	$66,830.43	78.5	$794.82
Challenger	15	$7,030.00	4.6	$706.57
Open Seat	29	$31,474.65	25.0	$917.74

2012 Elections

HOUSE	# OF CANDIDATES	AVG PAC$	# OF PAC CONTRIBS	AVG PAC AMT
Democrat	48	$15,232.48	28.0	$565.97
Republican	92	$23,051.88	33.8	$758.95
Winner	100	$24,179.02	41.0	$543.63
Loser	40	$11,005.74	10.0	$1,065.68
Incumbent	82	$22,635.22	40.3	$496.35
Challenger	20	$11,630.55	9.4	$918.66
Open Seat	34	$21,216.40	24.2	$1,059.85

SENATE	# OF CANDIDATES	AVG PAC$	# OF PAC CONTRIBS	AVG PAC AMT
Democrat	13	$29,531.11	44.2	$651.22
Republican	40	$29,583.58	33.3	$979.71
Winner	26	$50,892.50	62.0	$839.20
Loser	27	$9,468.07	9.7	$957.60
Incumbent	16	$52,190.05	69.4	$729.17
Challenger	8	$12,536.90	10.1	$1,117.60
Open Seat	29	$21,960.55	23.6	$933.34

money. They both did not have any challengers and *together* they raised $300 for their two campaigns. Thus, of the 126 winning candidates, 124 were able to get some PAC money, for a whopping percentage of 98.4%. With the losers, there is a different story; only 71 of the 139 losing candidates received any PAC money, for a percentage of only 51.1%. Of the 139 losers, only nine were able to raise more than $20,000 in PAC money, with no candidate receiving over $60,000. By contrast, among the 126 winners, 70 of them raised over $20,000 in PAC money, and sixteen of them raised over $60,000, including Representative T.W. Shannon and Senator Dan Newberry who each raised over $100,000.

Examining the Different PACs by Categories

Finally, once PAC information is collected by candidate, it is now possible to examine the PACs by categories. For the first time, we can truly see how much money is donated by various interests in Oklahoma. Table 11–11 shows PAC contributions for the 2010 and 2012 elections divided by category. Within each category, the total amount donated, the number of donations, the percentage of that total amount, and the average donations are given because each column truly yields different information. In looking at the percentages, some interests are clearly more powerful than others. Three of the most powerful interests stayed the same, although they switched order. These interests were health, Native American, oil/gas and business. Health went from being the top PAC category in the 2010 elections to #2 in the 2012 elections. A newcomer to the top PAC list is the Native American category, which only had 1.8% of the contributions in 2006, but 14% of the contributions in 2010 and 14.1% of the contributions in 2012 (#3). Oil/gas PACS which were third on both lists in 2006 and 2010 were first in 2012 with 16.0% of the contributions.

As noted previously, the Republican Party PACs which were first on the 2006 election almost disappeared in the 2010 elections and were only just a bit more evident in 2012 with 4.2% of the contributions. Moreover, the Democrats were even worse, representing a measly .6% of the contributions in 2010 and .3% of the contributions in 2012. These changes in political party contributions are significant for several reasons. First, political party PACs give a lot more money on average than these other types of PACs. The candidates depend on these large donations to get elected. It also makes it easier when fundraising when a contributor gives a large amount because it means that fewer donors have to be sought. Second, this has significant partisan implications because as can be seen in the chart, the Democrats continued to keep their dismal percentage, and instead, the most notable change came with the Republicans, from 2.8% in the 2010 elections to 4.2% in the 2012 elections.

In looking at Table 11-11, the first categories to notice are those with the large average donations. The Democratic and Republican Ideology PACs, the Labor PACs, and the Other PACs, and the Public Employee PACs all

Table 11–11

2010 vs 2012 Elections—Type of PAC—Which Ones Give the Most and Least?

Type of PAC	2010 Elections				2012 Elections			
	Avg Contrib	#	Total	% Total	Avg Contrib	#	Total	% Total
Agriculture	$478.96	587	$281,150.00	5.2	$612.59	480	$294,045.00	6.1
Banking	$511.19	367	$187,605.28	3.5	$548.67	318	$174,476.92	3.6
Business	$804.51	694	$558,330.00	10.3	$696.01	671	$467,023.76	9.7
Construction	$684.59	266	$182,100.00	3.4	$725.63	302	$219,141.50	4.6
Education	$540.34	295	$159,400.00	2.9	$560.59	206	$115,481.40	2.4
Environment	$342.86	7	$2,400.00	0.0	$192.31	13	$2,500.00	0.1
Fire	$740.00	165	$122,100.00	2.3	$791.77	243	$192,400.00	4.0
Guns	$291.67	12	$3,500.00	0.1	$0.00	0	$0.00	0.0
Health	$603.86	1382	$834,530.96	15.4	$650.81	1,177	$766,009.88	15.9
Ideology-D	$1,672.40	84	$140,481.82	2.6	$1,074.33	30	$32,229.92	0.7
Ideology-R	$1,875.76	132	$247,600.00	4.6	$1,754.61	234	$410,579.68	8.5
Indian	$1,971.17	385	$758,900.00	14.0	$2,122.34	320	$679,150.00	14.1
Labor	$1,090.96	177	$193,100.00	3.6	$1,024.44	208	$213,083.00	4.4
Oil and Gas	$755.28	997	$753,010.79	13.9	$721.03	1071	$772,226.90	16.0
Other	$1,343.28	233	$312,983.95	5.8	$1,150.75	264	$303,797.78	6.3
Party-D	$853.97	39	$33,305.00	0.6	$445.16	32	$14,245.00	0.3
Party-R	$940.75	162	$152,401.00	2.8	$1,355.37	149	$201,950.00	4.2
Professional	$345.97	124	$42,900.00	0.8	$428.05	123	$52,650.00	1.1
Pub Emp	$1,871.71	76	$142,250.00	2.6	$1,537.04	81	$124,500.00	2.6
Telecomm	$462.24	237	$109,550.00	2.0	$570.45	132	$75,300.00	1.6
Tobacco	$395.00	50	$19,750.00	0.4	$314.88	84	$26,450.00	0.5
Transport	$613.10	126	$77,250.00	1.4	$516.77	164	$84,750.00	1.8
Utilities	$378.32	309	$116,900.00	2.2	$106.45	31	$3,300.00	0.1

gave average contributions greater than $1,000 in both the 2010 and 2012 elections. The newcomer in 2012 was the Republican Party, which gave $1,355.37 on average to candidates. Again, this is more bad news for the Democrats. Not only did they have a significantly smaller average donation than the Republicans ($445.16), but the Health and Ideology PACs gave most of their money to Republicans as well. While the Democrats had narrowed the gap in Ideology average donations in 2010 ($1,672.40 to $1875.76 for the Republicans), that gap widened again in 2012 to $1,074.33 to $1,754.61 for the Republicans. Even more alarming though for the Democrats were the total number of donations and total amount spent. Ideology Democrat PACs spent only $32,229.92 on 30 candidates in the 2012 elections while the Republicans spent a gigantic $410,579.68 on 234 candidates. Most surprising here was the below average donations given by guns, tobacco, and even agriculture interests in both elections. Oklahoma is typically known nationally as a "gun and pickup" state, with lots of cowboys riding the plains, but these numbers show that these groups are not big contributors in Oklahoma. That's probably because they know that Oklahoman legislators will already be supportive of those interests.

One other notable trend evident on Table 11-10 was the growth in Fire PACs. While the average amount only marginally increased (from $740.00 in 2010 to $791.77 in 2012), the real growth came in the number of donations and the aggregate amount. Fire PACs gave to 165 candidates in 2010 with a total amount of $122,100, but in the 2012 elections, they gave $192,400 to 243 candidates. What also changed was the number of Fire PACs. In the 2010 elections, Oklahoma City and Tulsa fire organizations contributed the bulk of the donations, but in the 2012 elections, there were fourteen different fire organizations that contributed money.

In comparing the House versus the Senate on Table 11-12, other trends emerge. Because of the smaller size of the state Senate, its prestige, and the four-year terms, it was expected that PACs would give more to Senate candidates than House candidates. In fact, there were only four exceptions to this, and really only one of any significance—Fire PACs. The other categories, environmental PACs, Native Americans, and Public Employees had only minor differences in the averages. With Fire PACs, however, there was a difference in the average ($834.37 in the House, but $554.05 in the Senate), but there were even bigger discrepancies in the number of candidates (206 in the House and 37 in the Senate, as well as the amount—$171,900 in the House and only $20,500 in the Senate). These differences are even more than one would expect given the difference in size in the two bodies. With all the other PAC categories, senate candidates received more than house candidates in the 2012 elections. This was similar to the 2010 elections where only environmental PACs gave more to house candidates, but a change from the 2006 election when Banking PACs, Gun PACs, and Youth PACs were exceptions. In the 2012 elections, though, there were several interests, where the difference between the average House and Senate donation was substantial. Education PACs ($804.13 versus $469.67), Other

Table 11–12

2012 Election PAC Contributions by Type of PAC, Divided by House and Senate

	House			Senate		
	Average	#	Total	Average	#	Total
Agriculture	$575.60	334	$192,250.00	$697.23	146	$101,795.00
Banking	$511.46	216	$110,476.28	$627.46	102	$64,000.64
Business	$634.89	456	$289,510.92	$825.64	215	$177,512.84
Construction	$641.21	217	$139,141.50	$941.18	85	$80,000.00
Education	$469.67	150	$70,450.00	$804.13	56	$45,031.40
Environment	$220.00	10	$2,200.00	$100.00	3	$300.00
Fire	$834.47	206	$171,900.00	$554.05	37	$20,500.00
Guns	$0.00	0	$0.00	$0.00	0	$0.00
Health	$585.22	829	$485,150.00	$807.07	348	$280,859.88
Ideology-D	$477.44	9	$4,296.93	$1,330.14	21	$27,932.99
Ideology-R	$1,672.69	151	$252,576.68	$1,903.65	83	$158,003.00
Indian	$2,145.87	242	$519,300.00	$2,049.36	78	$159,850.00
Labor	$997.34	157	$156,583.00	$1,107.84	51	$56,500.00
Oil & Gas	$675.01	768	$518,409.90	$837.68	303	$253,817.00
Other	$993.06	167	$165,840.28	$1,422.24	97	$137,957.50
Party-D	$417.17	23	$9,595.00	$516.67	9	$4,650.00
Party-R	$1,247.45	98	$122,250.00	$1,562.75	51	$79,700.00
Professional	$416.28	86	$35,800.00	$455.41	37	$16,850.00
Pub Emp	$1,558.33	60	$93,500.00	$1,476.19	21	$31,000.00
Telecomm	$467.89	95	$44,450.00	$833.78	37	$30,850.00
Tobacco	$301.64	61	$18,400.00	$350.00	23	$8,050.00
Transport	$403.67	109	$44,000.00	$740.91	55	$40,750.00
Utilities	$97.62	21	$2,050.00	$125.00	10	$1,250.00

PACs ($1,422.24 versus $993.06), Health PACs ($807.07 versus $585.22), and Telecommunication PACs ($833.78 versus $467.89) gave much more on average to senate candidates than they gave to house candidates.

Table 11-13 also shows the different categories of PACs broken down by political party. For many interests, the Democrats and Republicans received roughly the same amount in terms of the average donation, with perhaps Republicans having the slight advantage. This was true for Agriculture PACs, Banking PACs, Business PACs, Construction PACs, Oil/Gas PACs, Health PACs, Professional PACs and Transportation PACs, among others. There were a couple of notable exceptions to this, however. Probably the most striking were the donations by Labor. Democrats typically get more from Labor PACs than do Republicans and that certainly was the case here with $1,102.27 on average for Democrats and only $524.11 for Republicans. But even more important were the differences in the number of donations and the total amount ($198,408 for 180 contributions for Democrats, but $14,675 for 28 contributions for Republicans). This makes up somewhat for the huge discrepancy in both political party and ideological PAC giving, but not entirely because the differences were so large. All the Democratic Party PACs only gave $14,245 for an average donation of $445.16, while the Republicans received $1,355.37 on average in $201,950 worth of donations. The ideological PAC donations were even more lopsided with $38,229.92 given to 35 Democrats, but $404,579.68 given to 229 Republicans. The Democratic total even included $6,000 the Democrats received from mostly Republican Ideological PACs!

Table 11-14 compares the PAC donations received by the winners and the losers in the 2012 elections. In looking at this table, two items need to be viewed simultaneously, the total amount given by an interest and the average donation. The reason for this is that if one just looks at the average donation, there will be some surprising results. In 60.9% of the categories, or 14 of 23, the loser received an average higher donation than the winner. This was especially the case for the Construction PACs, Fire PACs, Indian PACs, Labor PACs, Other PACs, Professional PACs, and the Telecommunication PACs. The most notable among these are the Education PACs ($481.29 for the winners but $1,215.22 for the losers), the Fire PACs ($582.98 versus $1,182.38), and Professional PACs ($388.98 versus $1,350.00). For a few interests, the average donation was higher for the winners, including the Agriculture PACs, Banking PACs, Tobacco PACs, and Utility PACs. But the most notable ones were the Republican Ideology PACs and the two political party PACs. The Republican Ideology PACs, for example, gave $1,853.48 to 159 winners, but only $1,545.03 to 75 losers. With the parties, the Democrats actually gave contributions to more losers (28 to 4 winners), the average contribution was slightly higher for winners ($523.75 for winners to $433.93 to losers). The Republicans chose a different strategy, giving to more winning Republicans than losers (110 to 39), but also a much higher average donation ($1,466.36 for winners to $1,042.31 for the losers). This is probably the result of having a

Table 11–13
2012 Election PAC Contributions by Type of PAC, Divided by Democrats and Republicans

	Democrats			Republicans		
	Average	#	Total	Average	#	Total
Agriculture	$561.75	166	$93,250.00	$639.47	314	$200,795.00
Banking	$408.75	80	$32,700.00	$595.70	238	$141,776.92
Business	$545.86	145	$79,150.00	$737.40	526	$387,873.76
Construction	$684.94	83	$56,850.00	$741.06	219	$162,291.50
Education	$667.48	103	$68,750.00	$453.70	103	$46,731.40
Environment	$209.09	11	$2,300.00	$100.00	2	$200.00
Fire	$675.50	149	$100,650.00	$976.06	94	$91,750.00
Guns	$0.00	0	$0.00	$0.00	0	$0.00
Health	$506.91	313	$158,661.41	$702.95	864	$607,348.47
Ideology-D	$1,074.33	30	$32,229.92			
Ideology-R	$1,200.00	5	$6,000.00	$1,766.72	229	$404,579.68
Indian	$2,358.02	131	$308,900.00	$1,958.99	189	$370,250.00
Labor	$1,102.27	180	$198,408.00	$524.11	28	$14,675.00
Oil & Gas	$524.98	261	$137,018.98	$784.21	810	$635,207.92
Other	$1,202.39	66	$79,357.50	$1,134.21	197	$223,440.28
Party-D	$445.16	32	$14,245.00			
Party-R				$1,355.37	149	$201,950.00
Professional	$365.52	29	$10,600.00	$447.34	94	$42,050.00
Pub Emp	$1,404.76	21	$29,500.00	$1,583.33	60	$95,000.00
Telecomm	$498.28	29	$14,450.00	$590.78	103	$60,850.00
Tobacco	$250.00	21	$5,250.00	$336.51	63	$21,200.00
Transport	$362.50	60	$21,750.00	$605.77	104	$63,000.00
Utilities	$100.00	18	$1,800.00	$115.38	13	$1,500.00

Table 11–14
2012 Election PAC Contributions by Type of PAC, Divided by Winners and Losers

	Winner			Loser		
	Average	#	Total	Average	#	Total
Agriculture	$472.21	511	$241,300.00	$528.00	75	$39,600.00
Banking	$504.53	332	$167,505.28	$574.29	35	$20,100.00
Business	$870.46	417	$362,980.00	$938.00	50	$46,900.00
Construction	$659.31	231	$152,300.00	$851.43	35	$29,800.00
Education	$458.58	239	$109,600.00	$703.72	74	$52,075.00
Environment	$375.00	4	$1,500.00	$300.00	3	$900.00
Fire	$397.50	100	$39,750.00	$1,266.92	65	$82,350.00
Guns	$295.45	11	$3,250.00	$250.00	1	$250.00
Health	$617.91	1244	$768,680.96	$477.17	138	$65,850.00
Ideology-D	$567.50	21	$11,917.50	$2,040.70	63	$128,564.32
Ideology-R	$1,870.09	107	$200,100.00	$1,900.00	25	$47,500.00
Indian	$1,909.21	331	$631,950.00	$2,350.93	54	$126,950.00
Insurance	$648.07	207	$134,150.00	$565.00	20	$11,300.00
Labor	$847.18	71	$60,150.00	$1,290.78	103	$132,950.00
Oil & Gas	$759.41	923	$700,935.79	$703.72	74	$52,075.00
Other	$1,321.24	177	$233,858.95	$1,412.95	56	$79,125.00
Party-D	$300.63	8	$2,405.00	$975.00	32	$31,200.00
Party-R	$925.64	119	$110,151.00	$998.81	42	$41,950.00
Professional	$350.00	107	$37,450.00	$320.59	17	$5,450.00
Pub Employee	$1,900.79	63	$119,750.00	$1,730.77	13	$22,500.00
Telecomm	$433.57	213	$92,350.00	$716.67	24	$17,200.00
Tobacco	$398.81	42	$16,750.00	$375.00	8	$3,000.00
Transport	$587.38	103	$60,500.00	$728.26	23	$16,750.00
Utilities	$376.87	281	$105,900.00	$387.93	29	$11,250.00

very comfortable Republican majority in the Oklahoma legislature and few competitive contests for the Republicans.

As with the differences between the winners and losers, a similar pattern emerges with the PAC donations to incumbents and challengers as shown in Table 11-15. Once again, the number of contributions and the total amount of contributions become very important because challengers and open seat candidates get very few donations. Most PACs are only willing to give donations to those candidates who are likely to stay in office. Thus, most of the usual sources of PAC money were just not there for challengers in the 2012 elections, including Agriculture PACs, Business PACs, Banking PACs, Construction PACs, Oil & Gas PACs, Health PACs, and Transportation PACs, who all gave very small numbers of contributions. Thus, the challengers only got 6.6% of the PAC contributions, the open seat candidates got 30.3% of the contributions, and the incumbents got 63.1% of the PAC contributions. In fact, of the 23 categories, only four, the Republican Party PACs, Republican Ideology PACs, Fire PACs, and Health PACs, gave more than 20 contributions to the challengers.

Despite all these problems, challengers did get some PAC money. Of the four types of PACs above, three were willing to give both a significant number of contributions along with a hefty average contribution amount. As an example, Fire PACs not only gave 27 challengers contributions, but they also donated an average amount of $1,740.74. Also notable are both the Republican Party and Ideology PACs. For challengers, party/ideology money can act as seed money for a campaign, providing the crucial early amount that can jump start a political campaign. The Republican Party PACs gave $1,075.00 on average to 26 candidates, while the Republican Ideology PACs gave $1,580.65 on average to 62 candidates.

Although Republican Party and Republican Ideological PACs did give large average sums to challengers and that was most of their money, those PACs gave even more to the open seat candidates. The Republican Party gave $1,462.80 on average to 82 open seat candidates, while donating $1,318.29 on average to 41 incumbents. The Ideological Republicans gave $1,845.00 on average to 114 open seat candidates, but gave $1,762.43 to its incumbents. Political party and ideology PACs are usually very willing to give to open seat candidates even more so than challengers or incumbents because challengers can be seen as a risky choice because the PAC might not want to offend the incumbent and because open seat races are often the most competitive and typically are more likely to take office than challengers.

Conclusions

The numbers of interest groups and the numbers of lobbyists in Oklahoma have increased. These interest groups have been very active on numerous measures appearing before the legislature. At the same time, Oklahoma strengthened its ethics laws for lobbyists, interest groups, and

TABLE 11-15
2012 Election PAC Contributions by Type of PAC, Divided by Incumbent, Challenger, and Open Seat

	CHALLENGER			INCUMBENT			OPEN SEAT		
	AVERAGE	#	TOTAL	AVERAGE	#	TOTAL	AVERAGE	#	TOTAL
Agriculture	$431.25	8	$3,450.00	$701.76	340	$238,600.00	$587.15	86	$50,495.00
Banking	$655.56	9	$5,900.00	$534.31	231	$123,426.44	$586.81	72	$42,250.48
Business	$1,108.33	12	$13,300.00	$659.78	502	$331,210.92	$805.49	148	$119,212.84
Construction	$825.00	12	$9,900.00	$683.29	204	$139,391.50	$807.74	84	$67,850.00
Education	$1,320.16	9	$11,881.40	$422.70	163	$68,900.00	$1,090.32	31	$33,800.00
Environment	$625.00	2	$1,250.00	$100.00	9	$900.00	$116.67	3	$350.00
Fire	$1,740.74	27	$47,000.00	$491.14	158	$77,600.00	$1,232.41	54	$66,550.00
Guns	$0.00	0	$0.00	$0.00	0	$0.00	$0.00	0	$0.00
Health	$650.00	21	$13,650.00	$630.40	893	$562,948.25	$738.98	244	$180,311.63
Ideology-D	$1,617.98	4	$6,471.93	$1,100.00	4	$4,400.00	$993.24	21	$20,857.99
Ideology-R	$1,580.65	62	$98,000.00	$1,762.93	58	$102,250.00	$1,845.00	114	$210,329.68
Indian	$2,444.44	9	$22,000.00	$2,091.44	222	$464,300.00	$2,150.57	87	$187,100.00
Labor	$902.52	23	$20,758.00	$885.51	107	$94,750.00	$1,293.33	75	$97,000.00
Oil & Gas	$1,653.42	15	$24,801.32	$670.86	869	$582,973.60	$898.88	177	$159,101.98
Other	$1,393.33	15	$20,900.00	$953.76	157	$149,740.28	$1,459.42	91	$132,807.50
Party-D	$429.17	12	$5,150.00	$650.00	2	$1,300.00	$433.06	18	$7,795.00
Party-R	$1,075.00	26	$27,950.00	$1,318.29	41	$54,050.00	$1,462.80	82	$119,950.00
Professional	$433.33	3	$1,300.00	$383.51	97	$37,200.00	$615.22	23	$14,150.00
Pub Emp	$1,750.00	4	$7,000.00	$1,695.00	50	$84,750.00	$1,212.96	27	$32,750.00
Telecomm	$425.00	2	$850.00	$590.00	110	$64,900.00	$500.00	18	$9,000.00
Tobacco	$250.00	1	$250.00	$320.42	71	$22,750.00	$287.50	12	$3,450.00
Transport	$1,000.00	4	$4,000.00	$484.47	132	$63,950.00	$612.96	27	$16,550.00
Utilities	$0.00	0	$0.00	$108.62	29	$3,150.00	$0.00	0	$0.00

ONLINE RESOURCES

General interest group information:	http://web.syr.edu/~jpcammar/intgroup.htm
The Tulsa World:	http://www.tulsaworld.com
Lawton Constitution:	http://www.lawton-constitution.com
The Daily Oklahoman:	http://www.oklahoman.net
Political Sites:	http://www.vote-smart.org

candidates, placing much deeper restrictions on how money can be raised and spent in Oklahoma. By examining the candidate's contributions and receipts, every Oklahoman can find out whether winning or losing candidates raise more money, whether Democrats or Republican have been more successful in the money game, and how various interests give their PAC money in Oklahoma.

NOTES

1. All lobbying statistics from 1997 were calculated by the author from the "Oklahoma Registered Lobbyists 1997-1998" report published by the Oklahoma Ethics Commission. Statistics from earlier years came from Morgan, England, and Humphreys (1991). 2004 and 2007 figures came from the Oklahoma Registered Lobbyists report as listed at www.state.ok.us/~ethics.

2. In trying to measure the number of lobbyists by categories of interest, some methodological issues arose. Since several lobbyists reported working for multiple associations or corporations that were not in the same issue area, the number was more difficult to measure. Percentages of time figures are not available, nor are the amounts paid by these groups to hire these lobbyists. Thus, the only way to measure the number of lobbyists by category was to count the number of associations or corporations listed and to categorize them, instead of doing it by the number of lobbyists. Also, I divided the time for each individual lobbyist based on the number of groups represented and then looked to see how many persons represented each association, as done by many human resource firms. The results were almost identical, particularly for the major categories represented.

3. Some of the other holdings of the Disney Corporation include 37.5% of A&E, 50% of Lifetime, four film studios in addition to Walt Disney (Touchstone, Hollywood, Caravan, and Miramax), several newspapers, several magazines including Los Angeles and Discover, a cruise line, and some vacation clubs.

4. These states require disclosure, but do not place any limits on the amounts that non-candidate individuals and groups may donate to campaigns: Oregon, Utah, Virginia, Idaho, and Illinois (Council of State Governments, 1996).

THE OKLAHOMA TAX SYSTEM

Loren C. Gatch

The income tax has made more liars out of the American people than golf has.

Will Rogers

I. INTRODUCTION

Taxes represent the main way that governments fund their commitments and responsibilities to citizens. In this chapter we examine briefly the types and patterns of taxation in Oklahoma. After some general remarks about the different forms of taxation and their relation to American federalism, this chapter describes the various taxes that Oklahoma imposes upon its citizens, and how Oklahoma's tax system differs in basic ways from those of other states. State finances can easily become a complicated topic, and this chapter takes a broad approach that seeks to describe the fiscal 'forest' rather than the 'trees.'

The Oklahoma tax system is shaped by a few fundamental rules. First, like practically all other American states, Oklahoma cannot run a budget deficit and must strive each year to bring its taxes and expenditures into balance. In addition, the Oklahoma state legislature is allowed to appropriate only 95% of the projected revenue collection certified in a given year by the **State Board of Equalization.** Actual revenues in excess of 100% of this estimate flow into the **Constitutional Reserve Fund** (also known as the **"Rainy Day Fund"**). Finally, Oklahoma's finances are particularly influenced by the constraints imposed by the passage, in 1992, of **State Question 640,** which severely limits the ability of state government to raise taxes.

More recently, lawmakers have repeatedly sought to cut the state's income tax, with the long-term goal of eliminating this tax from Oklahoma's fiscal mix. The consequences of the national financial crisis of 2008–9 have been severe for state finances across the country, including Oklahoma's, and the state's tax take has only barely recovered to pre-crisis levels. In the longer run, Oklahoma's tax system faces challenges posed by the continuing shift towards a service economy, and the rise of online commerce. We will look at these developments and their implications for Oklahoma government.

II. TAXATION AND AMERICAN FEDERALISM

Within American federalism, some taxes are excluded either from state or national control by the U.S. Constitution. Other methods are shared by both levels of government. National control over tariffs means that states cannot use them a source of revenue. Similarly, national commerce powers prevent states from taxing the export of each others' products across state lines. Conversely, the Constitution originally prohibited the national government from laying **capitation**, or "direct" taxes that focused directly upon individual wealth and income (Art. I, sec. 9). Although modified by the Sixteenth Amendment establishing a national income tax, the national government does not otherwise tax property directly. Instead, the property tax remains a mainstay of state and especially local governments. Otherwise, the power to tax income is shared by the national and state governments and, in a few cases, cities.

Sales tax authority is likewise divided between the national, state and local levels, with the national level limiting itself to selective sales or **excise taxes** upon items like gasoline, cigarettes, and liquor—the sorts of things that people are either addicted to or cannot do without. Despite the occasional proposal to establish a national sales tax, broad-based levies on an *ad valorem* basis are traditionally reserved for the states. In addition, states like Oklahoma which possess significant natural resources like minerals or fossil fuels will tax their extraction.

Finally, as a matter of tradition, the states raise revenues by selling permission to engage in certain activities, such as practicing a profession, driving a car, and owning a dog; or by charging for access to certain benefits, such as state parks, public higher education, turnpikes, or museums. State sponsored lotteries, a growing revenue source for state governments and available in Oklahoma since a vote of the people in 2004, charge their customers for access to dreams of instant wealth! Taken together, **licenses** and other miscellaneous **user fees** constitute a significant revenue source for many states.

As a practical matter, then, within the American federal system, state and local governments enjoy three main sources of tax revenue: **property taxes, sales taxes, income taxes,** with non-tax licenses and fees representing a fourth source. Finally, a fifth important source of revenue is **intergovernmental transfers,** or money given by a higher level of government to a lower level for specific purposes. Of course, money coming from the national government has to be raised somehow. But that issue is beyond the scope of this chapter.

The ability of any government to raise taxes depends upon economic conditions, and these may vary from state to state even within a broader context of expansion or recession in the national economy. For example, in the same fiscal year ending June 30, 2010, compared to the previous year, state tax collections rose about 10% in North Dakota but fell by 24% in Wyoming (Braybrooks, Ruiz, & Accetta, 2011). Beyond this variation, however, the broad historical trend in American federalism has affected all states in a similar direction. With the expansion of the national government since the 1930s, federal revenues have come overwhelmingly from personal and corporate income taxes, as well as social security contributions (a form of income tax). From the point of view of the national authorities, income taxes are the ideal source of revenue in that the government's share of this income grows automatically with an expanding economy. In contrast, the main sources of 19th century revenue for the national government, the tariff and excise taxes, have dwindled to relative insignificance.

For their part, since the 1930s most states have left property taxes to the localities. Since immobile property like a house is easier to tax yet requires local knowledge and manpower to assess its value, this revenue source is most easily managed by local governments. This shift in tax authority was accelerated by the severe decline in property values during the Great Depression, which forced states to seek more stable sources of revenue. At the same time, states began introducing their own general sales and income taxes. Indeed, Oklahoma was one of the first states to introduce a general sales tax. Miscellaneous taxes and fees, as well as expanding intergovernmental transfers (grants in aid, revenue sharing) rounded off the main revenue sources for states up until the 1970s (Winters, 1996). Since then, tighter national finances and the return of financial responsibilities to the states have had major impacts upon state budgets. Intergovernmental transfers from the national level have declined as a percentage of state funding, as have sales and corporate income taxes, while states have relied more on personal income taxes, miscellaneous revenues and higher user fees to make up the difference (Rainmondo, 1996). Moreover, popular resistance to local property taxes has led to restrictions on their use in most states, forcing local governments into a greater reliance upon financial support from state governments for such critical functions as public education. In recent years, the growing pressures of healthcare, education, and pension costs have squeezed state finances at the same time that states' traditional sources of revenue have failed to keep pace with new fiscal demands (Boyd, 2006).

III. THE OKLAHOMA TAX SYSTEM

In the fiscal year ending June 30, 2013, the Oklahoma Tax Commission (OTC) reported that the state collected the precise amount of $9,175,334,9788.88, not including those sales tax revenues gathered on behalf of cities and counties but before deducting tax refunds. This amount includes $240 actually paid for "Controlled Dangerous Substance Tax Stamps" (while dealing in marijuana is illegal in Oklahoma, it is also a felony to do so without paying the relevant stamp tax!). That mighty $240 is earmarked as a statutory appropriation for the "Drug Abuse Education Revolving Fund."

Oklahoma tax revenues for FY 2013 were about $177 million more than those for FY 2012, reflecting the gradual recovery of tax revenues from the revenue shortfalls caused by the 2008-2009 crisis, as well as income tax cuts passed by the legislature (Oklahoma Tax Commission, 2014). Of course, Oklahoma spends more than this annually; significant revenues also come from non-tax sources (the lottery, for example) and intergovernmental transfers from the federal level. According to the Oklahoma Office of Management and Enterprise Services (OMES), total revenues from all sources, tax and non-tax, amounted to over $17 billion (2013). What major categories of tax does Oklahoma impose, and how does its tax system fit within national patterns? How heavy a burden does the Oklahoma tax system impose upon citizens? We will consider these questions in turn.

Tax Administration

With few exceptions, the administration, enforcement and collection of state taxes is handled by the **Oklahoma Tax Commission** (OTC), a three-person body appointed by the governor, subject to senate confirmation, and serving staggered six-year terms. Motor vehicle registration taxes and fees are collected by motor license agents (tag agencies) approved and regulated by the OTC. In addition, the OTC provides considerable assistance to county and local governments, and to the State Board of Equalization, as it assesses property values for *ad valorem* taxation. While about sixty-five percent of tax revenues flow into the state's **General Revenue Fund** for appropriation by the legislature, the rest are earmarked by statute for county, city, and other local uses such as roads or education and are disbursed through the OTC. Finally, the OTC handles under contract the collection of sales and use taxes for counties and cities. In particular, nearly 500 municipalities as well as most counties impose some sort of sales tax over and above that levied by the state. As a consequence, the effective sales tax rates in Oklahoma can range from five to ten percent depending on location.

The Main Types of Taxes

Oklahoma has two main types of revenue source at the state level: an income tax (individual and corporate) and sales and use taxes. Together, they represent over seventy percent of the state's tax revenues. Also important are taxes on motor vehicles and their fuels. A fourth source that is peculiar to Oklahoma consists of **severance taxes** imposed on the extraction of nonrenewable resources such as oil and gas. Apart from the multitude of user fees, Oklahoma's other main non-tax source consists of transfers from the national government. At the local level, municipalities rely on the property tax and supplemental sales taxes, as well as intergovernmental transfers from the state level.

We will briefly review the features of Oklahoma's major taxes.

LEADERSHIP PROFILE

KEN MILLER
Oklahoma State Treasurer

KEN MILLER is the 18th State Treasurer of Oklahoma, serving since January 10, 2011. He was elected with almost 67 percent of the vote in the November 2010 General Election. A Republican from Edmond, Miller served for six years in the Oklahoma House of Representatives where he led the Appropriations and Budget Committee and guided Oklahoma through the largest state spending cuts in state history while maintaining the delivery of core government services.

Miller holds a doctorate in political economics from the University of Oklahoma. He earned a Master's of Business Administration from Pepperdine University and a bachelor's degree in economics and finance from Lipscomb University. Miller is an economics professor at Oklahoma Christian University. He has been honored with the "Who's Who Among American Teachers" award and the Merrick Foundation Award for Excellence in Teaching Free Enterprise.

Prior to his election to the State Legislature, Miller served in the administration of Governor Frank Keating as chairman of the Legislative Compensation Board where he established a 10-year freeze on legislative salaries.

Prior to his public service, Miller gained practical experience in the private sector. He began his professional career in banking at First American National Bank before joining MediFax-EDS, where he served as financial operations manager.

1. The *income tax* represents the state's single largest source of revenue. For individuals, it is levied annually upon the net income of Oklahoma residents, whether from earnings, dividends, or capital gains, irrespective of whether it was received in Oklahoma or elsewhere. Conversely, nonresidents are subject to Oklahoma's income tax in proportion to their property interests or business activities within the state. For individuals, this tax is mildly progressive, ranging from 0.5% to 5.25% for the

highest earners. The corporate tax rate is a flat six percent upon that portion of a corporation's income obtained from Oklahoma operations. Most income tax revenues go into the General Revenue Fund.

2. *Sales and use taxes* have risen over the years from one percent in 1933 to four and one half percent in 1990. On top of the current basic statewide rate, counties and municipalities have been allowed since 1965 to add supplemental rates, the proceeds of which are collected by the OTC on the localities' behalf. Indeed, alongside of the property tax this has become an important source of revenue for local governments. In FY 2013, the OTC collected and reimbursed over $1.5 billion for counties and municipalities. The use tax is merely the sales tax applied to items bought outside of, but delivered to, Oklahoma. Between 1933 and 1987, sales and use tax proceeds were earmarked to the State Assistance Fund to fund various public welfare programs. Since 1987 these proceeds have been redirected for general revenue purposes. The sales tax applies both to the sale of tangible goods and personal property, as well as to other specified services such as transportation, meals, hotel lodging, and entertainment admissions. Exemptions to the tax are numerous, ranging from certain agricultural sales and prescription drugs to the transfer of intermediate manufacturing goods.

Many of these exemptions reduce the incidence of taxation on productive activities by business, and in particular aim to avoid the problem of **tax pyramiding**, or the building up of excessive tax burdens when taxes levied early in production are passed on as price increases of intermediate goods, which then are taxed again in later stages of processing and distribution. In other cases, exemptions represent concessions to politically-influential or connected constituencies. Other items already subject to tax, such as motor fuel (see below), are also exempt. The single most important exemption

---

TABLE 12-1
Major Exemptions to the Sales Tax

1. Items already subject to excise or other taxes (fuels, motor vehicles, petroleum production);
2. Sales by the state and federal governments, and nonprofit organizations such as churches;
3. Agricultural sales made directly on the farm to consumers, as well as farm implements and livestock feed;
4. Sales of prescription drugs;
5. Sales by residential utilities (electricity, gas);
6. Sales of items purchased for subsequent resale (wholesale inventories);
7. Sales of intermediate manufacturing goods and products (machinery and products used in the manufacture of products for final consumption);
8. Sales of corporations and other entities that reflect various forms of financial consolidation (mergers, consolidations, restructurings)

SOURCE: Oklahoma House of Representatives, *Legislative Guide to Oklahoma Taxes, Collections, and Apportionments* (2008).

concerns the sale of services, most of which (as opposed to goods) remain untaxed. In a modern economy increasingly driven by the service sector, this exemption has resulted in an increasing mismatch between the fiscal systems of all American states and the economy that sustains it.

3. *Gross production taxes*, including severance taxes on oil, gas, uranium and other minerals, are significant sources of revenue for Oklahoma. These reflect the lingering importance of natural resource extraction in the state's economic profile, and seldom play the same important role in other states' finances. These taxes are based upon a percentage of the value of resources taken from the ground. Raised to their present level in 1971, severance taxes take seven per cent of the gross value of oil and gas and five percent of the value of uranium. Also included among gross production taxes are small excise taxes placed upon gas and petroleum. One significant, and growing, tax exemption pertains to the rate imposed upon horizontal drilling. A once seldom used but now common drilling technique, horizontal drilling, is taxed at a reduced rate that will mean over $250 million in forgone revenues to the state in 2014 (Oklahoma Policy Institute, 2014). Gross production taxes are earmarked to the General Revenue Fund, to county spending for roads and schools and, in the case of severance taxes on gas, to the Oklahoma Teacher's Retirement System.

4. *Excise taxes* are placed upon gasoline and diesel fuels, meaning that their sale is taxed at a fixed rate per gallon, and not as a percentage of their price (as would an *ad valorem* tax). Since 1987, the gasoline tax has remained at 16 cents a gallon, and 13 cents for diesel fuel. An additional one-cent per gallon has been tacked on for environmental cleanup purposes. Other excise taxes relating to motor vehicle ownership and operation include a variety of registration, title and lien fees, an "in lieu" tax, and vehicle, boat and motor excise taxes. These taxes are collected for the state by gas stations and private tag agencies. The details of, and exemptions to, this tax category are numerous and complex. In particular, they include the exemption of motor fuel taxes on sales by Indian tribal authorities to tribal members. Most of the proceeds are earmarked to various transportation and road-building purposes.

A related set of excise taxes (sometimes called **sumptuary taxes** or **"sin taxes"**) are those applied to alcoholic beverages and cigarettes. Taxes on liquor are levied per liter of spirits and wine, and per barrel of beer; cigarettes are taxed by the pack. In Oklahoma, some of the wages of sin are the following: For hard liquor, you pay the state $1.47 per liter for the privilege; wines range from 19 to 55 cents per liter, while beer over 3.2% is taxed at $12.50 per 31-gallon barrel. If you smoke cigarettes, you pay $1.03 per pack. If you really must chew tobacco or use snuff, you are assessed 60% of the factory list price. Because of Native Americans' sovereign status, their tribal smoke shops sell tobacco products at a substantially lower tax rate than do retailers elsewhere in Oklahoma. The loss of revenue to the state has been a point of contention between the state and its Native American population.

5. *Vehicle Taxes and Licenses* generate revenue from a number of sources, the most important of which is the annual tax which motorists pay based upon the value of their vehicles. Owners of commercial and farm vehicles pay their own separate schedule of taxes. The sale of new and used vehicles is also subject to an excise tax (in place of a sales tax) of 3.25%. Included in this category of revenue are receipts from the taxing of car rentals and fees for drivers' licenses and plates. Revenue from these sources is apportioned in a complicated way, with the bulk of it split between the General Revenue Fund and school districts.

6. *Property taxes* are collected by local governments as an assessed percentage of the "fair cash value" of the property. By law, personal property other than homes is included in this tax, although in practice the application of this tax beyond real estate has been sporadic, since its collection would require very intrusive measures. Over the years, the property tax system has been the subject of much revision and litigation. Property tax collections are continually politicized by the fact that county assessors are elected officials who enjoy considerable autonomy in how they value property and assess taxes on it. The key issues concern the consistency (or **"equalization"**) of assessed valuation across counties and the widespread under-reporting of personal property other than real estate. A **State Board of Equalization** seeks to impose greater uniformity in the assessment of similar pieces of property across counties. Finally, as

TABLE 12–2		
Oklahoma State Taxes and Collections, Amount and as a Percentage of All Revenues, by Major Source, FY 2013		
TYPE OF TAX	AMOUNT COLLECTED	PERCENTAGE OF ALL TAX REVENUES
Income Tax, Gross Collection (Personal and Corporate)	$4,123,861,208	45.0%
Gross Production Taxes	715,072,537	7.8
Sales and Use Taxes	2,541,392,779	27.7
Vehicle Taxes and Licenses	681,413,069	7.4
Motor Fuel Taxes	444,068,748	4.8
Beverage and Tobacco Taxes	390,096,075	4.3
Other (Franchise Tax and Fees; Rural Electric Tax and License; Miscellaneous Taxes, Fees, Licenses)	279,427,360	3.0
Total Tax Collection	9,175,334,979	100.0

SOURCE: *Annual Report of the Oklahoma Tax Commission, FY 2013*

with other taxes, exemptions abound—particularly for "intangibles" such as financial assets and relatively easy treatment of agricultural land. Table 12–2 provides a more detailed breakdown of Oklahoma's major tax revenue sources.

Sixty-five percent of these revenues flow into the General Revenue Fund, to be allocated by the legislature according to its priorities. The remainder is divided up among a number of earmarked uses. Again, it should be stressed that these numbers describe the proceeds from Oklahoma's tax system. They do not include revenue that Oklahoma earns from non-tax sources, such as tuition charged to college students. Nor do they factor in grants and other financial transfers from the federal government to the state, which in FY 2013 were approximately 38% of total revenues (Oklahoma Office of Management and Enterprise Services, 2013b). What Table 12-2 does provide is a basic snapshot of the pattern and results of Oklahoma's tax system.

Oklahoma Taxes in Comparative Perspective

Comparisons among state tax systems seek to answer two basic questions. First, what sort of a burden does the Oklahoma tax system impose relative to other states? Second, how do their mixes of revenue sources vary, both among themselves and relative to the national average? Various authorities have attempted to rank states in different ways. While these numerical rankings are important exercises from a policy perspective, the relevance of these numbers for political debates means that we must take some care to specify what the rankings do and do not compare. In particular, the bases for many cross-state comparisons involve revenue figures that aggregate both state and local spending, and often include non-tax revenue sources. As a consequence, the aggregate revenues being compared are often more comprehensive than the snapshot of Oklahoma's state tax sources given above. The basis for many state comparisons is the U.S. Census Bureau's Survey of State and Local Government Finances, the most recent of which reflects data collected for FY 2011, providing a slightly older picture than the more recent tax and revenue numbers available from the OTC and the OMES. Other cross-state comparisons make use of data available in 2008. Nonetheless, the resulting comparisons are useful for situating Oklahoma within broad national patterns.

Above all, it must be stressed that these rankings by themselves do not tell us whether Oklahoma is an over- or under-taxed state, and thus whether taxes are too high or too low. Those are political judgments that depend upon what the public decides it wants from its governments. That said, other important questions do arise that can be answered by fiscal analysis. For example, does the Oklahoma tax system encourage or discourage economic development? Are revenue sources stable, diversified, and well adapted to the nature of the economy from which they are drawn? Is the mix of taxes fair, if fairness can be defined in a generally acceptable way? While we cannot

	TABLE 12–3 Burden of State and Local Taxes, Oklahoma, Neighboring States, and the National Average, FY 2008 (National Rank Out of 50 States, 1 = Highest)	
STATE	STATE AND LOCAL TAXES PER CAPITA	STATE AND LOCAL TAXES AS A PERCENTAGE OF PERSONAL INCOME
Oklahoma	$3379 (40)	9.2 (41)
Texas	3554 (35)	8.9 (45)
Arkansas	3280 (44)	10.5 (35)
Kansas	4246 (19)	10.6 (19)
Missouri	3336 (41)	9.1 (42)
U.S. Average	4371 —	10.7 —

SOURCE: Morgan and Morgan (2011), pp. 304, 306.

give complete answers to these questions in this chapter, we can at least understand the relationship between tax policy and these other issues.

The most basic comparative measure of the burden of state and local taxes can be expressed as a percentage of personal income or per capita.

Oklahoma's place in this ranking reflects a number of factors—the wealth of the state relative to others, its geography, population distribution and density, tax structures, legal limits on spending, degree of federal aid, and voter preferences. One important fact that affects Oklahoma's ranking in this and a number of other fiscal indicators is its relatively low per capita income. At just under ninety percent of the national average, the state's relatively low income sets an overall limit to the amount of money the state can raise, from whatever revenue source. That said, taxes are high and low only relative to what populations are able to pay, so per capita rankings by themselves may not adequately express the burden borne by Oklahoma's taxpayers.

A slightly more detailed picture emerges when we compare, in the same way, the relative burdens posed by the three largest tax sources: property, sales, and income taxes (see Table 12-4).

Missing from these data is any reference to gross production taxes, which, though important revenue sources to Oklahoma, have no counterpart in most other states. As for its two other significant tax revenue sources, Oklahoma ranked 43rd in the nation for its 17 cents per gallon gasoline tax, and first in the nation for its per capita motor vehicle registration fees, even after having reduced these substantially in 2000 (Morgan & Morgan, 2011). What this broad comparison suggests is that, much like Arkansas, Oklahoma's relatively low property tax burden is made up by

TABLE 12–4

Per Capita Property, Sales, and Income Taxes, FY 2008
(National Rank Out of 50 States, 1 = Highest)

STATE	STATE AND LOCAL PROPERTY	STATE AND LOCAL SALES (GENERAL)	INCOME* (INDIVIDUAL)
Oklahoma	$580 (47)	$991 (22)	$690 (32)
Texas	1380 (17)	1114 (14)	0 (NA)
Arkansas	510 (49)	1296 (8)	775 (26)
Kansas	1318 (19)	1094 (15)	969 (15)
Missouri	566 (48)	849 (29)	797 (24)
U.S. Average	1346 —	1000 —	803 —

*For FY 2009.
SOURCE: Morgan and Morgan (2011), pp. 308, 310, 336.

reliance upon other revenue sources. Regional contrasts are accentuated by the case of Texas, which has no income tax and correspondingly relies far more heavily on the other two remaining legs of the state tax "tripod."

Yet another way of expressing these contrasts is to compare the relative contribution of each major tax category—property, sales, and income—to the sum of all three revenue streams.

As Table 12-5 illustrates, Oklahoma relies disproportionately on its sales and income taxes in order to make up for a relatively low property tax burden. As a percentage of state and local revenues, Oklahoma's property tax burden is about 60% below the national average, while its sales

TABLE 12–5

Property, Sales, and Income Taxes as a Percentage
of the Three-Tax Revenue Total, Oklahoma and
Neighboring States FY 2011

STATE	STATE AND LOCAL PROPERTY	STATE AND LOCAL SALES (GENERAL)	INCOME (INDIVIDUAL)
Oklahoma	26.0%	46.0%	28.0%
Texas	59.2	40.8	0
Arkansas	23.4	47.2	29.4
Kansas	39.6	33.2	27.2
Missouri	37.5	31.6	31.0
U.S. Average	43.1	29.2	27.7

SOURCE: Calculated from US Census, 2011 *Survey of State and Local Government Finance.*

tax burden is 60% above the national average. Another consequence of this reliance follows from the inherently local nature of property taxes. Since fewer taxes are collected by localities, more taxes are collected by the state. Compared to the national average, Oklahoma's tax system is more centralized at the state level in the sense that the state government, as opposed to county and municipal governments, collects a greater proportion of overall tax revenues than is the case in other states. Compared to its neighbors, Oklahoma's finances are more concentrated at the state level than in Texas, Kansas, and Missouri, but less so than in Arkansas.

The wide range in ranking among Oklahoma's neighbors for this value does point to the structural consequences of a state's tax mix. As with other indicators provided in this chapter, Arkansas' ranking paints it as a somewhat more accentuated version of Oklahoma. Quite apart from whether a state's taxes are too high or too low, specialists in state finance recommend that a good tax system should attempt to do three things. First, it should seek diversity in its revenue streams, and not depend too much on any one source. Second, it should seek revenue streams that will grow with the needs of the state. Finally, for the sake of fairness it should impose its burdens equally on the largest number of people, resulting in broad but low tax rates. No state balances these three goals in exactly the same way.

Non-Tax Revenue Sources

In addition to the taxes and other revenues states raise from their own citizens, an important source of revenue is federal ("intergovernmental") funding. This consists of transfers from the federal government to the states. In the wake of the severe national economic downturn that began in 2008, intergovernmental transfers soared, reflecting federal economic

TABLE 12-6
Share of State and Local Tax Collections by State Governments,
Oklahoma and Neighboring States FY 2011

STATE	PERCENTAGE COLLECTED BY STATE
Oklahoma	64.8%
Texas	47.5
Arkansas	79.9
Kansas	57.6
Missouri	51.5
U.S. Average	56.8

SOURCE: Calculated from US Census, *2011 Survey of State and Local Government Finance*.

stimulus spending. Indeed, in FY 2010 intergovernmental revenue for Oklahoma even exceeded state government tax receipts, though that proportion has since receded. Apart from stimulus-related spending, the growth of intergovernmental revenues has been driven in particular by rising levels of reimbursements for Medicare (health insurance for the elderly), the cost of which is shared between the national and state governments.

In other respects, Oklahoma does very well by its fiscal relationship with the federal government. In 2009, the state received $1.54 from the taxpayers of all other states for every one dollar that Oklahomans sent to Washington D.C. (calculated from U.S. Census Bureau, 2011). This reflects the prominence of federal payrolls, particularly those on military bases. States like Oklahoma that are poorer than the national average also receive greater federal assistance than do richer states.

The other main non-tax revenue source available to Oklahoma consists of the many charges and fees that the state imposes on its citizens. The distinction between these charges and specialized taxes is sometimes one without a difference. Nonetheless, if it is not collected by the OTC (turnpike fees or college tuition, for example), then it falls into the non-tax category. Nationwide, such non-tax sources of revenue have become increasingly important, both because of popular opposition to tax increases and because of longer-term structural problems with states' traditional tax bases. In Oklahoma, for example, taxes are restrained by

Table 12–7
State and Local Revenue Sourced From the Federal Government, Per Capita (FY 2008) and as a Percent of State and Local General Revenue (FY 2011): Oklahoma and Neighboring States

State	Per Capita Revenues (FY 2008; highest = 1)	Percent of all State and Local General Revenue (FY 2011)
Oklahoma	1630 (20)	22.2 (13)
Texas	1360 (39)	16.8 (35)
Arkansas	1664 (17)	24.3 (8)
Kansas	1317 (45)	16.2 (39)
Missouri	1533 (27)	21.6 (16)
U.S. Average	1,582	18.1

Source: Morgan and Morgan (2011), pp. 299–300. US Census, *2011 Survey of State and Local Government Finances.*

constitutional limitations on property tax millages and the supermajority requirements of Proposition 640 (a tax increase requires 75% vote by the legislature). Nationwide in FY 2008, taxes accounted for 50.0% of all state and local revenues, a percentage that has been in decline over the last decade. In that same year, Oklahoma ranked 33rd with a tax take that was four percentage points below the national average (Morgan & Morgan, 2011). As these percentages go down, the proportion of non-tax revenue within the state and local revenue mix increases.

One final way of assessing Oklahoma's tax system is to compare the relative importance of its major components to those of other states, again using the latest U.S. Census data reporting for FY 2011.

This table contributes to our portrait of the Oklahoma tax system because its comparisons point in the same direction as do the earlier tables. Whether expressed as a percentage of personal income, taxes per capita, or as a percentage of all tax revenue sources, Oklahoma makes less use of the property tax than do other jurisdictions. If it were not for Oklahoma's gross production tax revenues (reflected in Oklahoma's high percentage value for "Other" taxes in Table 12-8), the state's reliance upon sales taxes and stiff motor vehicle-related taxes would appear even more pronounced. Finally, Oklahoma's resort to non-tax revenue sources, while part of a larger national trend, has been exacerbated locally by constitutional restrictions placed upon the ability of the state to raise revenues. It is to these restrictions, and the tax policy responses they have engendered, that we turn to by way of conclusion.

TABLE 12–8

Major State and Local Tax Sources as a Percentage of Total Tax Revenue, Oklahoma vs. Neighboring States and US Average, FY 2011

STATE	PROPERTY	SALES AND GROSS RECEIPTS*	INDIVIDUAL AND CORP. INCOME	MOTOR VEHICLE	OTHER
Oklahoma	18.0%	43.0%	23.0%	5.0%	10.0%
Texas	43.6	45.2	0	2.1	9.0
Arkansas	18.2	50.2	26.6	1.4	3.6
Missouri	29.9	37.4	26.6	1.4	4.7
Kansas	33.3	37.2	25.0	1.7	2.8
U.S. Average	33.1	34.5	25.0	1.7	5.8

*Includes general and selective sales, alcoholic beverages, tobacco, public utilities, and other taxes.

SOURCE: Calculated from US Census, *2011 Survey of State and Local Government Finance.*

IV. IS THIS TAX SYSTEM RIGHT FOR OKLAHOMA?

As a general matter, each state's revenue sources mirror in important respects the economic condition and structure of the state. For broad comparative purposes, some data are more useful than others. For example, it is commonly pointed out that, in per capita terms, Oklahoma ranks near the bottom of the fifty states in various categories of taxing (Blatt, 2014). Yet this is not surprising given that Oklahoma's per capita income lags the national average. Obviously, a relatively poor state will take in, and spend less, per capita than will a rich one. Some anomalous rankings reflect interesting policy alternatives, such as the lack of an income tax in Texas. In contrast, a neighboring state like Kansas possesses a tax system whose results come far closer to national averages. Indeed, to appreciate the Oklahoma tax system it is far more useful to compare its tax pattern with those prevalent nationwide.

Oklahoma's relatively low income means that it has historically relied to a greater extent than other states upon transfers from the national government, although Oklahoma's dependence in this regard has faded in recent years with the more general retrenchment in national government aid to the states. Gross production and other severance taxes naturally make an outsized contribution to state revenues since most states lack Oklahoma's mineral resources. Yet these are notoriously unstable, depending as they do upon changes in the international commodity markets. During periods of high energy prices like the early 1980s and the late 2000s, Oklahoma's gross production tax receipts grew rapidly, only to shrivel when energy prices retreated. A significant part of Oklahoma's budgetary shortfalls between 2008 and 2010 can be accounted for a decline by half in the state's gross production receipts. Ironically, it was the expansion of these tax receipts up through 2008 that encouraged Oklahoma's legislators to pass income tax cuts which have only made the most recent budgetary shortfall worse.

How Heavy a Burden Does the Oklahoma Tax System Impose?

As noted above, a low per-capita tax take does not necessarily mean that Oklahoma has a low tax *burden*. Even low taxes may be burdensome; depending upon how poor Oklahoma is relative to the rest of the country, its tax burden may actually be greater than elsewhere. Alternately, the relatively heavy reliance upon gross production taxes may overstate this burden, since those taxes typically fall upon out-of-state consumers. Analysts are divided over the question of whether or not Oklahoma is a low-tax state in relative terms. As we have seen, comparisons by tax category yield mixed results. Even including intergovernmental transfers and non-tax revenues, in FY 2008 Oklahoma ranked 40th in state and local general revenues per capita (Morgan & Morgan, 2011). Another approach to the question with great intuitive appeal is to ask how long Oklahomans collectively must work in a given year before they earn the sum of that year's state tax bill. This date, popularly known as **"Tax Freedom Day,"** as shown in Table 12-9 is regularly calculated by The Tax Foundation, a national anti-tax lobbying group. By this measure, Oklahoma has one of the lighter tax burdens in the nation.

Whatever position one argues, it remains the case that Oklahoma's tax structure in part reflects political decisions about how to exploit the state's tax base. The resulting tax structure expresses first and foremost what voters will tolerate. Of all the deviations from the national average, taxes on oil and gas are most understandable, since they allow Oklahoma to shift the tax burden onto the citizens of other states. Similarly, property taxes in Oklahoma are, as a percentage of the take, far below the national average—in large part because, since 1933, their assessment and administration have been left in the hands of local government and elected county assessors.

It seems proper that local resources fund local services. However, localities will skimp on their contributions if they can get the money from somewhere else. Voters will always want low property taxes. In Oklahoma, these incentives are sharpened by the relative autonomy that local assessors enjoy, despite the efforts of the State Equalization Board. Oklahoma's experience illustrates the basic problem of property taxes. As has long been recognized, a tax that is best administered at a local level is also a tax that local property owners will most resist (Oklahoma Academy for State Goals, 1985).

Ironically, one result of this local autonomy is that Oklahoma exhibits greater **fiscal centralization**—the financial dominance of state governments over localities—than other states (Murry, et al., 1996). This condition is also suggested by Table 12-5. In this regard, Oklahoma is hardly alone; the movement of power and money from the local to the state level is a national trend that began in the 1980s. As federal aid to localities has decreased, states have taken up the slack, either by substituting their own grant systems, or by assisting localities in the collection of taxes (Hanson, 1996). Yet, by relying less upon property taxes than other communities, Oklahoma localities depend even more upon state-level revenue sources than do localities elsewhere.

TABLE 12–9 "Tax Freedom Day" 2013		
STATE	DATE OF "TAX FREEDOM"	NATIONAL RANKING
Oklahoma	April 6	40
Texas	April 10	30
Arkansas	April 7	39
Kansas	April 9	33
Missouri	April 8	37
New Mexico	April 3	46
U.S. average	April 18	

SOURCE: http://www.taxfoundation.org/taxfreedomday

It should be stressed these various rankings do not imply what Oklahoma taxes ought to be. Rather, they describe Oklahoma taxes *relative to national patterns*. Like all tax systems, Oklahoma taxes reflect the history of the state. The distinctive features of Oklahoma's system include: low property taxes; relatively high sales taxes; high fees and licenses; and heavy reliance upon unpredictable tax revenues from oil and gas production. In addition, the property, sales and income taxes contain many exemptions that tend to reduce their revenues. Overall, Oklahoma's tax system exhibits a structural tendency towards **inelasticity.** That is, revenues do not grow proportionally with increases in state income. This is increasingly a feature of state tax systems nationwide (Murry et al., 1996; Fox & Luna, 2006). Oklahoma's tax system reflects both past choices and the influence of powerful constituencies. Are these choices and influences necessarily bad? In an ideal world, taxes would be simple, broadly based, minimal, and fair. Oklahoma's taxes do not fit this ideal, but neither do the tax systems of any of the other 49 states. Any tax system that responds to popular pressure or is used as a tool of public policy will become complicated. For their part, policy reformers have a disconcerting tendency to prefer tax systems whose revenues grow in a steady and automatic fashion, beyond the reach of political interference. Fortunately, democracies have a high tolerance for political imperfections. Besides, inefficient and inequitable tax systems are also ones whose burdens do not grow as quickly as the rational "ideal." That said, one should not hesitate to point out the fiscal consequences of the tax choices that Oklahoma has made.

Like all other American states save one, Oklahoma ties itself down in advance by having a constitutional commitment to a balanced budget. In addition, the details of the state's budgeting are disciplined by the State Board of Equalization, which must certify the amount of money the legislature may spend in the coming year. Together, both of these mechanisms limit the overall budget to incremental growth. In March 1992, Oklahoma voters approved State Question 640, which forces the state to submit all tax increases to popular approval if they pass either house of the legislature by less than a three-fourths margin. A popular reaction to the tax increases of the 1980s, this new requirement makes it hard for Oklahoma to raise taxes.

What does SQ 640 mean for Oklahoma's fiscal future? As long as the economy grows, the government's increasing tax take means that the bite will be little felt. However, over the long run, the interaction of Oklahoma's tax system—particularly its reliance upon sales and excise taxes—with the limits imposed by SQ 640 point to the emergence of a chronic, structural shortfall in revenue growth, especially if lawmakers persist in cutting income taxes. Unlike income tax receipts, sales tax receipts do not grow proportionally with increases in per capita income. Moreover, the absence of taxes upon *services*—an increasingly dominant sector of any modern economy—means that more and more of what is bought and sold in Oklahoma escapes taxation (Murry et al., 1996). The rise of web-based commerce only aggravates this trend. Within this long-term trend, the state will repeatedly face pressures from changes in the business cycle. The painful results of these pressures reappeared with a vengeance during the recession of 2008-9. Revenue collections fell by over twenty percent between FY 2008 and FY 2010, and the state avoided bigger budget cuts only by relying on federal stimulus funds and tapping the state's **"Rainy Day fund,"** a special fund reserved for when the state faces a severe budget shortfall.

This most recent fiscal predicament has once again prompted calls for modernization of the Oklahoma tax system. In particular, reform of the tax system might entail reducing the number of special-interest features of the tax code, such as the exemptions to the sales tax detailed in Table 12-1, or the tax breaks for horizontal drilling. Such features are generally termed **tax expenditures**, which the OTC defines as "the amount of state revenue that would have been collected but for the existence of each exclusion, deduction, credit, exemption, deferral or other preferential tax treatment allowed by law" (Oklahoma Tax Commission, 2012). An analysis of the OTC data concludes that there are at least 450 separate tax expenditures that reduce the state's tax take by $5.6 billion. In other words, had these various special interest provisions not been in the tax code, the state's tax revenues would have been that much higher (Blatt, 2010).

Yet another fiscal development with implications for Oklahoma's finances is the repeated attempts by lawmakers to cut, and even eliminate, the income tax. Since 2004, the income tax rate on top earners has been lowered from 6.65% to 5.25%. Most recently, the legislative and executive branches approved in 2013 further cuts in this rate to 5% and lower by 2016, a move that was overturned by the state's Supreme Court that same year only on the grounds that the legislation violated the single-subject rule (tax cuts were combined with a measure to fund repairs to the state capitol). With a governor who has expressed her aspiration to eliminate outright the income tax, and Oklahoma's statewide offices solidly in the hands of anti-tax majorities, it is likely that further moves to cut the income tax are in the offing.

In the meantime, existing restrictions on the ability of Oklahoma to raise taxes have encouraged lawmakers in recent years to consider fee-for-service revenue sources such as a lottery, tuition increases, and turnpike tolls. Non-tax revenue sources have their advantages and drawbacks. Lotteries in particular are politically popular because they are not seen as a tax, yet they are unreliable as revenue sources and their benefits can be overblown (Holmes, 2004). In its brief life so far, the Oklahoma lottery has produced lower revenues than anticipated. Lotteries are also faulted for encouraging civic irrationality and a spirit of gambling among those citizens who can least afford it, although with the proliferation of tribal gaming facilities, opposition to state-sponsored gambling looks increasingly quaint (Claunch, 2002). As the impact of past and future income tax cuts begin to bite, Oklahomans will have to think hard about where it will get the funds to pay for the things Oklahomans want.

MUNICIPAL AND COUNTY GOVERNMENT
IN OKLAHOMA

Deborah D. Ferrell-Lynn

All politics is local.

Thomas P. "Tip" O'Neill,
Speaker of the U.S. House of Representatives, 1977–1987

I. INTRODUCTION

Y ou can't miss it. Whether you are driving towards downtown Oklahoma City or flying into Will Rogers World Airport southwest of the city, you will notice the 845-foot-tall Devon Energy Tower, the crown jewel of that company's downtown Center complex. With 52 stories and 1.8 million square feet, the Devon Tower is the tallest building in Oklahoma and ranks among the nation's top 40 skyscrapers. Easily dominating the city skyline, the Tower is a symbol of economic vitality and community optimism. Oklahoma City residents look at the $750-million structure and see another example of how far the city has come since the 1980s. Oklahoma's economic future looked dismal in 1986 as the "Oil Bust" of the late 1980s negatively affected employment and sales tax collections statewide. Throughout the state, municipal business leaders and elected officials questioned whether their jurisdictions could emerge from the economic malaise that resulted from the dramatic drop in crude oil prices (from $ 37.60 per barrel in 1982 to $11.15 in 1986) and the subsequent failure of Penn Square Bank. As the largest city in the state, both in land area and population, Oklahoma City was particularly hard hit. Already generally overlooked as part of "fly-over country" (a derisive term for the middle section of the U.S.), Oklahoma City's downtown was in danger of becoming little more than a place where suburb-dwellers worked before returning to their "bedroom communities" and where lower income residents dealt with declining infrastructure and little economic opportunity. By 1993, the city's primary convention center, the "incomparable" Myriad was hardly that—national business organizations and trades shows rejected the outdated and increasingly run-down event locale in favor of other cities' newer structures and nearby quality hotels (downtown Oklahoma City had one), restaurants, concerts, sports venues, and community events. Civic and elected leaders hoped that landing a contract with a major employer would jump-start Oklahoma City's flagging economy. Instead, potential employers looked to other more economically progressive cities, despite the fact that Oklahoma City residents had approved dedicated sales tax initiatives to enhance public safety and the city's zoo; a 1989 infrastructure bond issue had also been approved by voters. These efforts were somewhat unusual, given that City voters traditionally rejected sales tax measures, but the local economy was severely hurt by the Oil Bust, and City leaders and residents realized that a major investment would have to be made in order for Oklahoma City to compete with other states for private sector and tourism dollars. This realization prompted voters in 1991 to approve several sales tax measures to entice two major air carriers—United and American—to build their new aircraft maintenance centers in Oklahoma City. Despite an aggressive campaign for the $1 billion United contract, Oklahoma City finished behind Indianapolis (which, ironically, faced the prospect of closing the facility in 2003).

The loss of the United Airlines contract turned out to be a blessing in disguise. Airline officials told Mayor Ron Norick that Oklahoma City was rejected because of its limited quality of life and a declining downtown area. Lack of public investment had contributed to the city's negative image. City leaders learned through a survey conducted by the Greater Oklahoma City Chamber of Commerce in the early 1990s that only 17 percent of residents held a favorable view of the City's image; 61 percent indicated a negative image. Chamber chairman Ray Ackerman summarized respondents' views in an article in *The Daily Oklahoman*: "If you asked people why they stayed here, they said they thought we had a good quality of life. But they also thought the grass was greener on the other side of the fence. They didn't have any pride" (Lackmeyer, 2003, p. 1A).

Norick, Ackerman, and other city elected and business leaders responded by proposing the **Metropolitan Area Projects (MAPS),** an aggressive plan to fund nine projects seen as critical to revitalizing the downtown area. Other cities had funded the building of sports stadiums and entertainment districts. Oklahoma City was proposing a comprehensive package that would include among other things construction of an indoor sports arena, a minor league ballpark, a new library, a recreational canal running through the city's burgeoning entertainment district, and renovation of several existing city structures vital to its arts and entertainment. Instead of serving simply as a "quick fix" or "band-aid" approach to economic malaise, MAPS was envisioned as a major revitalization effort that would permanently enhance the city's economy and its status as a major mid-sized U.S. city.

The campaign to win city voters over to the idea faced an uphill battle. Polling data indicated that only 37 percent of residents initially supported the plan and the attached tax. Similar redevelopment plans like the ill-fated **"String of Pearls"** (derisively dubbed the "String of Beads" by critics), a previous effort to develop parks along a twenty-mile stretch of river, were cited by critics as proof that Oklahoma City could not successfully undertake such massive endeavors. Some argued that it was foolish of Oklahoma City to attempt to emulate San Antonio's Riverwalk through the building of a canal that "went nowhere."

Norick and his allies were not discouraged by such criticism. Their persistence and dedication to the vision paid off. In 1993, voters approved a five-year, one-cent sales tax to fund the $254-million plan to renovate existing structures and build new ones also viewed as vital to the project's success. During the next 10 years, Oklahoma City witnessed the renovation of its Civic Center, State Fair Arena, and convention center. The 13,000-seat Bricktown Ballpark, recognized as one of the finest minor league baseball venues in the country, opened in 1998. The Bricktown Canal, constructed in 1993, began attracting restaurants, shops, and special community events, making it a major tourist attraction. The state-of-the-art $87-million Ford Center (now known as the Chesapeake Energy Arena), the largest of the MAPS projects, has become a primary concert venue and was built to NHL and NBA standards.

The MAPS investment paid off in multiple ways. In addition to the renovation of existing cultural facilities like the 1937-vintage art deco Civic Center and the State Fairgrounds Arena, the infusion of public and private sector dollars into the Ballpark and Canal have led to increased economic development in the Bricktown Area, making it downtown's entertainment center. A new four-star hotel was erected north of the "Cox Convention Center" and high dollar apartments sprang up in the Deep Deuce section of Bricktown. Other communities and nations looked to MAPS as an innovative way for cities to reinvigorate their downtown economies. Residents of Tulsa, Oklahoma, adopted the MAPS approach, passing an $885 million historic economic development tax package in September 2003. As Oklahoma City observed the 10th anniversary of MAPS, there was much to be proud.

Yet, there were also controversies and challenges. Critics pointed to a lack of government accountability despite the creation of a Citizens' Advisory Committee. Cost estimates for the Civic Center, Bricktown Canal, and convention center were higher than expected, leading the new mayor, Kirk Humphreys, to call for an extension of the sales tax to cover the $10 million shortfall. The public criticized the granting of naming rights of the Bricktown Ballpark to Southwestern Bell Telephone for an undisclosed amount. The 1995 bombing of the Alfred P. Murrah Federal building delayed MAPS projects as the City responded to the loss of 168 lives and destruction of several downtown buildings. The city failed to attract an NHL team to the Ford Center (this proved to be a blessing in disguise as the NHL canceled its 2004-2005 season over a labor dispute), and legal disputes delayed construction of the new downtown library. The City of Oklahoma City's decision to fund the building of a MAPS spinoff, a Bass Pro Shop just south of the Ballpark, drew criticism from those concerned about taxpayer-funded incentives to attract private investment, despite a refund requirement. Civil rights groups argued that lower income groups were not benefitting from MAPS success and jobs creation.

Still, MAPS has been successful. All nine projects have been completed, the last being the $24-million Ronald J. Norick Library that opened in 2004. Downtown investment is expected to reach into the billions. Already, millions of people have visited new downtown attractions such as Bass Pro and the multi-screen theater in Bricktown. Resolution of the NHL strike led the Edmonton Oilers to relocate their farm team to Oklahoma City. Now, the Barons hit the ice in the Cox Convention Center. The Ford Center became the temporary home of the New Orleans Hornets after Hurricane Katrina devastated the Gulf Coast in 2005. Oklahoma City sports fans responded overwhelmingly positive in terms of attendance and enthusiasm. The proven quality of the arena as a sports venue and the record fan attendance numbers enabled a small group of investors to gain NBA approval to purchase and relocate the flailing Seattle Supersonics to Oklahoma City. In anticipation of the team's arrival, Oklahoma City voters approved another temporary sales tax in 2008 to build out a variety of upgrades to the Ford Center which later would be rechristened as The Chesapeake Energy Arena. The once cellar-dwelling Oklahoma City Thunder reached the Western Conference Finals in 2011 and played in the 2012 NBA Finals with sellout crowds at all of its home playoff games. The Oklahoma City Barons, the top affiliate of the National Hockey League's Edmonton Oilers, hit the home ice of the Myriad Convention Center in 2010 and have made the playoffs twice.

Other indicators reflect Oklahoma City's successes. The Oklahoma City National Memorial and Museum was awarded accreditation by the American Association of Museums and its 2-millionth museum visitor walked through the museum's doors during the summer of 2011 (Dinger, 2011). **Project 180**, a $176-million redesign of downtown streets, parks, sidewalks, and plazas to enhance the downtown area's appearance and make it more pedestrian-friendly, was launched in 2010.

MAPS exemplifies an aggressive response to competition among American cities for private sector investment capital and jobs creation. The project's success illustrates how important Oklahoma's cities are in enhancing their own and the state's economic well-being.

This chapter provides an overview of the structure and functions of Oklahoma's municipal and county governments and the means by which they acquire and spend funds needed to meet basic services while responding to new challenges. While the focus is primarily on municipal government, the chapter will also discuss the role and responsibilities of county government and changes that have occurred and not occurred in response to a massive scandal involving corrupt county officials during the 1980s. The issue of proposed consolidation of county governments and services will also be discussed.

II. MUNICIPAL GOVERNMENTS: CITIES AND TOWNS

Population and Jurisdictional Demographics

Discussion of a state's population and jurisdictional demographics is fact-based and traditionally uninspiring. However, these facts are important indicators of a state's (and more specifically, a municipality's) attractiveness as a place where people want to work and live. Oklahoma's total population according to the U.S. Census Bureau's 2013 estimate stands at 3,850,568—a nearly 400,000-person increase since the 2000 Census. As part of the American "Heartland," Oklahoma is generally regarded as a primarily rural state. Population figures, however, show that the state has become more urbanized with 80% living in cities and surrounding communities. The U.S. Census Bureau identifies cities as any urban place with a population of 2,500 or more; a **"Metropolitan Statistical Area"** (MSA) consists of at least one urban area (a "central city") with 50,000 or more inhabitants and "adjacent communities" that are linked economically and socially with the central city. Oklahoma ranks 42nd (up from 47th) among MSAs in the U.S., and Tulsa ranks 55th (U.S. Bureau Census, 2014).

The two major cities in the state are Oklahoma City (also the state capital), and Tulsa, formerly a major oil center. Table 13–1 identifies the current 10 largest cities (Stillwater replaces the previous number 10, Muskogee; and Broken Arrow now ranks as the 4th largest city). It is important to note that for several cities, "population" must be considered in terms of both those citizens living in the cities themselves and those living in outlying metropolitan areas. In addition, three of the cities (Norman, Stillwater, and Edmond) on the "Top 10" list are "university towns" with significant student populations.

TABLE 13–1 Ten Largest Cities in Oklahoma by Population with Area			
	2012 POPULATION	MSA (2011–2012)	AREA (SQ. MILES) 2011
Oklahoma City	599,199	1,296,565	621.2
Tulsa	393,987	951,880	186.8
Norman	115,562		189.5
Broken Arrow	102,019		45.6
Lawton	98,376		81.0
Edmond	84,585		87.9
Moore	57,810		21.9
Midwest City	56,080		24.6
Enid	49,854		74.1
Stillwater	46,560		28.3

SOURCE: U.S. Census Bureau, 2014.

"Legal Existence" – Constitutional and Statutory Aspects

The American federal system distributes governing power between the national and state governments. It not only prevents one level of government from dominating all others but also provides U.S. citizens with numerous government access points and elected officials accountable to the public for government actions. Article I, Sec. 3 of the U.S. Constitution gives the national government authority to admit states into the union. Section 4 states that "The United States shall guarantee every State in this Union a Republican Form of Government." Scholars generally agree that this language is designed to ensure that the citizens of each state are provided the legal means of electing their representatives to their respective state governments. While not specifically expressed in the Constitution, states hold the power to grant legal existence to cities, counties, and towns. States have established unitary relationships, individually determining the extent of power exercised by their respective individual jurisdictions. This relationship between states and cities is governed by the so-called **Dillon's Rule**, named after a nineteenth-century judge from Iowa who articulated the concept that cities are creatures of the states. Over time, the unitary relationship has been modified to allow cities greater discretion in service delivery and expanded taxation authority.

In identifying the formal structures of and powers exercised by Oklahoma's municipalities, one need look no further than the state constitution and statutes. Oklahoma's Constitution, specifically Article XVIII dealing with "Municipal Corporations," empowers the state legislature to *incorporate*, that is, to grant legal existence and powers to local jurisdictions and their governments. Specific rules regarding the incorporation of towns and cities are articulated in Title 11 of the Oklahoma State Statutes. Those jurisdictions consisting of more than 25 but less than 1,000 inhabitants may be incorporated by the state legislature as a *town*. An incorporated *city* has more than 1,000 inhabitants. Offical records indicate that there are 600 city and town municipalities incorporated in Oklahoma (U.S. Census Bureau, 2010).

Cities containing more than 2,000 inhabitants may apply for *home rule* status, meaning that the city's inhabitants, through adoption of a *city charter*, are empowered to determine the form of municipal government that will operate in the jurisdiction. Home rule makes it possible for cities to engage in actions which can lead to successful economic development (like MAPS and Tulsa's pursuit of aerospace and energy development), enhanced public safety programs (such as neighborhood policing), and other problem solving and enhancement activities without first seeking state approval.

Municipal Government Structures

Municipal government structures in Oklahoma differ in three important ways: (1) how power is distributed among several elected officials, (2) the degree and type of formal and informal power exercised by the governing body's chief executive and its impact on governance, and (3) the use of professional administrators to manage municipal operations. State statutes establish the forms of government that can be adopted by cities and towns and articulate details regarding elected officials, powers, terms of office, and other structural matters.

Unlike cities, towns are restricted regarding the form of government that can be adopted. Towns use the *aldermanic* form of city government with a mayor elected at large and one or two council members elected from each city ward. The mayor is not considered a council member when it comes to achieving quorum or for purposes of voting unless the council vote is equally divided. In this case, he or she is permitted to cast the tie-breaking vote for "questions under consideration of the council" (Title 11, Article IX). Other important officials in the aldermanic form include the city clerk, city treasurer, marshal, and street commissioner.

The processes by which cities in Oklahoma select the desired form of government first depends on whether the individual city chooses the charter or state statute route. Cities choosing government by state statute follow the rules stipulated in Title 11. Cities wishing to adopt one the three available options must first adopt a charter and then select from among the forms of government provided by statute (Title 11, Articles IX, X, and XI).

The *council-manager* form of government provides for the election of one council member from each city ward and one elected at large. Council members elect a mayor and vice mayor (who acts as mayor during the regular mayor's absence, disability, or suspension), both of whom have almost no formal powers. For example, the mayor presides at meetings and is considered the city's chief representative for ceremonial purposes, but is essentially in a "weak" position as he or she does not possess the veto power generally found in "strong mayor" governments. In addition, the mayor does not exercise sole appointment power over department heads, another feature of the strong mayor structure, but shares this responsibility with council members. The mayor does have voting power equal to each council member and participates in all discussions and votes before the council. The council-manager form is popular in Oklahoma and in medium-sized cities throughout the U.S.

Oklahoma City uses the council-manager form, but with some differences. The mayor is elected at large while the vice-mayor position is held on a rotating basis by the eight members of the city council, each of whom is elected on a ward-based system. Professionalization of city services is facilitated by the use of a city manager, appointed by the council based on executive and administrative qualifications to appoint department heads and manage city operations. City managers are also selected based on actual experience in performing pertinent administrative duties and knowledge of accepted public management practices. It is not uncommon for city managers in major Oklahoma cities to possess master's degrees in public administration, finance or other professional areas. The current city manager of Oklahoma City, James D. Couch, holds several engineering degrees and previously served as the City's Director of Water/Wastewater Utilities.

The city manager directly supervises department heads and their departments' activities, but all city employees serve under the authority of the mayor and council who are ultimately accountable to the citizens of Oklahoma City. Three exceptions to the city manager's supervision are the city auditor, the municipal counselor, and the municipal court judges, who as "council appointees" answer directly to the mayor and council.

The *strong mayor-council* form of government includes a mayor elected at large (who serves as an ex officio council member at large), and one council member from each city ward. The strong-mayor model provides the mayor with greater authority. Not only does the mayor preside at council meetings, but he or she essentially has all of the rights, powers, and privileges of all council members, including the right to vote on questions before the council. The strong mayor is described in statute as the city's chief executive officer and the head of the administrative branch of city government and can appoint and remove department heads and administer city operations. The strong mayor-council form is used in most large U.S. cities of 1 million or more in population, although it is also popular in many medium-sized cities in the Midwest (Bowman & Kearney, 2012).

One unique feature of the strong mayor-council form is the existence of a 3-member personnel board, elected for staggered six-year terms by the council, to provide a measure of merit protection. The mayor and council are prohibited from appointing or promoting persons to city classified positions (full-time, merit-based) for political or non-merit reasons.

Tulsa originally used the once-popular **city commission** form of government which empowered multiple commissioners with both executive and legislative powers. This form of government fell out of favor due to its lack of a single executive and problems associated with commissioners having almost complete autonomy over their assigned departments with no charter requirements that they possess the relevant qualifications. Tulsa adopted the strong mayor model in 1990 following approval by city voters the previous year.

Services and Functions—What Cities Do

Oklahoma's constitution empowers cities and towns to provide services and perform functions associated with local governance. Basic traditional services include provision of police and fire protection, clean water and wastewater management, solid waste management, street and traffic maintenance, zoning and code enforcement, and in some cases (Edmond, for instance), electricity purchased from publicly regulated, private companies.

Cities provide more than public safety services, utilities, and infrastructure maintenance. Many cities also fund and coordinate services and

LEADERSHIP PROFILE

CINDY ROSENTHAL
Mayor, City of Norman, Oklahoma

CINDY SIMON ROSENTHAL'S first real job was as a newspaper reporter. She worked the city desk for the *Toledo Blade* in Ohio and covered county government for *The Monterey Peninsula Herald* in California. Her interest in government services began to grow. At some point she realized just reporting about government activities was not going to be enough. While working on her Master of Arts in Urban Studies, she served a year-long public affairs internship with the Coro Foundation. That fellowship provided her an opportunity to observe  civic leadership in the St. Louis, Missouri area. She became more fascinated with representative institutions such as state legislatures, county commissions, and city councils. She then became involved with Legis 50, an advocacy organization for the improvement of policymaking capacity of state legislatures. From there she moved to the National Conference of State Legislatures (NCSL) where she provided technical assistance to legislative leaders and their staffs. Rosenthal drew upon her journalistic skills once again as she became the editor-in-chief for *State Legislatures*, a professional magazine published by NCSL. At that time, the circulation of *State Legislatures* was over 14,000.

When her husband Jim accepted an academic appointment to the School of Social Work at the University of Oklahoma, the Rosenthals moved along with their young daughter to Norman. Soon thereafter, she became a Carl Albert Congressional Fellow and began work on her Ph.D. in Political Science which she earned in 1995. Subsequently she was hired by the University of Oklahoma to serve as an Assistant Professor of political science and public administration with a joint appointment to Women's Studies.

Rosenthal now serves as the Director and Curator of the Carl Albert Congressional Research and Studies Center at OU. She has become a noted scholar with a national reputation in the fields of legislative studies and women's leadership. Rosenthal has written the book *When Women Lead* (1998) and edited *Women Transforming Congress*

(2002). Her latest book is *Speaker Nancy Pelosi and the New American Politics* written with her colleague, Dr. Ron Peters, Jr. In addition, she has written dozens of journal articles and book chapters and presented at numerous professional conferences. Rosenthal directs the National Education for Women's Leadership (N.E.W.) program.

She was always been extremely involved in the Norman community and in the summer of 2004, she began her official service to the city as Council Member of Ward 4. "One of the nice things about academic life is that you have a great deal of flexibility of your own schedule—teaching in the evenings and writing on the weekends has allowed me to be able to balance my university commitments and my public service to the city," Rosenthal explains. "A lot of the city meetings are in the late afternoon and evenings . . . and the university is so close to City Hall—within five minutes."

Rosenthal was first elected as Mayor in 2007. Her campaign platform emphasized maintaining quality of life for the citizens of Norman by carefully managing commercial and residential development in the city. In her first term, she was instrumental in encouraging the adoption of curbside recycling, using alternative fuels in city fleet vehicles, and promoting city beautification efforts. In 2010, Norman residents once again voted Rosenthal to be their mayor.

The *Journal Record* awarded Mayor Rosenthal with its prestigious Woman of the Year 2010 Award. She was also the recipient of the Oklahoma Chapter of the American Society for Public Administration's 2009 Distinguished Public Service Award. It's given annually to a public servant whose career exhibits the highest standards of excellence, dedication and accomplishment.

Both Cindy and Jim continue teaching at OU and have two grown children. In what little free time Rosenthal enjoys, she plays golf with her husband and continues her twenty-year participation in a local women's reading group.

Brett S. Sharp

programs designed to enhance "quality of life" and promote economic growth and vitality; for example, the City of Edmond established a public arts program to beautify its downtown area and encourage business growth (state lawmakers adopted a similar program statewide in 2004). Norman offers several youth-based recreation events including a fishing derby. Lawton's Arts and Humanities Council is part of the city's government. Oklahoma City sponsors or manages numerous entertainment and cultural events including the nationally known Festival of the Arts. These

TABLE 13-2	
City of Norman Select Departments and Functions	
Police	Law enforcement, criminal investigation, crime prevention
Fire	Fire suppression and prevention, emergency, management
City Clerk	Records management, issuance of licenses and permits, records minutes of council meetings
Public Works	Construction, maintenance, and operation of street and drainage networks
Finance	Monitors organization's financial activities, initiates and manages investment activity, prepares and coordinates budget activity
Parks and Recreation	Manages maintenance and operations at city parks, community centers, pools, and various sports facilities
Human Resources	Manages the recruitment, hiring, and training of city personnel, manages employee benefits and risk management activity

SOURCE: City of Norman.

positive activities are designed to enhance community life and may translate into more dollars being spent in these jurisdictions by residents and visitors attracted to events and sights.

In sum, modern Oklahoma cities are no longer just concerned with picking up trash, making sure the water runs clean, and keeping city streets safe—they are now expected to provide events and programs which provide entertainment for residents and economic opportunities for downtown merchants.

The majority of general fund municipal expenditures are dedicated to personnel expenses—compensation, benefits, training, compliance with state and federal labor laws—which makes most departmental budgets "labor intensive." Fiscal year budgets, which run from July 1 of one year to June 30 of the following year, provide municipal officials with a complete breakdown of revenues, specific fund activity, and expenditures. Oklahoma law, specifically the **Municipal Budget Act**, prohibits expenditures for each fund to exceed the estimated revenues for each fund; in addition, no more than 10% of the total budget for any fund may be budgeted for miscellaneous purposes, such as the fund balance that carries over to the next fiscal year (Title 11). The Act and other legal controls are designed to prevent deficit spending and force municipalities to exercise fiscal discipline.

Pie charts for The City of Oklahoma City illustrate the type and amount of some of the spending activity in which municipalities might engage (Figures 13-1 and 13-2).

299

FIGURE 13-1 FY 2013-2014 City of Oklahoma City Operating Expenditures by Function

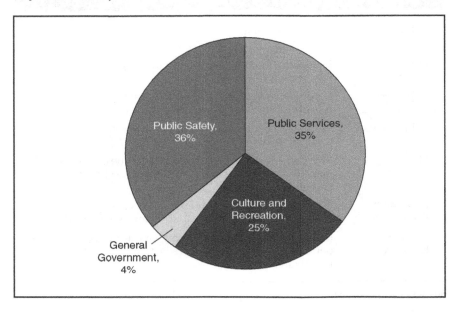

FIGURE 13-2 FY 2013-2014 City of Oklahoma City Operating Expenditures by Category

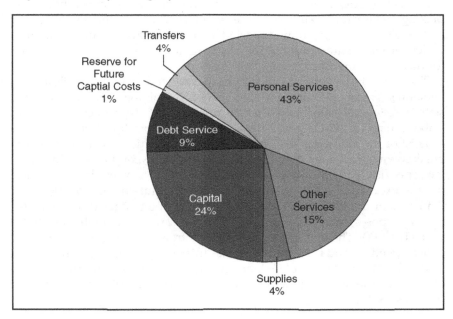

How They Pay For It –Municipal Finances

To meet service demands, municipal governments must collect and spend money. This money, commonly referred to as *revenue*, comes from multiple sources, including a variety of taxes and user fees needed to purchase equipment and materials and to meet employee payrolls and state and federal funding. Municipal governments also engage in capital projects to maintain and enhance infrastructure (streets, bridges, water/ wastewater lines, for example) and to build or restore public buildings. States authorize local governments to levy taxes, incur debt, and make expenditures, and the distribution of state and federal aid supplements the limited resources generated directly by individual municipalities. Municipal budgets reflect the complexities associated with multiple funds. A city's *general fund*, for example, designates expenditures associated with personnel costs–payroll, training, travel, benefits, etc.) and expenditure categories. Other funds are dedicated by law for specific uses; these may include funds that are to be spent specifically on public safety, street maintenance, public recreation, and other categories (see City of Broken Arrow in Figure 13-3). Oklahoma City, for example, has 18 designated operating funds (e.g. Airports Enterprise Fund, MAPS,

FIGURE 13–3 City of Broken Arrow Revenue Sources FY 2011-2012

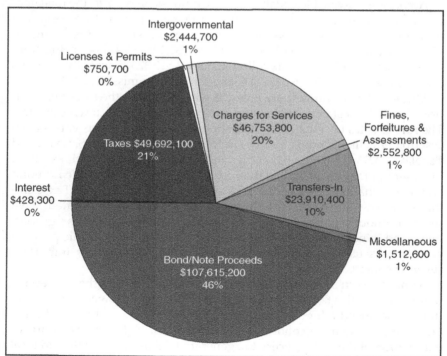

Emergency Management Fund, etc.) in addition to the general fund. Rigid budget and accounting rules are employed to ensure that dedicated funds are spent for specific purposes as required by state statutes.

Initially, municipal governments were not expected to provide many services, so *property taxes*, also known as "ad valorem" taxes, were the primary source of revenue. As urban populations grew and public demands for additional and expanded services increased, governments sought to identify new sources of revenue. Modern-day cities now tax a variety of sources including income, food and merchandise, tobacco and alcohol products, sales of goods, and certain services. In Oklahoma, property taxes are collected and used by state government. Municipalities do not derive any funding from this source. For Oklahoma cities and towns, the *sales tax* on food and merchandise is the primary *own source revenue*, that is, money that municipal governments raise through taxation of purchases made within their respective jurisdictions.

While cities and towns can raise some of the money needed to fund services, they generally do not have the tax base ("tax capacity") to raise all of the funds required to meet residents' service needs and expectations or federal and state policy mandates. Because of this, cities and towns must also rely on (1) state and federal fiscal assistance, i.e., intergovernmental transfers and revenue sharing, and for some, (2) home rule status, which provides municipal government with some autonomy in how revenues are generated and spent.

According to available Oklahoma Tax Commission reports, the total generated sales/use tax (the sale or rental of tangible personal property and from the furnishings of specific services) for the state of Oklahoma in FY 2012 was $2,427,637,700.23 with 91% (or $2,203,993,461.60) being from sales tax alone. Of the sales tax collected, $1,502,515,323.75 was city sales tax; $125,741,708.98 was city use tax (Oklahoma Tax Commission, 2013, p. 5).

Municipal governments are charged with collecting the sales tax, comprised of a 4.5% state sales tax and the individual city / town sales tax. The rate of sales tax charged by Oklahoma's cities and towns varies from .5% in towns like Schulter to 1.0% in towns like Burlington, Sawyer, and Texola to 4.5% in Beggs, Okarche, and Drumright. Larger cities tax at rates similar to each other. Oklahoma City charges 3.875%, while Edmond and Tulsa charge 3.75% and 3.167%, respectively (Oklahoma Tax Commission). The importance of the sales tax cannot be overstated. Two recent economic policy issues, elimination of the sales tax for grocery items and internet taxation, have featured prominently in municipal government discussions over how to protect and enhance this important revenue source.

Some concern has been raised in recent years over the **regressive** nature of the sales tax as it places a greater burden on lower income residents who spend a higher proportion of their income on food and other "non-luxury" items (alcohol and tobacco are not included). Support for elimination of the state grocery tax generated debate at the state and local level. SB 1328, passed in March 2010, would have eliminated sales tax on groceries when state revenue levels exceed 10% above spending levels. The elimination of grocery taxes to benefit low income Oklahomans would have devastated cities and towns which receive no ad valorem tax revenues for general operating purposes. One estimate was that passage of the legislation would result in the state losing $460 million in lost taxes with cities and towns losing $190 of that total in (rebated) sales tax received from the state. Fortunately for the bill's opponents, the measure was not considered in the Oklahoma House of Representatives.

Aside from the revenue loss associated with this proposal, many municipal leaders argued that this could force an increase in taxes on other goods and services or force reductions in municipal services for smaller municipalities which rely even more heavily on the sales tax than do the larger ones. The loss of this revenue source is particularly problematic. One suggested strategy for offsetting the loss of grocery sales tax was to expand the taxation of services (Oklahoma currently allows taxes of approximately 32 different types of services, such as utilities) to include dry cleaning, legal and medical services, barber and beauty shops, lawn maintenance, and other forms of professional and personal services. While most agree that eliminating the sales tax on groceries is justified because of its regressivity, there is disagreement regarding the impact that a sales tax on services would have on lower-income residents and concerns regarding the cost of municipal compliance and state administration of compliance activities (UCO College of Business Administration, 2001).

Related to the general sales tax issue and sales versus service debate is the issue of internet taxation. State and local governments lose an estimated $23 billion annually to online purchases not subject to state and local taxation (Lemov, 2011). According to a study by University of Tennessee economists, approximately $52 billion in internet sales tax will be lost during the period of 2006-2012 (Bruce, Fox, Stokely & Luna, 2009). A recent federal effort to tax internet purchases has some traction. The proposed Marketplace Fairness Act of 2013 would authorize state governments to collect sales taxes and use taxes from retailers (who would collect and remit sales and use tax to the states where the purchaser lives) with no physical presence in their state. The U.S. House and Senate proposed similar legislation in early 2013 with the Senate passing its version to be effective in May 2016. This controversial legislation act faces opposition from some legislative leaders at the federal and state levels and business leaders over the administrative and logistical burdens associated with collections and remittance that would be placed on small businesses ("Internet Sales Tax," 2013).

While other cities throughout the U.S. rely on *corporate and personal property* and *income* **taxes** to add to their revenue, Oklahoma restricts the imposing of these taxes to state government and, in the case of the property tax, for limited purposes. This tax can only be used to retire city debt for specific capital projects but not for day-to-day operations; otherwise, it is distributed to counties and school districts.

Other forms of revenue enhancement contribute to municipal coffers. *User fees*, generally accepted as the "fairest" form of taxation, are paid by the user for services (trash pick-up) and goods (water, parking garages) received. *Franchise fees* are paid by privately owned business establishments (ex: gas stations) located on city easements. *Fines and forfeitures* are collected for violation of criminal, parking, traffic, and code ordinances. Cities and towns charge for various *licenses* and *permits* (ex: garage sales and special events). *Interest* and *investment income* on collected revenues can also be generated.

Finally, local government may call upon residents to approve the issuance of **municipal bonds** through special elections for the purpose of funding long term capital projects that will require payment over time. Bonds, the most commonly-used form of long-term borrowing, are attractive forms of investment due to federal and state tax breaks for private investors. The attractiveness of bonds is also enhanced by a city's **bond rating**, a measure of the city's "fiscal health" as determined by the subjective/objective rating system established by the nation's top rating firms, Moody's Investor's Service and Standard and Poor's Corporation. The passing of a bond issue creates a debt obligation that municipal residents must assume until the debt is paid.

Two types of bonds are used by local governments to finance capital projects such as street construction and resurfacing, major computer systems, construction of new public facilities, and other one-time, non-recurring expenditures. **General obligation (G.O.) bonds** are secured by the "full faith and credit" of the local jurisdiction that issues them and are paid off with regular revenues. **Revenue bonds** are also paid off over time with the fees collected from those using the service or product (e.g., parking garages). The payment period for both types of bonds is usually between five and twenty years. While bond projects represent a rational approach to planning and spending (they force municipal elected and appointed leaders to plan and prioritize), there is no guarantee that the public will approve them in specially called elections.

Challenges for Municipal Governments

Oklahoma's municipal governments have faced numerous challenges, including fiscal uncertainty. Declining revenues associated with the impact that the September 11 attacks had on the national economy impacted state budgets (Oklahoma's tax collections dropped from approximately $6 billion to $5 billion between July 2001 and July 2003) forcing municipal leaders to cut city budgets leading to reductions in force. Oklahoma City, for example, estimated that mandatory budget cuts in city departments (2% for police and fire, 11% for other departments) would be needed to offset an estimated $4 million shortfall for

FY 2003–2004. The improved national economy prompted City officials to predict moderate sales tax gains for FY 2004–2005 (The City of Oklahoma City). However, the national recession beginning in 2008 took its toll on the states, and Oklahoma was no exception. Nationally, the economic downturn led to a drop in state revenues of $134 billion during the last quarter of 2009, and Oklahoma's revenues dropped by 26.9%. However, the state's cost of living made the state one of the most recession-proof in the nation, and by November 2010, state revenues increased to $383 million, a 2.5% increase over the previous year. Oklahoma's cities were able to offset some of their economic woes by streamlining budgets and relying on federal funds. Oklahoma City, for example, was awarded $45 million for capital projects via the American Recovery and Reinvestment Act. Increases in sales tax collections have lead The City of Oklahoma City to consider restoration of a number of FTE positions (including 51 public safety personnel) cut the previous year. Tulsa is also proposing increases in its budget from the previous year due to sales tax collections; however, some cities, such as Edmond, have proposed cuts (for FY 2011-2012, approx. 2.4% in cuts) due to rising fuels costs.

Oklahoma's state and municipal governments have responded to the national effort to deter and mitigate terrorist attacks. Already cognizant of the damage and loss of life associated with terrorism, the state of Oklahoma created the Oklahoma Office of Homeland Security (OKOHS) in 2002 to "develop and coordinate implementation of a comprehensive statewide plan to secure the State of Oklahoma from the results of terrorism . . ." As part of this effort, OKOHS distributes federal grant funds to local governments. An example of this was $32 million for programs associated with law enforcement terrorism prevention, interoperable communications, security, and continued funding of citizens' corps which render assistance in community emergencies.

Other challenges have prompted municipal governments to engage in ambitious and non-traditional efforts to respond to community needs. Tulsa's **"Vision 2025: Foresight for a Greater Tulsa"** was similar to MAPS as an economic development program, but unlike Oklahoma City's plan, Tulsa's includes regional as well as city improvements. Of the four proposed projects, two were approved by city voters leading to the construction of the BOK Tower, enhancements of several educational institutions (OU-Tulsa, OSU-Tulsa, Langston-Tulsa, NSU-Broken Arrow, and Tulsa Community College), and hundreds of millions of dollars dedicated to county roads and recreational infrastructure. **"Vision2,"** an extension of Vision 2025, failed to appeal to voters in November 2012 who were concerned about the funding (a tax that would begin when the original funding for Vision 2025 ended in 2017 but would not end until 2029) and vague language that caused confusion (Wertz, 2012). As a result of the proposal's defeat, Tulsa leaders turned to renewal of the city's **"Fix Our Streets"** program, a multi-billion dollar effort to improve infrastructure and transportation (Barber, 2012).

Oklahoma City partnered with the Oklahoma City Public Schools to develop and promote the **MAPS for Kids** plan designed to renovate dilapidated schools and provide enhanced academic programs through a $500 million tax initiative and $180 million bond issue passed by city voters in 2001. This partnership is unique in that The City of Oklahoma City has no formal role in the administration and funding of the city's public school system, but city leaders were persuaded to participate in development and passage of MAPS for Kids as the quality of the school system was seen as critical to the city's overall success.

While these do not encompass the entire scope of municipal challenges and are not an exhaustive accounting of what is happening at the municipal level, they do illustrate the fact that Oklahoma's cities are concerned with more than ensuring that routine operations are conducted efficiently.

Opportunities for Citizen Participation in Governance

The federal and unitary systems are intended to prevent one government from acquiring all power and to facilitate government accountability and public involvement. To that end, citizens enjoy "multiple points of access" to the two primary units of government, national and state, and the approximately 89,000 local governments that exist throughout the nation. Ideally, citizens would have a more prominent role in determining policy at the local level. National representatives work primarily in Washington, D.C., and but for a few months of the year, do not spend extended periods of time in their home districts or states. State legislators may spend more time with their constituents, but their focus may be on the activities at their state capitols. Local representatives, such as mayors, county commissioners, aldermen, and councilors, work and live in the same jurisdictions they represent. The proximity of these representatives to the people who elect them promotes the belief that local government is closest to the people, and is, therefore, more likely to be responsive to it. An oft-quoted remark by former U.S. Speaker of the House Tip O'Neill that "All politics is local" suggests that day-to-day actions and decisions by local government have a greater impact on the state's population and economic fortunes than some might think.

Yet, citizen participation at the local level is frequently marked by low voter turnout. While Oklahomans traditionally turn out in large numbers for presidential and some special elections (like MAPS and sales tax elections), their level of participation is sporadic for municipal and country elections. Less than a third of voters turned out for the highly competitive 2009 Tulsa Mayoral election. Lower turnout numbers are generally expected for school board and bond issues. This is not to suggest that municipal and town elections inspire little public interest. In fact, some elections, especially those involving candidates running on the basis of two clearly competing issues (the 1999 mayoral contest in Oklahoma City where the issue was extended funding of MAPS is an example) can result in higher-than-average turnout.

The problem of low voter turnout seems to stem from the great number of elections that city-county residents can participate in, a consequence of Oklahoma's populist heritage. Municipal and county elections for mayor, council members, county commissioners, sheriffs, school board presidents and members, education and general bond issues, tax measures, and special elections to fill vacancies occur throughout the year, making civic participation via voting a demanding responsibility.

While voting is generally regarded as the major form of public participation in governance, it is not the only means. Some Oklahoma cities provide additional opportunities for civic participation. Residents of Edmond can apply to the Citizens' Government Academy to learn about Edmond city government and the role played by citizens. Norman youth ages 14 to 20 can apply to the city's Police Explorers program to learn about law enforcement, possibly as a career. Oklahoma's Open Meetings Act requires that regular and special government meetings (like budget deliberations) be accessible to the public. City council meetings frequently designate a time specifically for citizen commentary in their weekly agendas. Citizen groups may form to support or oppose local government actions. "Citizens for a Better Edmond," an example of a citizens-based group, played an important role in influencing The City of Edmond's decision regarding the building of a Super Wal-Mart near a residential area while Oklahoma City's Neighborhood Alliance was a key player supporting the successful 3/4-cent sales tax for public safety. In short, municipal residents have multiple opportunities for accessing and influencing their governments, and in some cases, they are very successful in doing so.

III. COUNTY GOVERNMENT

County Government – Purpose and Functions

Oklahoma counties, established in Article XVII of the Oklahoma Constitution, are traditionally described as "creatures" or "agents" of state government; that is, they carry out the functions of state government at the local level. This makes it possible for state government to operate throughout the state without having to establish government offices with state employees in locations outside the capital. This decentralized system provides county officials with greater autonomy over how operations are to be managed but also provides local voters with the opportunity to elect their own county officials and hold them more accountable than they could state officials.

Nationally there are 3,066 of these "discrete subunits" of state government: Oklahoma has 77 counties, the largest by population are Oklahoma County (718,633) and Tulsa County (603,402). The two smallest counties are Cimarron

County (2,475) and Harmon County (2,992) (Barker, 2012; Carney & Morales, 2014). Many of Oklahoma's counties, including Choctaw, Comanche, Osage, Pottawatomie, and Pawnee, are named for Native American tribes. A rather detailed description of each county's jurisdictional boundaries is provided in Article XVII Section 8 of the Oklahoma Constitution.

Originally, Oklahoma counties consisted of 400 square miles of taxable area with at least 15,000 in population and $2.5 million in taxable wealth. Statutory changes expanded the area requirement to 500 sq. miles with the population requirement increased to 20,000; the taxable wealth requirement was also expanded to $4.0 million.

Oklahoma's counties engage in services determined via the state constitution and statutes. Traditional services have included road and bridge construction and maintenance (Oklahoma has over 84,000 county roads and 14,000 bridges that are 20 feet or longer), law enforcement and adjudication, and maintenance of county records, births, deaths, marriages, and land transactions. County services have expanded in recent years to include provision of health care and medical services, economic and industrial development, social services, and informal adult and youth education programs in science and agriculture, among others, often working with educational institutions located within country borders. For example, Payne County, in cooperation with Oklahoma State University provides courses in agricultural enterprises, natural resources and environmental management, and education in nutrition, food, and health safety through the Payne County OSU Cooperative Extension Center.

County services are supported through a variety of fiscal resources: tax levies (on personal property and real estate), aircraft registration fees, sales tax on some products and services, occupation taxes on liquor establishments outside municipal boundaries, and state collected fees used for county roads, bridges, and highways. Title 74 of the Oklahoma State Statutes authorizes counties to engage in interlocal agreements to share the cost of some road projects with adjacent municipalities and other counties. These agreements are used to combine fiscal, manpower, equipment, and material resources and planning expertise needed for construction of county roads and bridges that cross county and city jurisdictions. County road funds come primarily from state and federal fuel taxes, motor vehicle excise taxes, and gross production taxes.

The Structure of County Government

All counties in Oklahoma employ the "plural executive" system comparable to that used at the state level. The sharing of authority among several elected officials is seen as beneficial to citizens who can now hold multiple government figures accountable for what country government does. This is consistent with Oklahoma's populist tradition. However, like its state counterpart, the "plural executive," this can also impede coordination of policymaking and related activity.

The structure of county government is essentially the same throughout the state. Each county elects (on a partisan ballot) three **county commissioners** (administrative body with general supervision over fiscal affairs), a **sheriff** (county law enforcement and crime prevention), a **county clerk** (custodian of records, registrar of deeds, county's purchasing agent), an **assessor** (chief appraiser who determines the true worth of real and personal property for the purpose of taxation), and a **treasurer** (county tax collector and banker). All persons serving in these offices must, at the time of election or appointment, be qualified residents and voters in the county they serve. By statute, regular elections can only be held on Tuesdays in November. Commissioners serve four-year staggered terms. For example, the most recent election for Oklahoma County commissioners representing that county's Districts 1 and 3 was held in November, 2010. The election for the county's District 2 commissioner was held in 2012. In Oklahoma, a county's clerk, sheriff, and court clerk serve two-year terms while the assessor and treasurer serve four-year terms. Special elections can be held to fill vacancies (Title 19, Section 131).

The state's constitution and statutes empower county commissioners to assume responsibility for a variety of administrative duties. In addition to general management and administrative efficiency responsibilities, some of the more important commissioner duties are:

- Audit the accounts of all officers handling county money
- Exercise direct control over the county highway system
- Make general financial plans for the county including the county budget
- Approve bids for major purposes or construction projects
- Develop personnel policies for the county
- Sell or purchase public land to improve efficiency of county government

(Source: Association of County Commissioners of Oklahoma)

County commissioners, like their elected counterparts at the municipal level, must also deal with **unfunded mandates**, state and federal requirements that impose costs without reimbursement. These mandates include drug and alcohol testing for persons holding state-issued commercial driver licenses, meeting environmental requirements for roads and bridges, complying with ADA employment and public facilities access requirements, and providing training for various county personnel.

Recent Challenges - Scandal, Reform, and Consolidation

County government in Oklahoma has not always been viewed in a positive light. Statewide investigation of allegedly corrupt purchasing and expenditure practices in the early 1980s led to the conviction of 220 commissioners and other county personnel from 60 of the state's 77 counties in what federal prosecutors dubbed **"Okscam."** The scandal caused Oklahoma's citizens and lawmakers to take a hard look at the structure of county government and the system which facilitated such widespread corruption.

In their seminal study of the scandal, Holloway and Meyers determined that Okscam was *not* primarily a product of a "culture of corruption" that had existed in the state throughout its history or even at the time of the scandal (in fact, their research indicated that some, but not all county residents supported corrupt official behavior[1]). Rather, they argue that the structural and political environment fostered corrupt activity. Specifically, they found that county commissioners had a significant amount of funding and discretion available to them for road construction with few checks on how county money was spent or for what purpose (1993, p. 18).

In response to the scandal, the Oklahoma State Legislature and then-Governor Nigh launched separate efforts to identify the causes of such widespread corruption and develop suggestions for reform of the county commissioner system. Examination of the system revealed that there was a "virtual lack of accountability." Commissioners acted on their own with little effort made to comply with state statutes governing revenue collections and expenditures.

Suggestions for reform concentrated on restructuring county government through professionalizing administration and depoliticizing elective offices. The creation of full time positions (comparable to a city administrator) responsible for administration of road construction, maintenance activities, and county purchasing was proposed. Depoliticizing county government would occur through expansion of the number of commissioners (beyond the existing three) and consolidation or abolition of some elected positions (Holloway & Myers, 1993, p. 19).

A strong county lobby was effective in getting the state legislature to reject these proposals as interfering with the commissioner-constituent relationship. Ultimately, the state approved reforms proposed by Government Nigh that altered the procedures, but not the structure:

- Create a county purchasing position (end the commissioner control of this activity).
- End commissioner authority to lease or purchase heavy equipment and machines (now done through central purchasing at the state level).
- Completely fund county District Attorneys' offices though the state and empower District Attorneys to investigate allegations of corruption.

Interestingly, the proposal to professionalize county administration through the hiring of engineers and long range planning was "urged" but not mandated (Holloway & Myers, 1993, p. 19). Although these reforms fell short of some lawmakers' expectations (commissioners still retained control over road projects and authority was still fragmented among several county officers), the limited institutional modifications did reduce commissioner discretion. A significant change was the legislature's passage of the County

Budget Act in Title 19 which authorized the county clerk to ensure that county funds are legally spent and tracked. These, along with the successful prosecution of corrupt county officials, contributed to public support for reform (Holloway & Myers, 1993, p. 19).

Another recent major issue for counties is **city-county consolidation**, the merging of similar functions and operations engaged in by counties and area jurisdictions into single countywide government. Forty of these regional forms of government exist in the U.S. Some of the more prominent ones include Indianapolis-Marion County (Indiana), Jacksonville-Duval County (Florida), and Nashville-Davidson County (Kentucky). Despite the rationality of having one administrative body manage and provide like operations—police, fire, water and sewer systems, etc.–voters may reject the proposal as limiting their contact with those persons directly responsible for supplying needed services (Bowman & Kearney, 2012).

While some municipal leaders have at times indicated support for consolidation as a way to reduce duplication of services, Oklahoma's county commissioners have been generally resistant to the idea of sharing or even giving up administrative and decision making authority. Arguments against consolidation have included the belief that county government works well under the current system and that the at-will status of county workers reduces personnel problems (a view that is debatable given that several successful lawsuits have been filed due to illegal personnel practices). Suggestions that efficiency could be enhanced through county performance reviews are countered by arguments that the state already audits county operations. Because of these conflicting views, the possibility of city-county consolidation seems remote (Association of County Commissioners of Oklahoma, 2005).

Notes

1. My mother, former Canadian County Commissioner Penny Duncan Ferrell, encountered the corrupt practices that her predecessor, a convicted commissioner, had engaged in when she received an angry note from a county resident who demanded to have her driveway paved after Ferrell refused. The resident had sent a check for payment and a request for service because that is how the last commissioner did business. Ferrell insisted on complying with state law and was scolded for it.

PUBLIC POLICY

Dana K. Glencross and Sharon Vaughan

I had always hoped that this land might become a safe and agreeable asylum to the virtuous and persecuted part of mankind, to whatever nation they might belong.

George Washington

A simple way to take measure of a country is to look at how many want in . . . and how many want out.

Tony Blair

Your life depends on a random stranger who could kill you, will probably disrespect you, and will most likely pay you much less than you deserve. But even those prospects are better than the ones you used to have. This is the life of los jornaleros—the day laborers.

Gustavo Arellano *Ask a Mexican*

I. INTRODUCTION

Joel Menchaca, a student at Oklahoma State University-Oklahoma City, has no guarantee that the college degree he will earn one day will result in his employment. He was born so sick that doctors feared he wouldn't live beyond a few months. His father had left the family. In desperation, his mother illegally immigrated with him to the United States when he was just one-year-old. Growing up, Joel knew that he had to stay out of trouble and that at any time both he and his mother could be deported. His Spanish is weak and it is doubtful that he could depend upon it if he had to do so. He has no close family to return to in Mexico (Allen, "Undocumented OSU-OKC student").

Another undocumented immigrant, Ulises Serrano just might realize his dream of a career in the music business because of the U.S. Department of Homeland Security's Deferred Action for Childhood Arrivals program (a/k/a the **"Dream Act"**). An undocumented immigrant who came to the United States at age ten, Ulises' education at Oklahoma City

313

University is paid for largely by scholarships. This is fortunate considering that undocumented students are not legally entitled to federal financial aid. He is free to work, have a bank account, and travel out of the country to visit relatives. He is one of only 500,000 undocumented immigrants possessing **"deferred action status,"** however, and this is because of the program's age requirement when entering the United States. This status is only valid for two years (Allen, "Undocumented Oklahoma City University Student").

How can something be termed as "illegal" when it is so seemingly disregarded by government as a matter of practice? The presidents of Oklahoma colleges and universities sent a letter to the state's five representatives in the U.S. House asking them to pass immigration reform in 2013. The letter requested the delegation's help to aid graduate students born abroad working on degrees in science, technology, engineering and math (STEM). It states that "In 2009, 55 percent of Oklahoma's graduate students in those fields were temporary residents with no clear path to stay in the country after graduation" (Fox News Latino, 2013). The loss of these highly-educated graduates limits Oklahoma's ability to attract quality businesses requiring such skilled employees (Lackmeyer, 2008). As a result, it is detrimental to the state's economic future.

Overwhelmingly, public sentiment decries this broken immigration system but resists appeals for public policy that will result in the mass deportation of illegal immigrants. For Oklahoma, that would mean a loss in revenue of $580.3 million dollars in economic activity and the loss of 4,680 jobs. In Oklahoma, 5.5 percent of the state's residents are foreign-born, with 10.9 percent identified as Latino or Asian. More relevant to the issue, however, is that 89.1 percent of children with immigrant parents are U.S. citizens, 85.7 percent of children with immigrant parents are English proficient, and only 3 percent of the workforce is unauthorized (Sanders, 2013).

In Arizona, controversial **Senate Bill 1070** received national attention and withstood a constitutional challenge all the way to the U.S. Supreme Court. Among the law's provisions, it permitted law enforcement to make traffic stops of persons who were suspected of being undocumented immigrants and required them to produce legal identification. This resulted in an ironic consequence of the resignation of an illegal immigrant who had worked for the Arizona Department of Public Safety for 13 years. She unknowingly presented a fake or forged birth certificate to secure employment. Her true status was discovered when her brother applied for a visa to remain in the U.S. legally (McNamara & Birmingham, 2013). Problems in immigration policy such as these persist despite a history of attempts to address them.

On November 1, 2007, the **Oklahoma Taxpayer and Citizen Protection Act** went into effect. Commonly known as HB 1804 (Oklahoma House Bill 1804), it was the toughest illegal immigration policy passed and signed by a governor at that time (Mock, 2007). The bill made it illegal to transport or shelter an illegal immigrant and required proof of legal residence when getting identification cards at schools, registering to vote or applying for public assistance. In addition, it included strict provisions for employers such as prohibiting a business to retain an undocumented worker if a legal worker was fired. These provisions were not only passed to prevent future illegal immigrants from coming to Oklahoma but also, and some would argue more importantly, to send a strong signal that it was time for anyone living illegally in Oklahoma to leave. Other states, like Arizona (as noted above), were watching the process from the beginning since some of their elected officials also wanted to pass strong illegal immigration laws and Oklahoma was proving to be a great test case for this public policy.

To understand how this public policy came about and was implemented in Oklahoma, one has to follow the complicated process that actually began long before any legislation was introduced. While the public policy process is often fraught with many twists and turns, there are a series of foreseeable steps that all policies go through and Oklahoma's HB 1804 is no exception. This chapter begins by discussing the three dimensions (economic, moral, and political) to policymaking that frame arguments surrounding its formulation, passage, and implementation. In addition to these dimensions, the creation of public policy has a step-by-step process that political scientists have defined. It is necessary to identify and discuss these six steps. They are: 1) Problem Identification, 2) Agenda Setting, 3) Policy Formulation, 4) Policy Adoption, 5) Policy Implementation, and 6) Policy Evaluation (Geer, et al, 2014). Finally, these six steps will be considered in relationship to HB 1804.

II. The Economic, Moral, and Political Dimensions of Policymaking

In addition to the six predictable steps noted above, the process of public policymaking should always consider the three dimensions of every public policy. These are the economic, moral, and political dimensions. One way to look at these three dimensions is to think of them as analytical prisms through which one may evaluate a given policy such as HB 1804.

The first way that one may analyze a policy choice is by using economics as an analytical tool to judge whether or not a given policy will be cost-effective or good for the economy. In the case of HB 1804, much of the debate centered on whether the laws would save Oklahoma taxpayers money by keeping illegal immigrants from using publicly-funded social services, enrolling their children in Oklahoma public schools, and taking jobs away from legal residents. In addition, it was argued that illegal immigrants were willing to work for inadequate wages, which in turn drove the wages down for all Oklahomans and caused other unintended consequences typical of public policy implementation.

Opponents of the bill argued that it would be an economic disaster for the state, as previously mentioned, because it would affect such

LEADERSHIP PROFILE

AMY COULTER
Fiscal Analyst, Oklahoma State Senate

As a Fiscal Analyst for the Oklahoma State Senate, Amy Coulter is getting a firsthand look at the inner workings of political deliberation in the state. It's the perfect job to apply the skills she learned from earning her bachelor's degree in political science with a minor in business administration from the University of Central Oklahoma.

Coulter and other members of the fiscal staff analyze the state budget and the financial implications of proposed legislation. It's a great foundation for getting an overview of state government. Her most recent responsibilities include working with the standing committee on education which represents over half the state budget. She remembers one year when she worked in the natural resources area, and a series of extremely bad wildfires erupted all over the state. Monies had to be diverted to help the rural volunteer fire departments.

While the legislature is in session, her typical day is helping members draft bills, tracking proposed legislation as it moves through the process, and monitoring any amendments that may have financial impact. While out of session, she helps prepare interim studies, staffs new task forces, and of course awaits the October 1 deadline when executive agencies turn in their budgets.

"Every year, you learn something new," she says, "and then you don't hear about it for five years, until some new member asks the question, and you have to go research it."

Coulter comes from a large family. She was the second of nine kids and many of them are now starting families of their own. The occasional family reunions are getting even more crowded. She says that her biggest influence was her Mom.

"She would always talk politics and I was one of the few kids that would sit and listen," Coulter explains. She shares her interest in politics with her husband who is himself politically active. He's even run for office, a fact that Coulter downplays since she works in a nonpartisan position.

She loves the experience she's getting with the State Senate, but she doesn't have any plans to run for office any time soon.

"I'm never going to rule that out," she admits, but seeing her political representatives at work reinforces the idea she really needs to gain more life skills and hopefully spend a few years working in the private sector as well.

Brett S. Sharp

consequences as to discourage new businesses from locating in Oklahoma. Moreover, groups like the Oklahoma City and Tulsa Chambers of Commerce argued that while the bill was designed to encourage illegal residents to leave the state, it would have the effect of making others depart even though they were legal residents. These groups predicted that Oklahoma businesses would suffer financially when their supply of labor left the state once HB 1804 went into effect.

Indeed, that consequence was realized. The Oklahoma Bankers Association requested a study after members reported businesses in trouble that employed foreign-born workers. A few businesses stated that their labor supply disappeared after the bill took effect (Mecoy, 2008). Other accounts included an immigration law attorney in Oklahoma City who came to work the day after the law took effect only to find several of his employees gone. Portillo Construction, a Tulsa company which specializes in masonry and stone work employed about 15 immigrants. That is, until the law took effect November 1, and as co-owner Nataniel Portillo stated, "Not one employee showed up for work" (Bazar, 2008).

The reported decrease in the illegal immigrant population was estimated at 10,500 (Walker, 2008b). This number represented only a small part of the overall economic effect. However, as Oklahoma State Senator Harry Coates surmised,

Since the passage of House Bill 1804, we've seen a mass exodus of undocumented immigrants who have taken up residence in Texas and other surrounding states where they pump millions of dollars into those economies. House Bill 1804 did little more than put Oklahoma companies at a disadvantage by sending dedicated, knowledgeable workers to competing companies in other states. Losing that workforce has been devastating for many of Oklahoma's industries including agriculture, energy and construction ("Oklahoma State Senator," 2011).

The second analytical dimension is the moral or ethical one. Using the moral dimension, one would ask whether or not this is a good, principled policy that is morally correct. In other words, is it the right thing to do? For example, in a newspaper article (*The Oklahoman*, March 26, 2008) business writer Don Mecoy provides the following quote from Representative Randy Terrill speaking about HB 1804: "It's about fundamental respect for the rule of the law, about upholding our state and national sovereignty, about the morality of employing illegal alien labor. Those are things that are difficult if not impossible to express in economic terms."

Likewise, opponents of HB 1804 framed their arguments against the legislation in moral terms. For example, Hispanic community leaders and some clergy members argued that the legislation would have devastating effects on undocumented families by forcing them to make tough choices and jeopardize their children's futures. Moreover, the argument continues, many of these undocumented individuals and families left Mexico because of the lack of employment and their inabilities to provide any type of secure future for their children. In addition, the fear of the violence that has escalated since Mexican President Felipe Calderon began using federal police in 2006 to crack down on drug cartels has driven more individuals to decide that living illegally in the United States is safer than staying in Mexico. Morally, some may ask, can we deny these individuals and families the opportunities for a better life or any life? The words of Reverend Michael Chapman, pastor of Holy Angels Catholic Church in Oklahoma City, clearly demonstrate the moral dimension of the opposition to HB 1804. Rev. Chapman said, "It's definitely against the law to be here illegally. To that extent, Rep. (Randy) Terrill is correct. But we are making the statement that there is a higher law—a law of charity and helping your fellow man" (Hinton, 2007).

In addition, there is a fear among some law enforcement officials that legislation like HB 1804 will encourage violent crimes against Hispanic immigrants who are afraid to report crimes (Walker, 2008a). Oklahoma City Police Chief Bill Citty in 2007 stated that "We've had a series of armed robberies where Hispanics have been targeted. We think we are just getting a portion of it. We think they've been targeted because the suspects know they are less likely to report the crimes at this point" (Walker, 2008a).

Finally, the political prism of this three-part analysis is designed to ascertain whether or not the policy has **political feasibility.** That is to say, on the one hand, is there sufficient political support for this legislation to pass and then be implemented? Or, on the other hand, is there more political support against the legislation, which makes passing it politically impossible? One significant political argument for states taking the lead was that in the case of immigration reform, the United States Congress had failed to engage the issue and had not passed any meaningful immigration reform legislation since 1986 when President Ronald Reagan signed the **Immigration Reform and Control Act** (IRCA) into law. Inaction on the part of the federal government in response to illegal immigration made for fertile grounds for states to take the lead. States, like Oklahoma, where the number of illegal residents had increased significantly saw the lack of action on the federal government's part as a failure in government to deal with a pressing problem. Vallery Brown, a staff writer for *The Oklahoman* (May 30, 2010) cites a 2003 report by the U.S. Immigration and Naturalization Service, which states that the "illegal population in Oklahoma increased more than 200 percent between 1990 and 2000." So, the argument is that since the federal government is not doing its job, states like Oklahoma and Arizona are forced to seek legislative relief on their own. When voters see numbers like the one mentioned above coupled with an economic downturn, they view it as a call to political action. In addition, national and state interest groups like the Federation for American Immigration Reform and Immigration Reform for Oklahoma Now provided political support for stricter state laws by using their resources to bolster support for the legislation.

Opponents of the legislation tried to rally political support against the bill. Protests, candle light vigils, and rallies were organized by Hispanic leaders and groups like the Oklahoma Catholics for Life organization, to draw attention to the negative consequences of the bill (Walker, 2007a). Moreover, these groups, like supporters of HB 1804, used economic and moral arguments to try to generate political pressure against the legislation. In addition, in the same way as interest groups supported the legislation, there were also interest groups opposed to it. Organizations like the National Coalition of Latino Clergy and Christian Leaders and business organizations like the National Association of Homebuilders weighed in against HB 1804. These groups and others lent their names and resources to oppose the legislation.

Pastor Lonnie Vaughan, a member of the United Front Task Force, a group opposed to HB 1804, continued to provide shuttle rides to immigrants without driver's licenses to church. This was in direct violation of 1804's provisions. Vaughan said, "Every time I get in the van, I'm committing a felony." Despite the consequences and the law's tough reputation, he doubted that anyone would charge him with a felony for driving people to church. A person noted, "Once they [immigrants] realized Oklahoma had not turned into a Gestapo state, they thought they would come on home" ("HB 1804–Where's the," 2008). When business leaders like Tom Price Jr., senior vice president of corporate development for Chesapeake Energy, voiced concern to state legislators about the economic impact of so many Hispanic immigrants leaving the state, legislators who voted to pass the legislation admitted "we didn't allocate any enforcement dollars" and thus they should not worry about the bill ("Tom Price," 2008). The Oklahoma Supreme Court defended itself against charges of rendering "political" decisions when it upheld provisions of the state law making it illegal to knowingly transport undocumented immigrants and requiring proof of citizenship to qualify for government benefits, "It is not the place of the Supreme Court or any court to concern itself with a statute's propriety, desirability, wisdom or its practicality as a working proposition.. . . Such questions are plainly and definitively established by fundamental laws as functions of the legislative branch of government" (Korbe, 2011).

All three appeals—the economic, the moral, and the political—are used together often to make strong arguments to garner support for or against a specific policy. By using economic and moral arguments against or for the legislation, both groups are trying to rally political support for their side. While certain individuals or groups may focus on one aspect of a given policy, most often it is a mixture of arguments that pulls evidence from all three dimensions. As this chapter turns to the six steps of policymaking, one should keep in mind that economic, moral, and political arguments continue *throughout* the policymaking process.

III. THE POLICYMAKING PROCESS

Like the federal government, there are many political and judicial actors who contribute to policymaking in Oklahoma. The state legislature, the executive branch, the state and federal judiciary along with interest groups, the media, political parties, agency bureaucrats, and voting citizens may influence and participate in making public policy in Oklahoma. Political scientists know that because of the many factors influencing policy decisions, studying the process is a complex endeavor. It takes place in a multi-stage cycle that may not be well-defined in all cases. In addition, the process may continue for many years. One way to approach public policymaking is to define the six stages, which may not appear to be well-defined in a given policy study because often they overlap and may have interruptions in the process (Geer, et al., 2014). Keeping that in mind, identifying these six stages is critical to understanding how public policy decisions come about in Oklahoma state government.

1. Problem Identification

The first step is identifying the problem, i.e., a need for a change to an existing policy or an entirely new one. Who defines the problem varies. Legislators, the governor, interest groups, and political parties may identify the problem. In some instances, it may be citizens who contact their elected officials or the media directly. Defining the problem and articulating it clearly is the first step in the process. Once problem identification has taken place, the process can move to the second stage.

As stated in earlier in this chapter, the federal government's failure to engage the problem of illegal immigration elevated this issue to be recognized as a problem that needed attention from state lawmakers. Coupled with a 200-percent increase of undocumented immigrants living in Oklahoma between 1990 to 2000 and the public's overwhelming support for

FIGURE 14-1 Policy Making Process

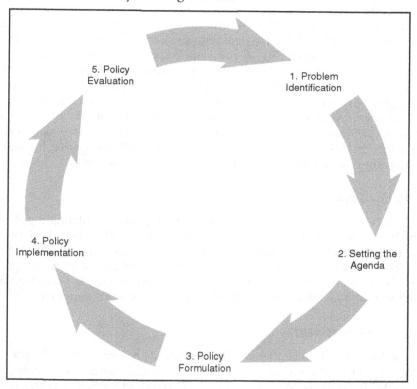

5. Policy Evaluation

1. Problem Identification

2. Setting the Agenda

3. Policy Formulation

4. Policy Implementation

policies designed to not only reduce the current number of undocumented immigrants in Oklahoma, but also to limit their future growth, the problem had been identified. With Oklahoma lawmakers and interest groups willing to support legislation, the policy moved on to the second step, getting on the legislative agenda.

2. Agenda Setting

State governments are confronted with myriad problems that need to be addressed and solved. All of these problems, however, will not get the same attention or may come up too late in the legislative session to make it on the agenda. The agenda is the set of issues that government wishes to resolve. What is not included on the agenda is sometimes as important as what makes the list. Problems that receive attention from stakeholders, i.e., those who seek to influence legislative content and direction include interest groups, the media, political parties, or a particularly articulate legislator or governor. These individuals or groups are more likely to appear on the legislative or governor's agenda. If there is a particular event that receives a lot of media attention, it may well make its way onto the agenda also.

Relating this step to HB 1804, one can trace the growing momentum in Oklahoma for legislation to deal with the increasing number of undocumented immigrants living in the state back to 2002 when a bill was introduced to designate English as the official language in the state (Walker, 2007b). Although the former bill failed to pass, the idea of passing legislation to deal with undocumented immigrants in Oklahoma did not go away with subsequent attempts at passing tough immigration laws in 2005 and 2006 (Walker, 2007b). While HB 1804 was not introduced in the Oklahoma House until January 2007, the desire for state immigration laws had been on the agenda for several years.

3. Policy Formulation

At this stage, the stakeholders begin defining and articulating a policy, which will address the problem. As mentioned earlier there had been attempts to pass tough immigration laws before HB 1804 was signed by the governor in November 2007. Learning from the failures of previous proposed immigration legislation that died in committee, HB 1804 was formulated so that it avoided the pitfalls yet still appealed to its supporters.

4. Policy Enactment

The legislative branch passes a law that enacts one or more of the policy proposals. HB 1804 was filed in January 2007 and passed the Oklahoma House with a vote of 88-9. On April 16, 2007, it passed the Senate with a vote of 41-6. The House agreed with the Senate amendments and passed the final version of the bill with a vote of 85-13. Governor Brad Henry signed it into law on May 8, 2007 with the law going into effect on November 1, 2007.

5. Policy Implementation

Once the legislature has passed a law and the governor has signed it, the process of implementing the policy begins. The authority to execute the policy provisions as outlined in the legislation falls to the executive branch. Walker highlights two problems with the implementation of 1804, one at the federal level and one at the state level. Millions of workers' Social Security numbers could not be matched to a valid person, so-called "no match" numbers. HB1804's enforcement would deny in-state tuition rates for illegal immigrant students unless they provided proof of application for a number. However, the Social Security administration did not send out notification letters due to a lawsuit challenge. Walker explained actions taken by the Oklahoma Health Care Authority's governing board. The board, frustrated by years of attempting to get legislators to permit them to provide prenatal care to pregnant undocumented immigrants without success, voted a rule change that qualified the women for such care. Terrill, the bill's author, stated about the board's action, "It clearly runs contrary to state legislative intent" (Walker, 2007b).

6. Policy Evaluation

It takes time to evaluate a given policy's outcomes. The legislature may choose to revisit the issues in the policy at a later time to reevaluate them. Likewise, the governor may decide to put the reevaluation of the policy at the top of her or his agenda calling on the legislature to follow suit. Finally, since public policy should reflect the will of the people, it may be that voters demand revisions to make the policy work better. The media and interest groups also play critical roles in bringing issues to the public's attention that are not working well.

Recent evaluations of laws such as HB 1804 as well as Arizona's SB 1070 conclude that legislative policies such as these had little ultimate effect on remedying the undocumented immigration policy problem overall. Several realities are present that bolster the argument that the effects of the policies, from economic, moral and political perspectives, have resulted in little tangible resolution of the problem. In many cases, federal law superseded state law and rendered ineffective and redundant enforcement of policies like HB 1804. Many undocumented immigrants were not applying for federal public program benefits such as health care, education, and food stamps, because of federal law changes in the mid-1990s that already required proof of documentation prior to passage of HB 1804's provisions. In other instances, state legislative provisions have been nullified or placed on hold by federal court rulings and injunctions. The effects of the economic recession of 2008 also slowed illegal migration. Additionally, other efforts to decelerate illegal immigration have achieved their purpose, such as improved border security. Inaction on the issue from the federal government has certainly slowed down the process overall as states wait to see if anything develops in congress. Thus, policymaking may result in a status quo which is less than desirable and has consequences in itself. Chapman comments,

> What's wrong with that? Just about everything. It means 11 million people, including 1.7 million brought here as children (the 'dreamers') will go on living among us without the protections of the law. As a result, they are more likely to be underpaid, more apt to work off the books, more vulnerable to crime and less likely to pay the taxes they owe. There's not much upside for any of us. (2013)

Even the 2015 federal budget reflects this policy dilemma as it advocates creation of a path for undocumented workers to earn citizenship while also allocating money to improve border security and for the detention and deportation of those same workers.

Recently, a course change in policy is being noticed, however. Cities and states that at one time were destined to remove all undocumented immigrants now realize the effects of their policies from the perspectives discussed above. The Congressional Budget Office is on record stating that finding a remedy to this "shadow economy" situation would bring much-needed additional revenue to the federal budget and deficit. Punitive policies are now being replaced with pro-immigrant policies. Latino immigrants bring renewed economic benefits to areas desperately in need of them. Kolodziej cites the example of South Carolina which announced it would no longer arrest motorists to check immigration status because it was unconstitutional and unwise (2014). As noted in the introduction to this chapter, college presidents in Oklahoma are seeking relief from enforcement of rules which harm undocumented students and state economies. Efforts to keep the very persons once sought for removal are increasing.

These more positive movements in immigration policy are even being welcomed in public opinion polls, which indicate an attitude change in favor of legislation that would enable undocumented workers to obtain legal status. Non-deportation of persons that are related to legal citizens is a policy development welcomed by all. The federal "Dream Act" legislation which allows persons who entered the country at young ages to be protected from deportation, represents another example that efforts to positively address the issue may now take hold.

IV. CONCLUSION

This chapter on public policy has sought to provide not only information about Oklahoma's immigration policymaking process but also about the steps in policymaking in general. By outlining the analytical tools used to evaluate polices and the step-by-step process using Oklahoma HB 1804 as an example, the three dimensions, i.e., economic, moral, and political were explored. Using this analytical framework to investigate the arguments surrounding HB 1804's formulation, passage, and implementation, one could see how different political actors and interest groups framed their arguments in support of or in opposition to the legislation. Moreover, these arguments continued throughout the policymaking process and continue as part of the policy evaluation process.

In addition to these three dimensions, public policymaking has a step-by-step process defined by political scientists as including: 1) Problem Identification, 2) Agenda Setting, 3) Policy Formulation, 4) Policy Adoption, 5) Policy Implementation, and 6) Policy Evaluation. Again, these steps come into focus by showing how HB 1804 came into being and was transformed into law. The process for the passage of HB 1804 began long before any legislation was proposed. In the case of HB 1804, proponents learned from failed attempts to pass immigration laws in the Oklahoma legislature. Over six years have passed since HB 1804 went into effect and in spite of claims by supporters, it has had limited effect on undocumented residents in Oklahoma.

Debates about immigration policy have dominated much of the political discourse during the last eight years in Oklahoma and in many other states. While it will no doubt continue to produce animated debates, most Americans appear open to a new approach from the federal government. This approach may be less punitive than many state laws, including Oklahoma's. The question remains if and when the U.S. Congress will elevate serious immigration reform to the top of their policymaking agenda.

Oklahoma Environmental Policy: Complexity in a Traditionalist/ Individualist State

John R. Wood

Man is a complex being: he makes deserts bloom –and lakes die
Gil Stern

I. Introduction

Oklahoma is an ecologically diverse state. According to the Environmental Protection Agency, Oklahoma holds the nation's most diverse terrain per square mile in the nation (Western Ecological Region, 2007; Office of Secretary of the Environment, 2014). Oklahoma's environment is a mosaic of grazing land, cropland, woodland, forests, and abandoned farmland. It is one of only four states with twelve **eco-regions**, areas separated by type of environmental terrain or sub-climate. The state's land varies from the cypress swamps of the Southeast to Rocky Mountain foothills in the West, tall-grass prairies in the Central and Northeast, and hardwood forests to pine-covered mountains in the South and Southeast.

Environmental policy is the implementation of governmental actions to influence natural resource use and environmental quality (Kraft, 2010). From its beginning, Oklahoma's stance toward governmental policies has been largely populist with "traditionalistic overtones" often in conflict with its physical environment (Morgan *et al.*, 1991). From the Land Run to the Dust Bowl to the controversies over Tar Creek and poultry operations, Oklahomans struggle to square their political culture with the demands placed on them by their own state's environmental regulatory complexity. Oklahoma's environmental policy is complicated by more than ten Oklahoma state agencies overlapping in their authority over environmental questions (See Table 15–1).

Oklahoma's environmental policy is made up of the state's collective decisions to pursue certain environmental goals with particular tools to achieve them. Not only is environmental policy a description of what the state does about the use of natural resources and protecting environmental quality, but what it *does not* do. Oklahoma's environmental history was dominated by settlers' struggles to keep food on the table, *not* by

TABLE 15-1
Oklahoma State Environmental Agencies

Department of Environmental Quality	The state's primary environmental agency. Established in 1993. Responsible for point and some non-point source pollution; ground and surface water quality and protection, air quality, radioactive waste, solid and hazardous waste, and enforcement of Water Quality Standards. Administers Superfund, or the Comprehensive Environmental Response, Compensation and Liability Act of 1980.
Department of Labor	Regulates indoor air quality under the Oklahoma Occupational Health and Safety Act. It also regulates asbestos monitoring in workplaces.
Department of Mines	Deals with mining activities and corporations engaged in mining activities in the state. Deals with groundwater protection and the development of a Water Quality Standards Implementation Plan for these activities.
Department of Public Safety	Responsible for transportation of hazardous waste including inspection of vehicles and other carriers of hazardous waste.
Department of Wildlife Conservation	In charge of wildlife protection.
Oklahoma Corporation Commission	Authority over oil and gas conservation and exploration, drilling, development, production, processing, and underground storage tanks. It receives its jurisdiction from the Oklahoma Constitution.
Oklahoma Conservation Commission	Monitors, evaluates, and assesses waters to determine the impact of non-point source pollution. It also deals with erosion control, abandoned mines, wetlands, and environmental education.
Oklahoma Department of Agriculture	Covers both point and non-point source pollution, and runoff, from agricultural-related activities. Also enforces the Oklahoma Water Quality Standard, implementing a Water Quality Standard Implementation Plan as well as other agricultural storage facilities.
Department of Civil Emergency Management	Prepares for and deals with emergencies and disasters in the state. Also maintains an electronic emergency information system which provides access to information relating to the quantity and location of hazardous materials.
Oklahoma Scenic Rivers Commission	Establishes minimum standards for planning and other ordinances necessary to carry out the provisions of the Scenic Rivers Act. Main focus is preservation and protection of the beauty, scenic, history, archaeology,

	and scientific features of the Illinois River and its tributaries—Barren (Baron) Fork Creek, Lee Creek, Little Lee Creek, Flint Creek, and (Upper) Mountain Fork.
Oklahoma Water Resources Board	Enforces Oklahoma water quality standards. Lead agency to enforce the Clean Water Act's clean lakes program. Deals with ground and surface water rights and interstate stream compacts.
Secretary of the Environment	Charged with the protection and enhancement of Oklahoma's environment and natural resources. Administers Federal Clean Water Act funds as well as coordinates pollution control efforts to avoid duplication of state agency work.

conserving their resources for future use. This early history is not unlike colonists' concentration on land use (Andrews, 2006). Such a policy strategy, with an emphasis on use rather than conservation, seemed to work well for the first third of the state's history. However, this policy strategy's eventual failure means that present Oklahomans ultimately inherit its consequences.

II. History From the Land Run to the Dust Bowl

A long row of excited settlers, some 50,000 on race horses, others in wagons and on foot, toed the imaginary line of a new frontier – a new life. Little did these settlers know, but Oklahomans' policies regarding their fragile and yet often hostile environment would begin with an earsplitting trumpet call heard on April 22, 1889, at high noon. At this pivotal moment, the Oklahoma Land Run began and thousands of settlers from many states broke the line, dashing for their highly coveted prize of 160 acres of land. Overnight, Guthrie, Oklahoma swelled from nothing to 10,000 people (Oklahoma Territory Census, 1890). The *Harper's Weekly* in 1889 described the new birth of a community virtually overnight:

> *Unlike Rome, the city of Guthrie was built in a day. To be strictly accurate in the matter, it might be said that it was built in an afternoon. At twelve o'clock on Monday, April 22nd, the resident population of Guthrie was nothing; before sundown it was at least ten thousand. (Howard, 1889)*

Land was plentiful at a time when Native Americans held the land in common. But this soon changed as it was opened up to homestead settlement. Poor settlers poured into the once barren territory, lured by "free land." They failed to understand that without a way to deal with this immediate and immense overpopulation, the result would be poverty and conflict (Morgan *et al.*, 1991).

More than 60 years prior, Indian tribes were uprooted from their homes east of the Mississippi River in a series of land confiscations under the **Removal Act of 1830**. Over several decades they moved to what was then called Indian Territory. Today this is recognized as the eastern portion of Oklahoma. Their new home would not last for long (Heidler & Heidler, 2007). After the Native Americans settled the territory, frontiersmen eyed the area, often complaining that these Native people and only a few cattlemen were the sole occupants of these sixty-million acres of treaty lands. Many government officials as well as frontiersmen felt that the Native Americans were not civilized and that they would assimilate as farmers if given individual land holdings. In his 1881 address to Congress, U.S. President Chester Arthur explains:

> . . . *there is reason to believe that the Indians in large numbers would be persuaded to sever their tribal relations and to engage at once in agricultural pursuits. Many of them realize the fact that their hunting days are over and that it is now for their best interests to conform their manner of life to the new order of things. By no greater inducement than the assurance of permanent title to the soil can they be led to engage in the occupation of tilling it. (Richardson, 2001)*

As a result, the General Allotment Act of 1887, also known as the **Dawes Act** or Dawes Severalty Act, authorized the President of the United States to survey Native American commonly-held tribal land and break it up into allotments for individual Native Americans (Debo, 1949). During this process, the "Indian Nations" were stripped of their communally-held lands. For Native Americans, the Dawes Act was the most important method of gaining citizenship prior to 1924 (Baird & Goble, 1990). The Dawes Act tied Native American citizenship to the ultimate proof of citizenship – individual land ownership. The Dawes Act supporters not only wanted to destroy the tribal loyalties and the reservation system, but also to open up white settlement of Indian Territory. The Dawes Act opened up hundreds of thousands of acres of land after the individual 160-acre allotments had originally been made to Native Americans. These land parcels were then sold for prices to land-hungry whites through the **Homestead Act,** which like the Dawes Act, allowed individuals to claim up to 160 acres of publicly owned lands. Those who lived on and improved their claims over a five-year period owned this land outright.

Land ownership through the Homestead Act, however, would later come to haunt Oklahomans (Egan, 2006). The soil erosion during the Dust Bowl was a result of not only farming technique and climate, but also Oklahomans' approach to environmental policymaking. Agronomists and others advised Congress members that for Indian Territory, the division of 160 acres per settler would not work. Farmers could not make enough money to feed their families on the arid Oklahoma soils with only

160 acres of land. However, Debo (1981) argues, Congress members wanted to boost their popularity by helping as many families as possible and stuck with the 160-acre allotments.

> *Oklahoma had a bad condition to start with: light, thin soil; large areas too rough for agriculture; and violent extremes of flood and drought. Then the method of settlement, although in the American tradition, was the worst possible method for the land. All the bad practices inaugurated at Jamestown and repeated on successive frontiers were intensified in Oklahoma. (p. 74)*

Settlers became conscious of the land's fragility soon after statehood in 1907. Farmers watched their fields become pockmarked with gullies filled with stagnant water, but did little because they were forced to squeeze every last ounce of each acre's production to feed their struggling families. By 1931, 13 of 16 million acres, or more than 80 percent of Oklahoma cropland, had been damaged with water wearing down the once fertile soil. After grasses and trees were removed to create farmlands, the resulting sandy Indian Territory soils were susceptible to erosion (Phillips & Harrison, 2004). The circumstances only grew tougher as depression hurt the economic outlook of much of the United States. The "Black Tuesday" crash of the stock market pushed people from the economic hardship in the cities to the already struggling farm lands (Carson, 2006). To make things even worse, severe drought hit the Great Plains in the mid-1930s. These problems piled up on the backs of farmers who could not plant their crops, leaving the land even more exposed to the wind. More than 300 **"Black Rollers,"** or major dust storms, windswept what was left of the once fertile soil already worn down by standing water. Along with environmental conditions unkind to crop farming, eastern methods of farming such as straight-row farming, often plowed up and down hillsides, created gullies in the lowlands from rainfall runoff. When it did rain, it often fell at the wrong time of year to help crops. As a result of a ten-year drought, Oklahoma started to look more and more like a desert by the mid-1930s. Not surprisingly, more than 75,000 farmers abandoned their unproductive farms for other states like California in search of employment (Phillips & Harrison, 2004). As a result, U.S. environmental policy toward Oklahoma changed from **laissez faire**, or a hands-off approach, to a focus on erosion control.

Policy Reaction

Environmental policy appeared in the forefront for the first time as the government recognized soil erosion in 1929 with the Buchanan Amendment to the Agriculture Appropriation Bill enacted by Congress (Egan, 2006). In an effort to keep farmers on the farm, the federal government created the **Agricultural Adjustment Act of 1933,** a forerunner to today's

Farm Bill. This Act paid farmers to limit producing certain crops when prices were low and store them during times of crisis (Carson, 2006).

In response to the "Black Rollers," the federal government took a more active role by enacting the **Soil Conservation Act of 1935,** which created the Soil Conservation Service (SCS) within the U.S. Department of Agriculture. This is now referred to as the Natural Resources Conservation Service. Hugh Bennett, who headed the Service, took over the largest soil conservation service project called "Operation Dust Bowl." Bennett's strategy attacked the drifts of sand with contour-plowing, creating furrows or grooves in the soil to protect it from the gusting wind. In these furrows, he planted African grasses, not to grow crops, but to bring the Oklahoman desert back to life (Mundende, 2004).

By 1937, Oklahoma took a more direct role in working with landowners and acted as an intermediary for federal soil conservation assistance. The resolution called for states to enact a law establishing a state soil conservation agency and procedures whereby local soil and water conservation districts could be established.

These environmental policies were a reaction to the Dust Bowl crisis and a way in which to deal with it. In debate at the time was whether the Dust Bowl was a hundred-year cycle or manmade. In 1936, Bennett delivered the Great Plains Drought Area Committee to President Roosevelt concluding that it was both. The study says that only 20 inches of rainfall or less would not support dry land farming. The report noted that: "Mistaken public policies have been largely responsible for the situation." The report more specifically, made reference to "a mistaken homestead policy, the stimulation of war time demands which led to over cropping and over grazing, and encouragement of a system of agriculture which could not be both permanent and prosperous"(Egan, 2006, p. 267). This report shows how environmental policy can be flawed. But, the story of the government's response shows how such tragedy can be turned around. The Dust Bowl coupled with the Great Depression convincingly demonstrates that state efforts alone were inadequate for dealing with the national economic and environmental problems. Although the New Deal itself did not adequately address the environmental problems, it transformed current notions of federalism by creating a presumption that national regulation was necessary for responding to national problems.

Counter to this trend, Oklahoman's painful Dust Bowl history has contributed to a largely traditionalist political culture resistant to change, placing a premium on "business as usual" (Morgan, England, & Humphreys, 1991, p. 4). This might help explain why the Resource Renewal Institute's *State of the States* report finds that Oklahoma ranks 46th out of 50 states in its policy innovation to improve the state's environmental programs, and in the bottom five states in pollution prevention performance in a study by the Environmental Defense Fund. Furthermore, Oklahoma ranks 37th in energy efficiency (American Council for an Energy-Efficient Economy, 2013).

In addition, *Governing* magazine cites U.S. Census Bureau data showing that Oklahoma ranks 45th in environmental spending per capita with more than $660 million dollars in 2004. *Governing* also finds that Oklahoma at 3.8% beats only Mississippi and South Dakota in the percent of residents' garbage recycled. Both these state residents' recycling efforts are miniscule— less than a tenth as compared to Minnesota at 42.3%, the nation's top recycler. Oklahomans' negative sentiments toward recycling reflects the fact that the state's landfill tipping fees are the lowest in the nation at an inexpensive $18 per ton compared to Vermont's hefty $98 per ton, which gives that state much more incentive to recycle. In lieu of recycling, Oklahoma is fond of landfilling and is the country's 10th biggest landfiller per capita ("*Governing's State and Local Sourcebook,*" 2006). What is more, Oklahoma is among the 5 states with only one school participating in the **"Recycle Bowl Competition,"** well behind Texas with 205 schools, Arizona with 132, and Ohio with 102 (Keep America Beautiful, 2014). The K-12 competition establishes new recycling programs within schools, increases recycling rates, and creates teaching opportunities ("SustainLane," 2008).

On the city level, Tulsa and Oklahoma City's ecological footprints rank a mere 90th and 93rd, out of 100 cities, respectively, measuring the human demand on the Earth's ecosystems, according to SustainLane's 2008 Sustainability Ranking.

III. Recent Policy Controversies

Controversies in Oklahoma as well as elsewhere often stem from diversity and complexity. This chapter briefly discusses two cases, representing major environmental controversies. The first is the rise of Oklahoma poultry farmers, who contract with large poultry corporations in Arkansas and the second is Tar Creek, one of the nation's most polluted places. Environmental policy from the Land Run to the Dust Bowl was relatively simple because at the time little was known about the environment. But as Oklahomans and their federal counterparts have had to deal with the Dust Bowl and thereafter, policy decisions on all levels of government have become more complicated and controversial.

Poultry

The poultry house's aluminum door whirrs as it opens, revealing a dark, dank, and stale "other world." The barn's intoned vibration betrays the community of 50,000 chickens therein. The unwieldy smell of chicken waste quickly penetrates the senses without warning. "You'll get used to it, they're just chickens," the farmer says as he notices my grimace. As we enter, the chickens cluck and cluster together away from our feet as we walk across the barn. A foot thick of chicken waste has finely matted over the last six weeks as the chickens have grown to maturity. Within a week, all these chickens will ship and be slaughtered at the contractor's plant just across the state line in Arkansas. We cross to the other end of the barn to adjust the watering system. Soon, a line of chickens greedily suck on the holes neatly carved in the bottom of the long PVC pile strung alongside the length of the barn. "Man, they're a thirsty this mornin,' mighty hot out there already," the farmer says as he wipes his brow with his grimy cap in hand.[1]

In an adjacent pasture, this poultry farmer sells his chicken waste to his neighbor, a cattle rancher, in order to fertilize the land's nutrient-starved soil. The payoff is a nice stand of wheat for the neighbor's cattle. This practice has alarmed politicians, residents and scientists alike. Scientific reports have indicated that increased phosphorous from various sources, like chicken waste, has caused the Illinois River to turn abnormally green and brown from **algal blooms**.[2] These blooms take up too many nutrients, starving fish and other wildlife from precious, life-giving oxygen.

`The Illinois River in Northeast Oklahoma is considered by many to be the state's most prized, scenic and pristine river. It provides numerous social benefits to the citizens of the state and region. It is a source of drinking water for Tahlequah and Watts and irrigates plant nurseries and farms in the region. It also provides a home to an abundance of wildlife, including several threatened and endangered species of plants and animals. It is additionally a popular tourist and recreation attraction and was the first river designated as a **Wild and Scenic River**[3] by the state. More than 180,000 tourists annually float the Illinois River by raft, canoe or kayak. Nearly 350,000 people swim, fish, camp, hike, bird watch and hunt, infusing $9 million into the local economy by bringing in tourists from not only Oklahoma, but also Arkansas, Missouri, Kansas and Texas (Bality *et al.*, 1998). In 2006, only 113,763 people floated the river, because of low stream levels and excessive heat (Kelly, 2007). However, Tahlequah Tourist Director Kate Kelly said, floaters and other tourists still contributed nearly a $12 million boost to the local economy that year.

Several large corporations contract with nearly 2,000 farmers just within 20 miles of the Oklahoma/Arkansas border. Over the course of the last 20 years, many farmers in the economically-depressed northeastern section of Oklahoma have eagerly undertaken chicken and turkey farming as a lucrative alternative to traditional crop farming. Increased large-scale poultry feeding operations are on the increase, numbering 45 million in Oklahoma and another 125 million in Arkansas (Cooper *et. al.*, 1994). Recent studies have indicated that the water quality in the Illinois River has deteriorated, particularly from chicken waste's nutrients, especially phosphorous, which seeps down into the soil and then runs off into the river (Palmer, 1994). Ed Fite, director of Oklahoma's Scenic Rivers Commission (OSRC) describes the Illinois River's headwaters as highly developed. He says, "My windshield impression is that the river's quality is spiraling downward" (Money, 2002). The OSRC board members are responsible for overseeing the state's river water quality. Therefore, it concerns these members when cattle ranchers buy chicken waste from poultry operators to apply to nutrient-starved pasture land. Unfortunately, the chicken waste is not applied consistently and often too liberally, creating excess nutrients that seep into the river. Legislation passed in 1997 requires soil tests on lands where farmers want to apply chicken waste. This test is to be sent to a stipulated lab in order to assess phosphorous levels. Land over the designated 250 phosphorous index has enough nutrients already; therefore chicken waste cannot be applied (Stephens, 1997). Too many nutrients, such as phosphorus from chicken waste, can cause a shortage of oxygen leading to **blue baby syndrome,** a condition that is sometimes fatal to humans. It can also create algal blooms that take up a great deal of oxygen, subsequently hurting **biodiversity** – basically the numbers and types of different species available in the water (Palmer, 1994). More specifically, biodiversity is the representation of the variety of living organisms, their differences in genetics, and the communities and their interrelation in their associated physical environment (Oklahoma Conservation Commission, 1998).

The nutrients from chicken waste trickles into the water from multiple places, but is not seen by the naked eye. Such a phenomenon is what policy experts call **non-point source pollution.** Non-point source pollution is an undefined or diffuse source from fields to urban streets from fertilizers, pesticides, or sediment (Oklahoma Conservation Commission, 1998). Because this movement of nutrients into the water is over time and invisible, often people who live in the area play the blame game, creating conflict over what to do. For example, tourists and farmers blame each other for the decline in water quality. Riverfront property owners also blame tourists for trespassing, littering, and rowdy behavior. Many in Oklahoma blame Arkansas poultry operations and wastewater treatment run-off from Fayetteville. Oklahoma's fight with Arkansas eventually led to a U.S. Supreme Court decision in 1992.[4] Five years later, citizens of Tulsa worried about a perceived threat to their city water supply and pushed for a law to address poultry (Hinton, 1997). At the same time, small-scale poultry farmers face large economic pressures because when they comply with more rules and regulations, their operational costs go up. However, passing costs off to consumers is only one problem farmers face. For example, Tyson Foods, located in Fayetteville, Arkansas, as well as other corporate poultry corporations, often threaten to pull their business and contracts with small farmers raising chicken and turkeys if costs go up (Kershen, 1997). These poultry farmers could lose their livelihoods.

In 2005, Attorney Drew Edmondson brought a lawsuit against several out-of-state poultry operators declaring that they are polluting the state's rivers and in turn, its drinking water and public health. His lawsuit alleged multiple violations of federal law including the Comprehensive Environmental Response Compensation and Liability Act (CERCLA), also known as **Superfund,** as well as state and federal nuisance laws, trespass and Oklahoma Environmental Quality and Agriculture Codes.

LEADERSHIP PROFILE

JEANETTE M. NANCE
Executive Director, Keep Oklahoma Beautiful

JEANETTE NANCE began her career in state government as one of former Governor Brad Henry's designated liaisons to the rest of the executive branch. She had never really thought about the hodgepodge of agencies assigned to her. Why, for example, did she have the Department of Agriculture and the Department of Transportation; or Public Safety, Corporation Commission, Insurance Department, Turnpike Authority, and the Secretary of the Environment? Then the necessity to coordinate these disparate state agencies became crystal clear to her. A series of back-to-back ice  storms hit the state. Ice and snow paralyzed large parts of Oklahoma. Nance found herself at the virtual center of a rapidly developing communications network linking these agencies to changing events on the ground. In a sense, she became eyes and ears for a host of decision makers inside and outside of the governor's office.

Nance received countless calls from citizens across the state who were facing critical needs. Thousand of homes were without power. Bitterly cold temperatures continued for days creating a host of problems. Power outages were forcing some people to lose food. Roads and highways were extremely slick and hazardous over widespread areas. The storms affected nearly every aspect of public policy in the state.

State agencies swung into action. The Corporation Commission channeled hourly updates about power outages to the governor's office. The Oklahoma Highway Patrol would then know where to keep state troopers assigned to distribute emergency water and generators. The Department of Agriculture gathered hay to deliver to assist ranchers and farmers who couldn't feed their cattle. A Chinook helicopter from the National Guard and a plane from the Highway Patrol dropped hay to cattle stranded due to the storms. Road crews worked day and night clearing ice and salting highways to keep open the transportation arteries of the state. The governor declared a state of emergency for all 77 counties of the state allowing local governments to get reimbursed for recovery expenses.

As a junior staff member, Nance realized that she was doing something important. She had face-to-face contact with several cabinet members, the chief of staff, and even the governor himself. She fielded dozens of calls per day, worked long hours and weekends all through the month. Storms of this magnitude make it impossible to fully address the needs of each and every citizen. But as Nance says, "I had the satisfaction of knowing I at least helped some of the people some of the time." She remembers a political proverb proffered by one of her mentors, Mike Turpen, who told her, "The rule of constituent service is the people that you specifically help specifically remember, and the people you generally help generally forget."

Prior to her service in government, Nance had worked mostly in the nonprofit sector and had just recently completed her bachelor's degree in political science from the University of Central Oklahoma. As part of her educational career, Nance made a special effort to take advantage of internship opportunities. Her first internship experience was as a Carl Albert Intern for the State of Oklahoma Office of Personnel Management. Later, she served as an intern on the inaugural committee for Brad Henry. Nance also was selected to be a Carl Reherman City Management Intern for the City of Edmond. Finally, she spent a summer internship in the scheduling office for Governor Brad Henry which ultimately led to her job as Agency Liaison and Public Policy Specialist. Toward the end of her tenure in the Governor's office, she was promoted to Director of Constituent Services.

After serving in the governor's office, Nance worked as the External Affairs Specialist and Legislative Liaison for the Oklahoma Department of Environmental Quality (DEQ). When legislators or the governor's office or members of their staffs needed assistance to address constituent concerns, she would connect them to the right resources.

Currently, Nance serves as the Executive Director and spokesperson for the nonprofit Keep Oklahoma Beautiful, the state affiliate to the national Keep America Beautiful. She works to foster positive relationships with sponsors, partners, affiliates, state agencies, board of directors, local authorities across the state, and national Keep America Beautiful staff. She helps coordinate these diverse organizations and people to help improve Oklahoma's quality of life through community development and environmental sustainability.

Nance and her husband Bob, a well respected attorney, are the proud parents of three children: Joy, Julie, and Daniel. She and her two daughters graduated at nearly the same time from the University of Central Oklahoma with degrees in political science.

Brett S. Sharp

"It all comes down to pollution," Edmondson says in a press release. "Too much poultry waste is being dumped on the ground and it ends up in the water. That's against the law. The companies own the birds as well as the feed, medicines and other things they put in their birds. They should be responsible for managing the hundreds of thousands of tons of waste that comes out of their birds" (Edmondson, 2005). Arkansas responded in 2006 by seeking the U.S. Supreme Court to intervene based on Constitutional grounds, but the Court rejected the state's claims (Demillo, 2006).

It is not clear whether new Attorney General Scott Pruitt will pursue the case that has been marked with fits and starts (Case Closed, 2010). Some say that the lawsuit's unpopularity with Eastern Oklahoma poultry growers was a potential factor in his primary loss, which may portend little progress in the area. By late 2012, the case was still pending in U.S. District court (Smoot, 2012).

There's been a great deal of conflict over whether poultry waste is the primary problem in the watershed, but there is little debate that the water quality in the area has degraded significantly over the last several years.

Tar Creek

"The Lawyer" and "The Sooner" are the names of two of many heaping 10-story piles of rock, dispersed throughout Pitcher, Oklahoma, drawing dirt bikers and children (Gillham, 2006). Over the years, the townsfolk named these massive mounds of rock by ordinary and familiar names instead of by the term most everyone else outside the region uses—**chat piles**. These massive piles of crushed rock like the mound locals call "Saint Joe," were left behind by miners long ago. These huge piles loom over residents and often blow contaminated dust on the populace and in school yards. These chat piles, some towering 200 feet in the air, are contaminated with heavy metals that pose a threat, especially to children (CCEH & DP Research, 2007).

Although Tar Creek in Northeast Oklahoma was once a vibrant mining area where many citizens in the area patriotically produced lead and zinc for the soldiers in World War II, today the battle lines are closer to home. U.S. Senator Inhofe explains that the government must act now because abandoned mining companies were not held responsible long ago for the hazardous waste from the mines that leaked into the groundwater (Inhofe, 2003). However, he says, federal agencies have engaged in interagency battles over who is responsible for the clean-up. The EPA, the Army Corps of Engineers, the Department of Interior, officially admit responsibility for the clean-up.

Battle lines have also been drawn between those residents who want to remain to clean up their home areas and those residents who want a "buyout" plan. Senator Inhofe, formerly held the chairmanship of the Senate Environment and Public Works Committee, which gave him huge sway over any legislation affecting Tar Creek. In 2003, the Senator asserted that instead of a buyout, he supported a $45 million plan to have the University of Oklahoma lead an effort focusing on the periphery of the Tar Creek area to remove tons of chat located in the site's epicenter (Myers, 2003). Inhofe's plan was in spite of then Governor Frank Keating's Tar Creek Superfund Task Force in 2000, which recommended a "world class wetlands." The conception of a wetlands created a backlash among residents who feared that they may be forced from their homes. In response, the Environmental Protection Agency (EPA) backed off a wetlands plan soon after (Myers, 2003).

Tar Creek, in Picher, Oklahoma, is part of the Tri-State Mining District – Northeast Oklahoma, Southwest Missouri, and Southeast Kansas. Eighty-three abandoned water supply wells along with dozens of exploratory drills mined the Boone Formation, which was particularly rich in zinc and lead. Despite the mineral riches found, the drills punctured the underlying deep Roubidoux aquifer, which serves as the drinking water supply for a large portion of Northeastern Oklahoma. The drill holes serve as pathways for abandoned toxic metals left by the mining companies as late as the 1970s when mineral deposits were exhausted. Underneath roughly 2,500 acres of this site are nearly 300 miles of tunnels and in excess of 1,300 mineshafts (CCEH & DP Research, 2007). By 1980, the contaminated water flowed down the stream, turning it bright orange, bringing media attention to the plight of Picher for the first time.

The Tar Creek Superfund site was added in 1983 to the EPA's **National Priority List** (NPL), which is a list of nation's dirtiest sites and eligible for funding to clean it up. Although Tar Creek was Oklahoma's first Superfund site, it is now only one of fourteen statewide. The Imperial Refining Company in Ardmore, for example, became Oklahoma's latest NPL list member in 2000. Clean up of the refining company's **underground storage tanks** began in 2005. These tanks also leaked oil into the groundwater, often the source for drinking water. The Oklahoma Department of Environmental Quality (ODEQ) oversees, maintains, and cleans up Superfund sites. ODEQ's website notes that Tar Creek is the state's "most challenging of the Oklahoma sites" (Land Protection Division: Tar Creek Section, 2014).

Ignoring groundwater contamination can have its consequences. For example, an Indian Health Services study found that 34% of the area's Native American children had lead blood levels in excess of the Centers for Disease Control (CDC) and Prevention standards. By 1996, the EPA removed and replaced contaminated soil from residents' yards with soil that is not contaminated. It took more than $40 million to clean up more than 1500 yards, with an estimated 600 left (Focht & Hull, 2004).

Resistance to a "world class wetlands" has dwindled in the area as a *Washington Times* article from February 2006 reported a collapse of a West Virginia coal mine. It reminded Oklahoma residents that the abandoned mine shafts and caverns underground could also give way. Before a jammed gymnasium at Picher-Cardin High School, the *Times* reported further, the results of an 18-month "subsidence" study which was released two weeks prior. The in-depth study produced by six state and federal agencies–U.S. Corps of Engineers, U.S. Geological Survey, U.S. Interior Department, U.S. Bureau of Indian Affairs, the Oklahoma Department of Environmental Quality and Geological Survey–shocked locals. The study described 286 mine shafts and caverns in danger of giving way, endangering 162 occupied homes, 16 public facilities, 18 businesses and 33 locations beneath major highways or streets (Aynesworth, 2006).

Because of this change, Senator Inhofe seemed to change his position from cleaning up the area to the "buyout" plan.

> *With the new facts provided by the recent subsidence report we simply cannot risk the safety of Oklahomans in the Tar Creek area and that is why we are moving forward with this plan. Buying out these residents and removing them from Tar Creek will eliminate a very serious risk to these Oklahoma families. (Inhofe, 2006)*

Tar Creek residents living with the greatest risk of cave-ins were the first to receive the buyouts. More than 870 buyout offers were made in total with 96% of those accepted. The state of Oklahoma sponsored the buyouts prior to 2005 and then thereafter the federal program purchased the remaining buyouts. A total of $46+ million was spent by the federal government. The end result after the buyout is that Picher and Cardin, two towns that had 1,640 and 150 residents respectively, had only about a dozen residents remaining after the buyouts (http://www.nativetimes. com/index.php/news/environment/6451-buyouts-in-tar-creek-superfund-area-winding-down).

Gary Garrett, a longtime resident, who lives in a nearby town of Cardin, says he would take a buyout if offered. "My house is situated above one of the risk sites identified by the Corps," Garrett explains. "I have lived here 40 of my 60 years but I would move. I am afraid for my safety and for my health. It would probably scare us to death if we really knew all the risks" (Gillham, 2006).

Tar Creek, a 2010 documentary had the tagline "The story of the worst environmental disaster you've never heard of: the Tar Creek Superfund site" (Myers, 2010). On the website, Myers describes the movie as a spotlight on how Superfund sites "aren't just environmental wastelands; they're community tragedies, too. Until the community fights back."

Both Tar Creek area communities—Picher and Cardin—have been dissolved as incorporated municipalities, after their infrastructure was largely bulldozed after the federally funded buyout (Stogsdill, 2013).

IV. Future Directions for the State

Many scientists, environmentalists and business leaders are focusing on **sustainable development** in the state. According to the Brundtland Commission, "Sustainable development is development that meets the

needs of the present without compromising the ability of future generations to meet their own needs." This definition focuses on finding the
middle ground between the present and future.

However, Governor Mary Fallin, reorganized her cabinet by combin-
ing the Department of the Environment and the Department of Energy
with the appointment of Michael Teague. "Strong energy policy is strong
environmental policy," Fallin said. "In Col. Teague's new role, his mission
will be to help develop policies that encourage energy exploration and
production as well as responsible environmental stewardship" (Wilmoth,
2013). This combination is not surprising in a state with individualist tendencies. The state's population tends to see government limited to
encouraging private initiative (Elazar, 1972) and discourage regulatory
action, especially when it comes to the environment (Kraft, 2010). Then it
is not surprising that Oklahoma ranks 18th as the most business-friendly
state and rating an A- in overall "regulatory friendliness" (Allen &
Daniels, 2013, p. 18).

However, this new emphasis may have consequences. The previous
Secretary of the Environment Michael Tolbert (2004) pointed out many of
Oklahoma's wildlife species are in decline, including the Prairie Chicken
with a 90% drop in numbers in just a few years. Even some birds are disappearing. For example, the Arkansas River Shiner is almost extinct.
Tolbert said that species decline is a result of habitats disappearing due to
human development. To illustrate, he said, 70% of the original wetlands
have been drained or filled and tall grass prairies have all but vanished.
In addition, 95% of Oklahoman lands are in the hands of private owners,
which means that state government is limited in its ability to enforce federal regulations on those lands. Even some hunters are thinking of closing
down quail hunting season because the Wildlife Department reports the
number of quail harvests have dropped yearly since its peak in 1987
(Godfrey, 2012).

Tolbert recommends a voluntary program of riparian buffers on public
and private land. **Riparian buffers** are the planting of native vegetation
along stream banks to filter nutrients from getting into the stream. This
simple plan benefits the environment in six major ways because it: 1) filters
pollutants from heading into the river; 2) decreases stream bank erosion;
3) reduces the number of cattle eroding the stream bank; 4) lowers temperatures of the stream; 5) improves habitats for wildlife and; 6) makes the
stream look better. There are different government programs, Tolbert says.
Few farmers have been aware of what the state has to offer in the past. He
says he would like to enhance the visibility of these programs.

Focht (2004) finds sustainable solutions have fallen by the wayside in
Oklahoma because there is a dearth of research on how to achieve sustainability and how to measure it. On top of this, people need to be a part of
the process and policymakers need to know what people want and will
accept to move forward toward a sustainable Oklahoma. It is also likely
though, as the history of Oklahoma in this chapter reveals, Oklahomans'

traditionalist worldview makes for slow change, especially when it is perceived that government is the force behind that change.

Change is not only coming from state government but from business. ConocoPhillips President J.J. Mulva says that his company is planning for a sustainable Oklahoma with a focus on protecting bird habitats (Mulva, 2004). The company has also moved to **double hulls**[5] and other environmental and safety features. Additionally, ConocoPhillips supports the Nature Conservancy's work to preserve the Tall Grass Prairie in Northeast Oklahoma. ConocoPhillips was named a top 100 Best Corporate Citizen by Corporate Responsibility Magazine (CR's 100 Best Corporate Citizens 2012).

State and local organizations

Sustainable change is also coming from nonprofit citizen groups like the Oklahoma Sustainability Network (OSN), which has made sustainability a focus of its work. The OSN's mission is to connect and educate the people of Oklahoma concerning the many aspects of sustainability. OSN is a catalyst and a resource for the improvement of Oklahoma's economy, ecology and equity (OSN, 2011). Eight OSN chapters focus on local sustainability issues across the state. In addition, the Oklahoma chapter of the Sierra Club has been active through its three local groups—Green Country, Cimarron Group, and the Red Earth Group. The Sierra Club's lobbyist as well as volunteers fought legislation at the state capitol during the 54th Legislative Session. For example, the Club helped block "a bill to forbid the EPA from enforcing any rules in Oklahoma," another bill on allowing the manufacture and use of chlorofluorocarbons (CFCs) in the state as well as bills to create constitutional amendments preventing the regulation of genetically modified foods, CAFOs, and other industrial agricultural practices (Oklahoma Sierra Club, 2013).

Universities

In addition, the Environmental Protection Agency (EPA) recognized the University of Central Oklahoma as the "2009-2010 Individual Conference Champion" for using more green power than any other school in the Lone Star Conference ("UCO Receives Green Power Partnership," 2010). Similarly, Oklahoma State University (OSU) saved $11.5 million by reducing energy and water consumption over the course of three years, according to the University's website (Energy Conservation Program, 2010). OSU replaced more than 45,000 lights with more efficient T5 bulbs/ballasts in 97 buildings (Climate Change and Energy, 2010). Additionally, OSU is working to retrofit heating, ventilation and air-conditioning (HVAC) systems in the years to come. OSU received a $288 rebate check from Oklahoma Gas & Electric Co. because it increased efficiency by 20% by investing in two new chiller units (Oklahoman Staff Reports, 2013).

V. Conclusion

As the state moves through the 21st century, environmental conflicts and controversies may become more apparent and serious. How Oklahoma's citizens approach these environmental problems will determine the state's direction. Oklahoma's environmental policy is complicated from the land's once fertile beginnings during early statehood to dealing with the environmental consequences of focusing on other prominent goals, such as making a living.

Deep down, environmental policy is about disagreements over values, which are basically abstract concepts evaluating what is worthwhile or right. At first blush, these conflicts might be fights about technical disagreements, for example, when a farmer is forced to test his land for phosphorous or another person is forced off his or her land to make way for a "world class wetland." Environmental conflict is actually about differences in opinions on how people should interact with the environment. Often government politicians and policymakers have to step in when there are concerns over pollution and subsequently when there has to be something done about it. However, government, business, and nonprofit groups can work together to facilitate change toward a more sustainable future.

NOTES

1. From the author's experience touring poultry houses in the Illinois River basin during the spring and fall of 1999.

2. An algal bloom is caused by a relatively quick increase in the population of phytoplankton algae in an aquatic system, such as a river or lake. Some algal blooms are the result of too many nutrients, i.e., phosphorus and nitrogen in a water environment. A higher concentration of these particular nutrients in the water creates an increased growth of algae and green plants. When the concentration is higher, it often causes other plants and animals to die out.

3. The Wild and Scenic Rivers Act was passed in 1968. The Act was to balance river development with river protection. In order to have this designation, Congress created nationwide the Wild and Scenic Rivers System. The Illinois River pushed in 1979 to be a candidate for Wild and Scenic designation. However, it needed a management plan. The river is considered a State Wild and Scenic River today. See Oklahoma Scenic Rivers Website http://www.oklahomascenicrivers.net/programs_next3.asp

4. An agreement was reached in 2003 between Oklahoma and Arkansas. Both states agreed to reduce phosphorus output from their waste water treatment plants by 75% over the next ten years, although the agreement did not address poultry-farm runoff.

5. Simply, a double-hulled tanker is a ship with a hull within a hull, basically a double skin of steel separated by a distance of 2 to 3.5 meters, depending on a ship's size. A hull like this can reduce the risk of a tanker oil spill (Valenti, 1999).

Oklahoma Towns and Cities in Cyberspace: Progress in Local E-Government in the Sunbelt

Tony Wohlers

Longevity isn't a hallmark of the CIO profession, and it certainly isn't for IT leaders who work in government. Oftentimes, CIOs must spend political capital in order to push through technology projects and policy changes, and with IT departments expected to produce more with fewer dollars, the job isn't exactly low stress.

Matt Williams, Associate Editor of *Government Technology*

I. Introduction

The wave of intensified economic globalization, increasing density of networked computers, and the rise of the Internet since the fall of the Berlin Wall in 1989 have become major forces across the industrialized countries and touched all levels of government. As a result, the adoption of information communications technologies (ICTs) via the Internet has become standard operating procedure at the local level of government in this country. Cities, counties, parishes, townships, municipalities, boroughs, and other local government units throughout the United States have adopted ICTs to modernize their modus operandi, thereby giving rise to innovative forms of interaction between municipal governments and citizens in this country. Within the context of ICTs, new functional avenues of information dissemination, service delivery and citizen engagement via interactive local government websites have become visible hallmarks of electronic government or **e-government.** Most of the existing research analyzes the breadth of e-government above the county level, but a systematic analysis of e-government progress at the city-and-town level remains scant. Closest to the people, we interact knowingly, and often unknowingly, with our town and city governments on a regular basis. And so we need a better understanding as to how these relatively new ICTs are used at the local level to facilitate citizen-government interaction.

Based on a detailed content analysis of a random sample of local government websites, this chapter analyzes the progress of e-government presence and functionality at the local level of government in the Sunbelt between 2010 and 2014 by comparing Oklahoma to its neighboring states, Arkansas, Louisiana, and New Mexico. This chapter argues that increasing population size and the presence of city or town chief administrators as well as increasing levels of financial resources available to local government improve e-government presence and functionality. Following a brief review of the literature about some of the basic trends and approaches to conceptualize local e-government, this study defines the relevant concepts, and introduces the methodological framework. Using a series of benchmarks to assess local e-government, the third part of this chapter analyzes progress of e-government presence and functionality across a representative sample of towns and cities in the selected states.

II. Trends in Local E-Government

Across the globe, many industrialized countries have embraced e-government to encourage the use of the Internet as an interactive tool of information retrieval, communication, transaction, and citizen outreach (Hernon, 2006; Nilsen, 2006; Petroni & Tangliente, 2005). The use of ICTs by local government in the United States aimed at designing and establishing official sites on the World Wide Web began in the mid 1990s. The availability of official local government Internet websites jumped from an estimated nine percent of American cities in 1995 to about 84 percent in 2000 (Norris, 2007; Holden, Norris, & Fletcher, 2003). More recent data indicates that local government website presence rose from 87.7 percent in 2002 to 95.0 percent in 2005 (Norris, 2007; Norris & Moon, 2005). Today, the implementation of an informative and interactive website has become standard operating procedure for most large- and mid-sized cities in the United States. Rising citizen expectations, increased technological capacity, and competition from other local governments drive continuous website upgrading. Recognized as a means to transform public administration and its interaction with the community through ICTs, e-government "aims at optimizing the provision of services, at increasing participation by citizens and enterprises..." (Petroni & Tagliente, 2005, p. 24).

Research has identified a number of factors to explain the adoption and expansion of e-government by local government in the United States. Typically, they include city size, type of city government, and city executives' support for e-government. Though there have been those defying the odds, as illustrated by the relatively small Californian city of San Carlos, a pioneer in local e-government and named Best of the Web for Local Government in 1997, size remains critical (Stowers, 2009). Large governmental units, especially those with city or metropolitan status and based on the council-manager form of government, which combines the strong political leadership of elected officials with the strong managerial experience of an appointed chief administrator, adopted e-government earlier. Moreover, local governments characterized by the professionally-driven council manager form have been able to expand and maintain the relevant e-government applications to a greater extent than those communities that lack financial resources, technical expertise, substantial infrastructure, and the ability to address security-related issues (Wohlers, 2009; Brown & Schelin, 2005; Holden, Norris, & Fletcher, 2003; Moon, 2002; Moulder, 2001). Lack of Internet access across certain segments of society (the so-called **"digital divide"**) as well as the allocation of scarce financial and technological resources, resistance within organizations, and cultural barriers in local governments have been identified as major barriers to local e-government (Mossberger, Tolbert, & McNeal, 2008; Hernon, 2006; Seifert, 2006; Petroni & Tagliente, 2005; Snellen, 2005; von Haldenwang, 2004; Wong & Welch, 2004).

Major categories to conceptualize functionality of local government websites include dissemination of information, delivery of services, and opportunities to interact with and participate in government. At the level of information dissemination, local government websites in the United States are mostly informative and limited to providing a range of basic one-way services rather than transactional services. Local government websites in the United States remain mostly informative and limited to providing a range of basic one-way services rather than transactional services including officials' contact information, government meeting schedules, election results, tourism information, and job postings (Garrett & Jensen, 2011; Wohlers, 2009; Coursey & Norris, 2008; Norris 2007; Haug, 2007; Norris & Moon, 2005; Holden, Norris, & Fletcher, 2003; Ho, 2002; ICMA/PTI, 2000, 2001, 2002). From a service-delivery perspective, an increasing percentage of cities offer web portals and online financial services and non-financial transactions, including the ability to pay utility bills, parking tickets, and taxes; request services and to apply for building permits, license renewals, and jobs with the city; and to register property (Center for Digital Government, 2008; Moon, 2002). Research reveals that improved online service delivery can improve citizens' trust and confidence in their government (Tolbert & Mossberger, 2006; Nugent, 2001). Despite these potential benefits, resources and expertise must be available for local government to provide effective on-line services (Schwester, 2009; Holden, Norris, & Fletcher, 2003; Moulder, 2001).

If it is highly sophisticated, e-government can enhance citizen participation in decision making and build the foundation for stronger democracy or e-democracy. At this stage in their development, local government websites are much more than highways flanked by billboards and a series of service stops along the way. Such sites are beginning to offer interactive online tools that can "extend public space [promoting] consultation and dialogue between citizens and their governments" (Lenihan, 2005, p. 274). For example, focusing on the extent to which the U.S. municipal websites support public involvement within the context of e-democracy, Scott (2006) analyzes the Web presence of the country's 100 largest metropolitan areas. The findings show that most sites facilitated interaction with officials via email or e-comment forms, but very few encouraged citizen engagement in the local public sphere through direct participation or dialogue. Though new ICT applications, such as Web 2.0, have the potential to realize both direct and representative democracy in cyberspace, several obstacles remain regarding e-democracy. (Hilbert, 2009; Holzer, Hu, & Song, 2004). They include the lack of making sustained human capital investments in municipal information technology departments and technology expertise to reduce errors and tampering with the system, the limited access of the poor to e-government, and the uneven telecommunication infrastructure across the country (Schwester, 2009; Moynihan, 2004; Toregas 2001; Cavanaugh, 2000).

In addition to the practical feasibility and implementation of e-democracy, there is also a philosophical debate about the merits of it. Advocates generally stress e-democracy as an extension of governance, while others perceive the implementation of it as running counter to a liberal democracy (Johnson, 2006; Knowles, 2005; Clift, 2004). The optimists argue that e-government can contribute to a more open, responsive, and democratic government (Meijer, 2012; Christensen and Laegreid, 2010). In this sense, the Internet can be used to "enhance our democratic processes and provide increased opportunities for individuals and communities to interact with government for the government to seek input from the community" (Clift cited in Riley & Riley 2003, 11). Similar to the argument made by Putnam (2000) about the relationship between technology and the loss of social connectedness, the critics claim that the impersonal dialogue encouraged by e-government and the cultural values associated with the Internet-based technologies undermine the participatory nature of a democratic political system (Johnson, 2006). Nevertheless, research points to promising advances made by local governments in e-democracy. The City of St. Paul, Minnesota, offers an email notification and personalization option while the Village of Hastings, New York provides an online input system (Clift, 2004).

III. RESEARCH DESIGN

As suggested by existing research, a variety of simple and advanced online features have been adopted by large metropolitan communities. Moreover, the regional location of municipalities, the availability of resources in terms of infrastructure, funding and expertise, and the form of local government influence the scope and functionality of local e-government. While the current research is impressive, gaps remain. Research on the current progress of regional e-government functionality across a wide range of municipalities in terms of population size remains rare. Furthermore, literature has mostly ignored the role of professional chief administrators not only in the context of the manger-council form of government, but across different forms of local governments. This study analyzes the progress of e-government presence and functionality across small, midsized, and large municipalities in the Sunbelt of the United States. It argues that increasing population size, the presence of city or town managers (chief administrators), and increasing wealth of towns and cities (annual revenues per capita) have a consistent impact on improving e-government presence and functionality.

Typically, the assessment of e-government functionality builds on different categories that reflect this increasing complexity and scope (Coursey & Norris, 2008; Haug, 2007; Rho, 2007; Scott, 2006; Petroni & Tagliente, 2005; Chadwick & May, 2003; Moon, 2002). Accordingly, local e-government functionality is defined as the ability of local government websites to communicate information, offer a range of online services, and facilitate citizen participation and deliberation in government. Increasing in complexity and scope, city e-government functionality for the purpose of this study is categorized as follows: 1) billboards; 2) service delivery; 3) citizen participation; and 4) citizen deliberation.

At the lowest level of e-government functionality, the **billboards** level emphasizes the display of relevant information that residents can use to learn about and gain access to a city's administrative departments and elected officials. More complex and broader in scope, the **service-delivery** level includes features that allow residents to engage in financial transactions online or to derive tangible benefits from the use of online services. The **citizen participation** level offers a range of interactive features that facilitate and encourage citizen input in government decision-making and involvement in the community. The final and most advanced level, **citizen deliberation,** allows residents to discuss specific issues on the local policy agenda. Table 16-1 identifies the corresponding indicators for each functional level and, assigning one point per indicator, results in a simple additive *Evaluation Index of Local E-Government Functionality.*

To analyze the progress of local e-government presence and functionality in light of the propositions and assessment approach, this study conducted a detailed content analysis of municipal websites in 2010 and 2014. Based on five population categories to capture small, medium-sized, and large municipalities, a disproportionate stratified sample of 160 incorporated towns and cities in the states of Arkansas (AR), Louisiana (LA), New Mexico (NM), and Oklahoma (OK) forms the basis to identify the specific functionality items across billboards, service delivery, citizen participation, and citizen deliberation. Given the quantitative nature of content analysis in conjunction with data obtained from the latest United States census and respective municipal state associations to determine municipalities' size, wealth, and the presence of chief administrators, descriptive statistics were used to analyze and present the data. With that in mind, we now turn to the analysis of local e-government presence and functionality between 2010 and 2014.

TABLE 16-1	
The Evaluation Index of Local E-Government Functionality	
FUNCTIONALITY LEVEL	INDICATORS
Citizen Deliberation Index Score (1)	• Discussion Forums
Citizen Participation Index Score (3)	• E-Comment Forms • E-Polling • Enabled Links to Civic Organizations
Service Delivery Index Score (4)	• Financial Transactions • Request for Services • Request for Records • Municipal Employment Opportunities
Billboards Index Score (8)	• News and Notices • Council Meeting Agendas • Council Meeting Minutes • Regulations and Ordinances • Finances and Budget • Background of Officials • Email Elected Officials • Email Notification

IV. PRESENCE AND FUNCTIONALITY OF LOCAL E-GOVERNMENT IN THE SUNBELT

Website presence at the local level in the Sunbelt relative to population size has increased between 2010 and 2014, especially for municipalities with a population between 100 and 30,000. As expected, prevalence of municipal websites generally increases for those localities included within the larger population categories. Based on the sample, only about 12 percent of towns between 100 and 2,000 citizens had a website presence in 2010. Though website presence for small towns increased to about 17 percent in 2014, their website presence remains considerably lower compared to their larger counterparts. Municipalities between 2,001 and 10,000 made the greatest leap in website presence increasing from 67 percent in 2010 to 79 percent in 2014. For the same time period, their next larger counterparts, i.e. 10,001-30,000, jumped from 93 percent to 96 percent. As such, the findings illustrate that the presence of local government in cyberspace has increased steadily, especially among the smaller municipalities. Based on established trends, towns and cities in Arkansas, Louisiana, New Mexico, and Oklahoma with a population of more than 30,000 residents continued to offer a fully developed website presence (see Figure 16–1 below).

The descriptive analysis regarding e-government functionality across the selected population categories generally confirms the previous patterns that indicate a relationship between population size and Internet presence.

FIGURE 16–1 Website Presence by Population Category in 2010 and 2014 (in percent)

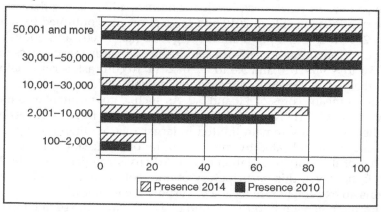

However, there are also some surprises. As indicated by the respective billboards, service delivery, and citizen participation mean scores in Figure 16-2, small municipalities with a population between 100 and 2,000 residents are generally characterized by low e-government functionality in 2010 and 2014. In fact, the data show that billboard functionality is basically stagnating at a low level. Through posted news and notice, meeting minutes and agendas minutes, email access to elected officials, and other means, only a small fraction of small municipalities provide and facilitate access to relevant government information, government departments, and elected officials. Given these findings, it is not surprising that small municipalities with a population between 100 and 2,000 rarely expand into the more sophisticated service delivery and interactive citizen participation levels.

While there is a clear upward trend, a visible expansion into billboards functionality and especially the more sophisticated service delivery and citizen participation levels is clearly visible for towns and cities larger

FIGURE 16–2 E-Government Functionality by Population Category in 2010 and 2014 (mean scores)

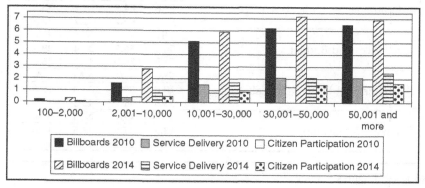

than 2,000. However, significant improvements in these areas occur for municipalities with a population of more than 10,000. In fact, the respective mean scores reach peak levels for municipalities larger than 50,000. These trends are visible in 2010 and have generally continued to accelerate in 2014. For these population categories (i.e. 10,001 and above) and based on a maximum mean score of 8.0, the billboards mean scores range from 5.3 to 6.5 in 2010 and 5.9 to 7.2 in 2014. In contrast, service delivery and citizen participation remain considerably below their respective maximum mean scores of 4.0 and 3.0. As such, e-government as a tool to allow for service delivery and citizen participation in both government and the community remain limited in larger metropolitan areas. Citizen deliberation, as indicated by the availability of discussion forums, exists in a handful of larger Oklahoma and Arkansas municipalities in 2014. Overall, however, this participatory online tool to enhance e-democracy remains an extremely rare local e-government commodity.

With these general findings in mind, we now turn to specific trends of e-government functionality in the selected states. Over the past four years, municipalities in the Sunbelt have generally continued to strengthen the billboard level of local e-government, especially those in Oklahoma and Arkansas. As indicated by Figure 16-3, this level of e-government functionality

FIGURE 16–3 Billboards by State Ranking in 2010 and 2014 (in percent)

	NM	AR	OK	LA
News and Notices	**88.2**	**87.0**	**81.1**	**76.5**
	90.9	75.0	75.8	68.8
	OK	AR	NM	LA
Regulations and Ordinances	**86.5**	**82.6**	**70.6**	**58.8**
	81.8	70.8	53.3	62.5
	AR	NM	LA	OK
Council Minutes	**78.3**	**70.6**	**64.7**	**62.2**
	70.8	63.6	62.5	42.4
	OK	AR	NM	LA
Council Agendas	**94.6**	**78.3**	**73.0**	**64.7**
	84.8	75.0	72.7	56.3
	AR	OK	NM	LA
Email Elected Officials	**69.6**	**64.9**	**64.7**	**58.8**
	58.3	66.7	72.7	37.5
	OK	AR	NM	LA
Finances and Budget	**54.1**	**56.5**	**29.4**	**29.4**
	51.5	50.0	45.5	25.0
	OK	AR	NM	LA
Background Elected Officials	**40.5**	**39.1**	**35.3**	**17.6**
	33.3	41.7	45.5	9.6
	AR	OK	NM	LA
Email Notification	**43.5**	**37.8**	**23.5**	**17.6**
	16.7	24.2	18.2	12.5

NOTE: 2014 figures in bold

at the local level remains the most developed area compared to the more sophisticated service delivery and the citizen participation levels in Arkansas, Louisiana, New Mexico, and Oklahoma. With Oklahoma and Arkansas municipalities leading most of the billboards categories in first or second place, municipalities in the south continue to offer a variety of information services, ranging from information about the history of the municipality and government structure to information about the missions and services provided by the municipal departments. The most prevalent and consistent information provided via the Internet includes council agendas, news and notices, regulations and ordinances as well as council minutes. Less prevalent are the possibilities to sign up for city or town news via email notifications and access background information about elected officials.

Though the service delivery and citizen participation levels are the least developed areas, municipalities were able to improve these areas of local e-government functionality. Municipalities in Oklahoma and Arkansas made considerable advances in these areas of e-government functionality, especially in regards to service deliver. Leading the pack, Figures 16-4 and 16-5 illustrate that Oklahoma residents are increasingly able to take advantage of specific services and citizen participation tools on a consistent basis over the past four years. The most prevalent service delivery items across municipalities include the search for employment opportunities within government and financial transactions. In both of these areas of service delivery, Oklahoma continues to outperform its neighbors. A visible proportion of municipalities, especially those in New Mexico and Oklahoma, allow residents to request services. In contrast, the possibility of requesting records via a government website remains virtually non-existent; only a small number of municipalities in Arkansas offer that online service (see Figure 16-4).

Despite some clear patterns of improvement coupled with consistent decline in e-government functionality to some extent, a large segment of

FIGURE 16-4 Service Delivery by State Ranking in 2010 and 2014 (in percent)

	OK	**AR**	**NM**	**LA**
Employment Opportunities	**86.5**	**73.9**	**70.0**	**52.9**
	81.8	70.8	63.6	50.0
	OK	**LA**	**NM**	**AR**
Financial Transactions	**64.9**	**47.1**	**41.2**	**39.1**
	48.5	31.3	36.4	25.0
	NM	**OK**	**AR**	**LA**
Request for Services	**29.4**	**27.0**	**17.4**	**11.8**
	18.2	18.2	8.3	6.3
	AR	**LA**	**NM**	**OK**
Request for Records	**8.7**	**0.0**	**0.0**	**0.0**
	8.3	0.0	0.0	0.0

NOTE: 2014 figures in bold

353

communities in the Sunbelt remains in the early stages of facilitating citizen participation. Again, Oklahoma and Arkansas municipalities continue to both dominate and improve citizen participation via the Internet, while municipalities in Louisiana have consistently fallen behind. Through enabled links, numerous municipalities across the Sunbelt and especially in Oklahoma allow residents to learn about and get involved in civic organizations, such as churches, youth organizations, sports clubs, and other civic organizations. Other common interactive citizen participation features are the availability of e-comment forms to ascertain input from residents and the explicit encouragement by city halls to volunteer for services on government and civic organization committees or boards (see Figure 16-5). In contrast to four years ago, the opportunity to provide input on local government matters through e-polling has emerged across the selected states. Though in its infancy, this is an important milestone towards e-democracy that also underscores an increasing inter-regional gap in offering citizen participation tools via local government websites. While Oklahoma and Arkansas municipalities tend to be the leading innovators in this area, their counterparts in Louisiana are falling behind and those in New Mexico, except for e-polling, are continuing to catch up.

The specific management perspective provided by city or town managers (chief administrators) makes a difference overall and in every state. The favorable local e-government environment created by chief administrators is obvious for communities across all states and is associated with considerable and consistent gains across the three levels of local e-government functionality in 2010 and 2014. As indicated by Table 16–2, the presence of chief administrators has a visible impact on strengthening billboards and especially both the service delivery and interactive citizen participation levels. In the latter areas the respective mean scores for 2010 and 2014 jump considerably. The degree of local e-government functionality in each state also varies considerably with the presence or lack of chief

FIGURE 16-5 Citizen Participation by State Ranking in 2010 and 2014 (in percent)

	OK	AR	LA	NM
Enabled Links to Civic Org.	67.6	56.5	41.2	23.5
	72.7	54.2	50.0	9.5
	AR	OK	LA	NM
E-Comment Forms	39.1	32.4	29.4	11.8
	33.3	30.3	31.3	18.2
	NM	AR	LA	OK
E-Polling	11.8	8.7	5.9	5.4
	0.0	0.0	6.3	0.0

NOTE: 2014 figures in bold

administrators. Though the differences have narrowed in Oklahoma, the presence of chief administrators continues to make a considerable impact on the level of e-government functionality, especially in Louisiana where respective mean scores more than double across e-government functionality levels.

Finally, the influence of town and city wealth on e-government functionality reveals consistent findings over the past four years that are comparable to the positive influence of chief administrators. Categorizing town and city wealth into low, medium, and high, the data in Table 16-3 generally show that e-government functionality improves as local revenues per capita increase. Except for Arkansas in the areas of billboards and service delivery and New Mexico in the area of service delivery, the respective mean scores based on wealth categories for the remaining states of Louisiana and Oklahoma, in contrast to 2010, increase consistently in 2014. With the noticeable exception of New Mexico and Oklahoma, the most visible increases tend to occur as towns and cities move from the low to the medium categories of wealth. In many cases, the mean scores double or even quadruple, illustrating a positive relationship between wealth of municipalities and e-government functionality.

TABLE 16–2				
Local E-Government Functionality by Chief Administrator in 2010 and 2014 (mean scores)				
LOCAL E-GOVERNMENT FUNCTIONALITY				
STATE	CHIEF ADMINISTRATOR	BILLBOARDS	SERVICE DELIVERY	CITIZEN PARTICIPATION
AR	With	**7.00**	**2.00**	**1.16**
		6.50	2.20	1.20
	Without	**4.76**	**1.17**	**0.79**
		3.90	1.10	0.78
LA	With	**7.33**	**2.66**	**2.33**
		7.00	2.30	2.30
	Without	**3.14**	**0.78**	**0.42**
		2.70	0.46	0.54
NM	With	**6.14**	**1.85**	**0.57**
		4.00	2.25	0.50
	Without	**3.40**	**0.87**	**0.40**
		2.45	0.71	0.29
OK	With	**5.70**	**2.03**	**1.18**
		5.32	1.76	1.16
	Without	**3.90**	**1.10**	**0.67**
		2.26	0.75	0.63

NOTE: Figures in bold reflect 2014 and those in normal fonts 2010

		TABLE 16–3 Local E-Government Functionality by Town/City Wealth in 2010 and 2014 (mean scores)		
		LOCAL E-GOVERNMENT FUNCTIONALITY		
STATE	TOWN/CITY WEALTH	BILLBOARDS	SERVICE DELIVERY	CITIZEN PARTICIPATION
AR	Low	**3.66**	**0.66**	**0.33**
		2.60	0.60	0.20
	Medium	**6.63**	**1.90**	**1.45**
		6.18	2.00	1.27
	High	**5.66**	**1.66**	**1.66**
		5.33	1.67	1.67
LA	Low	**3.25**	**0.83**	**0.41**
		2.67	0.50	0.50
	Medium	**5.25**	**1.75**	**1.50**
		6.00	1.67	2.00
	High	**6.00**	**2.00**	**2.00**
		6.00	2.00	2.00
NM	Low	**4.00**	**1.33**	**0.33**
		3.20	1.20	0.20
	Medium	**4.66**	**1.16**	**0.50**
		5.75	1.50	0.50
	High	**6.50**	**2.50**	**1.00**
		6.50	1.00	0.50
OK	Low	**4.30**	**1.15**	**1.00**
		4.40	1.20	1.20
	Medium	**5.11**	**2.00**	**1.05**
		4.00	1.62	0.94
	High	**7.14**	**2.42**	**1.14**
		6.23	1.71	1.00

NOTE: Figures in bold reflect 2014 and those in normal fonts 2010

V. CONCLUSION

The research presented in this chapter represents one of the first extensive and systematic analyses of government websites across small, medium, and large municipalities in Oklahoma and the benchmark Sunbelt states of Arkansas, Louisiana, and New Mexico. Guided by the literature on e-government functionality and based on a random sample of 160 municipalities, this study analyzes the ability of local governments to provide information, services, and democracy-enhancing tools via the Internet in 2010 and 2014. This chapter argues that increasing population size, presence of chief administrators, and increasing levels of municipal wealth improve e-government presence and functionality at the local level.

Based on both content analysis of government websites and descriptive statistics, the findings illustrate the presence and progress of local e-government functionality within the last four years. While the findings support the study's propositions, the analysis also illustrates mixed results with respect to the advances made in local e-government functionality.

Larger towns and cities managed by chief administrators and characterized by more wealth tend to attain relatively high levels of e-government functionality. These municipalities, in contrast to their smaller, less wealthy counterparts, and without chief administrators at the helm of government, do particularly well in terms of providing a wide array of information on their websites concerning the structure, function, and operation of government. Though municipalities in Oklahoma and Arkansas continue to lead innovation in local e-government compared to those in New Mexico and Louisiana and online service delivery in conjunction with citizen participation via the Internet have improved, a relatively small proportion of municipalities provides online services or facilitates a meaningful level of e-participation in government. Particularly apparent is the virtual lack of citizen deliberation via online forums to discuss policies and provide input across the sampled municipalities. Only very few municipalities in Arkansas and Oklahoma offer this advanced level of local e-government functionality. Despite these mixed results, overall local e-government functionality, i.e. the combination of billboards, service delivery, and citizen participation, has improved since 2010, especially in New Mexico and Oklahoma (see Figure 16-6).

FIGURE 16–6 Overall Local E-Government Functionality in 2010 and 2014

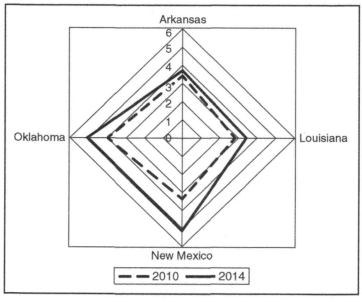

As indicated, towns and cities continue to improve their presence in cyberspace as a means to inform their residents. With respect to providing online services and enhancing citizen involvement in government and community through the new information communication technologies, local governments like the City of Fort Smith in Arkansas and the City of Enid, Oklahoma are on the verge of moving beyond the billboards and service delivery stages of e-government functionality. In contrast, municipalities in New Mexico continue to catch up, while their counterparts in Louisiana are generally falling behind. Despite the advances made in information communication technologies in recent decades, local governments in the Sunbelt, similar to many municipalities across the country, have not fully embraced and implemented the range e-government possibilities, especially in the area of e-democracy. Given the results of this study and the potential of e-government to expand into e-democracy, scholars interested in the subject matter should discuss and study the practical and theoretical implications of e-government as a means to facilitate citizen engagement in democratic decision making.

HIGHER EDUCATION POLICY IN OKLAHOMA

Elizabeth S. Overman and Markus S. Smith

You can't have a high standard of scholarship without having a high standard of integrity, because the essence of scholarship is truth.

John Hope Franklin[1]

I. INTRODUCTION

I n the summer of 2014, Davida Michels was awarded a bachelor's degree from an Oklahoma university following three years of study. She was able to achieve this feat because she accepted student loans and took as many courses as possible every semester, every intersession, and during the summer. Today she is in her first year of graduate school planning to graduate in 2016. When she graduated as salutatorian from her Oklahoma high school her son was one and a half years old. Unlike many young single mothers, Davida resisted the urge to drop out of high school and instead continued to pursue her education. As a new single mother she got a job to support her family. Her job enabled her to get her own apartment and she made enough to afford child care. But, working as an agent for a car rental company, Davida was paid by the hour and did not have any benefits including health insurance. If she did not work she would not get paid. The worst happened. She got sick, and unfortunately, she had no health insurance and little in savings. She ended up without a job and had to move in with her parents. Her next option was to get a college degree. Student loans enabled her to move, once again, into her own apartment. To date she has taken out $62,000 in student loans. She plans to complete her graduate program in the spring of 2015. Davida is seeking her college degrees at a time when state funding for higher education has been deeply cut and student tuition and fees are climbing sharply. This chapter examines higher education policy in Oklahoma through a consideration of its impact, the social role of public goods, origins, and the substantive role of the state's community colleges, higher education governance, the politics of funding, and the underlying philosophical debate.

II. THE IMPACT OF OKLAHOMA HIGHER EDUCATION

In the 2012-2013 academic year, a record 186,000 students enrolled in Oklahoma colleges and universities. The vast majority of college students in Oklahoma attend public institutions of higher education. Public colleges and universities were created and are supported by state government. For many residing in the state of Oklahoma, the opportunity to get a college education is possible only because the state created and funded a system of higher education. The state enjoys a handsome return on this investment. The Oklahoma State Regents for Higher Education estimate that for every $1 of state funding, Oklahoma public higher education returns $4.72 to the state. In the aggregate, expenditures from Oklahoma public higher education generate $9.2 billion in economic output and support more than 85,000 Oklahoma jobs (Oklahoma State Regents for Higher Education, 2014). Oklahoma higher education has a positive impact on the state and its citizens.

Education is a Public Good

Higher education is a unique public good in American society. Thomas Jefferson argued that the survival of a free people depends upon an educated citizenry (Berkes, 2011). In addition to preparing students for their tasks as democratic citizens, studies show that in the contemporary world "there is no longer an alternative path to prosperity than through higher education" (Oklahoma State Regents for Higher Education, 2012, p. 2). Oklahoma's Governor, Mary Fallin, acknowledges this. As the 2013-2014 president of the National Governor's Association, she released a report that extolls the advantages of a college education both for individuals and for the economy of their state (National Governors Association, 2013). Yet, today only one in four Oklahoma students graduate from high school prepared for college or careers (Ramirez, 2013).

Why does the state want more Oklahomans to earn postsecondary degrees? College graduates make higher personal income tax contributions because they have increased earnings. They suffer fewer bouts of unemployment. This, in turn, fosters local and state economic development. Further, college graduates are usually politically engaged. They are healthier, volunteer more, and commit fewer crimes. All of this contributes to the common good. Urban economic research shows that communities with concentrations of highly educated and highly skilled people tend to boost wages not only for themselves but even for those without degrees (Selingo, 2013, p. 168).

III. ORIGINS OF OKLAHOMA HIGHER EDUCATION

Although early higher education in the United States was the province of elites, the tie between democratization and economic development was a reality decades before Oklahoma entered its territorial phase of 1890. The Cherokee National Female Seminary, founded in 1851, was purchased by the 1909 Oklahoma State Legislature from the Cherokee Government. Benedictine monks established St. Gregory's University in 1875 in Atoka as a mission school. Soon it was relocated to Konawa as an abbey. With permission from the Vatican, Sacred Heart College appeared in 1877. By 1883 it was approved by the territorial government, and as the Catholic University of Oklahoma it moved in 1910 to Shawnee, a strategic location between the capitals of the Citizen Potawatomi Nation and the Seminole Nation. In 1922, it would be renamed St. Gregory's College.

The Creek and Cherokee Nations together with the American Baptist Churches of America, founded Bacone College in 1880 as the Indian University in Muskogee, Oklahoma. Today, it is the oldest continuously operating institution of higher education in the state. The antecedents of the University of Tulsa appeared in 1882 in Muskogee with the founding of the Presbyterian School for Indian Girls. The institution was rechartered in 1894 by the Presbyterian Women's Board of Home Missions. Renamed and relocated as the University of Tulsa in 1920 it became Oklahoma's largest private university.

The Congress of the United States issued territorial laws in 1889 that called for the establishment of a liberal arts and professional education college, an agricultural and mechanical arts college that would come under the land grant **Morill Act of 1862**, and a normal school college. The first meeting of the territorial legislature in Guthrie was so consumed with locational disputes for these three prizes that the territory's first governor, George Steele from Indiana, appointed by President Harrison, packed up in disgust and returned to his Hoosier home. Before he left, however, he signed, under the provision of the Oklahoma Territory Organic Act, the 1890 laws creating three institutions of higher education.

Norman would be the site of the Oklahoma Territorial University known today at the University of Oklahoma, officially founded by law on December 19, 1890. It was to provide liberal arts and professional education. Provisions for the Oklahoma Territorial Normal School at Edmond, renamed the University of Central Oklahoma and the Stillwater Oklahoma Territorial Agricultural and Mechanical College which became Oklahoma State University were signed into law on December 25, 1890. The following year, 1891, university classes would convene in Edmond and Stillwater. Students began studying on the Norman campus in 1892.

In the four years from 1897 to 1901, the Territorial Legislature authorized the Colored Agricultural and Normal University at Langston, renamed Langston University; Normal School for Teachers at Alva, today known as Northwestern Oklahoma State University; the Normal School for Teachers at Weatherford becoming Southwestern Oklahoma State University; and the Oklahoma University Preparatory School at Tonkawa, now Northern Oklahoma College which was established in 1901. Though

Northern Oklahoma College would serve as a preparatory school for those who would attend the University of Oklahoma in Norman, college-level courses were not added to its curriculum until 1921 (Smithheisler, 2007).

When the Oklahoma territory attained statehood in 1907, the State Legislature established the Industrial Institute and College for Girls (what would later be called the University of Science and Arts of Oklahoma) at Chickasha and the School of Mines and Metallurgy at Wilburton. It is known today as Eastern Oklahoma State College, which was established in 1908, making it one of the oldest community colleges in the state.

Origins and Roles of Oklahoma Community Colleges

Oklahoma community colleges have a longstanding history. The majority of Oklahoma's community colleges were established within the first four decades of the 1900s. Northern Oklahoma College (NOC) was established in 1901. Eastern Oklahoma State College was established in 1908 and only offered degrees in mining and engineering. In 1927, the school would eventually change its name to Eastern Oklahoma State College, where they would offer pre-college level instruction. The Miami School of Mines was established with the passing of SB 225 in 1919. In 1924, a special legislative session changed the name to Northeastern Oklahoma Junior College and general education courses were added to the curriculum. In 1943, the college officially changed its name to Northeastern Oklahoma A&M College (commonly referred to as NEO), which is located in Miami, Oklahoma (Birdsong, 2007). Murray State College, located in Tishomingo, Oklahoma, first opened its doors in 1908 to roughly 100 students who were primarily Chickasaw and Choctaw. The institution was not actually granted college status until 1922 (Rodden, 2007). Altus Junior College was established in 1926. After the passing of SB 492 in 1974, the college officially changed its name to Western Oklahoma State College. Connors State College became an accredited 2-year college in 1927. Seminole Junior College was established in 1931. The first college classes were actually offered at Seminole High School. In 1969, the Oklahoma State Regents for Higher Education recommended that all public-funded junior colleges separate themselves from their local high school connections. The separation was finalized in 1971. In 1996, Governor Frank Keating signed SB 836, which authorized the college's name be changed to Seminole State College (Wilson, 2007b). Poteau Junior College first enrolled students in 1933. In 1971, the college changed its name to Carl Albert State College, named in honor of Carl Albert (from Oklahoma) who had served as the Speaker of the U.S. House of Representatives (1971-1976) (Wilson, 2007a). El Reno Junior College was established in 1938. In 1991, the college officially changed its name to Redlands Community College (Tabor, 2007).

The remaining and current community colleges would be established after the 1960s starting with Oklahoma State University Technical Institute renamed Oklahoma State University-Oklahoma City in 1961. In 1970, Mid-Del Junior College was built and would become Oscar Rose Junior College and finally Rose State College. Tulsa Community College was formed in 1970. And, South Oklahoma City Junior College became Oklahoma City Community College in 1972. Throughout the past century these Oklahoma community colleges have been extremely important in providing great opportunities for thousands of students. Community colleges are one of the most important options for higher education. They are vital for providing an opportunity for nontraditional students–that is, high school dropouts, adults interested in seeking knowledge but not obtaining a degree, first-generation college students, and especially those seeking a wide-range of technical or professional certification programs and applied degrees such as nursing, occupational therapy assistant, paralegal, physical therapist assistant, or auto mechanics to name a few. These types of college degrees often lead to significant economic gains. For example, students awarded associate degrees often "earn 15% to 30% more in annual income than high school graduates of similar race and ethnicity, parental education, marital status, and job experience" (Ballantine & Spade, 2008). In Oklahoma, students who graduate from a community college are employed at a higher rate, 18.7%, than the 12.2% for U.S. as a whole (Oklahoma Association of Community Colleges, 2014).

Community colleges are also important due to their great numbers in terms of campuses spread throughout the U.S., open-admissions access, and growth. According to the U.S. Department of Education, roughly 62% of the nearly 1,700 community colleges in the U.S. have an open-admissions policy. In addition, nearly 50% of all college students enrolled in public institutions are enrolled at community colleges (U.S. Department of Education, 2001). Oklahoma community colleges are experiencing heightened enrollment. From FY2000 to FY2010, community colleges in Oklahoma increased enrollment from 88,000 students to nearly 118,000 – an astounding increase of 34%. The factors contributing to this dramatic growth are "not only returning adult students, but also significant increases in recent high school graduates, international students, and students who already have college degrees" (Oklahoma Association of Community Colleges, 2014).

IV. HIGHER EDUCATION GOVERNANCE

Today, the largest provider of higher education in Oklahoma are those public institutions governed by the Oklahoma State Regents for Higher Education (OSRHE). The state of Oklahoma has 28 public colleges and universities, 13 of which have more than one campus. Fourteen of the colleges and universities are independent and three are proprietary or for profit institutions. All institutions supported completely or in part by direct legislative appropriations from the Oklahoma State Legislature are governed by OSRHE. Each governor makes one nine-year appointment to the regent's board annually. OSRHE was organized in 1941, a time when the state began to professionalize and upgrade organizational systems through a public vote that amended the state's constitution adding Article XIII-A. The newly configured Oklahoma State System of Higher Education extended the state's reach by authorizing OSRHE to prescribe academic standards for all public and private institutions of higher education in Oklahoma. State institutions are funded by monies allocated to each institution by OSHRE once the state legislature votes on the total appropriation to higher education. The courses of study, tuition and fees within limits imposed by the state legislature, degrees granted, the Oklahoma Guaranteed Student Loan Program, and the scope of activities on each public campus are subject to permission and review by OSHRE. A chancellor appointed by the board of gubernatorial appointees manages OSHRE. Title 70 of the state constitution created trustee boards that deal directly with operations management on each campus.

OSHRE, following the U.S. Department of Education Higher Education Classification Guidelines, developed a three-tier categorization framework. Institutions are classified as either research, teaching, or community colleges. The 12 community colleges are charged with the provision of a general education for all students through one to two year technical or occupational programs that lead directly to jobs in the immediate area. To provide this sort of training means that the community colleges leaders work with local employers and state officials who monitor employment trends and employer needs. At the same time, community colleges provide university-parallel study for students intending to transfer to institutions that grant bachelor's degrees. And these institutions develop a variety of continuing education programmatic activities for adults and out-of-school youth.

V. The Politics of Higher Education Funding

In 2010, the Republicans swept into state office controlling two of the three main branches of state government. Mary Fallin assumed the governorship and her fellow Republicans held 32 seats in the Oklahoma Senate and 70 seats in the Oklahoma House of Representatives. This large majority expanded to become a supermajority in both chambers in 2012 with the party holding 36 seats in the Senate and 72 in the House (McNutt, 2010b). Wayne Greene, editor of *The Tulsa World* points out that today the Republicans enjoy "complete numerical dominance of both chambers, control of all statewide elective offices and the entire congressional delegation" (2014, p. G6). This dramatic political shift was driven by the state's Tea Party activists and others who believed that government was too big, costly, and intrusive. Big government, according to the Governor is "not the Oklahoma way "as she has set about reshaping the agenda for higher education funding with the concurrence of the State Legislature. This has fueled an unprecedented drop in the annual state appropriation for public colleges and universities that began when Democratic Governor Brad Henry faced The Great Recession of 2008. Between 2008 and 2013 there was a 26.2% decrease in finding per student in Oklahoma (Olif, et al, 2013). Robert Daufennbach, Director of the Center for Economic and Management Research at Price College of Business at the University of Oklahoma notes that the funding decline for higher education also comes at a time

> when Oklahoma significantly lags the nation in the proportion of adults 25 and older who have bachelor's or advanced graduate degrees and ranks 40th overall. Of the state's adult population, 23.8 percent has a bachelor's or advanced degree compared to a national average of 28.6 percent. (Winslow, 2014, p. E6)

Although the nation is slowly pulling out of the Great Recession of 2008 and Oklahoma's tax collections are on the rise, the situation for students and colleges and universities is getting worse. In 2014, the Governor submitted a budget to the state legislature calling for a 5% across the board reduction in all state spending. This comes at a time when Oklahoma's "gross revenue collections are at an all-time high, but funds for the state's discretionary budget have a $188 million shortfall." As Gene Perry of the Oklahoma Policy Institute points out, this comes at a time when Oklahoma's "gross revenue collections are at an all-time high, but funds for the state's discretionary budget have a $188 million shortfall." Perry continues to say that even though some of the revenue is going to individuals and to corporations, "the lost revenue is going mostly to transportation spending and oil and gas industry tax breaks" (2014). Meanwhile, the oil and gas industry is getting large tax breaks for deploying horizontal drilling or "fracking."

Paying for the provision of broadly accessible educational opportunities requires a state subsidy coupled with tuition charges paid by enrollees. When the state subsidy falls, tuition rates rise. Even if one attends a private college, the state government may still play a significant role in covering the costs of the education. Students at private, nonprofit and for-profit schools receive grants or other forms of financial aid directly funded by state governments. In fact, undergraduates at private colleges receive on average more than $2,500 in state grants or other financial aid from state and local government. Not including tuition, that amount of financial aid is several hundred dollars more than the average undergraduate at a public college receives from the state.

The National Center for Budget and Policy Priorities points out that lowering state appropriations leads to tuition increases. One of the questions students face today is whether or not college is affordable even though data show that college graduates make much more money, suffer lower unemployment rates, and generally have a better quality of life, from stronger marriages to living longer (CollegeStats, 2013). Another question for society is whether or not the reduction in college affordability and the massive shift in tuition from the state of Oklahoma to the students compromises our democracy. Public higher education has traditionally been regarded as the great equalizer, the mechanism by which people make something out of themselves. How many potential students are shut out, not because they aren't capable, but because they are unwilling or unable to take on the heavy burden of student loan debt?

In 2011-12, well over half of Oklahoma college and university students were in debt with student loans averaging $23, 636 (Institute for College Access & Success, 2014). Economists worry about the impact of college student debt on the state's economy. Unlike other forms of debt, student loans cannot be discharged through bankruptcy. Such debt means big box purchases such as homes and cars may be deferred as former students, now graduates, remain at home or in cheap housing in order to pay off their loans. They may defer or even forgo graduate school. The irony is that as little as thirteen years ago, tuition for one year at a public university in Oklahoma was as little as $5,000 annually (Arnold, 2014). It is fair that this generation of college students must assume so much debt?

State funding decreases not only lead to rising tuition rates. The cuts also result in fewer tenure-track faculty positions, limited course offerings, deferred maintenance of campus facilities, reduced library holdings and services, elimination of open computer labs and printing centers. Whether or not a professor is full or part-time, tenured or on a tenure track may not seem important. However, studies show that the chances of completing a college degree in a timely fashion is directly related to the tenure status of one's professor. "Freshmen who have many of their courses taught by adjuncts are less likely than other students to return as sophomores" (Jaschik, 2010).

Outside of academia, few understand the role of the professorate in society. First, all faculty, whether full or part time, are officers of the university. They are responsible for sharing in the governance of the institution. In addition to teaching, they are charged with carrying out research and other forms of scholarship, as well as service to the university, the community in which they reside and their profession. The core value for the professorate is the search for truth. To do this faculty must be allowed to do research and speak freely while upholding the rights of their students to do the same. Ideally, the three primary responsibilities of the professorate are seamless and reinforce each other to the benefit of students and institutions. When the state cuts funding to institutions, class sizes swell and the faculty are unable to spend as much time with each individual student.

The Underlying Philosophical Debate

Behind the fundamental changes in state funding of higher education is an argument about the role of government. The guiding neo-liberal open market philosophy was adopted by the Oklahoma Republicans since Ronald Reagan captured the presidency in 1981. Proponents of free-markets think that people are "utility-maximising rational egoists." Each of us, as individuals, always act in our own best interests if markets are open and free. From this perspective, education is not a common good that benefits the whole of society, but a private good that solely benefits the individual. Therefore, education is a commodity and sold individually like a smart phone or a laptop.

Those who oppose this view see education as a common good that benefits society as a whole. Because, in the aggregate, the college educated make so many contributions to society, they create goods for everyone. Conceptually, the common good originated over two thousand years ago in the writings of Plato, Aristotle, and Cicero. John Rawls, a contemporary ethicist, defines the common good as "certain general conditions that are . . . equally to everyone's advantage" (1971, p. 246) From the end of World War II until 1980, education was regarded as a common good. In the 1980s, with the advent of supply side economics, the conception began to shift.

Everyone agrees that the state needs to develop a skilled workforce as rapidly as possible. But, we face a choice between a society where people accept modest sacrifice for a common good or a more contentious society where individuals and groups protect their own benefits.

NOTE

1. Dr. John Hope Franklin (1915 – 2009) was born in Tulsa, Oklahoma. In 1995, he was awarded the Presidential Medal of Freedom, the nation's highest civilian honor. He was an American historian of the United States and former president of Phi Beta Kappa, the Organization of American Historians, the American Historical Association, and the Southern Historical Association. Franklin is best known for his work *From Slavery to Freedom*, first published in 1947, and continually republished. More than 3 million copies have been sold.

BIBLIOGRAPHY

Abramson, Paul R., Aldrich, John H. and Rohde, David W. (2014). *Change and Continuity in the 2008 and 2010 Elections*. Washington, D.C.: Congressional Quarterly Press.

ACE Book 2011: Accountability for a Competitive Economy. State Chamber of Oklahoma. http://www.okstatechamber.com/additional/21stCentury/2011AC EBook.pdf.

ACE Book 2014: Accountability for a Competitive Economy. State Chamber of Oklahoma. http://www.okstatechamber.com/additional/researchfdn/2014%20 ACE%20Book_WEB.pdf.

ACT. (2013). *ACT Profile Report-Oklahoma*. Iowa City, IA: ACT, Inc. Retrieved from https://www.act.org/newsroom/data/2013/pdf/profile/Oklahoma.pdf.

Agee, Steven C. (2011). *Oklahoma's Oil and Natural Gas Industry: Economic Impact and Jobs Report*. Oklahoma City, OK: Oklahoma Energy Resources Board. Retrieved from http://www.oerb.com/Portals/0/docs/2012%20OERB%20 Economic%20Impact%20Study%20FINAL.pdf.

Adkison, D.M. & McNair Palmer, L. (2001). *The Oklahoma State Constitution*. Westport, CT: Greenwood Press.

Agency Directory. (2014). Oklahoma City, OK: State of Oklahoma. Retrieved from http://www.ok.gov/agency.php.

Alderman, E. & Kennedy, C. (1991). *In Our Defense: The Bill of Rights in Action*. New York: William Morrow and Company, Inc.

Aldrich, G. (1973). *Black Heritage of Oklahoma*. Edmond, OK: Thompson Book and Supply Co.

Administrative Office of the Courts (Oklahoma). (1994). *Annual Report*. Oklahoma City, OK: Author.

Administrative Office of the Courts (Oklahoma). (1995a). *Annual Report*. Oklahoma City, OK: Author.

Administrative Office of the Courts (Oklahoma). (1995b). *The Supreme Court of Oklahoma* [Brochure]. Oklahoma City, OK: Author.

Administrative Office of the Courts (Oklahoma). (1995–1996). *The Oklahoma Court of Criminal Appeals*, Brochure. Oklahoma City, OK: Author.

Administrative Office of the Courts (Oklahoma), (1998). *Annual report*. Oklahoma City, OK: Author.

Administrative Office of the Courts (Oklahoma). (2011). *The Judiciary. Annual Report, FY-2011*. Oklahoma City, OK: Author.

Allen N. and S. Daniels. (2013). *2013 Thumback.com Small Business Friendliness Survey: Methodology & Analysis*. San Francisco, CA: Ewing Mario Kauffman Foundation. Retrieved from http://www.thumbtack.com/media/survey/ 2013/friendliness/v1/ThumbtackMethodologyPaper2013.pdf.

Allen, Silas. (2013, June 16). "Undocumented Oklahoma City University Student Sees Benefits of Federal Deferred Action for Childhood Arrivals Policy." *Daily Oklahoman*. Retrieved from http://newsok.com/undocumented-oklahoma-city-university-student-sees-benefits-of-federal-deferred-action-for-childhood-arrivals-policy/article/3852066.

Allen, Silas. (2013, June 16). "Undocumented OSU-OKC Student: 'Oklahoma is My Home.'" *Daily Oklahoman*. Retrieved from http://newsok.com/undocumented-osu-okc-student-oklahoma-is-my-home/article/3852064.

American Council for an Energy-Efficient Economy. (2013). *The State Energy Efficiency Scorecard*. Washington, DC: Author. Retrieved January 7, 2014. http://aceee.org/state-policy/scorecard.

Anderson, James, David Brady, and Charles Bullock. (1978). *Public Policy and Politics in America*. California: Wadsworth Publishing Company, Inc.

Anderson, James E. (2000). *Public Policymaking*. Boston: Houghton Mifflin Company.

Andrews, R. (2006). *Managing the Environment, Managing Ourselves: A History of American Environmental History*. New Haven, CT: Yale University Press.

Arizona. SB 1070. (2010). Phoenix, AZ: Arizona State Legislature. Retrieved from: http://www.azleg.gov/legtext/49leg/2r/bills/sb1070s.pdf

Arnold, Kyle. (2014, March 2). "Burdensome Student Loans a Society Ill. *Tulsa World*, p. E1.

Arnold, Peri. (1976). "The First Hoover Commission and the Managerial Presidency." *The Journal of Politics, 33.1*, 46–70.

Aspin, Larry. (1999). "Trends in Judicial Retention Elections, 1964–1998." *Judicature, 83*, 79.

Associated Press. (1998, September 30, AM Cycle). "Topless Snapshot Enrages Candidate." National Political, Dateline: Shawnee, Oklahoma.

Associated Press. (1999a, August 25, AM cycle,). "Man Given Suspended Sentence in Kidnapping and Torture of Common-law Wife." State and Regional, Dateline: Woodward, Oklahoma.

Associated Press. (1999b, October 18, PM Cycle). "Tide Turning Against Judicial Elections." State and Regional, Dateline: Oklahoma City.

Associated Press. (2000a, July 6, BC Cycle). "Appeals Court Disqualifies Judge from Case." State and Regional, Dateline: Oklahoma City.

Associated Press. (2000b, February 24, AM Cycle). "Judicial Retention Bill Fails in Legislative Committee." State and Regional, Dateline: Oklahoma City.

Associated Press. (2011, August 24). "Two Lawmakers Throw Support behind Tribes' Water Rights Case." *The Oklahoman*, 13.

Association of County Commissioners of Oklahoma. (2005). *Responsibilities of County Commissioners*. Oklahoma City, OK: Author. Retrieved from www.oklacco.com.

Attocknie, Dana. (2011, February). "arrior Nerd: Pawnee Fights for Native Rights." *Oklahoma Native Times, 1.4*, 6–9.

Aynesworth, H. (2006, February 20). "That Sucking Sound Would Be the Whole Town Going Under." *The Washington Times*. Retrieved from ttp://washingtontimes.com/national/20060220-121016-2913r.htm.

Bailey, Brianna. (2013, September 29). "Companies Cash in Oklahoma Job Creation Incentives Even After Layoffs." *Daily Oklahoman*.

Baird, D. & D. Goble. (1990). *The Story of Oklahoma*. Norman, OK: University of Oklahoma Press.

Baker, Dean & Deutsch, Rivka. (2009). "The State and Local Drag on the Stimulus" Washington, DC: Center for Economic and Policy Research. Retrieved from http://www.cept.net/documents/publications/stimulus-2009-05.pdf.

Bality, A., Caneday, L., Fite III, E., Wikle, T., & Yuan, M. (1998). *IRB Management Plan 1999*. Tahlequah, OK: Oklahoma Scenic Rivers Commission, 1–94.

Ball, Carolyn (2009, Fall). "What is Transparency?" *Public Integrity, 11.4,* 293–307.

Ballantine, Jeanne H. and Spade, Joan A. (2008). *Schools and Society: A Sociological Approach to Education (3rd Ed.).* Thousand Oaks, CA: Pine Forge Press (Sage).

Barber, Brian. (2012, November 8). "After Vision2, Tulsa Leaders Ready to Shift Focus onto Fix Our Streets Program." *Tulsa World.* Retrieved from Newspaper Source Plus database.

Barker, Steve. (2012). *2012 Demographic State of the State Report: Oklahoma State and County Population Projections Through 2075.* Oklahoma City, OK: Oklahoma Department of Commerce. Retrieved from http://okcommerce.gov/assets/files/data-and-research/Population_Projections_Report-2012.pdf.

Barrett, Edith J. (1995). "The Policy Priorities of African American Women in State Legislatures." *Legislative Studies Quarterly, 20,* 223–248.

Barrett, Katherine, Greene, Richard, Mariani, Michele, & Sostek, Anya. (2003, February). "The Way We Tax." *Governing, 16.5,* 20–31.

Baum, Lawrence. (2004). *The American Courts.* Boston, MA: Houghton Mifflin.

Baum, Lawrence & Kemper, Mark. (1994). "The Ohio Judiciary." In *Ohio Politics* (Chap. 13). Kent, Ohio: Kent State University Press.

Bays, Brad A. (2002). "Tribal-state Tobacco Compacts and the Motor Fuel Contracts in Oklahoma." In Bays, Brad A. and Erin Hogan Fouberg's *The Tribes and the States.* Lanham, MD: Rowman and Littlefield: pp. 181–210.

Bazar, Emily. (2008, January 9). "Strict Immigration Law Rattles Okla. Businesses." *USA Today.* Retrieved from http://usatoday30.usatoday.com/news/nation/2008-01-09-immigcover_N.htm

Bellmon, Henry. (1992). *The Life and Times of Henry Bellmon.* Tulsa, OK: Council Oak Books.

Benjamin, Gerald & Malbin, Michael J. (1992). "Term Limits for Lawmakers: How to Start Thinking about a Proposal in Process." In Gerald Benjamin & Michael J. Malbin (Eds.), *Limiting Legislative Terms* (Chap. 1). Washington, DC: Congressional Quarterly Press.

Berkes, Anna. (2011, August 24). "An Educated Citizenry is a Vital Requisite for Our Survival as a Free People (Quotation). *Thomas Jefferson Encyclopedia.* Charlottesville, VA: Monticello and the University of Virginia. Retrieved from http://www.monticello.org/site/jefferson/educated-citizenry-vital-requisite-our-survival-free-people-quotation

Birdsong, Jeff. (2007). Northeastern Oklahoma A&M College. *Oklahoma Historical Society's Encyclopedia of Oklahoma History.* Oklahoma City: Oklahoma Historical Society. Retrieved from http://digital.library.okstate.edu/encyclopedia/entries/N/NO013.html.

Bisbee, Julie. (2010, September 26). "Voters May be Surprised by Lengthy State Question Ballot in November," *Daily Oklahoman.*

Blatt, David. (2010, March 22). "Making Oklahoma's Tax Expenditures More Transparent and Accountable." *State Tax Notes,* 847–863. Retrieved from http://masswildlife.com/dor/docs/dor/stats/tax-expenditure-commission-materials/transparency-accountability-studies/tax-expenditures-more-accountable-oklahoma.pdf.

Boumediene v. Bush. (2008, June 12). No. 06-1195. U.S. Supreme Court.

Bowman, Ann O'M., & Kearney, Richard C. (2002). *State and Local Government* (5th ed). Boston, MA: Houghton Mifflin Company.

Bowman, Ann O'M., & Kearney, Richard C. (2012). *State and Local Government: The Essentials* (5th ed). Boston, MA: Wadsworth/Cengage.

Bowman, Ann O'M., & Kearney, Richard C. (2015). *State and Local Government: The Essentials* (6th ed). Stamford, CT: Cengage Learning.

Boyd, Donald J. (2006)."State Budgets: Recent Trends and Outlook." In *The Book of the States: 2005 Edition,* 401–407. Lexington, KY: The Council of State Governments.

Brace, Paul & Butler, Kellie Sims. (2001). "New Perspectives for the Comparative Study on the Judiciary: The State Supreme Court Project." *The Justice System Journal,* 22, 243–262.

Braybrooks, Melissa, Ruiz, Julio, and Accetta, Elizabeth. (2011, March). "State Government Tax Collections Summary Report 2010." *Governments Division Briefs.* Retrieved from http://www2.census.gov/govs/statetax/2010stcreport.pdf.

Brooks, Harold E. & Doswell III, Charles A. (2001). "Deaths in the 3 May 1999. Oklahoma City Tornado from a Historical Perspective." *American Meteorological Society,* 17.3, 354–361.

Brown, M. M. & Schelin, S. (2005). "American Local Governments: Confronting the E-Government Challenge." In H. Drüke (Ed.), *Local Electronic Government: A Comparative Study.* London, Routledge: 229–268.

Bruce, Donald, Fox, William F., Stokely, William B. and Luna, LeAnn. (2009, April 13). *State and Local Government Sales Tax Revenue Losses from Electronic Commerce.* Knoxville, TN: University of Tennessee. Retrieved from http://cber.utk.edu/ecomm/ecom0409.pdf.

Brus, Brian. (2007, May 25). "OKC's MAPS3 Survey Shows Strong Support for Mass Transit." *The Journal Record.*

Bureau of Labor Statistics. (2011). "Local Area Unemployment Statistics." Washington, DC: United States Department of Labor. Retrieved from http://data.bls.gov/pdq/SurveyOutputServlet?data_tool=latest_numbers &series_id=LASST40000003.

Busch, Andrew E. (1996). "Early Voting: Convenient, but …?" *State Legislatures,* 22.8, 25–27.

Button, James & Hedge, David. (1996). "Legislative Life in the 1990s: A Comparison of Black and White State Legislators." *Legislative Studies Quarterly,* 21, 199–218.

Caldeira, Gregory A. (1983). "On the Reputation of State Supreme Courts." *Political Behavior,* 5, 83–108.

Canon, Bradley C. & Baum, Lawrence. (1981). "Patterns of Adoption of Tort Law Innovations: An Application of Diffusion Theory to Judicial Doctrines." *The American Political Science Review,* 75, 975–987.

Carney, Kristen, and Morales, Anthony. (2014). *Oklahoma Demographics.* Austin, TX: Cubit Planning, Inc. Retrieved from http://www.oklahoma-demographics.com/counties_by_population.

Carp, Robert A., Stidham, Ronald, & Manning, Kenneth L. (2004). *Judicial Process in America.* Washington, D.C.: Congressional Quarterly Press.

Carson, J. (2006). *Oklahoma Agriculture: The First 100 Years.* Oklahoma City, OK: Oklahoma Department of Agriculture.

Carter, M. Scott. (2011, February 7). "Find a Way Forward." *The Journal Record.* Retrieved from http://journalrecord.com/2011/02/07/%E2%80%98find-a-way-forward%E2%80%99-capitol/.

Carter, M. Scott (2011, February 7). "New Workers' Compensation Law May Require a Few Tweaks." *The Journal Record.* Retrieved from http://journal record.com/ 2014/02/07/msc-workers-comp-again-capitol/.

"Case closed? Poultry lawsuit under review." (2010, November). Tulsa World. Editorial. Retrieved from http://www.tulsaworld.com/opinion/article.aspx?subjectid=61&articleid=20101109_61_A13_During754398&allcom=1.

Catalyst. (2004). "The Bottom Line: Connecting Corporate Performance and Gender Diversity." New York: Catalyst.

Cavanaugh, W. J. (2000, Fall). "E-Democracy: Thinking About the Impact of Technology on Civic Life." *National Civic Review, 89*: 229–34.

Center for Digital Government. (2008). *Digital Cities Survey*. Retrieved from http://www.govtech.com/dc/surveys/cities/89/2008.

Center for Immigration Studies. (2008 & 2011). Retrieved from http://cis.org.

Center for Responsive Politics. (2010). "Outside Spending." *OpenSecrets.org*. Retrieved from http://www.opensecrets.org/outsidespending.

Center for Worklife Policy (2007). New York. Retrieved from http://www.worklifepolicy.org.

Chadwick, A. & May, C. (2003, April). "Interaction Between States and Citizens in the Age of the Internet: 'E-government' in the United States, Britain, and the European Union." *Governance, 16*: 271–300.

Chapman, Steve. (2013, May 2). "Facing Facts About Illegal Immigration." Retrieved from http://www.creators.com/opinion/steve-chapman/facing-facts-about-illegal- immigration.html

Christensen, T. & Laegreid, P. (2010). "Civil Servants' Perceptions Regarding ICT Use in Norwegian central government. *Journal of Information Technology & Politics.* 7: 3–21.

City of Oklahoma City. (2004). "Who's Who on the Horseshoe?" Oklahoma City, OK: Author. Retrieved from www.okc.gov.

Clark, Blue. (2009). *Indian Tribes of Oklahoma: A Guide*. Norman, OK: University of Oklahoma Press.

Clark, W. (1988). "Constitutional Reform and Economic Development in Oklahoma." *State Policy and Economic Development in Oklahoma: 1988*. Oklahoma City, OK: Oklahoma 2000 Inc.

Claunch, Forrest. (2002, Spring/Summer). "Con: Is the Lottery a Good Gamble for Oklahoma? Not By a Clear Measure." *Oklahoma Policy Studies Review, 3.1*, 3, 6–7.

Clift, L. S. (2004). "E-Government and Democracy: Representation and Citizen Engagement in the Information Age." Retrieved from www.mail-archive.com/do-wire@lists.umn.edu/msg00161.html.

Climate Change and Energy. (2010). Oklahoma State University's Sustainability. Stillwater, OK: Oklahoma State University. Retrieved from http://sustainability.okstate.edu/index.php/applications/projects/climate-change-and-energy.

Cobb, Roger B. & Elder, Charles D. (1972). *Participation in American Politics: The Dynamics of Agenda-Building*. Baltimore, MD: Johns Hopkins University.

Colberg, Sonya. (2011, March 14). "Mental Health Budget Cuts Affect Communities," *The Oklahoman*, p. 1A.

Coleman, Bill. (2006). "Oklahoma Lobbyists' Job Salary." Retrieved from http://sw2.salary.com/salarywizard/layouthtmls/ok/sw21_compresult_state_ok)cm02000070.html.

CollegeStats. (2013). *The Happy State of College Graduates*. Retrieved from http://collegestats.org/articles/2013/05/the-happy-state-of-college-graduates.

Constitution Revision Study Commission. (1991). *The Constitution of the State of Oklahoma: Recommendations for Revision, Final Report.* Oklahoma City, OK: Author.

Cooper, M.S., J. Dahlgren, D. Barnes, M. Fram, R. West, & M. Smolen. (1994). *How Do We Improve Water Quality in the Illinois River Basin? A report by the Oklahoma Cooperative Extension Service.* Stillwater, OK: Oklahoma State University.

Copeland, Gary W. & Rausch, John David. (1993). "Sendin' Em Home Early: Oklahoma Legislative Term Limitations." *Oklahoma Politics, 2.1,* 33–50.

Copeland, Larissa. (2014, January). "Choctaw Nation Designated a 'Promise Zone.'" *Biskinik,* 1.

Corporation for Enterprise Development. (2014, February 19). "Asset and Opportunity Scorecard/Outcome Profile: Oklahoma." *Assets and Opportunity Scorecard,* Washington, DC: Author. Retrieved from https://dl.dropboxusercontent.com/u/19732897/outcome-profile-OK.pdf.

Council of State Governments (CSG). (1996). *Book of the states.* Lexington, KY: Author.

Council of State Governments (CSG). (2003). *Book of the states.* Lexington, KY: Author.

Council of State Governments. (2010). Retrieved from www.csg.org.

Council of State Governments. (2014). Retrieved from www.csg.org.

Coursey, D. & Norris, D. (2008, May June). "Models of E-Government: Are They Correct? An Empirical Assessment." *Public Administrative Review, 68:* 523–36.

Court Upholds Cockfighting Ban. (2004, March 31). *The Oklahoman,* p. 1A.

Cowger, Thomas. (1999). *The National Congress of American Indians.* Lincoln, NE: University of Nebraska Press.

CR's 100 Best Corporate Citizens 2012. (2012). *Corporate Responsibility Magazine.* Retrieved from http://www.thecro.com/files/100BestF.pdf

CRS Report for Congress. (2006). *USA PATRIOT Improvement and Reauthorization Act of 2005 (H.R. 3199): A Legal Analysis of the Conference Bill.* Washington, DC: Congressional Research Service. Retrieved from http://www.law.umaryland.edu/marshall/crsreports/crsdocuments/rl33239_01172006.pdf

Daffron, Brian. (2012, March 9). "Oklahoma Tribes Still Waiting for Governor Fallin's Native Liaison." *Native Strength.* Retrieved from: http://nativestrength.com/tag/gov-mary-fallin

Daffron, Brian. (2013). "Oklahoma's Power Brokers: The 26 Natives Holding State Positions." *Indian Country Today.* Retrieved from http://indiancountrytodaymedianetwork.com/2013/07/18/oklahomas-power-brokers-21-natives-holding-state-positions-150479

Dauffenbach, Robert C. (1994). *State Government Finance in Oklahoma After SQ 640.* Oklahoma City, OK: Oklahoma 2000 Inc.

Dauffenbach, Robert C. (2005, April). "Economy Watch—Focus on Oil and Gas." *Oklahoma Business Bulletin,* 1–8.

Dauffenbach, Robert C. (2006a, April). "Business Highlights" *Oklahoma Business Bulletin,* 1–7.

Dauffenbach, Robert C. (2006b). "The Skinny on Oklahoma's Personal Income." In *State Policy and Economic Development in Oklahoma: 2006,* 1–20. Oklahoma City, OK: Oklahoma 21st Century, Inc.

Dauffenbach, Robert C. (2014, February). "State Rankings on Key Economic Indicators, State and Local Finance, and K-12 Education Statistics: A Graphical Analysis." *Oklahoma Business Bulletin,* 6–18.

Davis, James A., Metla, Saiand Helan, Josh. (2006). "Profiles & Stereotypes of Lobbyists in Oklahoma." *Oklahoma Politics 15*, 1–18.

Debo, Angie. (1985). *Prairie City: The Story of an American Community*. Tulsa, OK: Council Oaks Books, LTD.

Debo, Angie. (1940). *And Still the Waters Run*. Princeton, NJ: Princeton University Press.

Debo, Angie. (1949, Reprint 1987). *Oklahoma: Foot-loose and Fancy-free*. Norman, OK: University of Oklahoma Press.

Del Barco, Mandualit. "California Ballot Measure Targets Illegal Immigrants." (2009, July 16). NPR. Retrieved from http://www.npr.org/templates/story/story.php?storyId=106657563

Delcour, Julie. (2004, March 28). "Bottom-of-the-Barrel Pay." *Tulsa World*, p. G1.

Demillo, A. (2006). "Supreme Court Denies Arkansas Permission to Sue Oklahoma in Dispute Over Water Pollution." *Associated Press*. 2–22.

Dinan, John. (2010). State Constitutional Developments. *In Council of State Governments, Book of the States 2010*. Lexington, KY: The Council of State Governments.

Dinger, Matt. (2011, June 19). "Oklahoma City National Memorial Museum Gets its 2 Millionth Visitor." *NewsOK*. Retrieved from http://newsok.com/oklahoma-city-national-memorial-museum-gets-its-2-millionth-visitor/article/3578537.

Doak, John. (2011, March 18). "Working to Provide Aid Following Catastrophes," *The Oklahoman*, p. 9A.

Dolan, Kathleen and Ford, Lynn. (1995). "Women in the State Legislatures: Feminist Identity and Legislative Behaviors." *American Politics Quarterly, 23*, 96–108.

Dresang, Dennis & Gosling, James J. (2002). *Politics and Policy in American States and Communities*. New York: Longman.

Durocher's OKC Business. (2004). Istook introduced bill to simplify taxes. Retrieved from www.okcbusiness.com.news.

Dye, Thomas R. & McManus, Susan A. (2012). *Politics in States and Communities* (14th Ed). Upper Saddle River, NJ: Pearson/Longman.

Eagly, Alice H. & Carli, Linda L. (2007, September). "Women and the Labyrinth of Leadership," *Harvard Business Review*, pp. 6–7.

Edmondson, Drew. (2005, June 13). "AG Sues Poultry Industry for Polluting Oklahoma Waters: Press Release." Retrieved from http://www.oag.state.ok.us/oagweb.nsf/0/2448aafc29ac39668625701f0067edbe?OpenDocument.

Economics of High Technology in Oklahoma. (1985). Stillwater, OK: Office of Business and Economic Research, College of Business Administration, Oklahoma State University.

Egan, T. (2006). *The Worst Hard time: The Untold Story of Those Who Survived the Great American Dust Bowl*. New York, NY: Houghton Mifflin Company.

Elazar, Daniel. (1966). *American Federalism: A View From the States*. New York: Thomas Y. Crowell Co.

Elazar, D. J. (1972). *American Federalism: A View From the States (2nd Ed.)*. New York: Thomas Y. Crowell.

Elazar, Daniel. (1982). "The Principles and Traditions Underlying State Constitutions." *Publius: The Journal of Federalism, 12*, 11–25.

Elbel, Fred. (2007). "Original intent of the 14th Amendment." Retrieved from http://www.14thamendment.us/birthright_citizenship/original_intent.html.

Ellis, Randy. (2004, November 4). Ballot Issues Meet Voter's Approval. *The Daily Oklahoman*, p. 14A.

Ellis, Randy. (2013, February 27). "Indian Gaming Revenues Continue to Climb in State." *The Oklahoman*, 1A.

Ellis, Randy. (2014, February 10). "Gov. Fallin's Reforms Progress." *The Oklahoman.* Retrieved from http://newsok.com/oklahoma-house-approves-state-employee-pay-raise-bill/article/3942200.

Emerson, Alicia R. (2002). *Legislator's Guide to Oklahoma Taxes.* Oklahoma City, OK: Oklahoma House of Representatives, Research Division.

Energy Conservation Program (2010, October). Oklahoma State University website. Retrieved from *http://www.okstate.edu/energy.*

EPIC. (2005). "USA PATRIOT ACT SUNSET." Retrieved from http://epic.org/privacy/terrorism/usapatriot/sunset.html

Epstein, Lee, Segal, Jeffrey A., Spaeth, Harold J., and Walker, Thomas G. (2003). *The Supreme Court Compendium: Data, Decisions & Developments.* Washington, D.C.: CQ Press.

Ernst and Young. (2009). Groundbreakers Study, Diversity an Equation for Success. London, UK. Author. Retrieved from http://www.cy.com/GI.en/Issues/Dirving-growth/Groundbreakers---Diversity---an--equation--for--success.

Eulau, Heinz, Wahlke, John C., Buchanan, William, and Ferguson, Leroy C. (1959, September). "The Role of the Representative: Some Empirical Observations on the Theory of Edmund Burke." *American Political Science Review, 53.3,* 742–756.

Fairbanks, Jenille, Plowman, Kenneth D., and Rawlins, Brad L. (2007, February). "Transparency in Government Communication." *Journal of Public Affairs, 7.1,* 22–37.

Fallin, Mary. (2014b, February 3). "State of the State Address." Retrieved from http://www.ok.gov/governor/documents/2-3-14%202014%20State%20of%20the%20State%20press%20copy%20final.pdf.

Federal Funds Information for States. (2004). *State Policy Reports, 22.* Washington, D.C.: Author.

Ferguson, Larry R. (1989). *Oklahoma Legislative Process—A Training Manual* (5th Ed.). Oklahoma City, OK: Minority Leader of the Oklahoma House of Representatives.

Fischer, LeRoy H. (1981). *Oklahoma Governors 1907–1929: Turbulent Politics.* Oklahoma City, OK: Oklahoma Historical Society.

Focht, Will. (2004). "A Research and Education Agenda." In *Oklahoma's Environment: Pursuing a Responsible Balance*, 7–12. Oklahoma City, OK: The Oklahoma Academy.

Focht, Will and Hull, J. (2004, Spring/Summer). "Framing Policy Solutions in a Conflicted Policy Environment: An Application of Q Methodology to a Superfund Cleanup. *Oklahoma Policy Studies Review, 1,* 30–37.

Former Haskell County Food Stamp Recipient Earns College Degrees. (2013, June 27). Oklahoma Department of Human Services, Office of Communications.

Fowler, Linda L. (1992). "A Comment on Competition and Careers." In Gerald Benjamin & Michael J. Malbin (Eds.), *Limiting Legislative Terms* (Chap. 9). Washington, DC: Congressional Quarterly.

Fox, William F. and Lune, LeAnn. (2006). "State Tax Collections: Eroding Tax Bases. In *The Book of the States: 2005 Edition* (411-16). Lexington, KY: The Council of State Governments.

Fox News Latino. (2013, September 21). "Oklahoma College Presidents Push for Immigration Reform." Retrieved from http://latino.foxnews.com/latino/politics/2013/09/21/oklahoma-college-presidents-push-for-immigration-reform/.

Friedrich, Carl. (1963). *Man and His Government.* New York: McGraw-Hill.

Gail, William & Harris, Benjamin. (2007, Dec. 14). "Savings and Retirement: What are Defined Plans?" *Tax Policy Center: Tax Policy Briefing Book.* Retrieved from http://www.taxpolicycenter.org/briefing-book/key-elements/savings-retirement/defined-contribution.cfm.

Galanter, Marc (1974). "Why the 'Haves' Come Out Ahead: Speculations on the Limits of Legal Change." *Law and Society Review, 9,* 95–160.

Garrett, Thomas A. and Rhine, Russell M. (2006, January/February). "On the Size and Growth of Government," *Federal Reserve Bank of St. Louis Review, 8.1,* 13–30.

Garrett, R. K. and Jensen, M. J. (2011). E-Democracy Writ Small: The Impact of the Internet on Citizen Access to Local Elected Officials. *Information Communication & Society, 14.2,* 177–197.

Gallup.Com. (2013). Gallup Politics. Fewer Americans Than Ever Trust Government to Handle Problems. Retrieved from http://www.gallup.com/poll/164393/fewer-americans-ever-trust-gov-handle-problems.aspx.

Geer, John G., Schiller, Wendy J., Segal, Jeffrey A., & Glencross, Dana K. (2014). *Gateways to Democracy, The Essentials: An Introduction to American Government.* Ohio: Cengage Learning, pp. 4–16.

Gerschenkron, A. (1962). *Economic Backwardness in Historical Perspective.* Cambridge, MA: The Belknap Press.

Gibson, Arrel Morgan. (1981). *Oklahoma: A History of Five Centuries.* Norman, OK: University of Oklahoma Press.

Gibson, Lorenzo Tucker, Jr. (1961). *The Political Significance of the Oklahoma Merit System.* (Unpublished master's thesis). Stillwater, OK: Oklahoma State University.

Gillham, O. (2006, December 1). "Picher Relief: Hometown Exodus." *TheTulsa World.* Retrieved from http://www.leadagency.org/modules.php?op=modload&name=News&file=article&sid=211&POSTNUKESID=da814c37235aab63aa27e02e2878c3f2.

Githens, Marianne, Norris, Pippa and Lovenduski, Joni. (1994). *Different Roles, Different Voices: Women and Politics in the United States and Europe.* New York: Harper Collins College Publishers.

Glick, Henry R. (1991). "Policy Making and State Supreme Courts." In John B. Gates & Charles A. Johnson (Eds.), *The American Courts.* Washington, DC: Congressional Quarterly Press.

Glick, Henry and Emmert, Craig. (1987). "Selection Systems and Judicial Characteristics." *Judicature,70,* 230.

Goble, Danney. (1980). *Progressive Oklahoma, the Making of a New Kind of State.* Norman, OK: University of Oklahoma Press.

Goble, Danney & Scales, J.R., Jr. (1983). "Depression Politics: Personality and the Problem of Relief." In Kenneth Hendrickson, Jr. (Ed.), *Hard Times in Oklahoma: The Depression Years* (pp. 3–21). Oklahoma City, OK: Oklahoma Historical Society.

Godfrey, E. (2012, September 8). "Declining Quail Population: Some Hunters Think Oklahoma Should Close Quail Hunting Season." *The Oklahoman.*

Retrieved http://newsok.com/declining-quail-population-some-hunters-think-oklahoma-should-close-quail-hunting-season/article/3708245/?page=1.

Goodsell, Charles T. (1994). *The Case for Bureaucracy: A Public Administration Polemic* (3rd ed.). Chatham, NJ: Chatham House.

Governing's State and Local Sourcebook 2006. (2006). "Environmental Spending" (p. 21). Retrieved from: http://www.census.gov/govs/www/estimate04.html.

Graham, Ginnie. (2011, March 22). "Children's Rights Group Releases Critical Reports on DHS," *The Oklahoman*, p. 5A.

Gray, Virginia & Peter Eisinger. 1997. *American States and Cities* (2nd Ed.). New York: Longman.

Greater Oklahoma City Chamber of Commerce. (2005). *MAPS for Kids Background.* Retrieved from www.okcchamber.com

Green, John Clifford, Rozell, Mark J., and Wilcox, Clyde (Eds.). (2004). *The Values Campaign? The Christian Right and the 2004 Elections.* Washington, DC: Georgetown University Press.

Greene, Wayne. (2011, May 31). "Majority of Bills Never Get to Starting Line in Legislature." *Daily Oklahoman*, p. A1.

Greene, Wayne. (2014, March 23). Legislative: The Quiet Before the Storm. *Tulsa World*, p. G6.

Greene, Wayne. (2014, March 30). "Fallin's Horror Show: It Came from Washington." *Tulsa World.* Retrieved from http://www.tulsaworld.com/opinion/waynegreene/wayne-greene-fallin-s-horror-show-double-feature-it-came/article_97d34450-54a4-5618-a64b-504607b2f034.html.

Greiner, John. (2003, July 28). "State Cuts Near Bone, Group Says." *The Daily Oklahoman*, p. 1-A.

Greiner, John. (2004, November). "Rooster Battle is Over: Supreme Court Declines Cockfighting Ban Appeal." *The Oklahoman.* Retrieved http://newsok.com/rooster-battle-is-over-br-supreme-court-declines-cockfighting-ban-appeal./article/2874268.

Hale, D. (1982). "The People of Oklahoma: Economics and Social Change." In Anne Hodges Morgan and H. Wayne (Eds.), *Oklahoma: The Views of the Forty-sixth State.* Norman, OK: University of Oklahoma Press.

Hale, Duane K. and Gibson, Arrell Morgan. (1991). *The Chickasaw (Indians of North America).* Chelsea House Publishers.

Halper, Alvin and McGreevy, Patrick. (2009, January 17). "California Controller Suspends Tax Refunds, Welfare Checks. *Los Angeles Times.* Retrieved from http://articles.latimes.com/2009/jan/17/local/me-budget17.

Hamdan v. Rumsfeld. (2006, June). Supreme Court of the U.S., No. 05-184.

Hamilton, Ann (Ed.). (2003). *Oklahoma Almanac 2003–2004.* Oklahoma City, OK: Oklahoma Department of Libraries.

Hamilton, Arnold. (2000, December 3). Artist-senator Prepares His Statue of an American Indian to Stand Atop Oklahoma's New Capitol Dome. *The Dallas Morning News*, p. 41A.

Hamm, Keith E. and Hedlund, Ronald D. (1990). "Accounting for Change in the Number of Committee Positions." *Legislative Studies Quarterly*, 15.2, 201–226.

Hanson, R. (1996). "Intergovernmental Relations." In Virginia Gray & Herbert Jacob (Eds.), *Politics in the American States.* Washington, DC: Congressional Quarterly Press.

Hardy, Richard J., Dohns, Richard R., and Leuthold, David. (1995). *Missouri Government and Politics*. Columbia, MO: University of Missouri Press.

Harrigan, John J. & David C. Nice. (2004). *Politics and Policy in States and Communities* (8th Ed.). New York: Pearson/Longman.

Hartz, Jim. (2014, Feb.15). "Jim Hartz: Will Rogers Memorial Museum Caught Unaware by Consolidation Plan." Retrieved from http://www.tulsaworld .com/opinion/readersforum/jim-hartz-will-rogers-memorial-museum-caught-unaware-by-consolidation/article_5c35cca2-e0ab-53eb-804d-2f48e0b16a53.html#user-comment-area.

Haug, V. A. (2007). "Local Democracy Online: Driven by Crisis, Legitimacy, Resources, or Communication Gaps?" *Journal of Information Technology & Politics, 4.2*, 79–99.

HB 1804—Where's the 'Shock and Awe? (2008, February 28). Oklahoma Political News Service. Retrieved from http://okpns.wordpress.com/2008/02/28/hb-1804-wheres-the-shock-and-awe/

Hedlund, Ronald D. (1992). "Accommodating Members' Requests in Committee Assignments: Individual Level Explanations." In Gary F. Moncrief & Joel A. Thompson (Eds.), *Changing Patterns in State Legislative Careers* (pp. 49–174). Ann Arbor, MI: University of Michigan Press.

Heeks, R. and Bailur, S. (2007). "Analyzing E-Government Research: Perspectives, Philosophies, Theories, Methods, and Practice." *Government Information Quarterly, 24.2*, 43–65.

Hegen, Dirk. (2009, April 22). "2009 Immigration-Related Bills and Resolutions in the States January-March 2009). *Immigrant Policy Project*. Denver, CO: National Council of State Legislatures (NCSL). Retrieved from http://www .ncsl.org.

Heidler, D. S. and Heidler, J. T. (2007). *Indian Removal*. New York: Norton.

Heintze, T. and Bretschneider, S. (2000). "Information Technology and Restructuring in Public Organizations: Does Adoption of Information Technology Affect Organizational Structures, Communications, and Decision-making?" *Journal of Public Administration Theory and Research, 10*, 801–830.

Hennessy-Fisk, Molly. (2013, September 5). "Oklahoma Governor Orders Father of 'Baby Veronica' Extradited." *Los Angeles Times*.

Henschen, Beth M., Moog, Robert, and Davis, Steven. (1990). "Judicial Nominating Commissioners: A National Profile." *Judicature, 73*, 329–333.

Hepner, Mickey. (2004). "Corporate Tax Shelters Cost Oklahoma $69 million." *Oklahoma Policy Digest, 2.1*, 7–8.

Hernon, P. (2006). "E-Government in the United Kingdom." In Hernon, R. Cullen & H. C. Relyean (Eds.), *Comparative Perspectives on E-Government*. Landham, MD: The Scarecrow Press, 55–65.

Hibbing, John R. (1991). *Congressional Careers: Contours of Life in the U.S. House of Representatives*. Chapel Hill, NC: University of North Carolina Press.

Hicks, John D. (1931). *The Populist Revolt*. Minneapolis, MN: University of Minnesota Press.

Hilbert, M. (2009, April/June). "The Maturing Concept of E-Democracy: From E-Voting and Online Consultations to Democratic Value Out of Jumbled Online Chatter." *Journal of Information Technology & Politics, 6*, 87–110.

Hinton, M. (1997, August 21). "Task Force Mulls Messy Problem of Chicken Waste." *The Daily Oklahoman*. Retrieved from http://www.newsok.com/theoklahoman/archives/.

Ho, Tat-Kei, A. (2002, July/August). "Reinventing Local Governments and the E-Government Initiative." *Public Administration Review. 62*, 434–44.

Holden, S. H., Norris, D. & Fletcher, P. (2003, June). "Electronic government at the local level: Progress to date and future issues." *Public Performance & Management Review, 26*: 325–44.

Holloway, Harry & Myers, Frank S. (1993). *Bad times for good ol' boys: The Oklahoma County Commissioner Scandal*. Norman, OK: University of Oklahoma Press.

Holmes, Alexander. (2004). "A Lottery for Oklahoma?" In *State policy and economic development in Oklahoma: 2004* (pp. 53–64). Oklahoma City, OK: Oklahoma 21st Century, Inc.

Holzer, Marc, Hu, Lung-Tung, Song, Seok-Hwi. (2004). "Digital government and citizen participation in the United States." In A. Pavlichev & G. D. Garson (Eds.), *Digital Government: Principle and Best Practices*. Hershey, PA: IDEA Group Publishing, 306–19.

Housel, Steve. (2013, November). "Oklahoma's Adoption of the Merit System: J. Howard Edmondson and Cooperative Federalism." *Oklahoma Politics, 23*, 65–83.

Hovey, Kendra A. and Hovey, Harold A. (Eds.). (2004). *Congressional Quarterly State Fact Finder 2004*. Washington, D.C.: Congressional Quarterly Press.

Hovey, Kendra A. and Hovey, Harold A. (2006). *Congressional Quarterly's Fact Finder 2006*. Washington, D.C.: Congressional Quarterly Press.

Howard, W. W. (1889, May 18). "The Rush to Oklahoma." *Harper's Weekly, 33*, 391–94. Retrieved from http://www.library.cornell.edu/Reps/DOCS/landrush.htm.

Immigration Reform and Control Act (IRCA) (1986). 8 U.S.C. § 1324.

Imperial Refining Company-National Priorities List. (2007). *Environmental Protection Agency*. Retrieved from http://www.epa.gov/earth1r6/6sf/pdffiles/0605091.pdf.

Inhofe, James. (2003). "Inhofe: Tar Creek Memorandum is Real Progress." Press Release of Senator Inhofe. Retrieved from http://inhofe.senate.gov/pressapp/record.cfm?id=203429.

Inhofe, James. (2006, May 4). "Inhofe-Henry-Boren announce Tar Creek buyout." Press Release of Senator Inhofe. Retrieved from http://inhofe.senate.gov/pressapp/record.cfm?id=255524.

Institute for College Access & Success. (2014). Student Loan Debt by State. *CollegeInSight*. Retrieved from http://college-insight.org/#explore/go&h=44b1 36f4d155362e46d5da65ab244409.

International City/County Management Association and Public Technology, Inc.

(ICMA/PTI). (2002). *Digital Government Survey*. Washington, DC: Author.

International City/County Management Association and Public Technology, Inc. (2001). *Is Your Local Government Plugged In? Highlights of the 2000 Electronic Government Survey*. Baltimore: University of Maryland. International City/County Management Association and Public Technology, Inc. (2000). *Digital Government Survey*. Washington, DC: Authors.

Internet Sales Tax Bill Faces Hurdles. (2013, June 19). *Governing*. Retrieved from http://www.governing.com/blogs/fedwatch/gov-internet-sales-tax-sponsor-outline-hurdles-facing-bill.html.

Interview with David Bond, Oklahoma House Communication Specialist. (2007). Author.

Ireland, Tim C., and Amos, Orly M. (2011, April). "Recent Trends in Oklahoma's Per Capita Personal Income" *Oklahoma Business Bulletin,* 5–13.

Ireland, Tim C., Snead, Mark C., and Steven R. Miller (2006, January). "Oklahoma: If We Aren't High-tech, Where are our Competitive Advantages?" *Oklahoma Business Bulletin,* 11–20.

Jadlow, J.W. & Lage, Gerald M. (1992). "Oklahoma in the Global Economy." In *Oklahoma Economic Outlook* (pp. 66–19). Stillwater, OK: Oklahoma State University Press.

Janda, Kenneth, Berry, Jeffrey M., & Goldman, Jerry. (1997). *The Challenge of Democracy: Government in America* (5th ed.). Boston, MA: Houghton Mifflin Co.

Jaschik, Scott. (2010, June 21). "Adjuncts and Retention Rates." *Inside Higher Ed.* Retrieved from http://www.insidehighered.com/news/2010/06/21/adjuncts#sthash.7RAHYOaI.dpbs.

Jewell, Malcolm E. & Olson, David M. (1982). *American State Political Parties and Elections.* Homewood, IL: Dorsey Press.

Jewell, Malcolm. (1982). *Representation in State Legislatures.* Lexington, KY: University of Kentucky Press.

Johnson, J. (2006). "The Illiberal Culture of E-Democracy." *Journal of E-Government,* 3.4, 85–112.

Jones, R.W. & McClure, N. (1997, August 20). *How Much Spending Money do Oklahoma Consumers Really Have Available?* Oklahoma City: Oklahoma Council for Public Affairs. Retrieved from http://www.ocpathink.org.

Jones, Stephen. (1974). *Oklahoma Politics in a State and Nation.* Enid, OK: The Haymaker Press.

Justice at Stake. (2014). "In Oklahoma Leadership Shuffle, Some Anti-Court Measures Die." *Gavel Grab.* Retrieved from http://www.gavelgrab.org/?p=69570.

Kagan, Robert, Cartwright, Bliss, Friedman, Lawrence M., & Wheeler, Stanton. (1977). "The Business of State Supreme Courts, 1870–1970." *Stanford Law Review, 30,* 121–156.

Kathlene, Lyn. (1995). "Alternative Views of Crime: Legislative Policymaking in Gendered Terms." *Journal of Politics, 57,* 696–723.

Keefe, William J. & Ogul, Morris. (1997). *The American Legislative Process: Congress and the States.* Upper Saddle River, NJ: Prentice Hall.

Keel, Jefferson. (2012). "State of Indian Nations." Retrieved from http://www.ncai.org/events/2012/01/26/2012-state-of-indian-nations.

Keep America Beautiful. (2014, January 7). "Recycle Bowl Competition." Stamford, CT: Author. Retrieved from http://recycle-bowl.org/state-ranking/.

Keller, M. (1987). "The Politics of State Constitution Revision, 1820–1930." In Kermit L. Hall, Harold Melvin Hyman, & Leon V. Sigal, *The Constitutional Convention as an Amending Device* (pp. 67–111). Washington, DC: American Historical Association and American Political Science Association.

Kelly, Kate. (2007, April 11). Personal Interview. Tourism Director for the Tahlequah Chamber of Commerce.

Kersch, Ken. (1997). "Full Faith and Credit for Same-sex Marriages." *Political Science Quarterly, 112.1,* 117–136.

Kershen, D. (1997). "An Oklahoma slant to environmental protection and the politics of property rights." *Oklahoma Law Review.* 50: 391–398.

Kettl, Donald F. (2005). "The Civil Service," In *The Politics of the Administrative Process,* Washington, D.C.: CQ Press, p. 209.

Killian, J.H. (Ed.) (1987). *The Constitution of the United States of America: Analysis and Interpretation.* Washington, DC: U.S. Government Printing Office.

Killman, Curtis, Hinton, Mick, & Hoberock, Barbara. (2007, February 5). "Report lists gifts to lawmakers" *Tulsa World.*

Kincaid, John. (Ed.). (1982). *Political Culture: Public Policy and the American States.* Philadelphia, PA: Institute for the Study of Human Issues.

King, L. J. (1982, January/February). "Local government use of information technology: The next decade." *Public Administration Review. 42,* 25–36.

Kirkpatrick, Samuel A. (1978). *The Legislative Process in Oklahoma: Policy Making, People, and Politics.* Norman, OK: University of Oklahoma Press.

Kirksey, Jason F. and Wright, III, David E. (1992). "Black Women in State Legislatures: The View from Oklahoma." *Oklahoma Politics, 1,* 67–80.

Klein, John Jay. (1963). *The Oklahoma Economy.* Stillwater, OK: Oklahoma State University Press.

Klos, Joseph J. (1965). *Public Welfare in Oklahoma.* Stillwater, OK: Oklahoma State University Press.

Knowles, T. (2005). "Digital Democracy in Alaska." In E. A. Blackstone, M. L. Bonanno & S. Hakim (Eds.). *Innovations in E-Government: The Thoughts of Governors and Mayors.* Landham, MD: Rowman & Littlefield Publishers (131–41).

Kolodziej, Matthew. (2014, March 5). "Local Anti-Immigration Laws Die as More States and Municipalities Pursue Pro-Immigration Policies." Retrieved from http://immigrationimpact.com/2014/03/05/local-anti-immigrant-laws-die-as-more-states-and-municipalities-pursue-pro-immigrant-policies.

Korbe, Tina. (2011, June 15). "Oklahoma Supreme Court Upholds State Anti-illegal-immigration Law." *Hot Air.* Retrieved from http://hotair.com/archives/2011/06/15/oklahoma-supreme-court-upholds-state-anti-illegal-immigration-law/.

Kraft, M. (2010). *Environmental Policy and Politics* (5th Ed.). Upper Saddle River, NJ: Pearson/Longman

Kraft, Michael E. & Furlong, Scott R. (2004). *Public Policy: Politics, Analysis, and Alternatives.* Washington, DC: CQ Press.

Krehbiel, Randy. (2003, April 13). "State Workforce is Up." *Tulsa World,* A23.

Krehbiel, Randy (2006, October 15). "Tax Breaks Increased Along with State's Revenues." *Tulsa World,* A-19.

Krehbiel, Randy. (2013, September 25). "Public Employees Wary of Plans to Reform Retirement Programs." *Tulsa World.* Retrieved from http://www.tulsaworld.com/news/government/public-employees-wary-of-plans-to-reform-retirement-programs/article_d4a6125d-2538-5e86-b496-4f2b5ca78a69.html.

Krehbiel, Randy. (2014, March 11). "Oklahoma House Approves State Employee Pay Raise Bill." *Tulsa World.* Retrieved on from http://www.tulsaworld.com/gov-fallin-s-reforms-progress/article_cd91e465-b9b8-548b-93b9-1ec995f91842.html.

Lackmeyer, Steve. (2003, December 7). 10 Years Later: Projects Put City on MAPS. *The Daily Oklahoman,* 1A.

Lackmeyer, Steve. (2008, March 2). "Economics, Politics are at Odds Over State's Immigration Law." Retrieved from http://newsok.com/article/3210714

Lage, Gerald M. (1996). "Restructuring of the Oklahoma economy." *Oklahoma Business Bulletin, 64.3,* 6–12.

Lage, Gerald M.. Moomaw, Ronald L., and Warner, Larkin. (1977). *A Profile of Oklahoma Economic Development: 1950–75.* Oklahoma City, OK: Frontiers of Science Foundation.

Lambert, Valerie. (2007). *Choctaw Nation: A Story of American Indian Resurgence.* Lincoln, NE: University of Nebraska Press.

Land Protection Division: Tar Creek Section (2014). Oklahoma Department of Environmental Quality. Retrieved from http://www.deq.state.ok.us/lpd-new/TarCreekindex.html.

Oklahoman Staff Reports. (2013). "Oklahoma State University to Receive Energy Efficiency Rebate." Retrieved January 7, 2014. http://newsok.com/oklahoma-state-university-to-receive-energy-efficiency-rebate/article/3890166

Law, Iris J. & McNichol, Elizabeth. (2009). "New Fiscal Year Brings No Relief From Unprecedented State Budget Problems," Washington, D.C.: Center on Budget and Policy Priorities. Retrieved October 12, 2010 from http://www.cbpp.org/cms/?fa=view&id=id=711.

Lawton, Millicent. (1992). "Oklahoma Votes Approve Tax Limitation Initiative." *Education Week.* Retrieved from http://www.edweek.org/ew/articles/1992/03/18/26okla.h11.html.

Leeds, Stacy. (2007). "Defeat or Mixed Blessing?: Tribal Sovereignty and the State of Sequoyah." *Tulsa Law Review, 43,* 5–17.

Legislative Candidates Listed. (1992, October 30). *NewsOK.com.* Retrieved from http://newsok.com/legislative-candidates-listed/article/2410843.

Lawler, James J. and Spurrier, Jr., Robert L. (1991). "The Judicial System." In David R. Morgan, Robert E. England, & George Humphreys (Eds.), *Oklahoma Politics and Policies* (Chap. 8). Lincoln, Nebraska: University of Nebraska Press.

League of Women Voters of Oklahoma, (1994). *A Resource Guide to Oklahoma Courts.* Oklahoma City, OK: Author.

Leavitt, Noah (2004). "Is Oklahoma a New Human Rights Hot Spot? Why the State's Judges and Governor were Right to Stop an Execution that Nearly Violated International Law." *Findlaw's Legal Commentary.* Retrieved from http://writ.findlaw.com/commentary/20040524_leavitt.html.

Lemov, Penelope. (2011, May 18). "States Look to Collect Internet Sales Taxes." *Governing.* Retrieved October 9, 2011 from http://www.governing.com/columns/public-finance/states-collect-internet-sales-taxes.html.

Lenihan, G. D. (2005). "Realigning Governance: From E-Government to E-Democracy."

In M. Khosrow-Pour (Ed.). *Practicing E-Government: A Global Perspective.* Hershey, PA: IDEA Group Publishing (pp. 250–88).

Lester, James P. & Stewart, Joseph. (2000). *Public Policy–An Evolutionary Approach.* CA: Wadsworth/Thompson Learning.

Lorch, Robert S. (2001). *State and Local Politics: The Great Entanglement.* Upper Saddle River, NJ: Prentice-Hall.

Lowi, Theodore J. (1972). "Four Systems of Policy, Politics and Choice." *Public Administration Review, 32,* 298–310.

Lusk, Chris. (2010, July 27). "Law Student Emily Virgin Wins Democratic Nod for District 44 Seat." *The Oklahoma Daily.* Retrieved from http://oudaily.com/news/2010/jul/27/emily-virgin-wins-democratic-nod-district-44-seat/

MacGillis, Alec. (2014, March 3). "Woke Up This Morning and All That Love Had Gone: The Rise and Fall of Chris Christie." *The New Republic, 244.23,* 14–25.

Maxwell, Amos. D. 1953. *The Sequoyah Constitutional Convention*. Boston: Meador Publishing Co.

Maxwell, William Earl, Crain, Ernest, & Santos, Adolfo. (2010). *Texas Politics Today 2009–2010 Edition*. Boston, MA: Cengage.

McClatchy-Tribune News. (2011, March 18). "Grants Available to Promote Specialty Crops." *NewsOK*. Retrieved from http://newsok.com/grants-available-to-promote-specialty-crops/article/3549733.

McCormick, Richard. (1986). "Progressivism: A Contemporary Reassessment." In *The Party Period and Public Policy* (pp. 263–288). Oxford, UK: Oxford University Press.

McGuigan, Patrick E. (2010, December 7). "New Year's Resolution: Kris Steele, the Right Hand, and the Other Hand." *Tulsa Today*. Retrieved from http://www.tulsatoday.com/index.php?option=com_content&view=article&id=2276:new-years-resolution-kris-steele-the-right-hand-and-the-other-hand&catid=54:tulsa-speaks&Itemid=147.

McGuire, Karen. (2013). "The Changing Nature of Energy in Oklahoma" (Oklahoma Economic Outlook Conference). http://economy.okstate.edu/caer/files/02-Maguire_TheChangingNatureOfResourcesInOklahoma.pdf.

McNamara, Tom and Birmingham, Paul. (2013, December 11). "Investigation Reveals Illegal Immigrant Working as DPS Officer." KVOA.com. Retrieved from http://www.kvoa.com/news/investigation-reveals-illegal-immigrant-working-as-DPS-officer/.

McNutt, Michael. (2010, March 24). "Poll Shows Support for Smoke-free Law." *The Oklahoman*, p. 17.

McNutt, Michael. (2010, November 7). Oklahoma's Legislative Leaders Pledge to Work with Democrats. *The Oklahoman*.

McNutt, Michael McNutt. (2011, February 7). "Oklahoma's Governor Asks for Reforms to Improve Oklahoma's Business Climate," *NewsOK*. Retrieved from http://newsok.com/oklahoma-gov.-fallin-asks-for-reforms-to-improve-oklahomas-business-climate/article/3538875#.

McNutt, Michael. (2011, March 25). "Agencies May Face Steeper Cuts,"*The Oklahoman*, p. 8A.

McNutt, Michael. (2012, February 11). *State Asks Supreme Court to Determine Water Rights*, 1A.

McNutt, Michael. (2012, August 7). GOP Registration in Oklahoma Continues to Grow. *The Oklahoman*. Retrieved from http://newsok.com/gop-registration-in-oklahoma-continues-to-grow/article/3698732.

McNutt, Michael. (2013, March 2). "Governor Fallin Calls for Major Overhaul of Oklahoma's Pension System. Retrieved from http://newsok.com/governor-fallin-calls-for-major-overhaul-of-oklahomas-pension-system/article/3760394.

McSuite, O.C. (2002). *Invitation to public administration*. M.E. Sharpe: Armonk, N.Y.

Mecoy, Don. (2008, March 26). "HB 1804 Could Hurt, Study Shows." *The Oklahoman*. Business 1A.

Meijer, A. (2012). "Open Government Connecting Vision and Voice." *International Review of Administrative Sciences, 78.1*, 10–29.

Melone, Albert P. and Karnes, Allan. (2003). *The American Legal System: Foundations, Processes, and Norms*. Los Angeles: Roxbury Publishing Co.

Meltabarger, Lucinda. (2013, December 16). Administrator, Human Capital Management Division, Oklahoma Office of Management and Enterprise Services. Letter to governor.

Membership of the Oklahoma Historical Society Would be Abolished Under Consolidation. (2014, April). *Mistletoe Leaves*, p. 8.

Milakovich, Michael E. and Gordon, George J. (2013). *Public Administration in America*. (11th Ed.). Boston: Wadsworth.

Mock, Jennifer. (2007, November 11)."Author of HB 1804 Says He's Proud Law is 'Setting the Standard for the Nation'." Retrieved from http://newsok.com/author-of-hb-1804-says-hes-proud-law-is-setting-the-standard-for-the-nation/article/3167532.

Moncrief, Gary F. & Thompson, Joel A. (Eds.). (1992). *Changing Patterns in State Legislative Careers*. Ann Arbor, MI: University of Michigan Press.

Money, J. (2002, June 23). "Scenic Rivers' Water Auality Brings Debate." *The Oklahoman*, 1. Retrieved from the Oklahoma Scenic River's Commission Website: http://www.oklahomascenicrivers.net/News/Illinois_debate.doc.

Money, Jack. (1996, August 26). "Independent Movement Growing." *The Daily Oklahoman*.

Monies, Paul. (2003, December 21). "Work Force Push a Priority Issue Under State Plan." *The Daily Oklahoman*, p. 3D.

Moomaw, Ronald L. (2006). "Education Reform in Oklahoma: A State at Risk?" In *State Policy and Economic Development in Oklahoma: 2006* (63–78). Oklahoma City, OK: Oklahoma 21st Century, Inc.

Moon, M. Jae. (2002, July/August). "The Evolution of E-Government Among Municipalities: Rhetoric or Reality?" *Public Administration Review*. 62.4, 424–33.

Moon, J. M. and Norris, D. (2005). "Does Managerial Orientation Matter? The Adoption of Reinventing Government and E-Government at the Municipal Level." *Information Systems Journal*, 15, 43–60.

"More Work is Needed to Make Oklahoma's IT Consolidation Initiative a Success." (2013, Oct. 2). *The Oklahoman*. Retrieved from http://newsok.com/more-work-is-needed-to-make-oklahomas-it-consolidation-initiative-a-success/article/3888725.

Morgan, David R., England, Robert E., and Humphreys, George G. (1991). *Oklahoma Politics and Policies: Governing the Sooner State*. Lincoln, NE: University of Nebraska Press.

Morgan, David R. (1991). "State and Local Spending in Oklahoma: Comparing Actual Expenditures to Service Needs." *Oklahoma Business Bulletin*, 59.3, 13–17.

Morgan, H. Wayne and Morgan, Anne Hodges. (1977). *Oklahoma: A History*. New York: W.W. Norton & Company, Inc.

Morgan, Kathleen O'Leary and Morgan, Scott (Eds.). (2002) *State Rankings 2002* Lawrence, KS: Morgan Quitno Press.

Morgan, Katherine O'Leary, and Morgan, Scott. (2011) *State Rankings 2011: A Statistical View of America*. Washington, DC: CQ Press.

Mossberger, Karen, Tolbert, Caroline J. and McNeal, Ramona S. (2008). *Digital Citizenship: The Internet, Society, and Participation*. Cambridge, MA: The MIT Press.

Mosher, W.E., Kingsley, J.D., and Stahl, O.G. (1950). *Public Personnel Administration*. New York: Harper & Brothers.

Moulder, E. (2001, September). "E-Government...If You Build It, Will They Come?" *Public Management, 83*: 10–14.

Moynihan, Donald P. (2004, September/October). "Building Secure Elections: E-Voting, Security, and Systems Theory." *Public Administration Review. 64.5*, 515–528.

Mulva, J. J. (2004). "Sustainability: Good business and good sense." In *Oklahoma's Environment: Pursuing a Responsible Balance* (5-26-28). Oklahoma City: The Oklahoma Academy for State Goals.

Mundende, D. C. (2004). "Saving the land: soil and water conservation in Oklahoma." *Chronicles of Oklahoma, 82*. 4–31.

Munger, Michael C. (2000). *Analyzing Policy: Choices, Conflicts, & Practices*. W.W. Norton.

Murry, Donald A. (1988). "The Legislative Development Efforts and Economic Diversification." In *State Policy and Economic Development in Oklahoma* (pp. 23–26). Oklahoma City, OK: Oklahoma 2000 Inc.

Murry, Donald A., Olson, Kent W., Holmes, Alexander, Warner, Larkin, Dauffenbach, Robert C., & Gade, Mary. (1996). *In Search of Smaller Government: The Case of State Finance in Oklahoma*. Oklahoma City, OK: Oklahoma 2000 Inc.

Myers, J. (2003, July 9). "Inhofe Still Firm on Tar Creek." *The Tulsa World.*, 1. Retrieved from http://www.leadagency.org/modules.php?op=modload&name=News&file=article&sid=36.

Myers, Jim. (1996). "Group Violated Law in State Races, FEC Claims." *Tulsa World.*

Myers, Matt. (2010). *Tar Creek*. Documentary. Retrieved from http://tarcreekfilm.com.

Nathan, R.P. (1996). "The role of the states in American federalism." In C.E. Van Horn (Ed.), *The state of the states* (pp. 13–32). Washington, DC: Congressional Quarterly Press.

National Conference of State Legislatures. (2007). Retrieved from http://www.ncsl.org.

National Conference of State Legislatures. (2011, July 22). "Absentee and Early Voting." Retrieved from http://www.ncsl.org/default.aspx?tabid=16604.

National Governors Association. (2013). *America Works: Education and Training for Tomorrow's Jobs, The Benefit of a More Educated Workforce to Individuals and the Economy*. Washington, DC: National Governors Association Center for Best Practices. Retrieved from http://ci.nga.org/cms/sites/ci/home/1314/index.html.

National Institute on Money in State Politics (2014). "Follow the Money" Database. Retrieved from ttp://www.followthemoney.org/database/State Glance/ierace.phtml?m=768&s=OK&y=2010.

National Priorities List Sites in the United States. (2007). Environmental Protection Agency. Retrieved from: http://www.epa.gov/superfund/sites/npl/npl.htm

National Science Foundation (2014). *Science and Engineering Indicators*. Washington, DC: Author. Retrieved from http://www.nsf.gov/statistics/seind14/.

NewsOK.com. (2005, October 24). "Quick poll." *The Daily Oklahoman.*

National Caucus of Native American State Legislators. (2014). Retrieved from www.nscl.org/collaboration/nativeamericanlegislators.

National Conference of State Legislatures. (2014). Retrieved from http://www.ncsl.org.

Nilsen, K. (2006). "E-Government in Canada." In P. Hernon, R. Cullen & H. C. Relyea (Eds.), *Comparative Perspectives on E-Government* edited by Landham, MD: The Scarecrow Press (66–83).

Norris, D. (2007). Electronic Government at the American Grassroots. In A. Anttiroiko & M. Mälkiä (Eds.), *Encyclopedia of Digital Government, Volume II E-H* (pp. 643–651). Hershey, PA: Idea Group Reference.

Norris, F. D. and Moon, M. Jae. (2005, January/February). "Advancing E-Government at the Grassroots: Tortoise or Hare?" *Public Administration Review, 65*, 64–75.

Nugent, D. J. (2001, Fall), "If E-Democracy is the Answer, What is the Question?" *National Civic Review, 90*, 221–33.

O'Connor, Karen & Larry Sabato. (2011). *American Government: Roots and Reform* (2011 Edition). Glenview, IL: Pearson/Longman.

Office of Secretary of the Environment. (2014). EcoRegions. Retrieved from http://www.state.ok.us/energy/Environment/Land/EcoRegions.

Office of State Finance. (2011). "Government Modernization: HB2140 - Consolidating the State of Oklahoma's Administrative Functions." Oklahoma City, OK: Author.

O'Harrow, R. (2005). *No Place to Hide.* New York: The Free Press.

Oklahoma 2000, Inc. (1996). *In Search of Smaller government: The Case of State Finance in Oklahoma.* Norman, OK: University of Oklahoma Printing Services.

Oklahoma Academy for State Goals. (1985). *Oklahoma Revenue: Sources and Uses, Final Report.* Oklahoma City, OK: Author

Oklahoma Advisory Committee to the United States Commission on Civil Rights. (1978, March). *The Quest for Equal Employment Opportunity in Oklahoma State Government.* Washington, D.C.: United States Commission on Civil Rights.

Oklahoma Association of Community Colleges. (2014). *Oklahoma's Community Colleges: Destinations of Choice.* Midwest City, OK: Author. Retrieved from http://oacc.onenet.net/pdf/CC-Presentation.pdf.

Oklahoma Center for the Advancement of Science and Technology, (2004) *Meeting Challenges in the New Economy: Recommendations to Improve Oklahoma's Position in Technology-based Economic Development.* Oklahoma City, OK: Author.

Oklahoma Center for the Advancement of Science and Technology (2007). *2007 Impact report.* Oklahoma City, OK: Author.

Oklahoma Center for the Advancement of Science and Technology. (2014). *2014 Impact Report.* Retrieved from http://www.ok.gov/ocast/documents/2014ImpactReport.pdf.

Oklahoma Conservation Commission. (1998). *Riparian Area Management Handbook. Oklahoma Cooperative Extension Service Division of Agricultural Sciences and Natural Resources,* E-952. Oklahoma State University.

Oklahoma Council of Public Affairs. (2013, July 26). "Oklahoma's History with Income Tax Cuts: A Story of Growth" *Memorandum.* Retrieved from http://www.ocpathink.org/articles/2415

Oklahoma Council of Public Affairs & Arduin, Laffer and Moore Econometrics. (2011, November). *Eliminating the State Income Tax in Oklahoma: An Economic Assessment.* Retrieved from http://www.ocpathink.org/articles/1647.

Oklahoma Department of Commerce. (2004). *Improving Your Community: Community County Profiles.* Oklahoma City: Author.

Oklahoma Department of Commerce (2006a, January 23). "Oklahoma Oil & Gas Briefing."

Oklahoma Department of Commerce (2006b, May 19). "High Technology Report."

Oklahoma Department of Commerce (2006, July 10). "Oklahoma Economic Briefing."

Oklahoma Department of Commerce (2007a). *Oklahoma Business Incentives and Tax Guide 2007. Oklahoma City, OK: Author.*

Oklahoma Department of Commerce (2007b). *Oklahoma Quality Jobs Program 2007 Guidelines.* Oklahoma City, OK: Author.

Oklahoma Department of Commerce. (2014). *Oklahoma Quality Jobs Program. 2014 Guidelines.* Oklahoma City, OK: Author. Retrieved from http://okcommerce .gov/assets/files/incentives/Quality_Jobs_Guidelines.pdf.

Oklahoma Department of Libraries. (1997). *The Oklahoma Almanac.* Oklahoma City: Author.

Oklahoma Department of Libraries. (1998). *The Oklahoma Almanac.* Oklahoma City: Author.

Oklahoma Economic Outlook. (2003). Stillwater, OK: College of Business Administration, Oklahoma State University.

Oklahoma Election Board. (2014, January 15). *Current Registration Statistics by County.* Retrieved from http://ok.gov/elections/documents/reg_0114.pdf.

Oklahoma Employment Security Commission (2014, February). *Oklahoma Economic Indicators.* Oklahoma City, OK: Author. Retrieved from http://www.ok.gov/ oesc_web/documents/lmiEconIndPub.pdf.

Oklahoma Ethics Commission. (1997). "Oklahoma Registered Lobbyists, 1997–1998." Oklahoma City, OK: Author.

Oklahoma Forum. (2014, February 23). KOED HD. Oklahoma Education Television Authority.

Oklahoma Governor's Consolidation Plan Warrants Careful Review. (2014, Feb. 14). *NewsOK.* Retrieved from http://newsok.com/oklahoma-governors-consolidation-plan-warrants-careful-review/article/3933418.

Oklahoma Governor's Office. (2014a, March 24). *Governor Mary Fallin Statement on Common Core Legislation* [Press release]. Retrieved from http://www.ok. gov/triton/modules/newsroom/newsroom_article.php?id=223&article_id =13860.

Oklahoma HB 1804. (2007) Retrieved from http://www.oscn.net/applications/ oscn/DeliverDocument.asp?CiteID=448995

Oklahoma House of Representatives. (2008). *Legislative Guide to Oklahoma Taxes, Collections, and Apportionments.* Retrieved from http://digitalprairie.ok.gov/ cdm/singleitem/collection/stgovpub/id/6957/rec/35

Oklahoma Office of Management and Enterprise Services. (2011). *Consolidating the State of Oklahoma's Administrative Functions.* Oklahoma City, OK: Author. Retrieved from http://www.ok.gov/ OSF/News/HB_2140_Consolidation_ Report.html.

Oklahoma Office of Management and Enterprise Services. (2013). *State of Oklahoma Total Remuneration Study.* Oklahoma City, OK: Author. Retrieved from http://www.ok.gov/OSF/ documents/TotalRemunerationStudy.pdf.

Oklahoma Office of Management and Enterprise Services. (2013). *Oklahoma 2103: Comprehensive Annual Financial Report.* Oklahoma City, OK: Author. Retrieved from http://www.ok.gov/OSF/documents/cafr13.pdf.

Oklahoma Office of Personnel Management. (2003a). *FY2004 Annual Compensation report*. Oklahoma City, OK: Author.

Oklahoma Office of Personnel Management. (2003b). *Fiscal Year 2003 Annual Report*. Oklahoma City, OK: Author.

Oklahoma Office of Personnel Management. (2006, December 1). *2006 Annual Compensation Report*. Oklahoma City, OK: Author.

Oklahoma Office of Personnel Management. (2007, March 28). *Oklahoma State Government Equal Employment Opportunity/Affirmative Action Status Report*. Oklahoma City, OK: Author.

Oklahoma Office of Personnel Management (2009). *Annual Compensation Report*. Oklahoma City, OK: Author.

Oklahoma Office of Personnel Management (2010, March). *Equal Employment Opportunity/Affirmative Action Status Report, Fiscal Year 2009*. Oklahoma City, OK: Author.

Oklahoma Office of Personnel Management. (2011). *FY2010 Annual Report and Workforce Summary*. Oklahoma City, OK: Author.

Oklahoma Policy Institute. (2011, March). *Fact Sheet: Oklahoma State Spending As Share of Economy Hits 30-Year Low*. Tulsa, OK: Author. Retrieved from http://okpolicy.org/files/State%20Spending%20Hits%2030-Year%20Low%20Fact%20Sheet.pdf.

Oklahoma Policy Institute (2013, October). *Action Items for Oklahoma: Education*. Tulsa, OK: Author. Retrieved from http://okpolicy.org/wp-content/uploads/2013/10/action-items-education.pdf.

Oklahoma Secretary of State. (2013a). *Administrative Rules*. Retrieved from https://www.sos.ok.gov/oar/.

Oklahoma Secretary of State. (2013b). *Administrative Rules – The Other Half of Oklahoma's Codified Laws*. Retrieved from https://www.sos.ok.gov/oar/oarRules.aspx.

Oklahoma Sierra Club. (2013, June 10). *2013 Environmental Report Card: Oklahoma Legislature*. Oklahoma City, OK: Author.

Oklahoma State Courts Network. (2004). Oklahoma Statutes Citationalized. Retrieved from www.oscn.net.

Oklahoma State Courts Network (2014), "Oklahoma Judicial Nominating Commission," Retrieved from http://www.oscn.net/Sites/JudicialNominatingCommission/default.aspx.

Oklahoma State Regents for Higher Education. (2012). *Higher Education Employment Outcomes Report 2012*. Oklahoma City, OK: Author. Retrieved from https://www.okhighered.org/studies-reports/employment-outcomes/employrpt-10-2012.pdf

Oklahoma State Regents for Higher Education. (2014). "Fast Facts." Oklahoma City, OK: Author. Retrieved from http://www.okhighered.org.

Oklahoma State Senator Proposes Guest Worker Program for Illegal Aliens. (2011, December 6). Retrieved from https://www.numbersusa.com/content/news/december-6-2011/oklahoma-state-senator-proposes-guest-worker-program-illegal-aliens.html

Oklahoma Sustainability Network. (2011). "Welcome." Retrieved from http://www.oksustainability.org/index.php.

Oklahoma Tax Commission. (2004) *Annual Report FY 2003*. Oklahoma City, OK: Author.

Oklahoma Tax Commission. (2006). *Tax expenditure report* 2005–2006. Oklahoma City, OK: Author.

Oklahoma Tax Commission. (2012). *Tax Expenditure Report 2011–2012.* Oklahoma City, OK: Author. Retrieved from http://www.tax.ok.gov/reports/Tax%20Expenditure%20Report%202011-2012.pdf.

Oklahoma Tax Commission. (2013). *Annual Report of the Oklahoma Tax Commission for FY 2012.* Oklahoma City, OK: Author. Retrieved from http://www.tax.ok.gov/publicat/AR2012.pdf

Oklahoma Tax Commission.(2014). *Annual Report of the Oklahoma Tax Commission for FY 2013.* Oklahoma City, OK: Author.Retrieved from http://www.tax.ok.gov/reports/AR2013.pdf.

Oklahoma Taxpayer and Citizen Protection Act of 2007. H.B 1804.

Oklahoma Territory Census of 1890. (2001). Oklahoma Historical Society via the *Internet Archive Wayback Machine.* Retrieved from http://web.archive.org/web/20060206034927/http://www.ok-history.mus.ok.us/lib/1890/1890index.htm

Oklahoma Ballot Access Reform. (2014). Retrieved from www.oklp.org/obar/issues.html.

Oklahoma Ethics Commission. (2014). Retrieved from http://www.ok.gov/oec/Rosenthal, Alan. (2004). *Heavy Lifting: The Job of the American Legislature.* Washington, D.C.: Congressional Quarterly Press.

Oklahoma Policy Institute. (2014, March 13). "Curb Unnecessary Tax Breaks" (March 13th). http://okpolicy.org/priority-oklahoma-curb-unnecessary-tax-breaks

Oklahoma Republican Party. (2014). Retrieved from www.okgop.com.

OKPolicy.org. (2014). "Limits on the Budget." Retrieved from http://okpolicy.org/resources/ online-budget-guide/budget-process/essentials-of-public-budgeting/limits-on-the-budget.

Olivarez, Jesse. (2007, December 11). "Capitol Hill Feels Effect of HB 1804." *The Oklahoman*, p. 16A. Retrieved from http://archive.newsok.com.

Olson, Kent. (1984). *Oklahoma State and Local Taxes: Structure, Issues, and Reforms: A Report to the Kerr Foundation.* Stillwater, OK: Oklahoma State University Press.

Olson, Kent. (2003). "The Oklahoma State Budget Crisis: Lessons from the Past, Policies for the Future." In *State Policy and Economic Development in Oklahoma: 2003* (pp. 1–20). Oklahoma City, OK: Oklahoma 21st Century, Inc.

Osborne, David, & Gaebler, Ted. (1992). *Reinventing Government: How the Entrepreneurial Spirit is Transforming the Public Sector.* New York: Penguin Books.

Osborne, David, & Hutchinson, Peter. (2004). *The Price of Government: Getting the Results We Need in an Age of Permanent Fiscal Crisis.* New York: Basic Books.

Peters, Thomas J. and Waterman, Jr., Robert H. (1982). *In Search of Excellence: Lessons from America's Best-run Companies.* New York: Harper & Row.

Padgett, John F. (1985). "The emergent organization of plea bargaining." *The American Journal of Sociology, 90.4,* 753–800.

Palmer, T. (1994). *Lifelines: The Case for River Conservation.* Covelo, CA: Island Press.

Penn D. (1990). "Measures of Diversification." In *State Policy and Economic Development in Oklahoma: 1990, A Report to Oklahoma 2000 Inc.* (pp. 33–38). Oklahoma City, OK: Oklahoma 2000 Inc.

Perry, Gene (2014, February 27). The Mystery of the Disappearing Revenue. *Oklahoma Policy Institute.* Retrieved from http://okpolicy.org/mystery-disappearing-tax-revenue.

Petroni, G. and Tagliente, L. (2005). "E-government in the Republic of San Marino: Some Successful Initiatives." In G. Petroni & F. Cloete (Eds.), *New Technologies in Public Administration* (23–37). Amsterdam: IOS Press.

Pevar, Stephen L. (2012). *The Rights of Indians and Tribes.* New York: Oxford University Press.

Phillips, D. and Harrison, M. (2004). *Out of the Dust: The History of Conservation in Oklahoma in the 20th Century.* Oklahoma City, OK: Oklahoma Association of Conservation Districts, Oklahoma Conservation Commission, and USDA Natural Resources Conservation Service.

Porto, Brian L. (2001). *May It Please the Court: Judicial Processes and Politics in America.* New York: Longman.

Potential Consequences of Arts Council consolidation. (2014, Feb. 7). *Oklahoma Arts Council News.* Retrieved from http://arts.ok.gov/News/2014/February/Potential_Consequences_of_Oklahoma_Arts_Council_Consolidation.htm.

Prah, Pamela M. (2012). "Oklahoma Among States Limiting Property Taxes." *Stateline.* Retrieved from http://www.pewstates.org/projects/stateline/headlines/oklahoma-among-states-limiting-property-taxes-85899431055.

Price, Marie. (1998, January 29). "Report Ranks Oklahoma's Tax Burden." *The Journal Record.*

Putnam, Robert D. (2000). *Bowling Alone. The Collapse and Revival of American Community.* New York: Simon & Schuster.

Rafool, Mandy and Warnock, Kae. (1996). "Let the Voters Decide." *State Legislatures, 22.8,* 33–50.

Rainmondo, H.J. (1996). "State Budgeting: Problems, Choices and Money." In Carl E. Van Horn (Ed.), *The State of the States* (pp. 33–50). Washington, DC: Congressional Quarterly Press.

Rainey, Hal G. and Bozeman, Barry. (2000). "Comparing Public and Private Organizations: Empirical Research and the Power of A Priori. *Journal of Public Administration Research and Theory, 10.2,* 447–469.

Ramirez, Martin. (2013, December 4). "Governor Fallin Champions Higher Standards. Oklahoma City, OK: Stand for Children Oklahoma." Retrieved from http://stand.org/oklahoma/blog/2013/12/04/governor-fallin-champions-higher-standards.

Rausch, David and Farmer, Rick. (1998). "Term Limits in Oklahoma." *The Almanac of Oklahoma Politics, 6,* 33–36.

Rainey, Hal G. and Steinbauer, Paula. (1999, January). "Galloping Elephants: Developing Elements of a Theory of Effective Government Organizations." *Journal of Public Administration Research and Theory, 9.1,* 1–32.

Rasul v. Bush. No. 03-334. (20014, December 28). U.S. Supreme Court. Print.

Rawls, John. (1971). *A Theory of Justice.* Cambridge, MA: The Belknap Press of Harvard University Press.

Rawls, Wendall. (2005). "Hired Guns: Ratio of Lobbyists to Legislators 2004." Retrieved from <http://www.hillnews.com/news/022304/ss_gelak.aspx=> on August 10, 2006.

Reagan, Michael D. (1987). *Regulation: The Politics of Policy.* Boston, MA: Little, Brown and Company.

Reilly, Thom., Schoener, Schaun. and Bolin, Alice. (2007). "Public Sector Compensation in Local Government: An Analysis." *Review of Public Personnel Administration, 27.1,* 39–58.

Reingold, Beth. (1992). "Concepts of Representation Among Female and Male State Legislators." *Legislative Studies Quarterly, 17,* 509–537.

"Repeal of Common Core Would Increase Federal Control." (2014, March 19). *Daily Oklahoman.* Retrieved from http://www.tulsalibrary.org:2141/iw-search/we/ InfoWeb?p_product=NewsBank&p_theme=aggregated5&p_action=doc&p_docid=14CC24DFE588B038&p_docnum=1&p_queryname=1.

Rho, S. (2007). "An Evaluation of Digital Deliberative Democracy in Local Government. In L. Al-Hakim (Ed.), *Global E-Government: Theory, Applications and Benchmarking* 200–213). Hershey, PA: Idea Group Publishing.

Richardson, J. (2001). "Archives of the West from 1877–1887." Indian Policy Reform Extract from President Chester Arthur's First Annual Message to Congress December 6, 1881. Retrieved from http://www.pbs.org/weta/thewest/resources/archives/seven/indpol.htm.

Richardson, Lillard, Jr., and Freeman, Patricia. (1995). "Gender Differences in Constituency Service Among State Legislators." *Political Research Quarterly, 48,* 169–179.

Riley, B. T. and Riley, C. G. (2003). "E-Governance to E-Democracy: Examining the Evolution." Retrieved from http://www.rileis.com.

Rodden, Kirk A. (2007). Murray State College. *Oklahoma Historical Society's Encyclopedia of Oklahoma History.* Oklahoma City: Oklahoma Historical Society. Retrieved from http://digital.library.okstate.edu/encyclopedia/entries/m/mu012.html.

Russell, Steve. (2010). *Sequoyah Rising: Problems in Post-Colonial Tribal Governance.* Carolina Academic Press.

Sanders, Larry D. (2013, July). "U.S. Immigration Policy & Impacts." PowerPoint presentation on behalf of Oklahoma State University to the Tulsa Regional Chamber of Commerce Policy Forum. Citing data from immigrationpolicy.org. Retrieved from http://www.google.com/cse?cx=0103174997107449 66587%3Asypiuj4tvpy&ie=UTF-8&q=larry+sanders+immigration&sa= Search#gsc.tab=0&gsc.q=larry%20sanders%20immigration&gsc.page=1

Schafer, Shaun. (2002, November 2002). "Blood Sport's Fans, Foes Take Aim," *Tulsa World,* p. A1.

Schmitt, John. (2010, May). "The Wage Penalty for State and Local Government Employees." Washington, DC: Center for Economic and Policy Research. Retrieved October 12, 2011 from www.cepr.net.

Schwester, R. (2009). "Examining the Barriers to E-Government Adoption." *Electronic Journal of e-Government, 7,* 113–122.

Scott, K. J. (2006, May/June). "'E' the People: Do U.S. Municipal Government Web Sites Support Public Involvement?" *Public Administration Review, 66,* 341–53.

Seifert, W. J. (2006). "E-Government in the United States." In P. Hernon, R. Cullen & H. C. Relyea (Eds.), *Comparative Perspectives on E-Government* (pp. 25–54). Landham, MD: The Scarecrow Press.

Selingo, Jeffrey J. (2013). *College (Un) Bound.* New York: Harvest Houghton Mifflin Harcourt.

Shafritz, Jay. (2005). *Introducing Public Administration.* New York: Pearson Education, Inc.

Shafritz, Jay M, David. H. Rosenbloom, Norma M. Riccucci, Katherine C. Naff, & Albert C. Hyde. (2001). *Personnel Management in Government: Politics and Process.* New York: Marcel Dekker.

Shapek, Raymond A. (1981). *Managing Federalism: Evolution and Development of the Grant-In-Aid System*. Charlottesville: Community Collaborators.

Simpson, Philip M., (2000). "The Judicial System of Oklahoma." In Christopher L. Markwood (Ed.), *Oklahoma Government & Politics* (pp. 119–138). Dubuque, Iowa: Kendall/Hunt Publishing Co.

Snead, Mark C. and Ireland, Tim C. (2002). "Oklahoma Regional and County Output Trends: 1980–1999." *Oklahoma Business Bulletin, 70,* 7–18.

Snead, Mark (2007). *The Oklahoma Economy. 2007 Economic Outlook.* Stillwater, OK: Center for Applied Economic Research, Oklahoma State University.

Snellen, I. (2005). "Technology and Public Administration: Conditions for Successful E-Government Development." In G. Petroni & F. Cloete (Eds.), *New Technologies in Public Administration* (5–19). Amsterdam: IOS Press.

Small, Jonathon. (2014, March 5). "Retirement Reform an Opportunity." *Tulsa World.* Retrieved from http://www.tulsaworld.com/opinion/readersfo rum/jonathan-small-retirement-reform-an-opportunity/article_62e01301-d4ca-5590-aa05-2f0b083664d2.html.

Smith, Christopher E. (1999). *Courts, Politics and the Judicial Process* (2nd Ed.). Chicago: Nelson-Hall Publishing Co.

Smithheisler, Marjilea. (2007). Northern Oklahoma College. *Oklahoma Historical Society's Encyclopedia of Oklahoma History & Culture.* Oklahoma City: Oklahoma Historical Society. Retrieved from http://digital.library.okstate.edu/ encyclopedia/entries/N/NO015.html

Smoot, D.E. (2012, October 20). "2 1/2 Years, No Poultry Case Ruling." *Muskogee Phoenix.* Retrieved from http://www.muskogeephoenix.com/local/ x688445298/2-1-2-years-no-poultry-case-ruling/?state=taberU.

State of the States: Assessing the Capacity of States to Achieve Sustainable Development Through Green Planning. (2001). San Francisco, CA: Resource Renewal Institute.

State Rankings: A Report by the Environmental Defense Fund. (1999). New York: Environmental Defense Fund. Retrieved from http://www.environmental-defense.org/article.cfm?ConentID=1560.

Stephens, Michelle. (1997). "Oklahoma Legal Changes in Animal Waste Management Precipitated by Citizens' Concern." Poteau, OK: Kerr Center for Sustainable Agriculture, Inc. Retrieved from http://www.p2pays.org/ ref/21/20034.htm.

State v. Walker. (1977). 568 P.2d 286.

Steady Climb: Legislative Staff Growth Makes Sense. (2004, March 1). *Daily Oklahoman,* p. 12A.

Stogsdill, S. (2007, March 6). "Tar Creek Residents Await Buyout Offers." *The Joplin Globe.* Retrieved from http://www.joplinglobe.com/neo_sek/ local_story_065011922.html.

Stogsdill, S. (2013, December 4). "Tar Creek Towns of Picher, Cardin Officially Dissolved." *Tulsa World.* Retrieved http://www.tulsaworld.com/news/ local/tar-creek-towns-of-picher-cardin-officially-dissolved/article_b17836c2-5cd7-11e3-9475-0019bb30f31a.html.

Stowers, G. (2009). "The Little City That Could: The Case of San Carlos, California." In C. Reddick (Ed.), *Handbook of research on strategies for local e-government adoption and implementation: Comparative studies. Volume II* (pp. 705–718). New York: Hershley.

Strain, Jack, Reherman, Carl F., and Crozier, Leroy. (1990). *An Outline of Oklahoma Government*. Oklahoma City, OK: Americanism Commission, American Legion Department of Oklahoma.

Strain, Jack L., Crozier, Leroy, and Reherman, Carl F. (1997). *An Outline of Oklahoma Government*. Edmond, OK: Department of Political Science, University of Central Oklahoma.

Strategic planning and budget requests. (n.d.) *Introduction*. Retrieved from http://www.ok.gov/OSF/Budget/Strategic_Planning_and_Budget_Request.html.

Strauss, Valerie. (2013, Nov. 27). "Gates Foundation Pours Millions into Common Core in 2013." *The Washington Post*. Retrieved from http://www.washington post.com/blogs/answer-sheet/wp/2013/11/27/gates-foundation-pours-millions-into-common-core-in-2013/.

Stumpf, Harry P. (1998). *American Judicial Politics* (2nd ed.). Upper Saddle River, NJ: Prentice-Hall Inc.

Sturm, Albert L. (1982). "The Development of American State Constitutions." *Publius: The Journal of Federalism, 12,* 57–98.

Summation of Oklahoma's HB 1804 Law. (2008). Oklahoma Immigration Reform for Oklahoma Now. Retrieved from http://okiron.org/HB1804Summary.html.

Support Our Law Enforcement and Safe Neighborhoods Act, S.B. 1070 (2010). Retrieved from http://www.azleg.gov/legtext/49leg/2r/bills/sb1070s.pdf.

SustainLane's 2008-Sustainability Ranking. (2008). Oklahoma City. Retrieved from http://www.sustainlane.com/us-city-rankings/cities/oklahoma-city.

Tabor, Michael. (2007). Redlands Community College. *Oklahoma Historical Society's Encyclopedia of Oklahoma History*. Oklahoma City: Oklahoma Historical Society. Retrieved from http://digital.library.okstate.edu/encyclopedia/entries/r/re017.html.

Thomas, Clive S. & Hrebenar, Ronald J. (1990). "Interest Groups in the State." In Virginia Gray, Herbert Jacob, & Robert Albritton (Eds.)., *Politics in the American States: A Comparative Analysis* (5th Ed.). Glenview, IL: Scott, Foresman/Little, Brown.

Thornton, Anthony. (2004, October 29). "3 Tribes Help Fund Lottery Campaign. *The Daily Oklahoman*, p. 1A.

Tolbert, J. C. and Mossberger, K. (2006, May/June). "The Effects of E-Government on Trust and Confidence in Government." *Public Administration Review, 66,* 354–69.

Tolbert, M. (2004). "This Generation's Problem." In The *Oklahoma Academy 2004 Town Hall – Oklahoma's Environment: Pursuing a Responsible Balance*, 6-24-25.

Tom Price Wants to Show Oklahomans "A Better Way." (2008, March 6). Oklahoma Political News Service. Retrieved from http://okpns.wordpress.com/2008/03/06/tom-price-wants-to-show-oklahomans-a-better-way/.

Toregas, C. (2001, Fall). "The Politics of E-Gov: The Upcoming Struggle for Redefining Civic Engagement." *National Civic Review, 90,* 235–40.

TRS. (2013). *State of Oklahoma Total Remuneration Study*. Retrieved from http://www.ok.gov/OSF/documents/TotalRemunerationStudy.pdf.

Tseng, Nin-Hai. (2011, March 7). "Tom Coburn: Government Employees are a Drag on the Economy," *Fortune*. Retrieved from http://finance.fortune.cnn.com/2011/03/07/tom-coburn-government-employees-are-a-drag-on-the-economy/.

Turpen, Mike. (2007). "Turpen's Top Seven: Why Being a Lawyer is the Greatest Job in the World." *Oklahoma Bar Journal.* Retrieved from http://www.okbar.org/obj/ backpage/090404.htm.

UCO College of Business Administration. (2001). *Sales Tax on Services.* Retrieved from: http://busn.ucok.edu/ole.

Unit to Target Voting Rights Infractions. (1996, November 2). *Tulsa World.* Retrieved from http://www.tulsaworld.com.

Uniting and Strengthening by Providing Appropriate Tools Required to Intercept and Obstruct Terrorism, USA PATRIOT Act. (2001). H.R. 3162. 107th Congress, 1st Session. Retrieved from http://epic.org/privacy/terrorism/hr3162.html.

University of Central Oklahoma Receives Green Power Partnership Individual Conference Champion Award. (2010, March 19). Press EPA Release. Retrieved from http://yosemite.epa.gov/opa/admpress.nsf/0/BF3D4F51857C10D08525770A004F998D.

Unshackle Upstate (2009). "New York' Double Standard: How Public Employee Pay and Benefits Have Outpaced the Private-Sector," Rochester, NY. Author. Retrieved October 12, 2011 from http://www.unshackleupstate.com/files/UUDSReport.pdf.

"Update on House Bill 3028." (2014, March 14). *Oklahoma Arts Council News.* Retrieved from http://www.arts.ok.gov/News/2014/March.html.

U.S. Census Bureau. (2000). Population statistics for towns and cities in Oklahoma. Retrieved from www.us-news-watch.com/population/Oklahoma-pop.html.

U.S. Census Bureau. (2010). "Table B-1: Metropolitan areas: Area and population. *Statistical Abstract of the United States.* Retrieved October 4, 2011 from www.us-news-watch.com/population/Oklahoma-pop.html.

U.S. Census Bureau. (2011), *2011 Survey of State and Local Government Finances.* https://www.census.gov/govs/local/.

U.S. Census Bureau (2014). "Population, 2013 Estimate." *State and County Quick-Facts.* Washington, DC: Author. Retrieved from http://quickfacts.census.gov/qfd/states/40000.html.

U.S. Bureau of Economic Analysis. (2004, September). *2004 Survey of Current Business, 84.* Washington, DC: Author.

U.S. Bureau of Economic Analysis (2007, April). *Survey of Current Business.* Washington, DC: Author.

U.S. Bureau of Economic Analysis. (2014, March). *Survey of Current Business.* Washington, DC: Author. Retrieved from https://www.bea.gov/scb/.

U.S. Bureau of Labor Statistics. (2006). *Career guide to industries, 2006–2007.* Washington, DC: Department of Labor.

U.S. Bureau of Labor Statistics. (2014, January 24). "Union Members -2013" *News Release.* Retrieved from http://www.bls.gov/news.release/pdf/union2.pdf.

U.S. Department of Education. (2001). *Community College Facts At a Glance.* Washington, DC: Author. Retrieved from https://www2.ed.gov/about/offices/list/ovae/pi/cclo/ccfacts.html.

U.S. Department of Justice, (2004, April 24) "Civil Cases and Verdicts in Large Counties, 2001," *NCJ 202803.* Washington, DC: Author.

U.S. Election Assistance Commission. (2010). *U.S. Election Assistance Commission Report 2010.* Washington, DC: Author. Retrieved from http://www.eac.gov/research/election_administration_and_voting_survey.aspx.

Utter, Jack. (2001). *American Indians: Answers to Today's Questions*. Norman: University of Oklahoma Press.

Valenti, M. (1999). "Double Wrapped." The American Society of Mechanical Engineers. Retrieved from http://www.memagazine.org/backissues/membersonly/january99/features/doublewrap/doublewrap.html.

Vigdor, Neil. (2011, September 28). "State GOP Moves Away from Winner-take-all Presidential Primary." *GreenwichTime.com*. Retrieved from http://www.greenwichtime.com/news/article/State-GOP-moves-away-from-winner-take-all-2193277.php.

Von Haldenwang, C. (2004, Summer). "Electronic Government (E-Government) and Development." *The European Journal of Development Research, 16*, 417–32.

Walker, Devona. (2007, November 1) "Crowd Protests Immigration Law." *The Oklahoman*. Retrieved from http://newsok.com/crowd-protests-immigration-law/article/3161766.

Walker, Devona. (2007, November 4) "From 9/11 to Present: How We Got to HB1804." *The Oklahoman*. Retrieved from http://newsok.com/article/3163329/1194193859.

Walker, Devona. (2008, May 11). Immigrants' Fear of Police Aids Criminals." *The Oklahoman*. Retrieved from http://newsok.com/immigrants-fear-of-police-aids-criminals/article/3241838.

Walker, Devona. (2008, September 14). "Are State's Immigrants Leaving?" *The Oklahoman*. Retrieved from http://newsok.com/are-states-immigrants-leaving/article/3297495.

Ward, Charles. (2010, January 21). "Two More OU Students Enter District 44 Race." *The Oklahoma Daily*. Retrieved from http://oudaily.com/news/2010/jan/21/two-more-ou-students-enter-district-44-race/.

Warner, Larkin. (1990). "Oklahoma Constitutional Revision 1988–89." In *State Policy and Economic Development in Oklahoma: 1990*. Oklahoma City, OK: Oklahoma 2000 Inc.

Warner, Larkin and Stephen Smith. (1991). "State Government Provision of Business Finance in Oklahoma", in *State Policy and Economic Development in Oklahoma*: 1991 (Oklahoma City, OK: Oklahoma 2000, Inc.), 1-17.

Warner, Larkin. (1995a). "An Overview of Oklahoma's Economic History: Part I." *Oklahoma Business Bulletin, 63.9*, 5–21.

Warner, Larkin. (1995b). "An Overview of Oklahoma's Economic History: Part II" *Oklahoma Business Bulletin, 63.12*, 5–13.

Warner, Larkin. (2002, July) "A Note on New Administrative Organization of Oklahoma Economic Development." *Oklahoma Business Bulletin, 70*, 5–10.

Warner, Larkin and Dauffenbach, Robert C. (2002, April). "Increasing Oklahoma's Competitiveness in the New/Global Economy: An Assessment." *Oklahoma Business Bulletin, 70*, 7–20.

Warner, Larkin and Dauffenbach, Robert C, (2004a) "Two Oklahoma Incentives for Economic Development: Introduction to Ad Valorem Tax Exemption and Quality Jobs Act." In *State Policy and Economic Development in Oklahoma: 2004* (pp. 1–12). Oklahoma City, OK: Oklahoma 21st Century, Inc.

Warner, Larkin and Dauffenbach, Robert C. (2004b) "Oklahoma's Ad Valorem Tax Exemption and the Quality Jobs Act: Analysis of Economic Impacts and Tests for Differential Growth" *State Policy and Economic Development in Oklahoma: 2004* (13–28). Oklahoma City, OK: Oklahoma 21st Century, Inc.

Warner, Larkin, and Dauffenbach, Robert C. (2006). "State Policy and Oklahoma High-Tech Economic Development." In *State Policy and Economic Development in Oklahoma: 2006* (49–62). Oklahoma City, OK: Oklahoma 21st Century, Inc.

Watson, Richard A. and Downing, Rondal G. (1969). *The Politics of the Bench and the Bar.* New York: Wiley.

Watson, Richard A., Downing, Rondal G., and Spiegal, Frederick C. (1967). "Bar Politics, Judicial Selection and the Representation of Social Interests." *The American Political Science Review, 61.1,* 54–71.

Wayne, Stephen J. (1997). *The Road to the White House—The Politics of Presidential Elections.* New York: St. Martin's Press.

Wertz, Joe. (2012, November 7). Two Reasons Vision2 Failed in Tulsa. *StateImpact: A Project of NPR member stations.* Retrieved from http://stateimpact.npr.org/oklahoma/2012/11/07/two-reasons-vision2-failed-in-tulsa-county/.

Western Ecological Region, Corvallis, Oregon. (2007). Environmental Protection Agency. Retrieved from http://www.epa.gov/wed/pages/ecoregions/ok_eco.htm.

What is strategic planning? (n.d.) Balance Scorecard Institute: Strategy Management Group. Retrieved fom https://balancedscorecard.org/BSCResources/StrategicPlanningBasics/tabid/459/Default.aspx.

What Parents Should Know. (2014). *Common Core State Standards Initiative.* Retrieved from http://www.corestandards.org/what-parents-should-know/.

White House, The. (2009, November). *The White House Project Report: Benchmarking Women's Leadership.* Washington, DC: Author.

Wildenthal, Bryan H. (2003). *Native American Sovereignty on Trial.* Santa Barbara, CA: ABC CLIO.

Wilkins, David E. and Heidi Stark. (2010). *American Indian Politics and the American Political System.* Lanham, MD: Rowman and Littlefield.

Wilmoth, A. (2013, August 16). "Gov. Mary Fallin Nnames Ssecretary of Energy and Environment." *NewOK.* Retrieved from http://newsok.com/gov.-mary-fallin-names-secretary-of-energy-and-environment/article/3872696.

Wilson, Linda D. (2007a). Carl Albert State College. *Oklahoma Historical Society's Encyclopedia of Oklahoma History.* Oklahoma City: Oklahoma Historical Society. Retrieved from http://digital.library.okstate.edu/encyclopedia/entries/C/CA055.html.

Wilson, Linda D. (2007b). Seminole State College. *Oklahoma Historical Society's Encyclopedia of Oklahoma History.* Oklahoma City: Oklahoma Historical Society. Retrieved from http://digital.library.okstate.edu/encyclopedia/entries/s/se015.html.

Winslow, Laurie. (2014, March 22). Researcher: Higher Education Still Pays Off. *Tulsa World,* p. E6.

Winters, R.P. (1996). "The Politics of Taxing and Spending." In Virginia Gray and Herbert Jacob (Eds.), *Politics in the American States.* Washington, DC: Congressional Quarterly Press.

Wohlers, Tony E. (2009, August/June). The Digital World of Local Government: A Comparative Analysis of the United States and Germany. *Journal of Information Technology & Politics. 6,* 111–126.

Wong, W. & Welch, E. (2004, April). "Does E-Government Promote Accountability? A Comparative Analysis of Website Openness and Government
Accountability." *Governance, 17*, 275–97.

Wood, John. (2013, November). "Fallin's Formal Powers in Transition." Paper
presented at the meeting of the Oklahoma Political Science Association, Norman, OK.

Wright, Deil S. (1988). *Understanding Intergovernmental Relations* (3rd Ed.). Pacific
Grove, CA: Cole Publishing.

Zizzo, David. (200, November 8). "State Voters Favor Tobacco Trust Fund," *The
Daily Oklahoman*, p. 6.